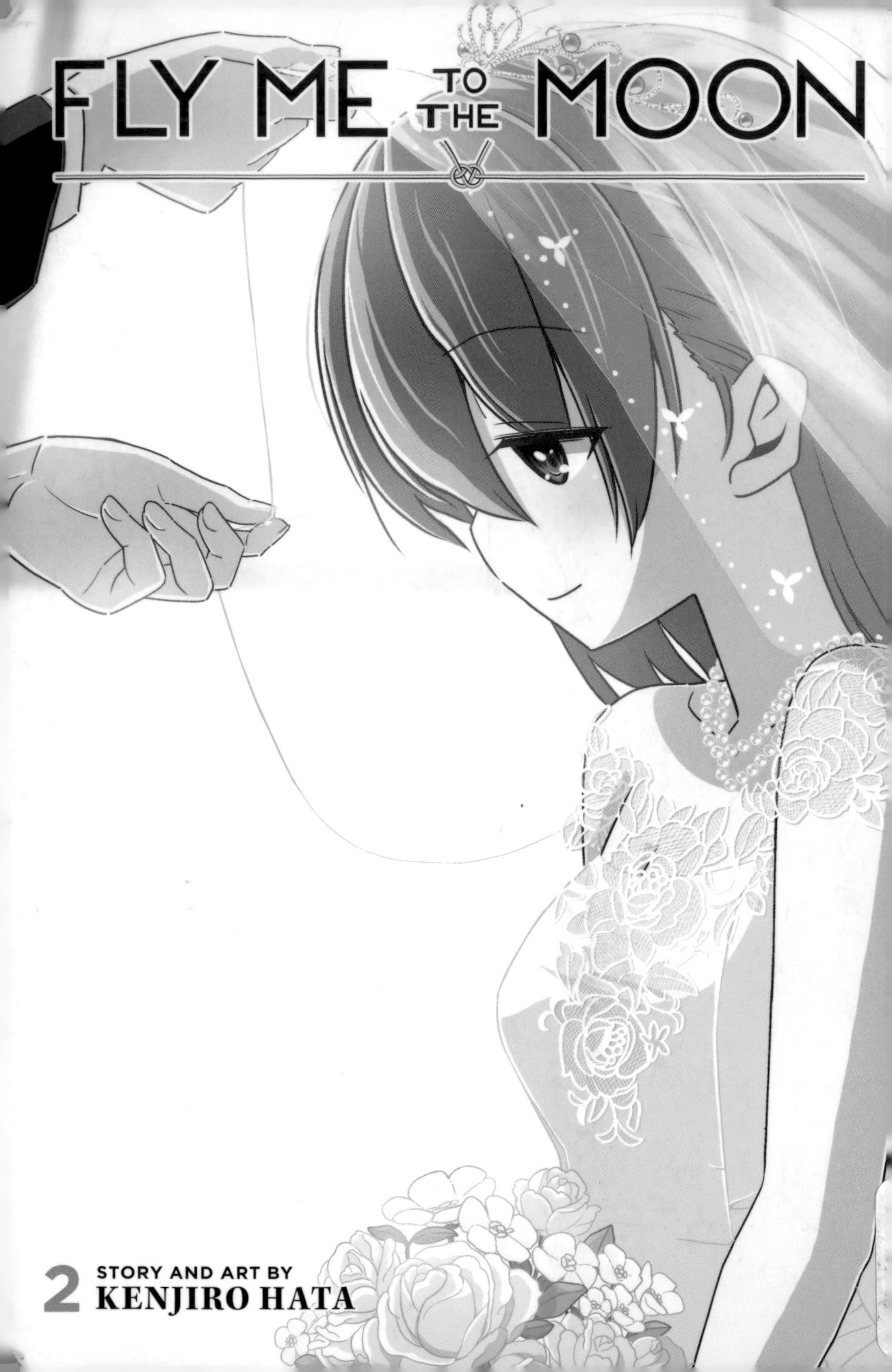
FLY ME TO THE MOON
2
STORY AND ART BY
KENJIRO HATA

FLY ME TO THE MOON

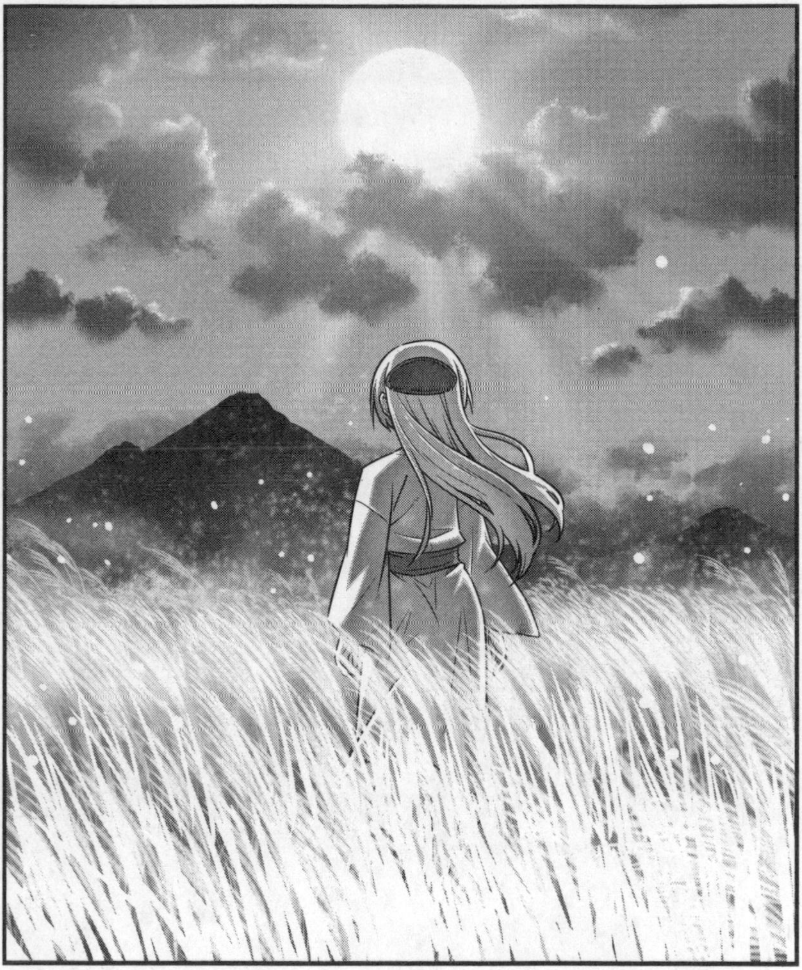

VOLUME 2

KENJIRO HATA

FLY ME TO THE MOON

Contents

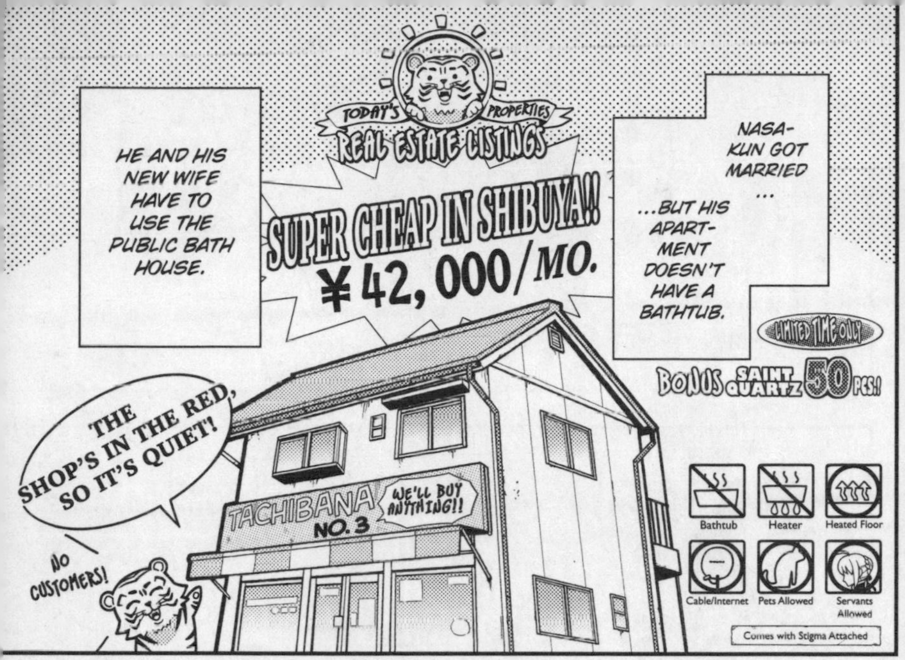
NASA-KUN GOT MARRIED ...
...BUT HIS APARTMENT DOESN'T HAVE A BATHTUB.
TODAY'S PROPERTIES
REAL ESTATE LISTINGS
SUPER CHEAP IN SHIBUYA!!
¥42,000/MO.
LIMITED TIME ONLY
BONUS SAINT QUARTZ 50 PCS.!
Bathtub
Heater
Heated Floor
Cable/Internet
Pets Allowed
Servants Allowed
Comes with Stigma Attached
HE AND HIS NEW WIFE HAVE TO USE THE PUBLIC BATH HOUSE.
TACHIBANA NO. 3
WE'LL BUY ANYTHING!!
THE SHOP'S IN THE RED, SO IT'S QUIET!
NO CUSTOMERS!

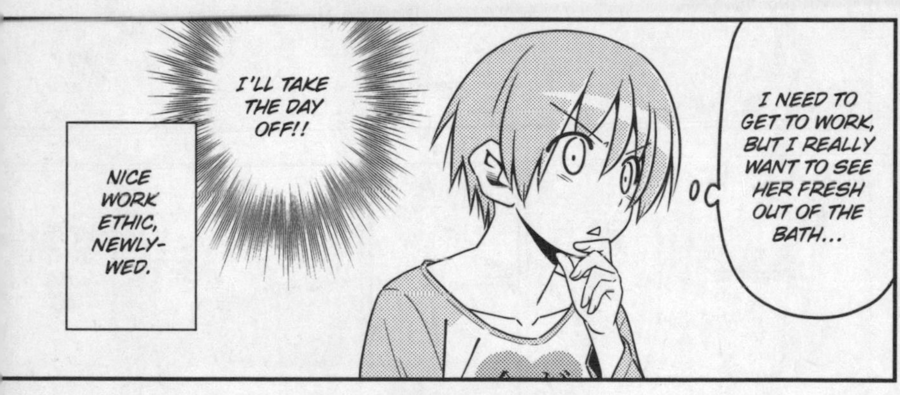
I NEED TO GET TO WORK, BUT I REALLY WANT TO SEE HER FRESH OUT OF THE BATH...
I'LL TAKE THE DAY OFF!!
NICE WORK ETHIC, NEWLY-WED.

Chapter 9: "I Like Young Folks to Be Spirited to a Fault (If They're Pretty Girls)"

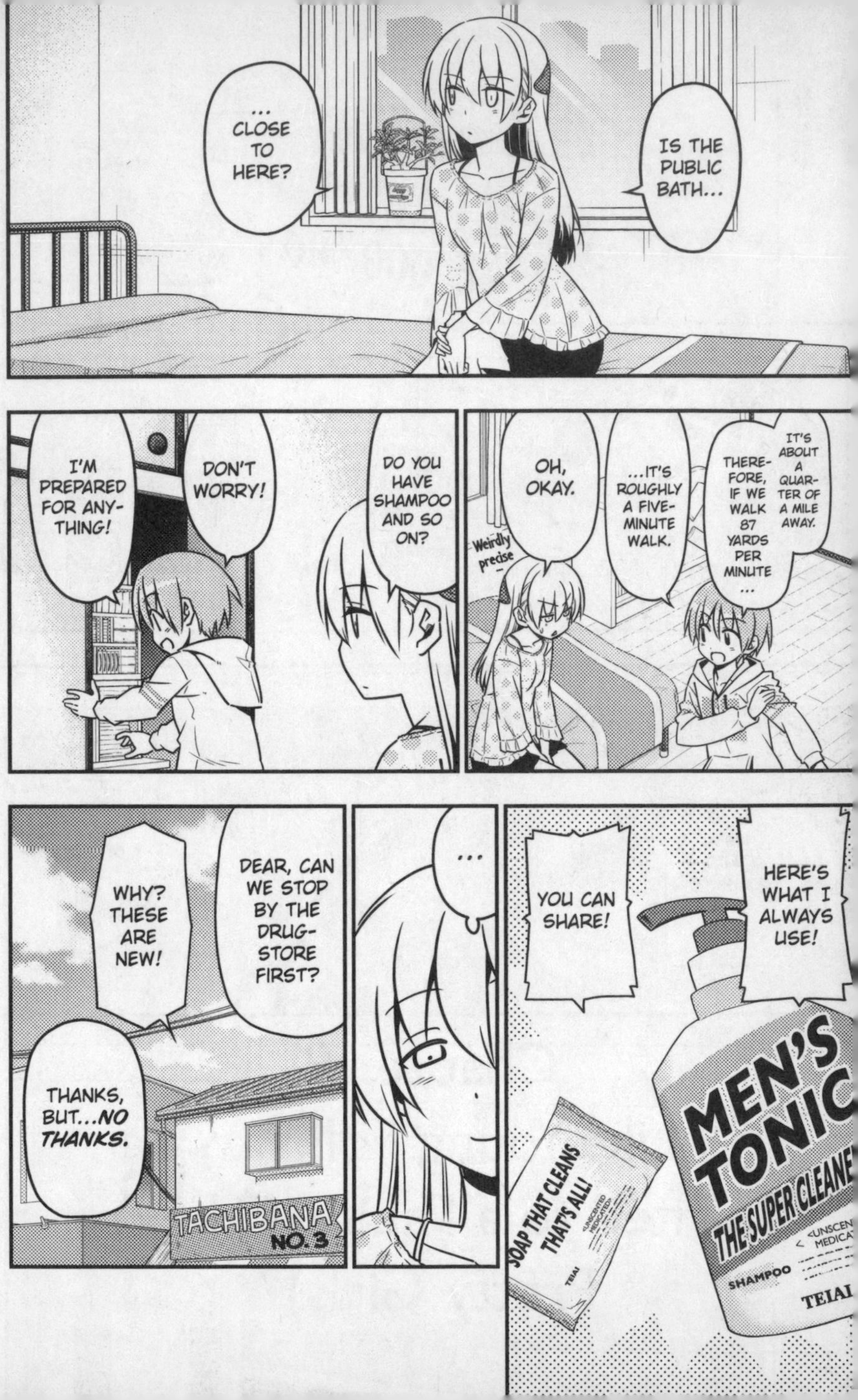
IS THE PUBLIC BATH...
...CLOSE TO HERE?
IT'S ABOUT A QUARTER OF A MILE AWAY.
THEREFORE, IF WE WALK 87 YARDS PER MINUTE...
...IT'S ROUGHLY A FIVE-MINUTE WALK.
OH, OKAY.
Weirdly precise
DO YOU HAVE SHAMPOO AND SO ON?
DON'T WORRY!
I'M PREPARED FOR ANYTHING!
HERE'S WHAT I ALWAYS USE!
YOU CAN SHARE!
MEN'S TONIC
SHAMPOO
TEIAI
SOAP THAT CLEANS THAT'S ALL!
UNSCENTED MEDICATED
TEIAI
...
DEAR, CAN WE STOP BY THE DRUGSTORE FIRST?
WHY? THESE ARE NEW!
THANKS, BUT...NO THANKS.
TACHIBANA NO. 3

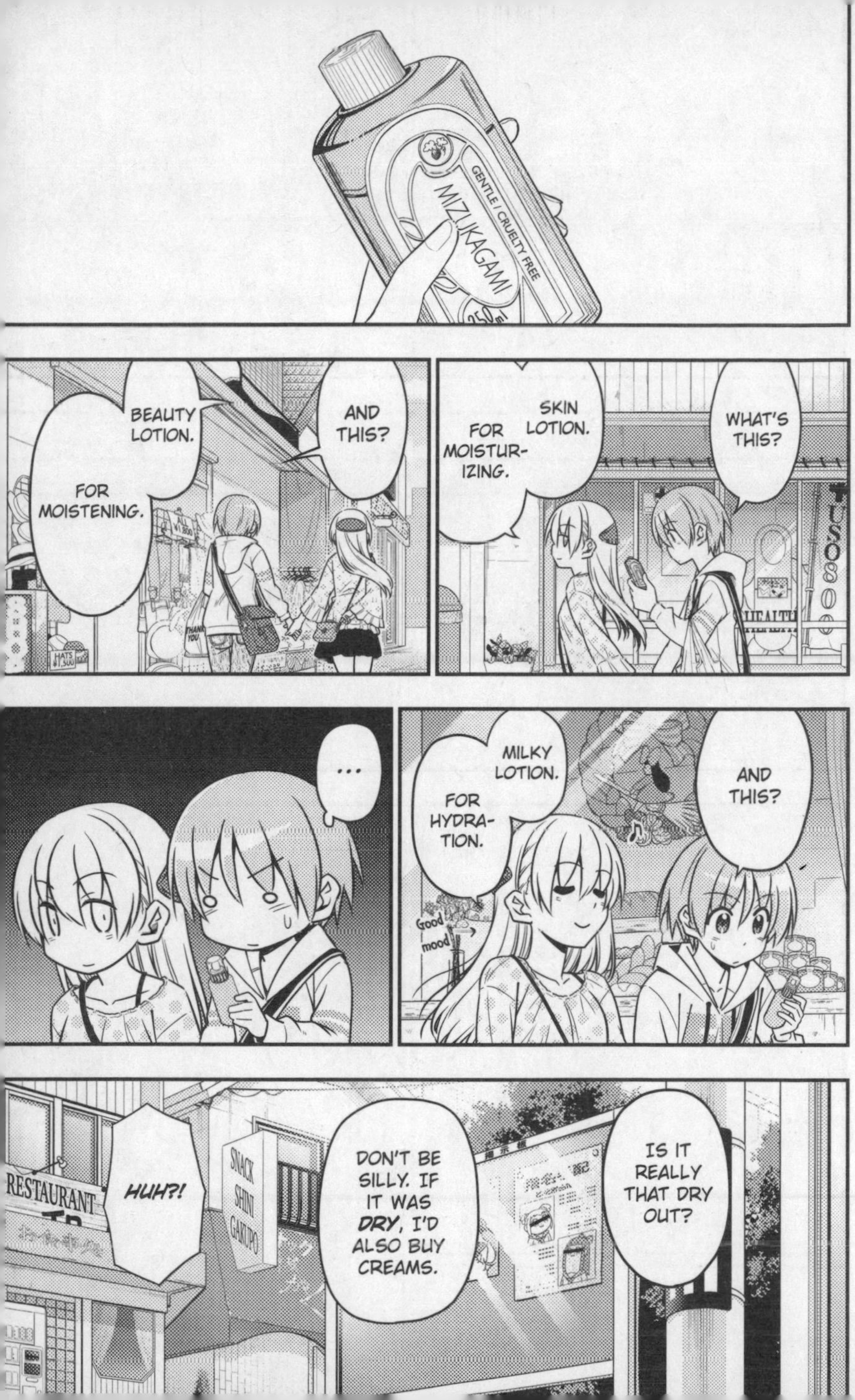
GENTLE / CRUELTY FREE
MIZUKAGAMI
250ml
WHAT'S THIS?
SKIN LOTION.
FOR MOISTURIZING.
USO800
HEALTH
AND THIS?
BEAUTY LOTION.
FOR MOISTENING.
THANK YOU
HATS ¥1,300
AND THIS?
MILKY LOTION.
FOR HYDRATION.
Good mood
...
IS IT REALLY THAT DRY OUT?
DON'T BE SILLY. IF IT WAS *DRY*, I'D ALSO BUY CREAMS.
HUH?!
SNACK SHINI GAKUPO
RESTAURANT

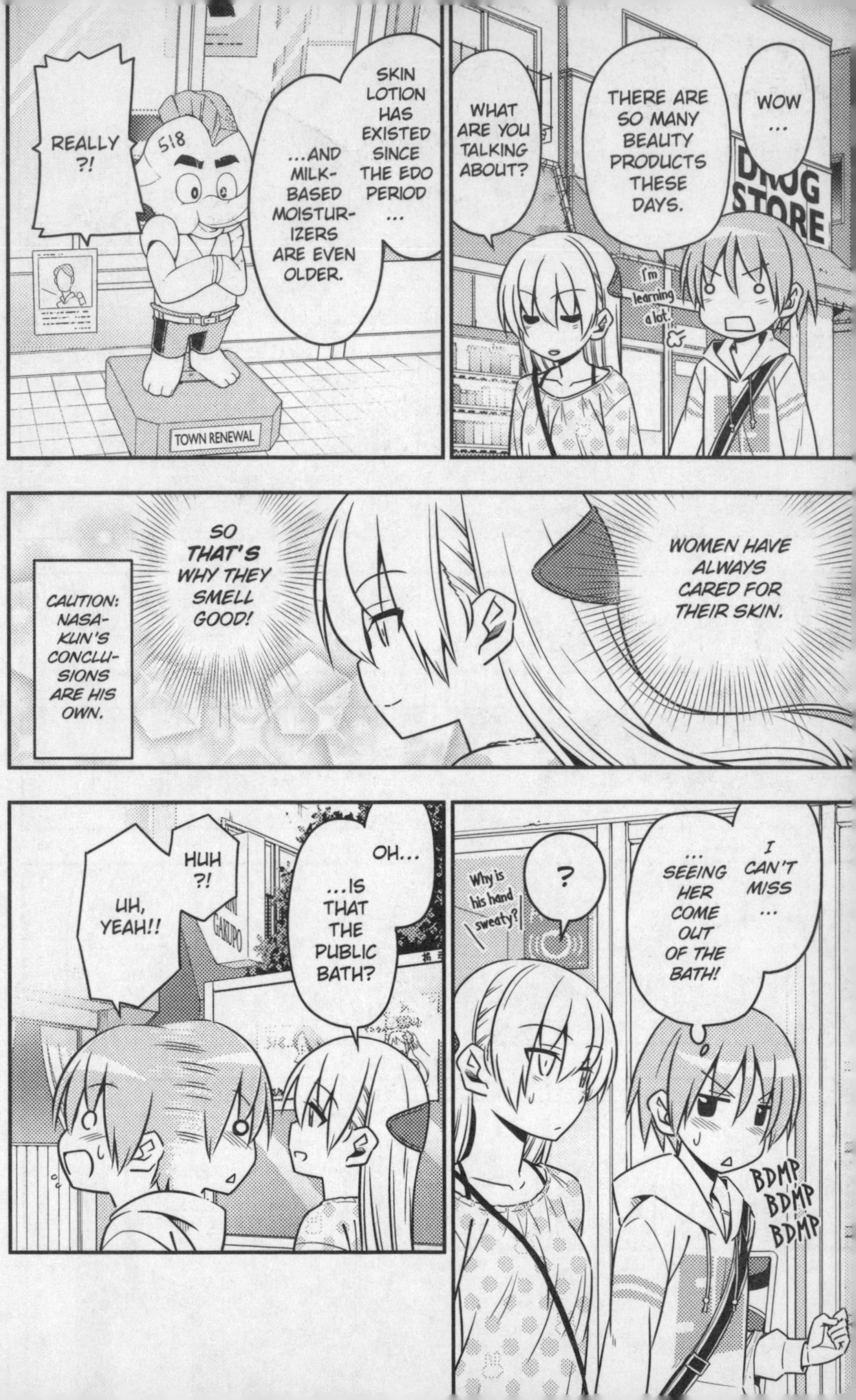
WOW ...
THERE ARE SO MANY BEAUTY PRODUCTS THESE DAYS.
WHAT ARE YOU TALKING ABOUT?
I'm learning a lot.
STORE
SKIN LOTION HAS EXISTED SINCE THE EDO PERIOD ...
...AND MILK-BASED MOISTURIZERS ARE EVEN OLDER.
REALLY ?!
518
TOWN RENEWAL
WOMEN HAVE ALWAYS CARED FOR THEIR SKIN.
SO THAT'S WHY THEY SMELL GOOD!
CAUTION: NASA-KUN'S CONCLUSIONS ARE HIS OWN.
I CAN'T MISS ...
... SEEING HER COME OUT OF THE BATH!
?
Why is his hand sweaty?
BDMP BDMP BDMP
OH...
...IS THAT THE PUBLIC BATH?
HUH ?!
UH, YEAH!!
GAKUPO

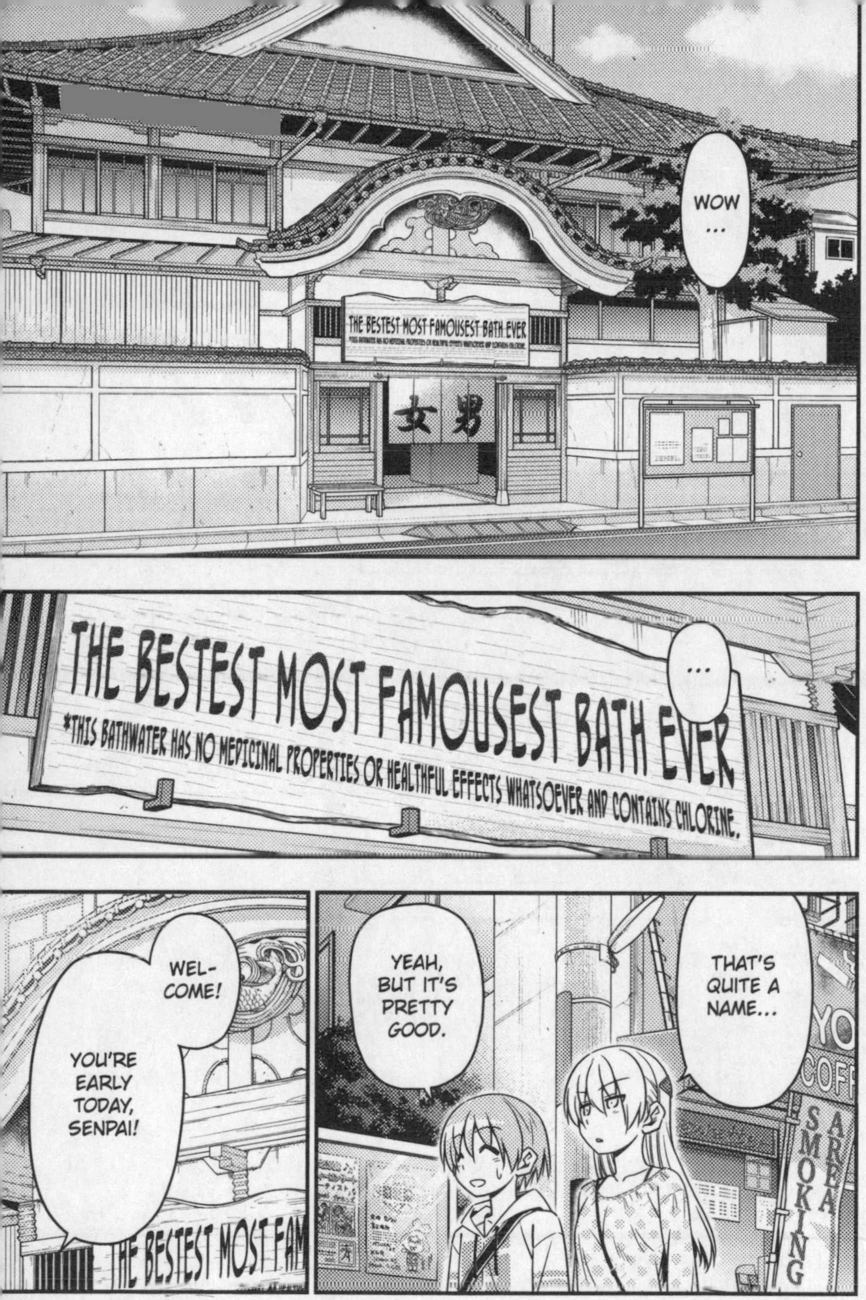
THE BESTEST MOST FAMOUSEST BATH EVER
男 女
WOW ...
THE BESTEST MOST FAMOUSEST BATH EVER
*THIS BATHWATER HAS NO MEDICINAL PROPERTIES OR HEALTHFUL EFFECTS WHATSOEVER AND CONTAINS CHLORINE.
...
THAT'S QUITE A NAME...
YEAH, BUT IT'S PRETTY GOOD.
SMOKING AREA
WEL-COME!
YOU'RE EARLY TODAY, SENPAI!

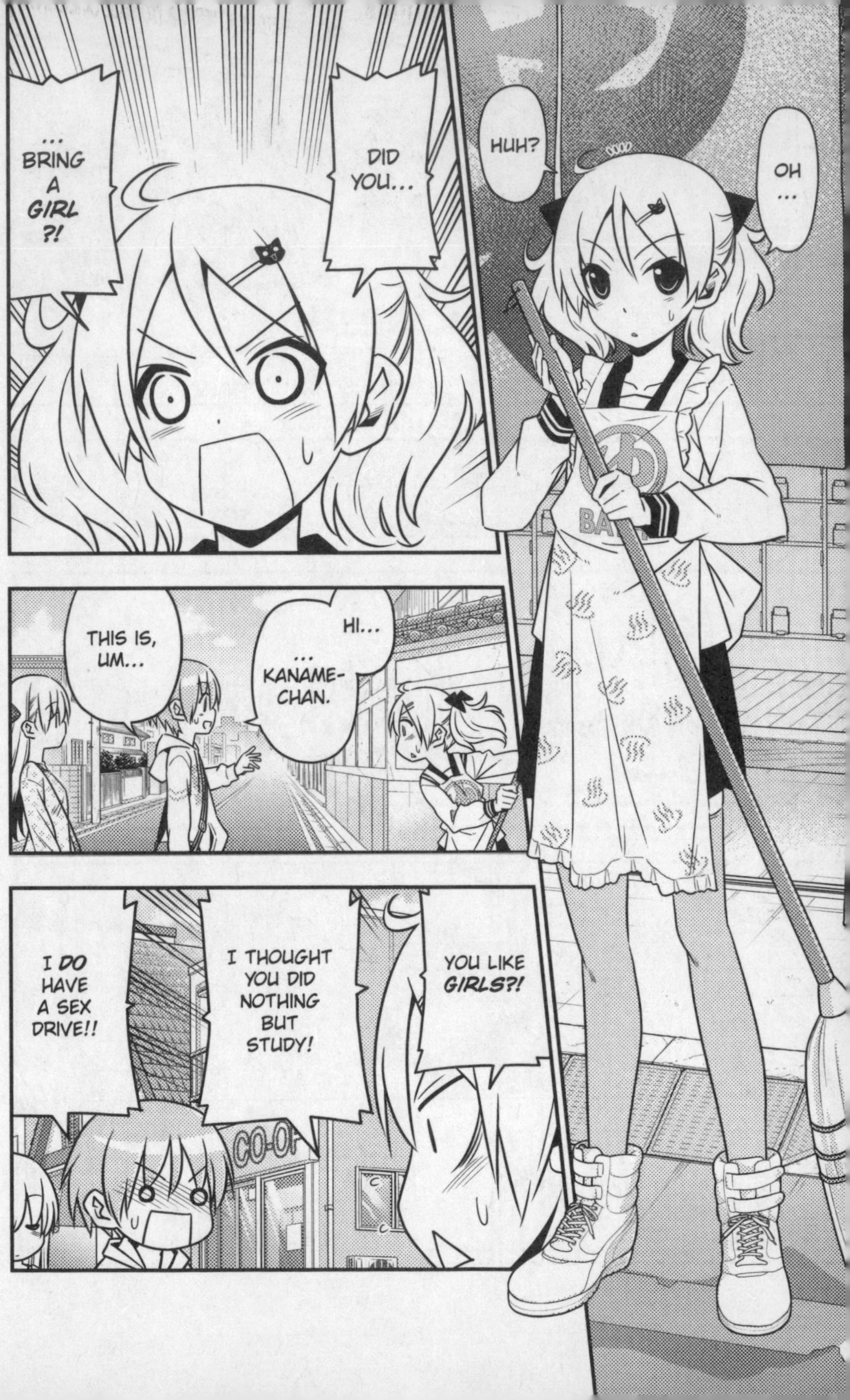
OH ...
HUH?
DID YOU...
... BRING A GIRL ?!
HI...
... KANAME-CHAN.
THIS IS, UM...
YOU LIKE GIRLS?!
I THOUGHT YOU DID NOTHING BUT STUDY!
I DO HAVE A SEX DRIVE!!

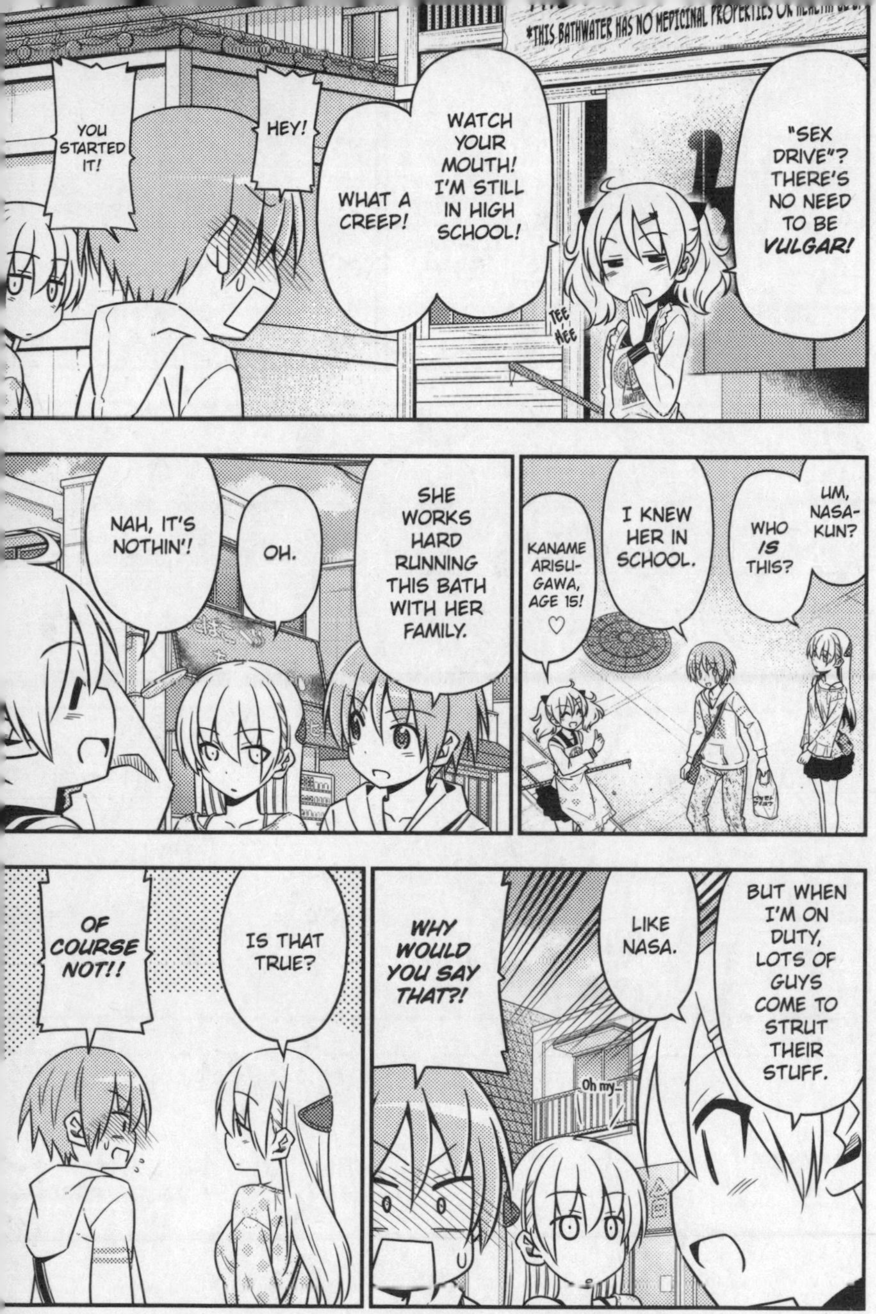
*THIS BATHWATER HAS NO MEDICINAL PROPERTIES OR
"SEX DRIVE"? THERE'S NO NEED TO BE VULGAR!
TEE HEE
WATCH YOUR MOUTH! I'M STILL IN HIGH SCHOOL!
WHAT A CREEP!
HEY!
YOU STARTED IT!
UM, NASA-KUN?
WHO IS THIS?
I KNEW HER IN SCHOOL.
KANAME ARISUGAWA, AGE 15! ♡
SHE WORKS HARD RUNNING THIS BATH WITH HER FAMILY.
OH.
NAH, IT'S NOTHIN'!
BUT WHEN I'M ON DUTY, LOTS OF GUYS COME TO STRUT THEIR STUFF.
LIKE NASA.
Oh my...
WHY WOULD YOU SAY THAT?!
IS THAT TRUE?
OF COURSE NOT!!

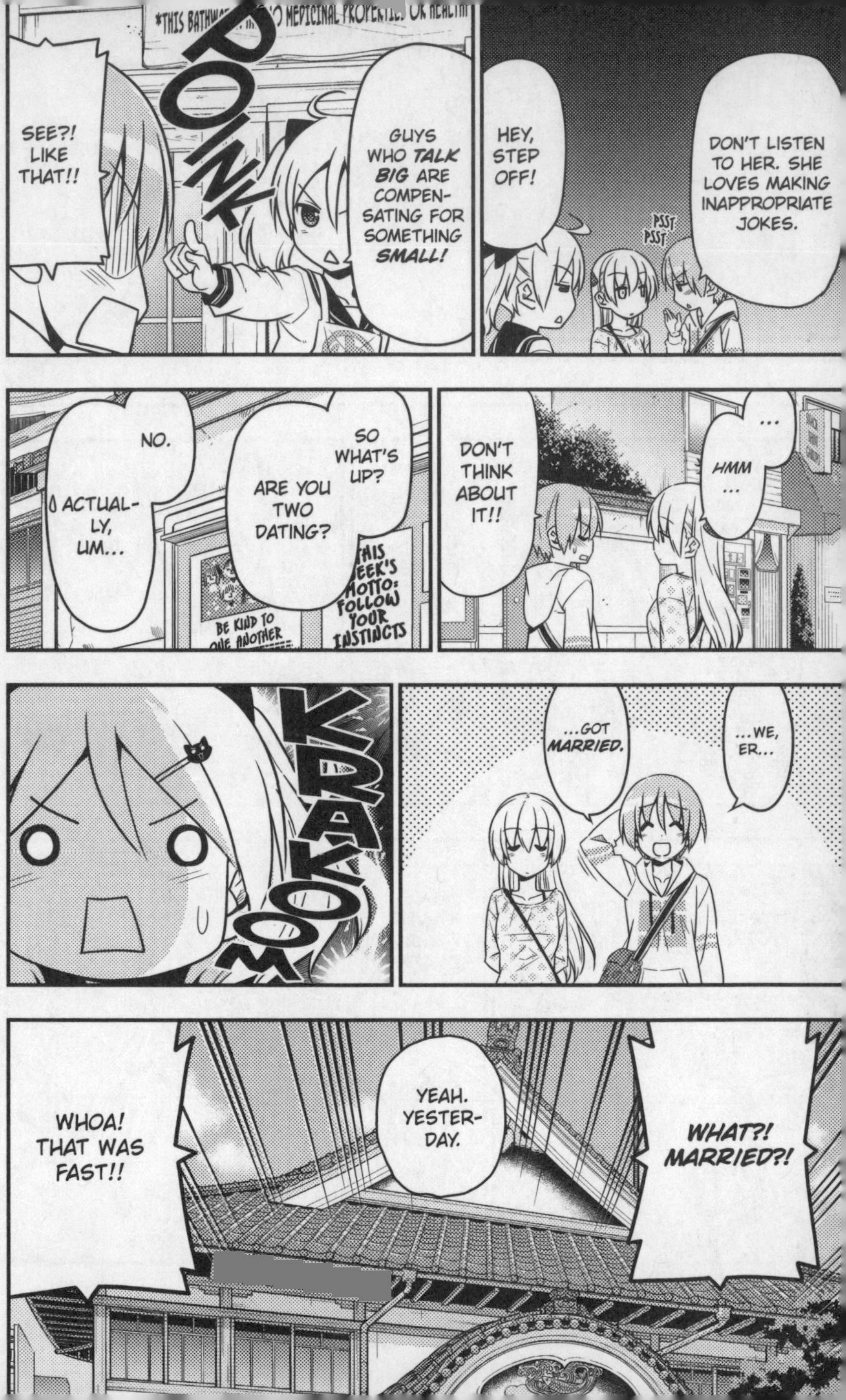
DON'T LISTEN TO HER. SHE LOVES MAKING INAPPROPRIATE JOKES.
PSST PSST
HEY, STEP OFF!
GUYS WHO *TALK BIG* ARE COMPENSATING FOR SOMETHING *SMALL!*
POINK
SEE?! LIKE THAT!!
...
HMM ...
DON'T THINK ABOUT IT!!
SO WHAT'S UP?
ARE YOU TWO DATING?
FOLLOW YOUR INSTINCTS
BE KIND TO ONE ANOTHER
NO.
ACTUALLY, UM...
...WE, ER...
...GOT *MARRIED.*
KABOOOM
WHAT?! MARRIED?!
YEAH. YESTERDAY.
WHOA! THAT WAS FAST!!

BATH HOUSE

7:00 A.M.—1:00 A.M.
EVERY DAY
FEES:
ADULT (JUNIOR HIGH
CHILD (ELEMENTAR
BABY (INFANTS AN

TICKETS

RULES
1. WASH BEFORE ENTERING.
2. DO NOT SIT ON THE EDGE OF THE
3. DO NOT LEAVE WATER RUNN
4. DO NOT WASH ITEMS.
5. NO INAPPROPRIATE TOUCHI
6. DO NOT EAT IN THE BATH.
7. DO NOT BATHE WHILE INTOX
8. PEEPING TOMS WILL BE EJECT
9. DO NOT ENTER IF SUFFERING FR
FOLLOWING CONDITIONS:
ZONAPHA SYNDROME, RABID KUG
FEVER, WINTER BLUES
10. NO CHEST ENGINES.
11. NO PSYCHOGUN ARMS.
12. WEAR SWIMSUITS OR NOTHING.
13. DO NOT OPEN WINDOWS, AS CHIMERA ANTS MAY ENTER.
14. NO PLAYING "DEFEAT KING JOE!" IN THE BATHTUB.
*PLAYING X-RIDER IS ALSO FORBIDDEN.
15. UNDER NO CIRCUMSTANCES BRING IN

REALLY? THANKS!

TO CELEBRATE, TODAY YOUR BATH IS ON THE HOUSE.

...BUT CONGRATS, I GUESS.

SEEMS WEIRD TO ME...

...NASA-KUN.

SEE YOU IN A BIT...

THANK YOU.

GO ON IN!

EH, NO BIGGIE. IT'S NOT SOME FANCY SPA.

NOT SO FAST!!

...I'LL WASH OFF TOO!

I GUESS ...

...

ER... YEAH!

Trembling with anticipation.

Has never seen him like this. →

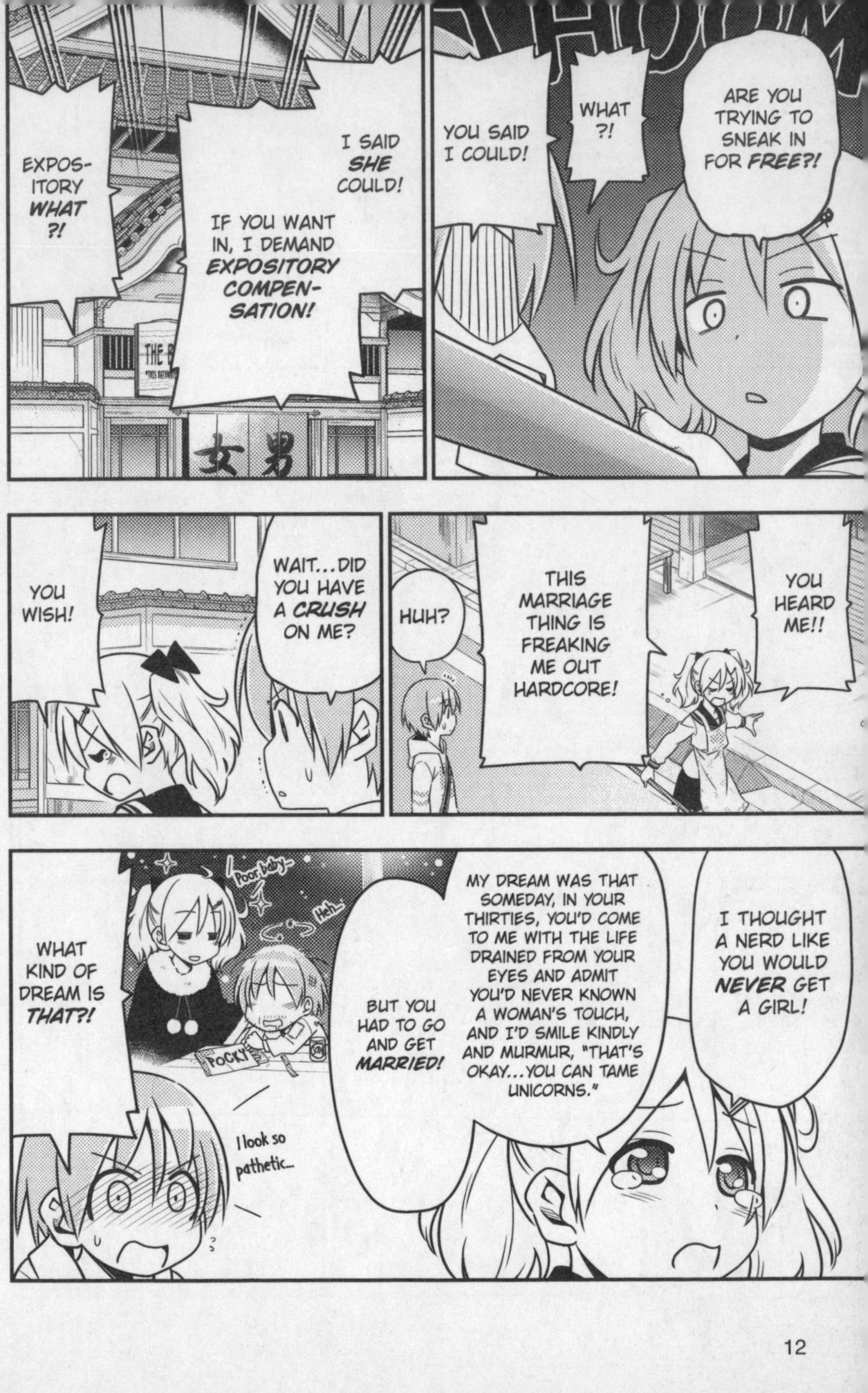
ARE YOU TRYING TO SNEAK IN FOR FREE?!
WHAT ?!
YOU SAID I COULD!
I SAID SHE COULD!
IF YOU WANT IN, I DEMAND EXPOSITORY COMPENSATION!
EXPOSITORY WHAT ?!
女 男
YOU HEARD ME!!
THIS MARRIAGE THING IS FREAKING ME OUT HARDCORE!
HUH?
WAIT...DID YOU HAVE A CRUSH ON ME?
YOU WISH!
I THOUGHT A NERD LIKE YOU WOULD NEVER GET A GIRL!
MY DREAM WAS THAT SOMEDAY, IN YOUR THIRTIES, YOU'D COME TO ME WITH THE LIFE DRAINED FROM YOUR EYES AND ADMIT YOU'D NEVER KNOWN A WOMAN'S TOUCH, AND I'D SMILE KINDLY AND MURMUR, "THAT'S OKAY...YOU CAN TAME UNICORNS."
BUT YOU HAD TO GO AND GET MARRIED!
Poor baby...
Heh...
POCKY
WHAT KIND OF DREAM IS THAT?!
I look so pathetic...

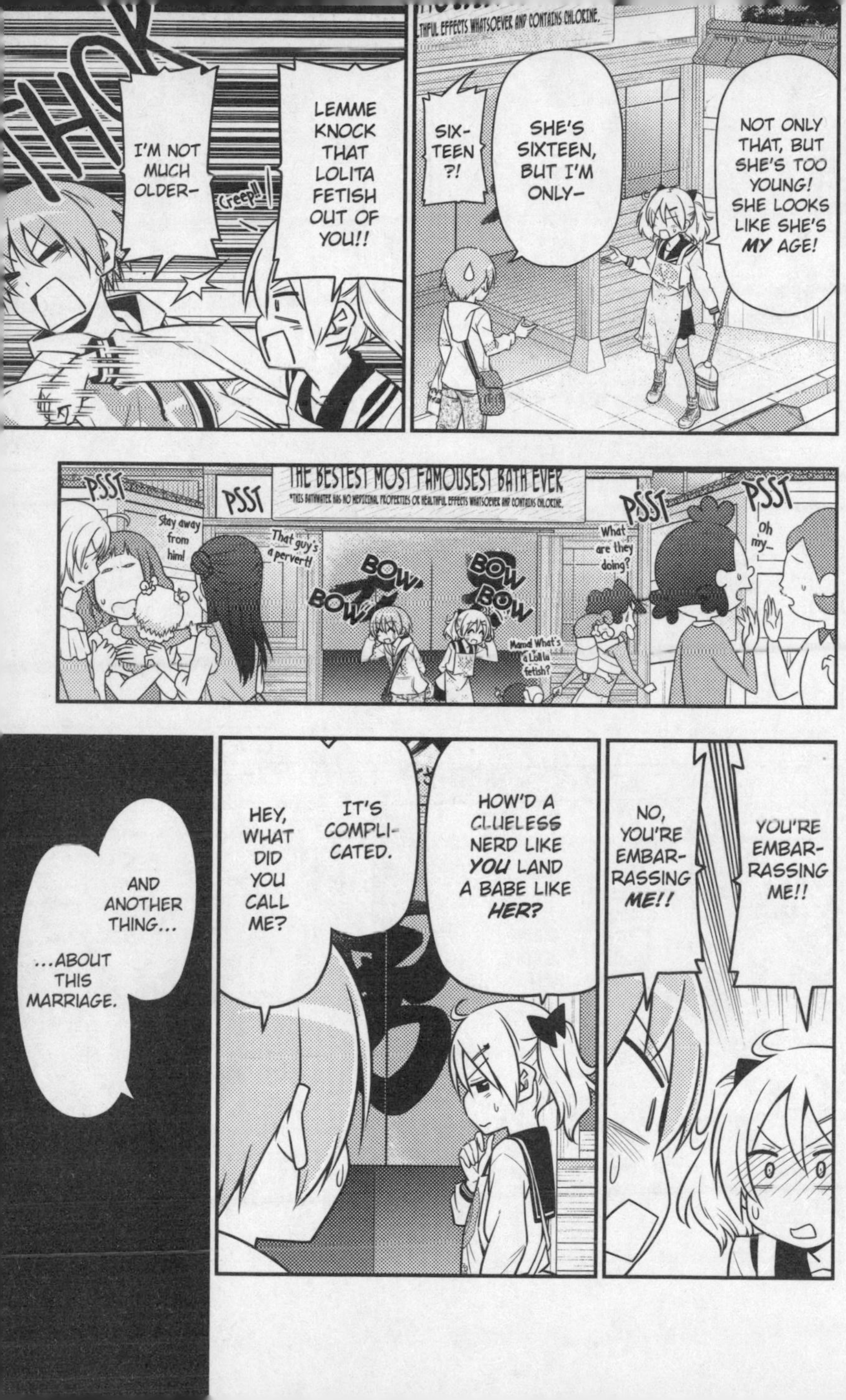
THFUL EFFECTS WHATSOEVER AND CONTAINS CHLORINE.
NOT ONLY THAT, BUT SHE'S TOO YOUNG! SHE LOOKS LIKE SHE'S MY AGE!
SHE'S SIXTEEN, BUT I'M ONLY-
SIX-TEEN?!
LEMME KNOCK THAT LOLITA FETISH OUT OF YOU!!
Creep!!
I'M NOT MUCH OLDER-
PSST
Oh my...
PSST
What are they doing?
Mama! What's a Lolita fetish?
BOW BOW
BOW BOW
THE BESTEST MOST FAMOUSEST BATH EVER
*THIS BATHWATER HAS NO MEDICINAL PROPERTIES OR HEALTHFUL EFFECTS WHATSOEVER AND CONTAINS CHLORINE.
That guy's a pervert!
PSST
Stay away from him!
PSST
YOU'RE EMBAR-RASSING ME!!
NO, YOU'RE EMBAR-RASSING ME!!
HOW'D A CLUELESS NERD LIKE YOU LAND A BABE LIKE HER?
IT'S COMPLI-CATED.
HEY, WHAT DID YOU CALL ME?
AND ANOTHER THING...
...ABOUT THIS MARRIAGE.

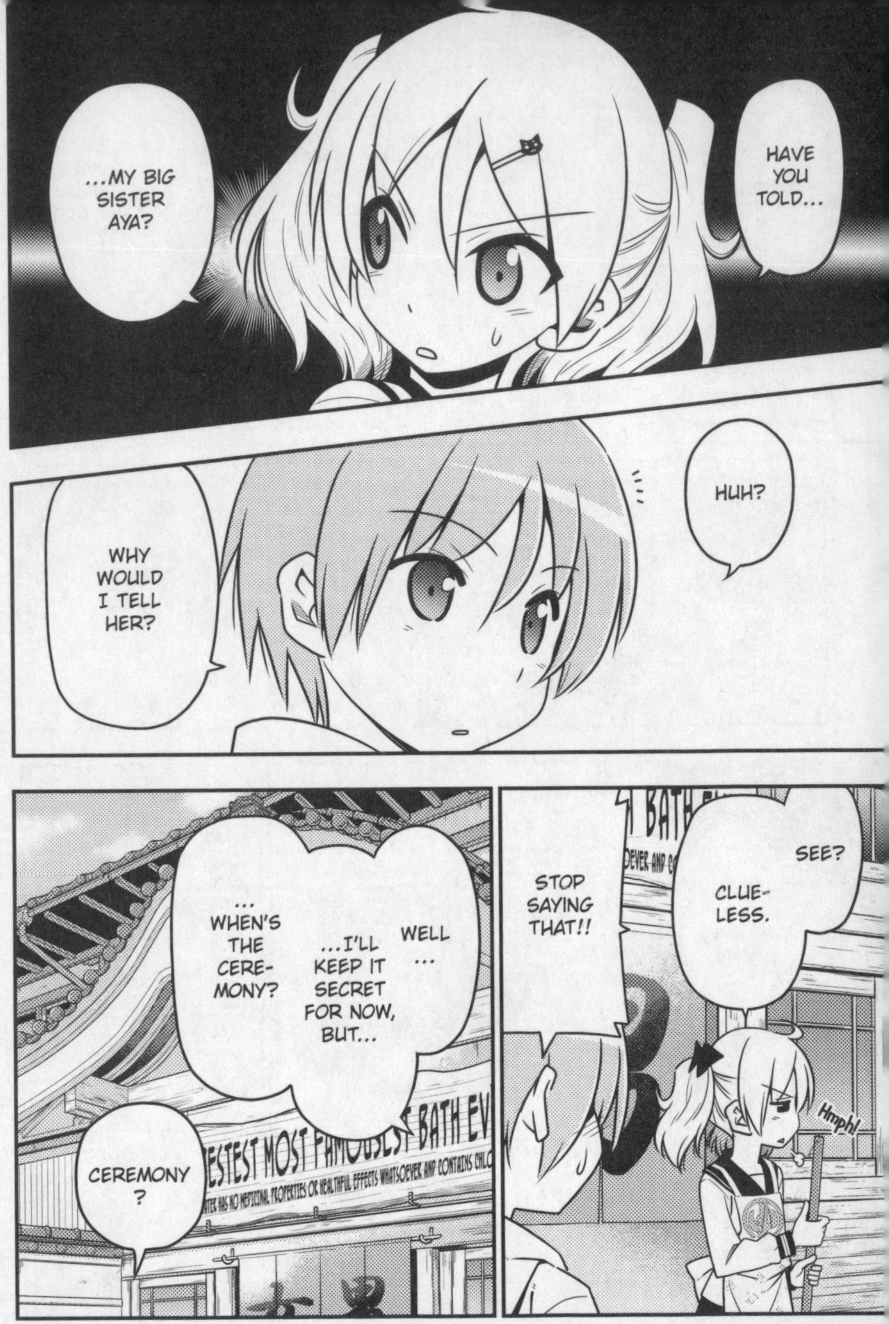
HAVE YOU TOLD...
...MY BIG SISTER AYA?
HUH?
WHY WOULD I TELL HER?
SEE?
CLUE-LESS.
Hmph!
STOP SAYING THAT!!
WELL ...
...I'LL KEEP IT SECRET FOR NOW, BUT...
... WHEN'S THE CERE-MONY?
CEREMONY ?

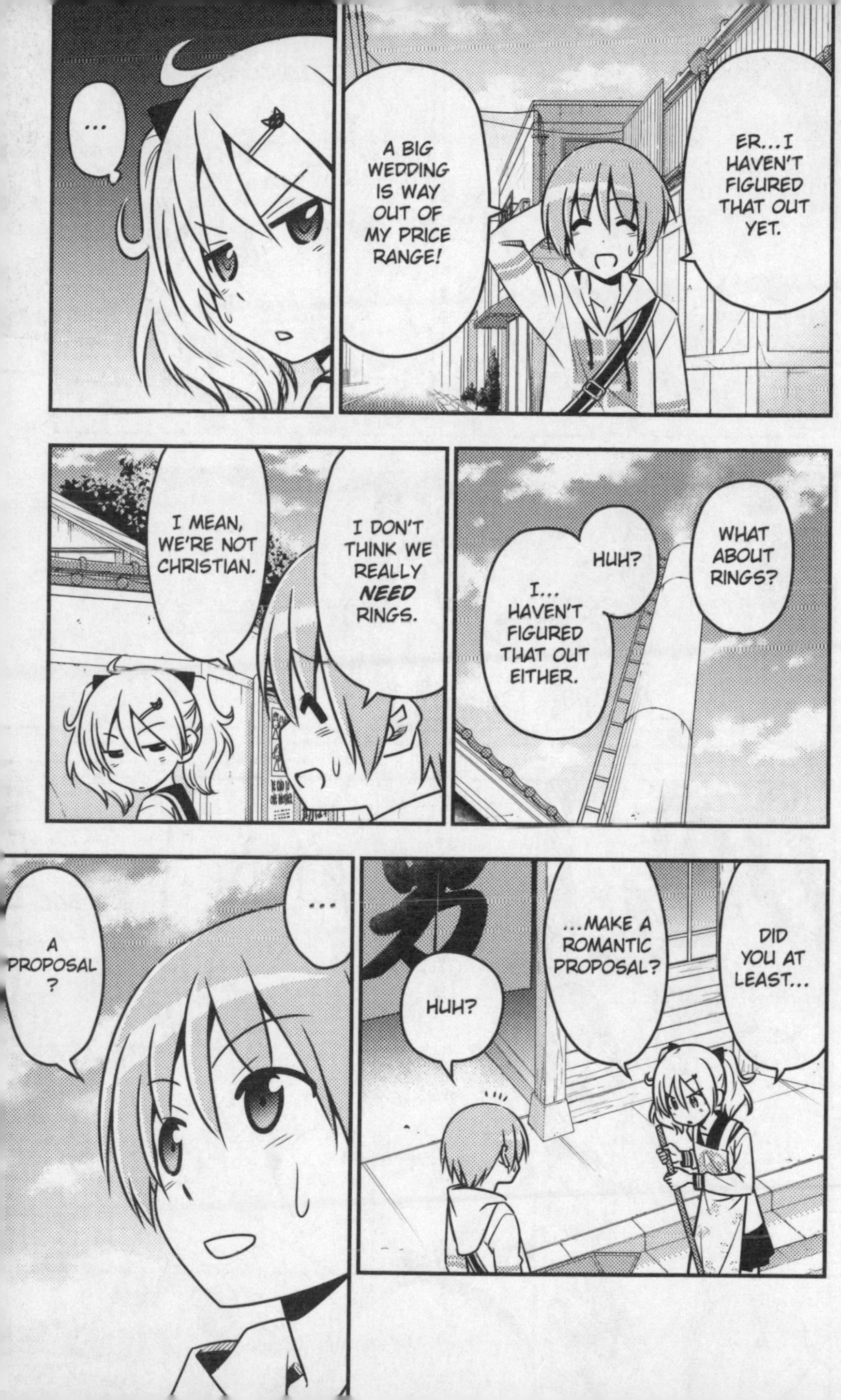
ER…I HAVEN'T FIGURED THAT OUT YET.
A BIG WEDDING IS WAY OUT OF MY PRICE RANGE!
…
WHAT ABOUT RINGS?
HUH?
I… HAVEN'T FIGURED THAT OUT EITHER.
I DON'T THINK WE REALLY NEED RINGS.
I MEAN, WE'RE NOT CHRISTIAN.
DID YOU AT LEAST…
…MAKE A ROMANTIC PROPOSAL?
HUH?
…
A PROPOSAL?

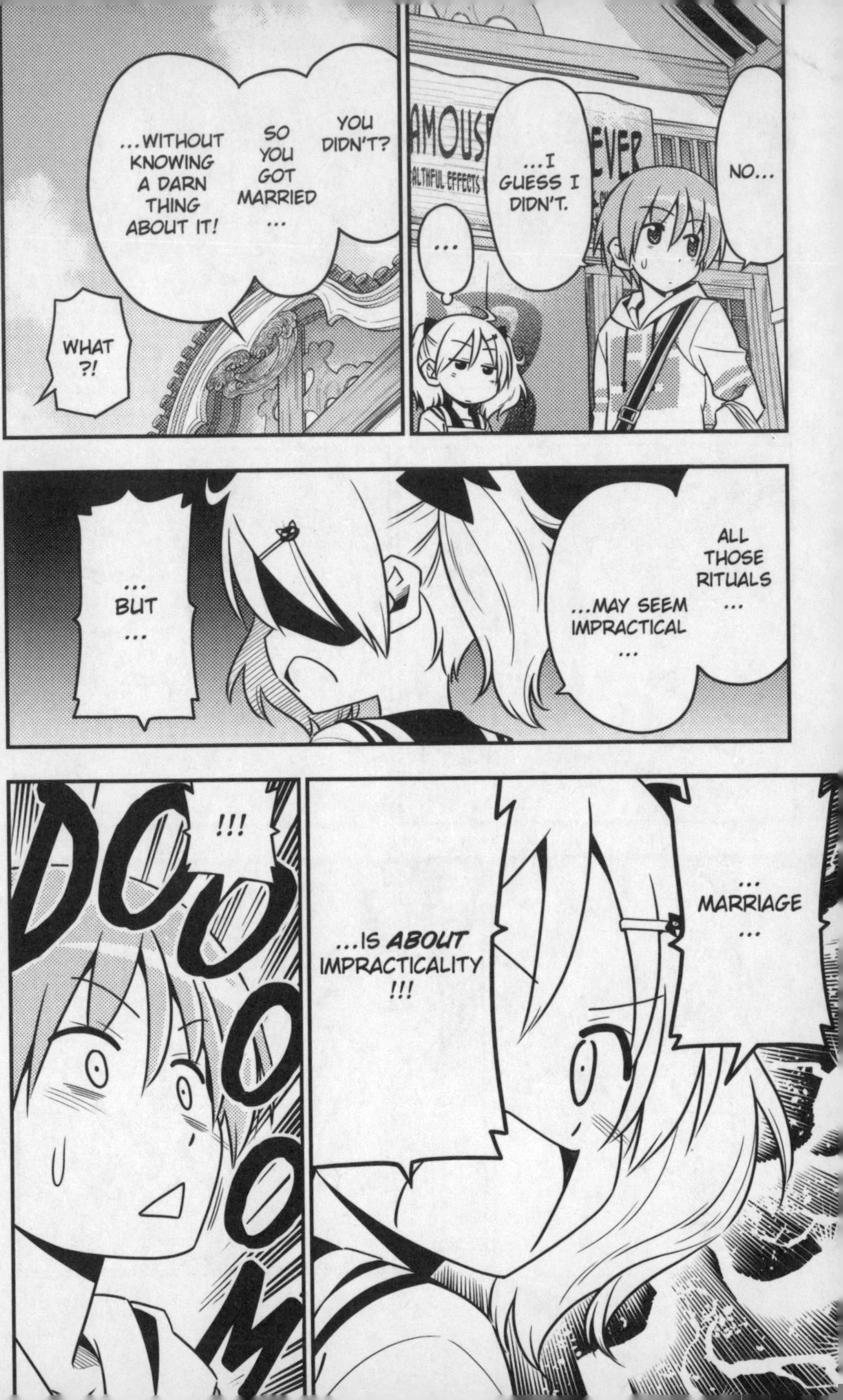
NO...
...I GUESS I DIDN'T.
...
YOU DIDN'T?
SO YOU GOT MARRIED ...
...WITHOUT KNOWING A DARN THING ABOUT IT!
WHAT ?!
ALL THOSE RITUALS ...
...MAY SEEM IMPRACTICAL ...
... BUT ...
... MARRIAGE ...
...IS ABOUT IMPRACTICALITY !!!
!!!

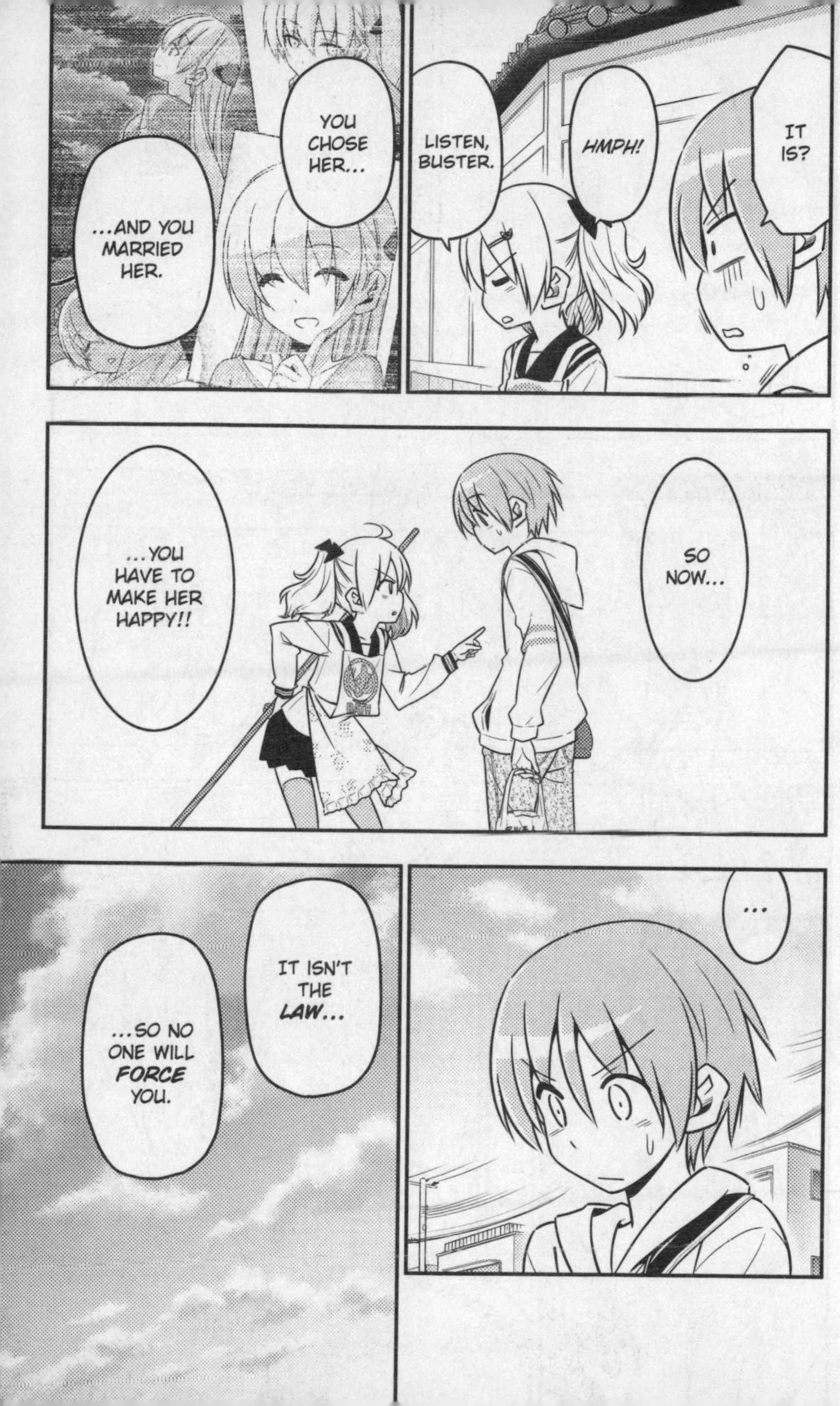
IT IS?
HMPH!
LISTEN, BUSTER.
YOU CHOSE HER...
...AND YOU MARRIED HER.
SO NOW...
...YOU HAVE TO MAKE HER HAPPY!!
...
IT ISN'T THE LAW...
...SO NO ONE WILL FORCE YOU.

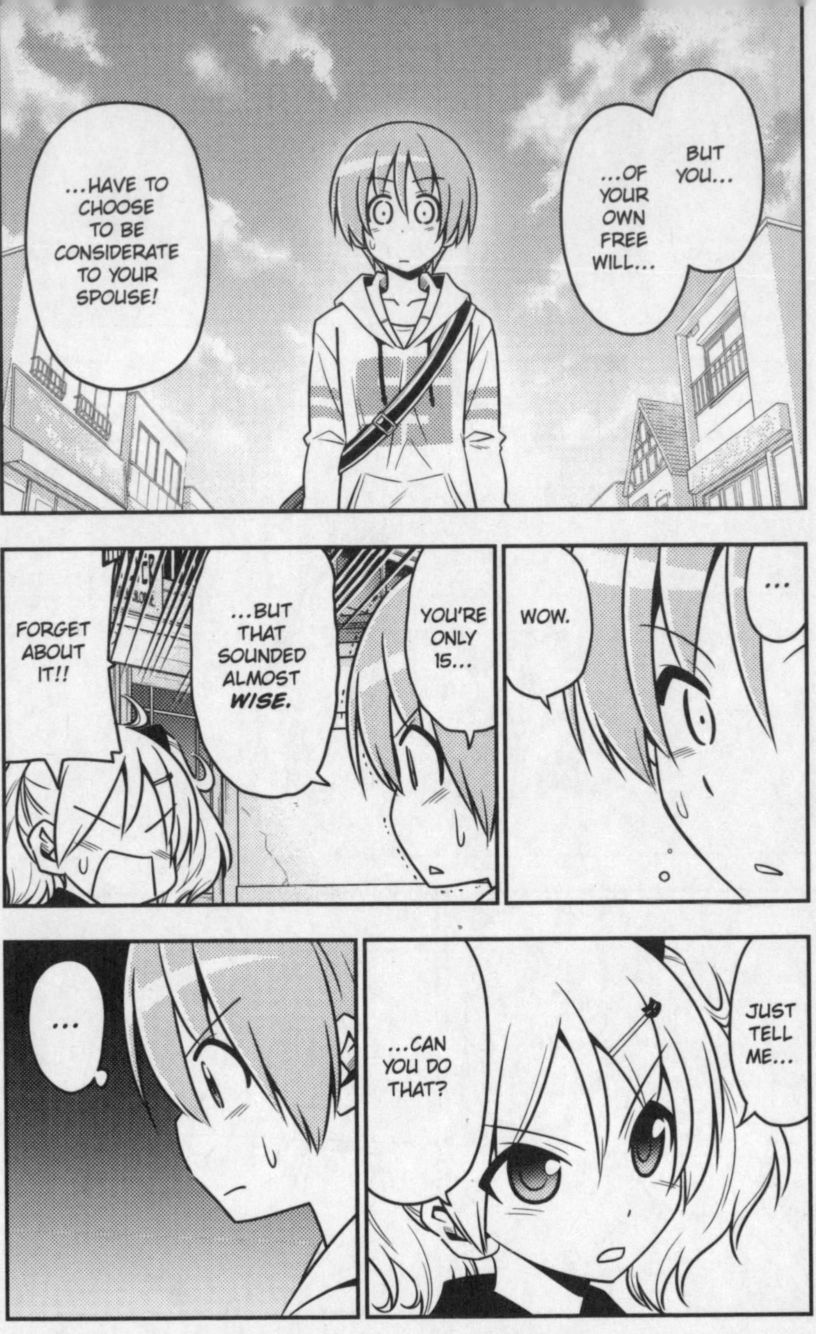
BUT YOU...
...OF YOUR OWN FREE WILL...
...HAVE TO CHOOSE TO BE CONSIDERATE TO YOUR SPOUSE!
...
WOW.
YOU'RE ONLY 15...
...BUT THAT SOUNDED ALMOST *WISE.*
FORGET ABOUT IT!!
JUST TELL ME...
...CAN YOU DO THAT?
...

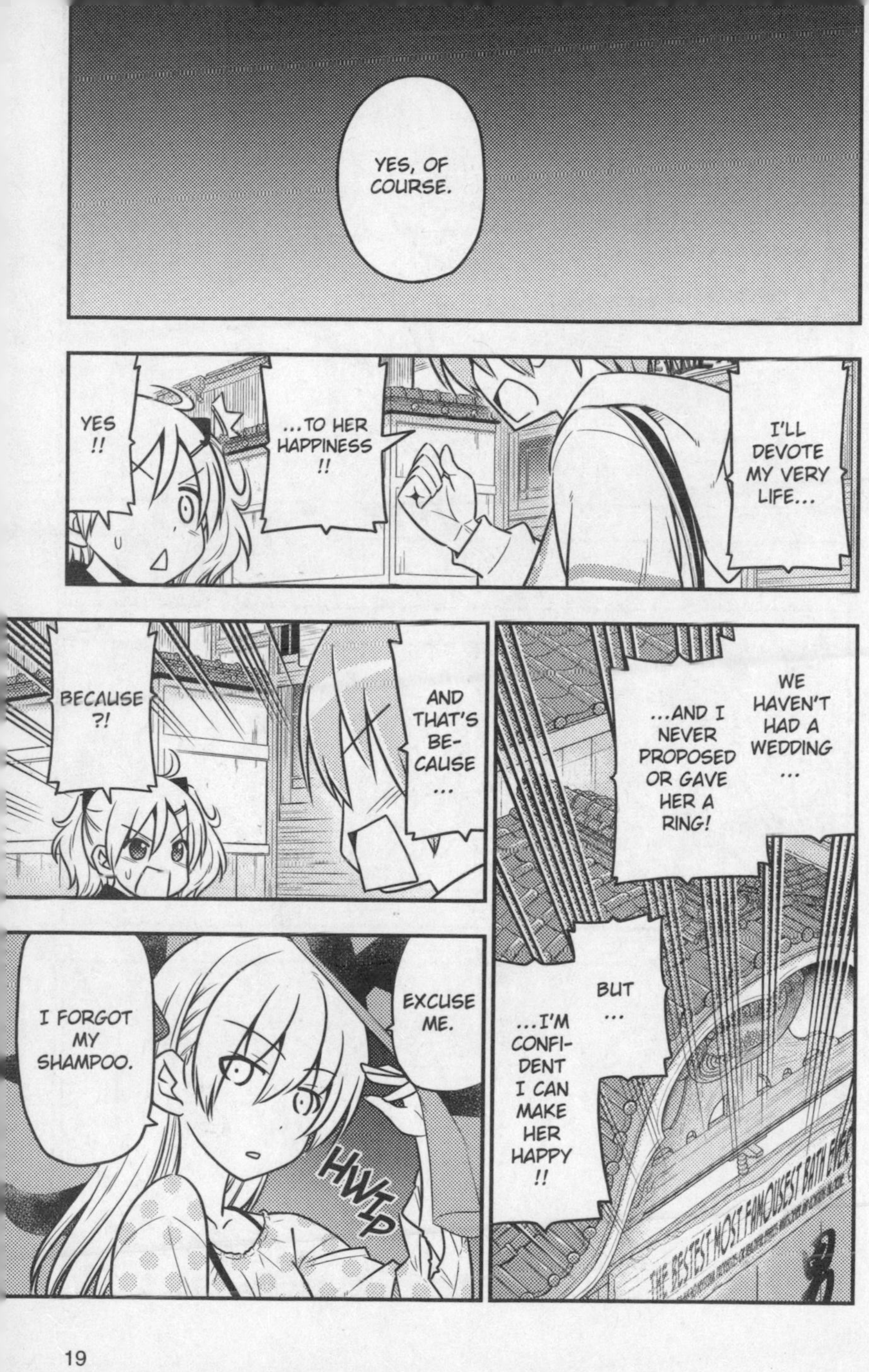
YES, OF COURSE.
I'LL DEVOTE MY VERY LIFE...
...TO HER HAPPINESS !!
YES !!
WE HAVEN'T HAD A WEDDING ...
...AND I NEVER PROPOSED OR GAVE HER A RING!
BUT ...
...I'M CONFI- DENT I CAN MAKE HER HAPPY !!
THE BESTEST MOST FAMOUSEST BATH EVER
AND THAT'S BE- CAUSE ...
BECAUSE ?!
EXCUSE ME.
HWIP
I FORGOT MY SHAMPOO.

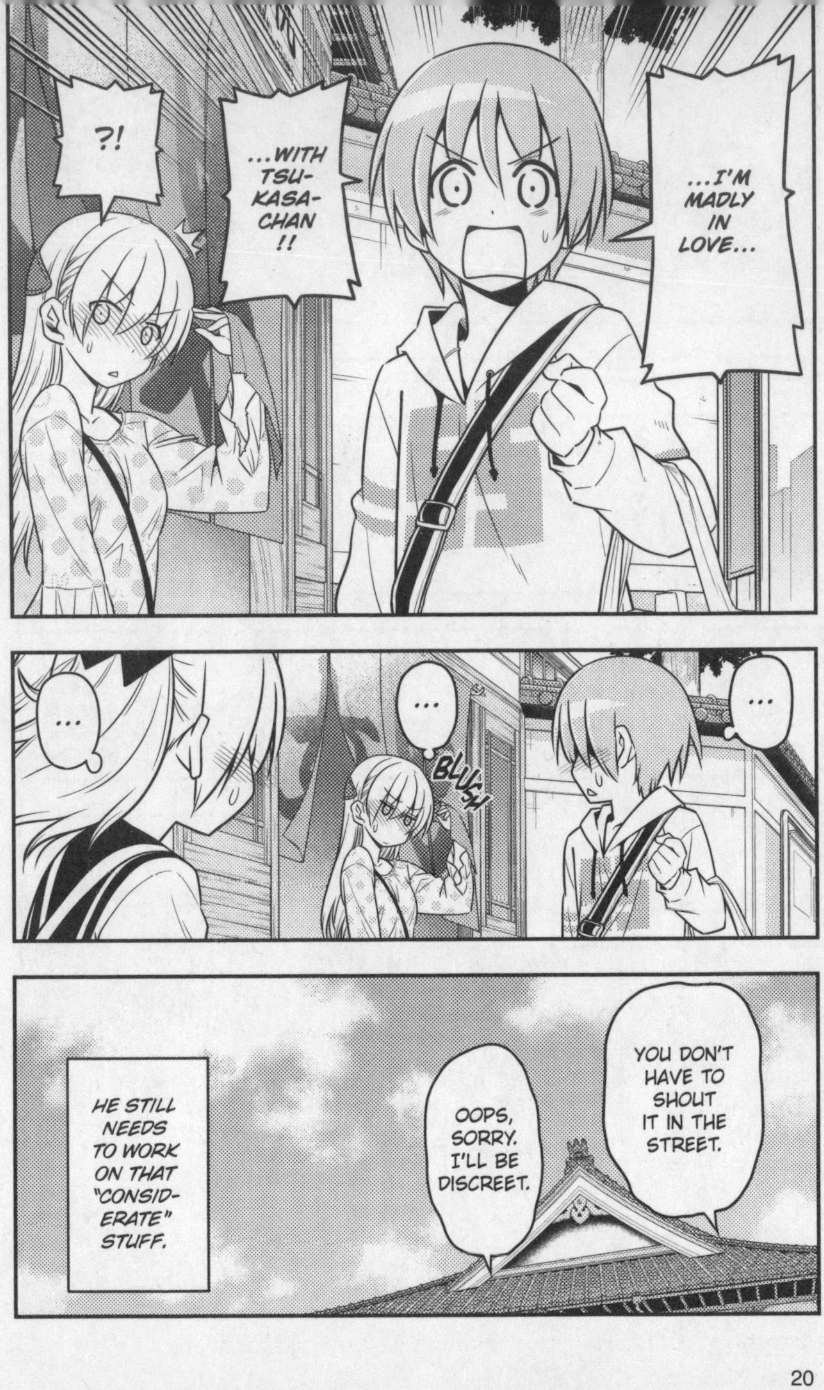
...I'M MADLY IN LOVE...
...WITH TSU-KASA-CHAN!!
?!
...
...
BLUSH
...
YOU DON'T HAVE TO SHOUT IT IN THE STREET.
OOPS, SORRY. I'LL BE DISCREET.
HE STILL NEEDS TO WORK ON THAT "CONSID-ERATE" STUFF.

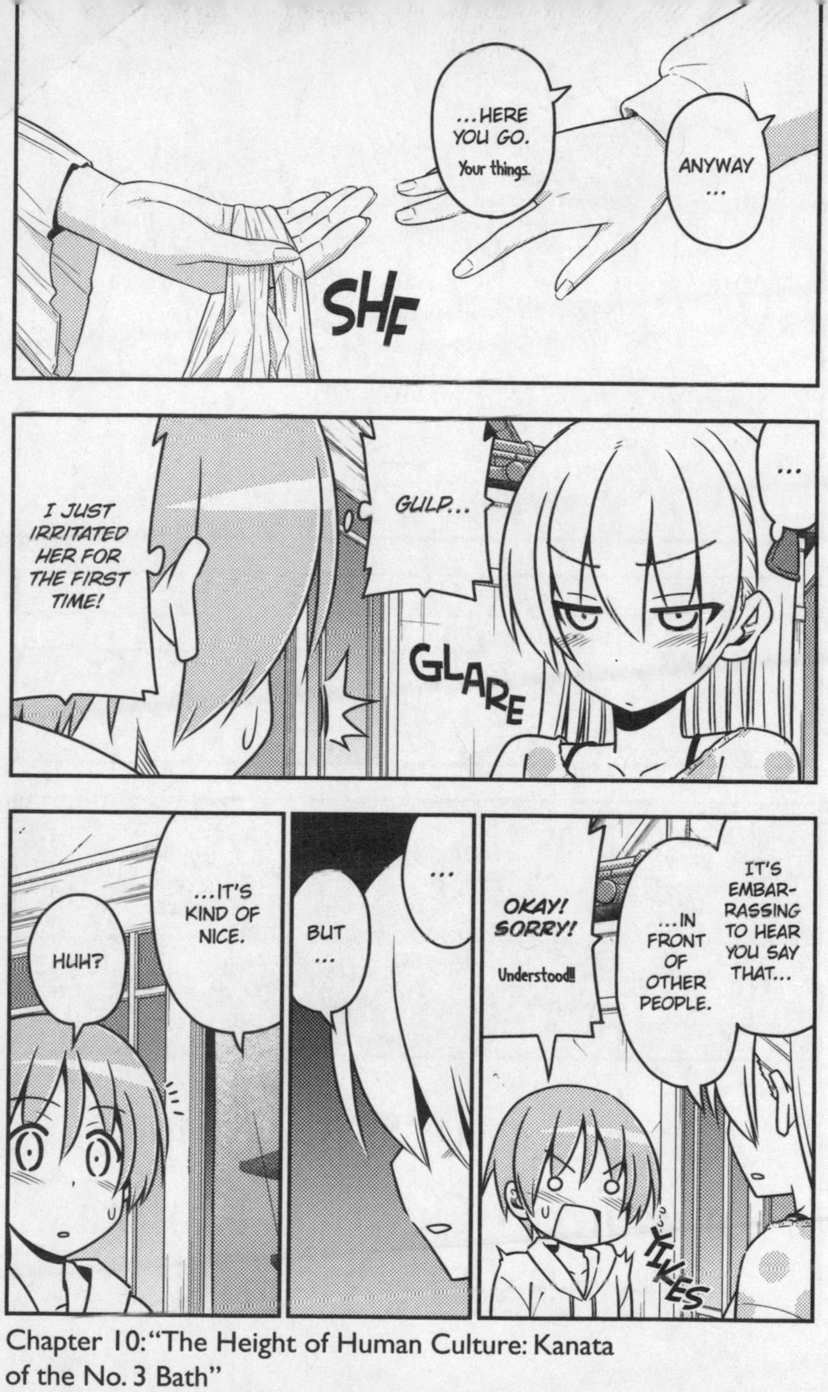
ANYWAY ...
...HERE YOU GO.
Your things.
SHF
...
GULP...
GLARE
I JUST IRRITATED HER FOR THE FIRST TIME!
IT'S EMBAR-RASSING TO HEAR YOU SAY THAT...
...IN FRONT OF OTHER PEOPLE.
OKAY! SORRY!
Understood!!
YIKES
...
BUT ...
...IT'S KIND OF NICE.
HUH?

Chapter 10: "The Height of Human Culture: Kanata of the No. 3 Bath"

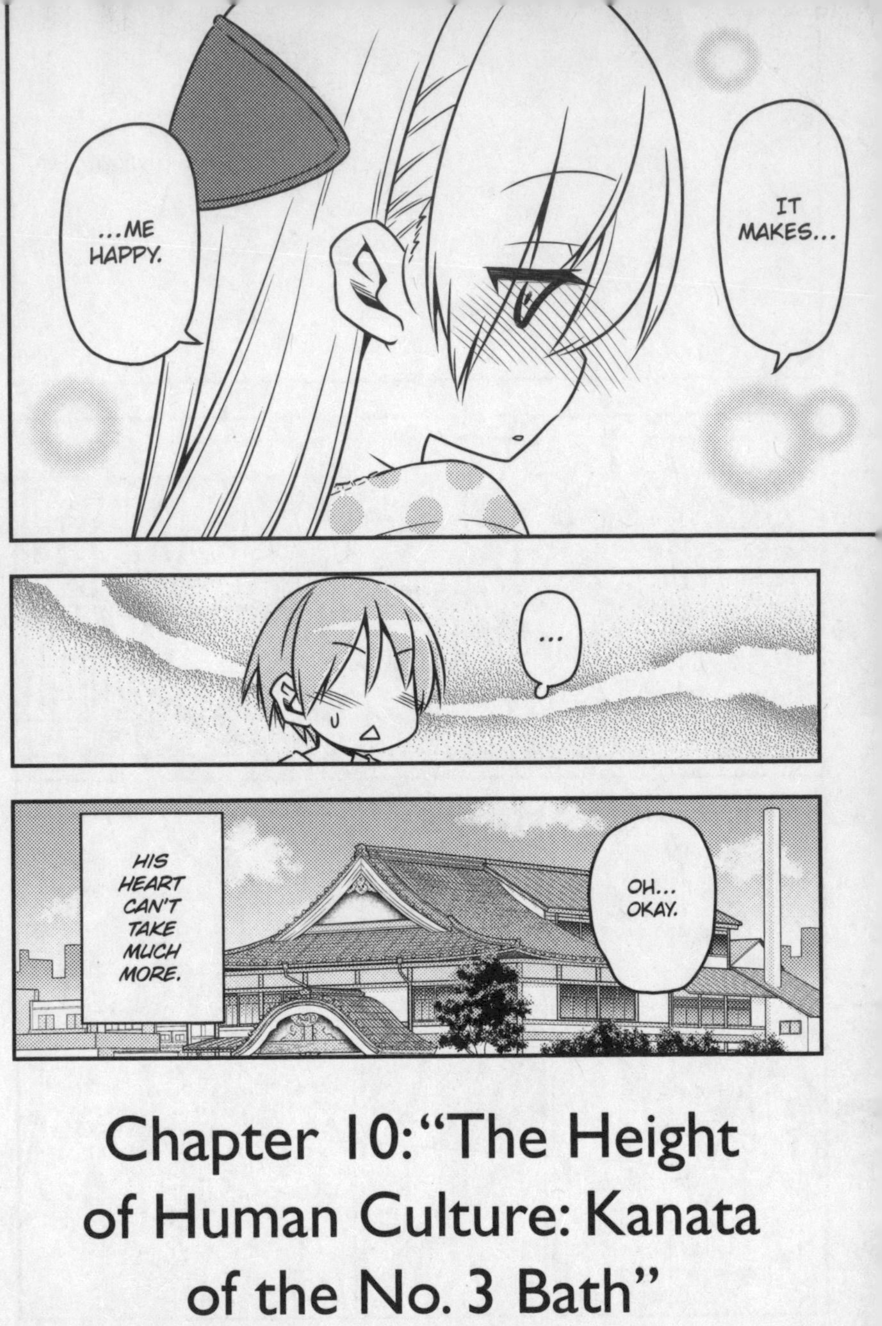
IT MAKES...
...ME HAPPY.
...
OH... OKAY.
HIS HEART CAN'T TAKE MUCH MORE.

Chapter 10: "The Height of Human Culture: Kanata of the No. 3 Bath"

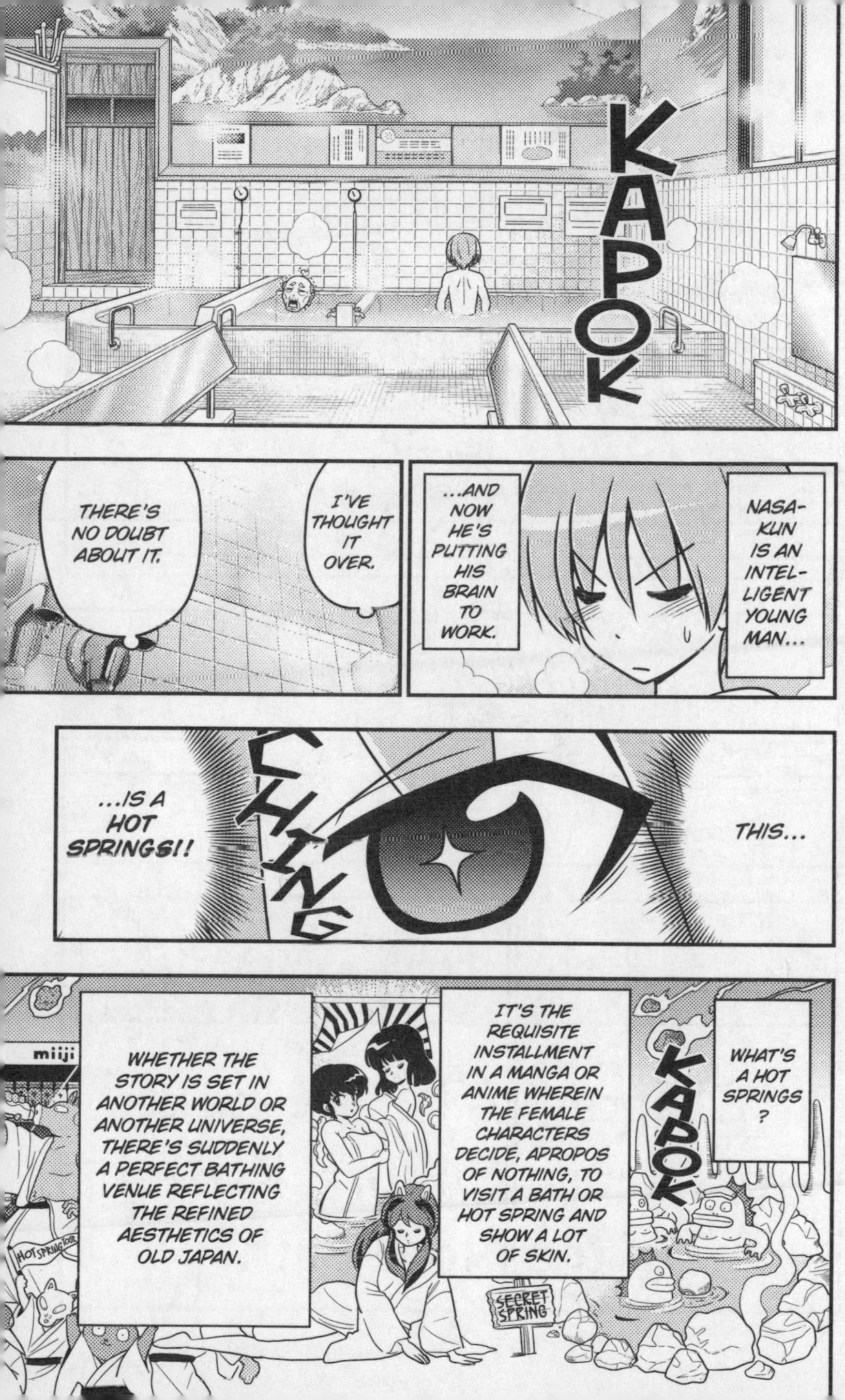
KAPOK
NASA-KUN IS AN INTELLIGENT YOUNG MAN...
...AND NOW HE'S PUTTING HIS BRAIN TO WORK.
I'VE THOUGHT IT OVER.
THERE'S NO DOUBT ABOUT IT.
THIS...
CHING
...IS A HOT SPRINGS!!
WHAT'S A HOT SPRINGS?
KAPOK
IT'S THE REQUISITE INSTALLMENT IN A MANGA OR ANIME WHEREIN THE FEMALE CHARACTERS DECIDE, APROPOS OF NOTHING, TO VISIT A BATH OR HOT SPRING AND SHOW A LOT OF SKIN.
SECRET SPRING
WHETHER THE STORY IS SET IN ANOTHER WORLD OR ANOTHER UNIVERSE, THERE'S SUDDENLY A PERFECT BATHING VENUE REFLECTING THE REFINED AESTHETICS OF OLD JAPAN.
miiji
HOT SPRING TOUR

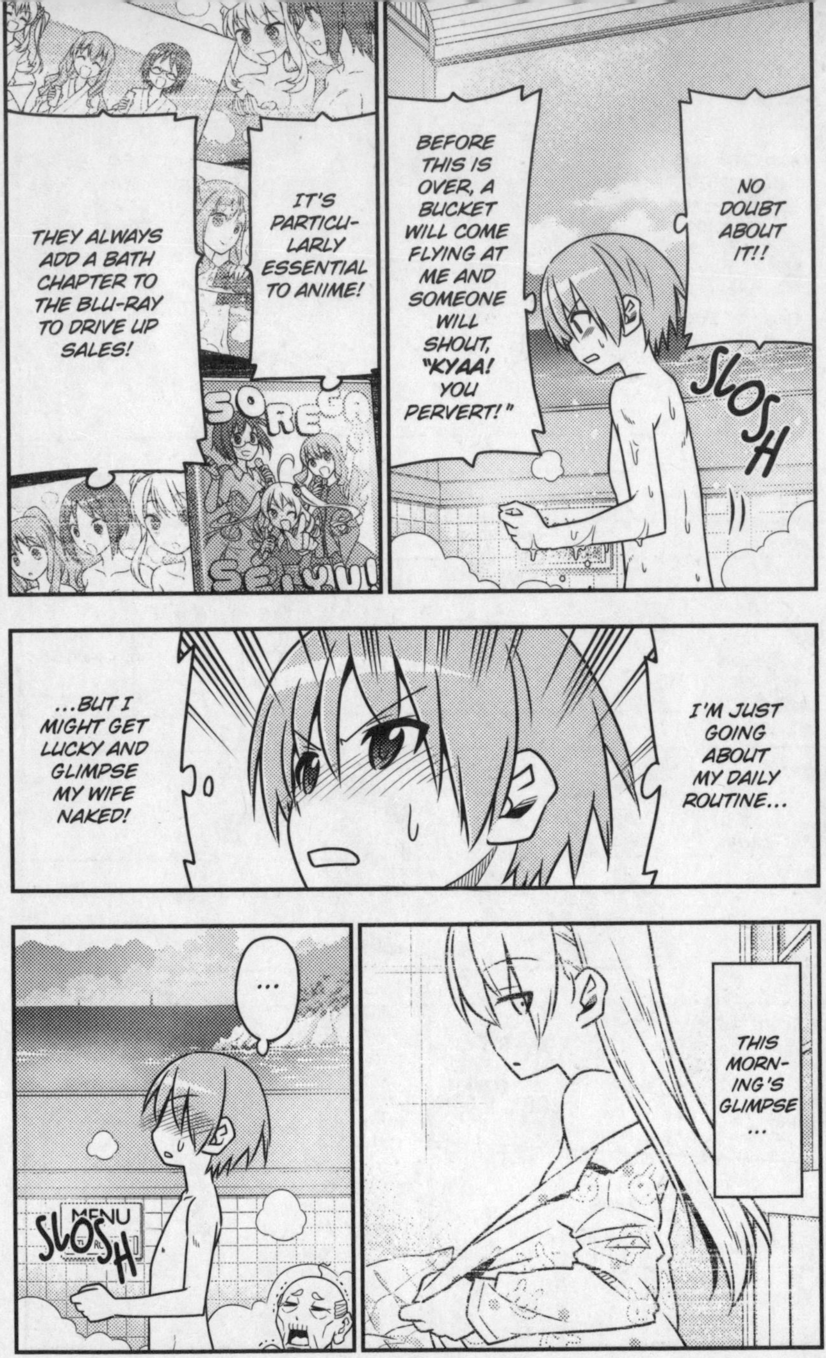
NO DOUBT ABOUT IT!!
BEFORE THIS IS OVER, A BUCKET WILL COME FLYING AT ME AND SOMEONE WILL SHOUT, "KYAA! YOU PERVERT!"
SLOSH
IT'S PARTICU-LARLY ESSENTIAL TO ANIME!
THEY ALWAYS ADD A BATH CHAPTER TO THE BLU-RAY TO DRIVE UP SALES!
SORE GA SEIYUU!
I'M JUST GOING ABOUT MY DAILY ROUTINE...
...BUT I MIGHT GET LUCKY AND GLIMPSE MY WIFE NAKED!
THIS MORN-ING'S GLIMPSE...
...
MENU
SLOSH

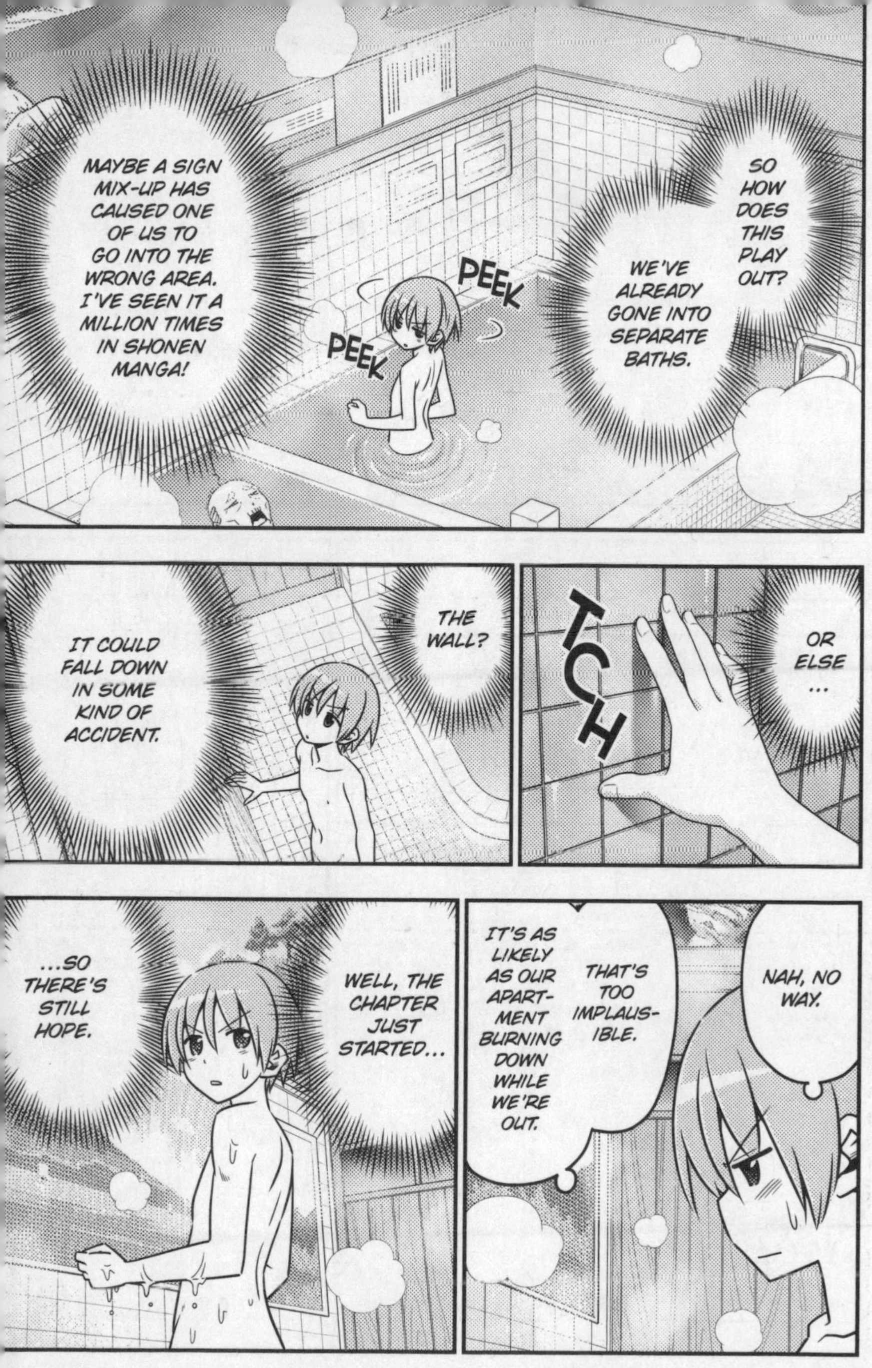
SO HOW DOES THIS PLAY OUT?
WE'VE ALREADY GONE INTO SEPARATE BATHS.
PEEK
PEEK
MAYBE A SIGN MIX-UP HAS CAUSED ONE OF US TO GO INTO THE WRONG AREA. I'VE SEEN IT A MILLION TIMES IN SHONEN MANGA!
OR ELSE ...
TCH
THE WALL?
IT COULD FALL DOWN IN SOME KIND OF ACCIDENT.
NAH, NO WAY.
THAT'S TOO IMPLAUS-IBLE.
IT'S AS LIKELY AS OUR APART-MENT BURNING DOWN WHILE WE'RE OUT.
WELL, THE CHAPTER JUST STARTED...
...SO THERE'S STILL HOPE.

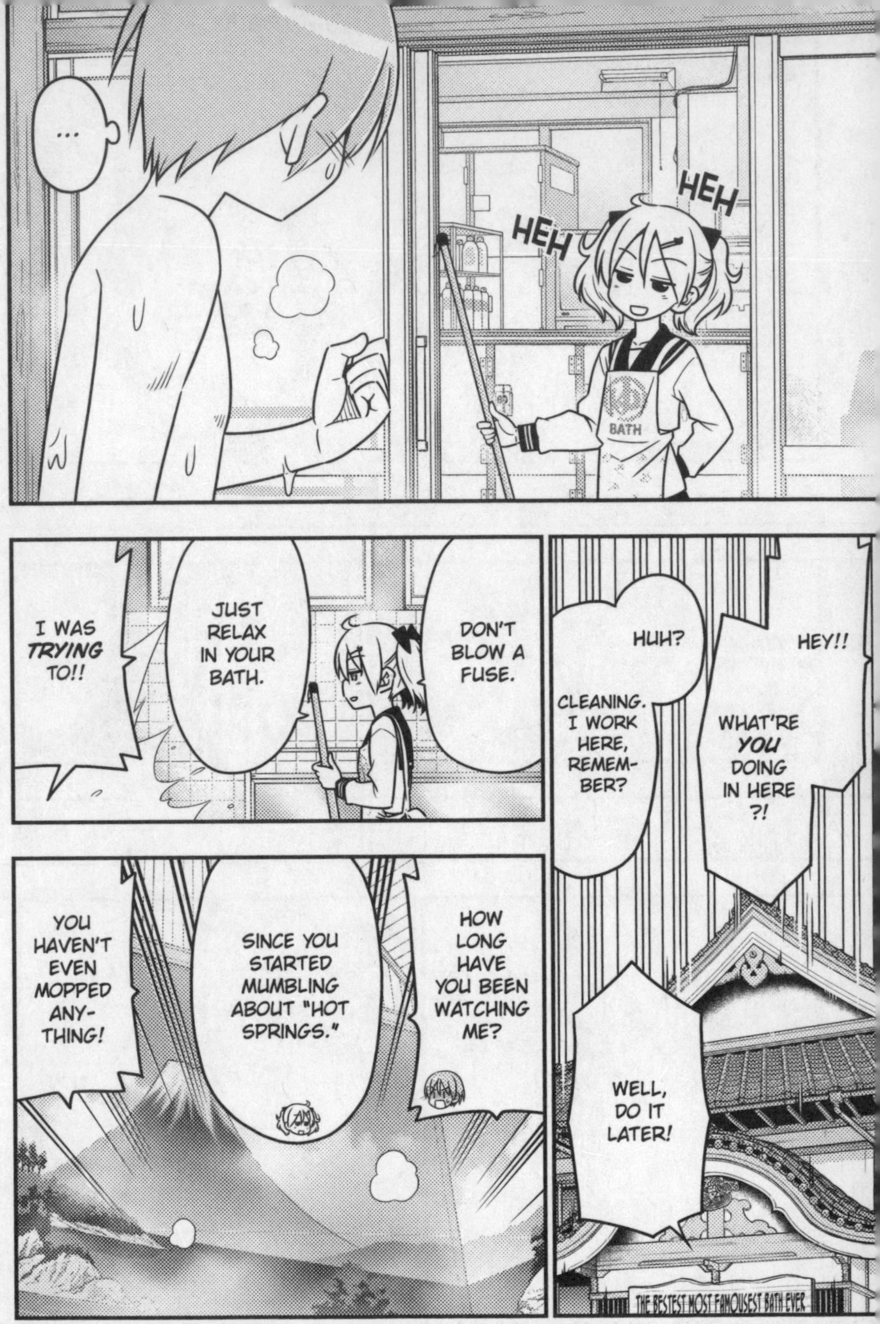
HEH HEH
...
BATH
HEY!!
WHAT'RE *YOU* DOING IN HERE ?!
HUH?
CLEANING. I WORK HERE, REMEMBER?
WELL, DO IT LATER!
THE BESTEST MOST FAMOUSEST BATH EVER
DON'T BLOW A FUSE.
JUST RELAX IN YOUR BATH.
I WAS *TRYING* TO!!
HOW LONG HAVE YOU BEEN WATCHING ME?
SINCE YOU STARTED MUMBLING ABOUT "HOT SPRINGS."
YOU HAVEN'T EVEN MOPPED ANY-THING!

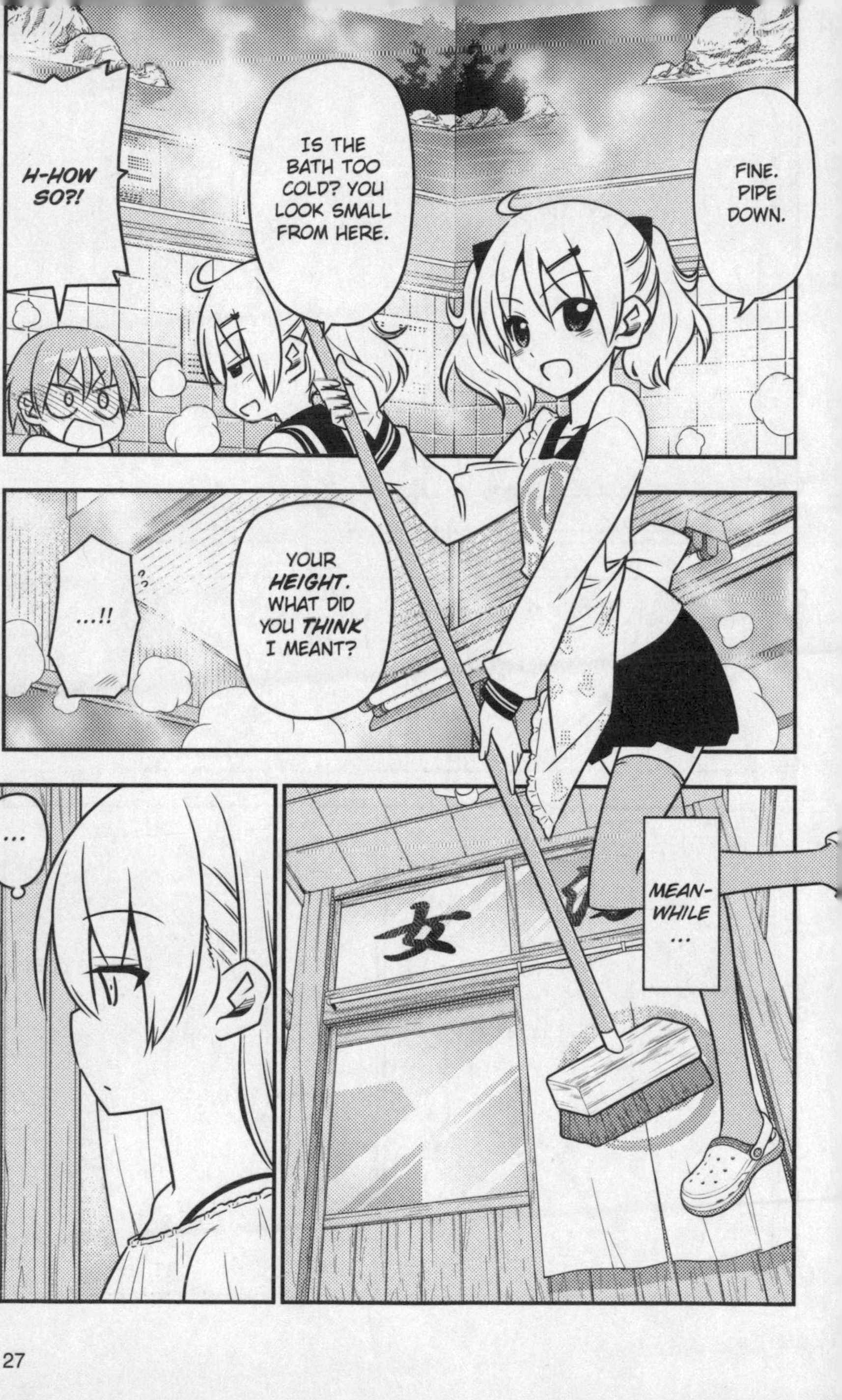
FINE. PIPE DOWN.
IS THE BATH TOO COLD? YOU LOOK SMALL FROM HERE.
H-HOW SO?!
YOUR HEIGHT. WHAT DID YOU THINK I MEANT?
...!!
MEAN-WHILE...
...

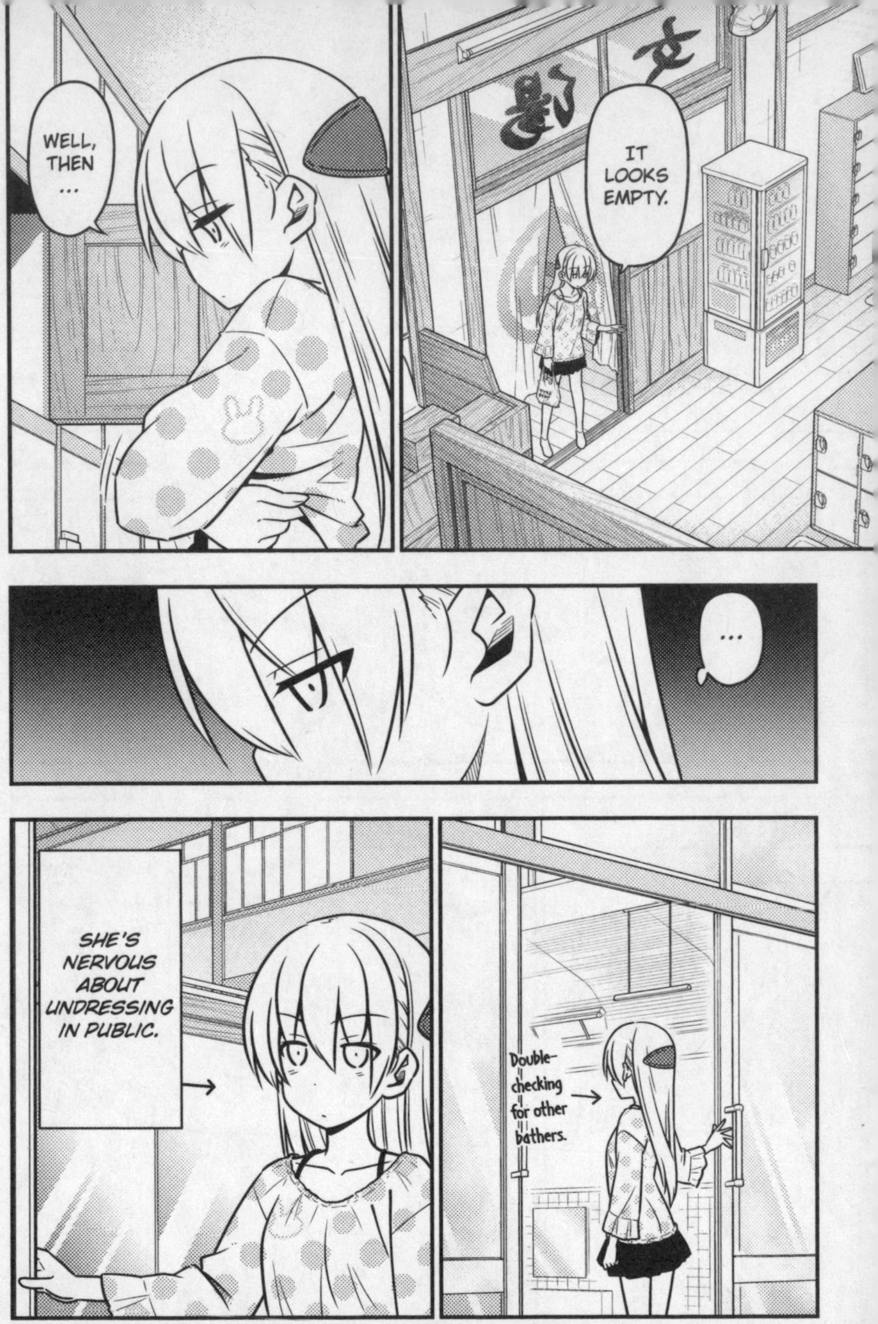
IT LOOKS EMPTY.
WELL, THEN ...
...
Double-checking for other bathers.
SHE'S NERVOUS ABOUT UNDRESSING IN PUBLIC.

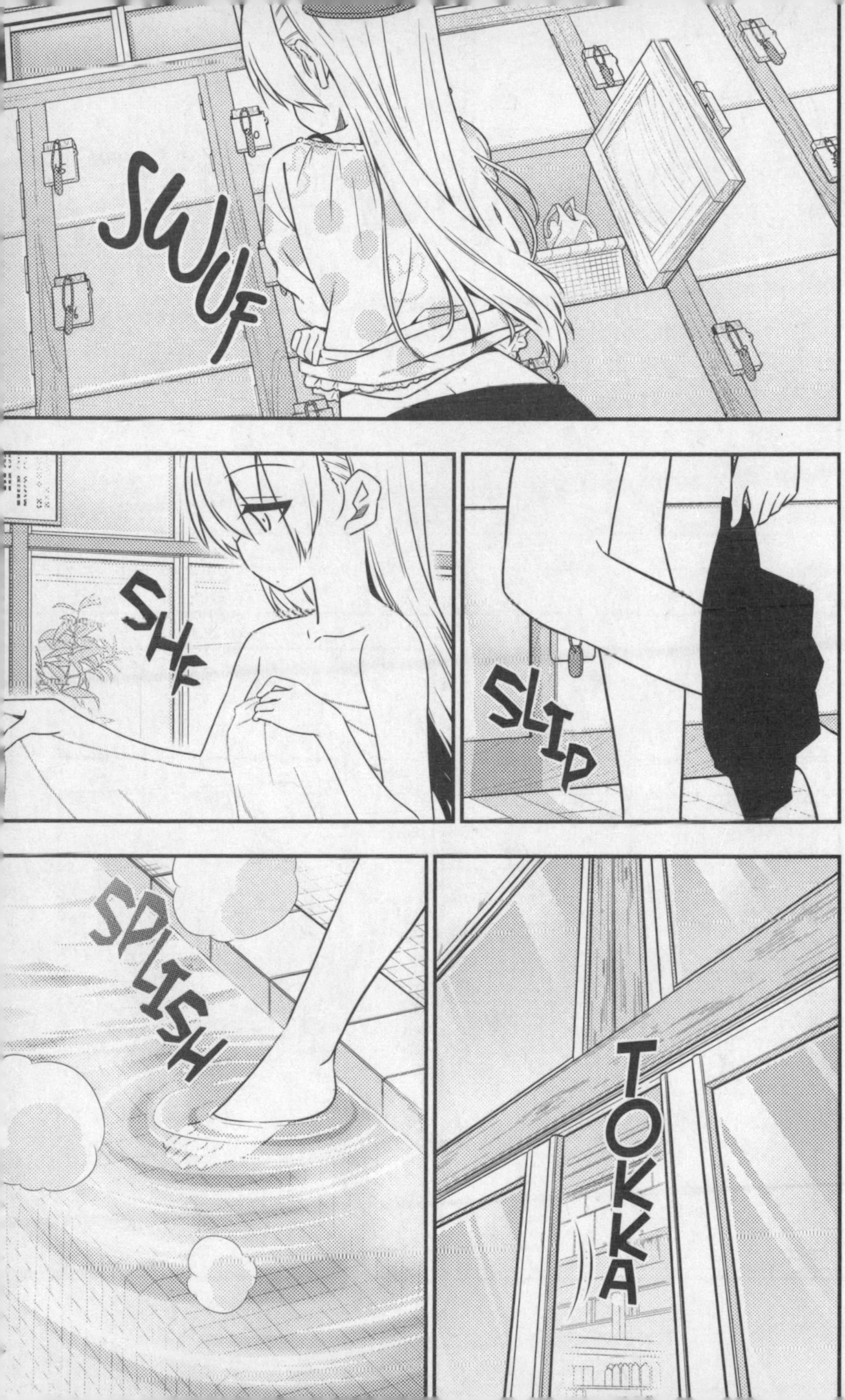
SWUF
SLIP
SHF
TOKKA
SPLISH

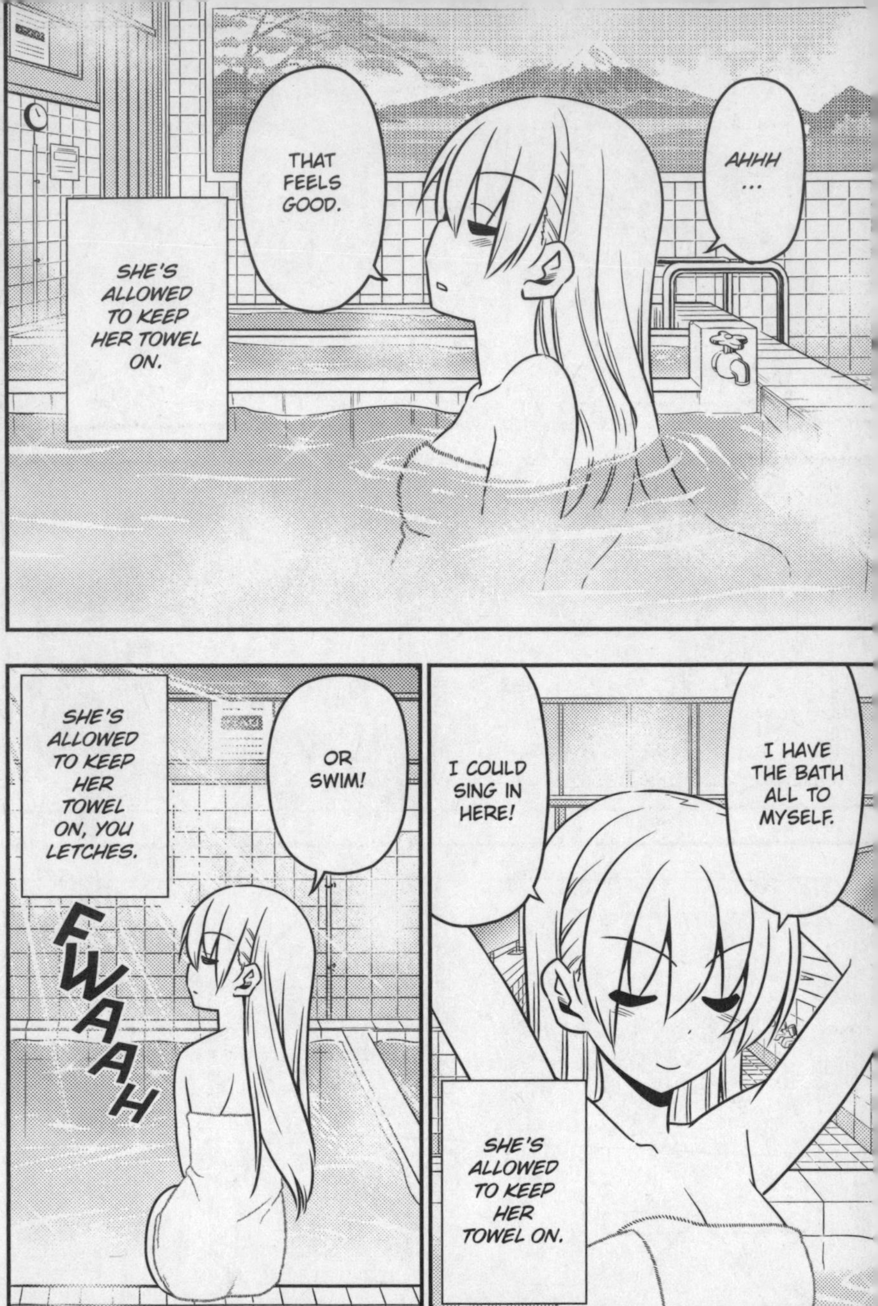
AHHH ...
THAT FEELS GOOD.
SHE'S ALLOWED TO KEEP HER TOWEL ON.
I HAVE THE BATH ALL TO MYSELF.
I COULD SING IN HERE!
SHE'S ALLOWED TO KEEP HER TOWEL ON.
OR SWIM!
SHE'S ALLOWED TO KEEP HER TOWEL ON, YOU LETCHES.
FWAAH

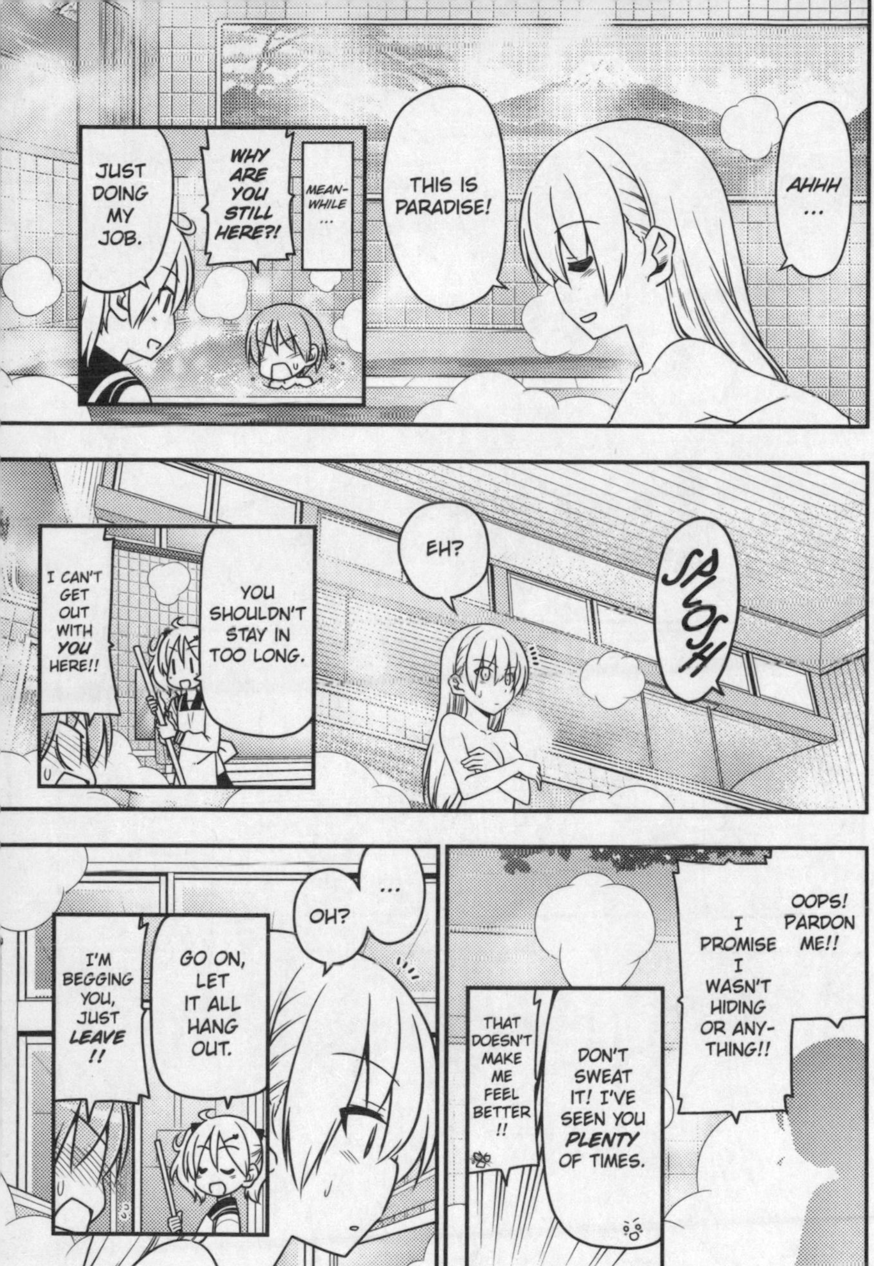
AHHH ...
THIS IS PARADISE!
MEAN-WHILE ...
WHY ARE YOU STILL HERE?!
JUST DOING MY JOB.
SPLOSH
EH?
YOU SHOULDN'T STAY IN TOO LONG.
I CAN'T GET OUT WITH YOU HERE!!
OOPS! PARDON ME!!
I PROMISE I WASN'T HIDING OR ANY-THING!!
DON'T SWEAT IT! I'VE SEEN YOU PLENTY OF TIMES.
THAT DOESN'T MAKE ME FEEL BETTER!!
... OH?
GO ON, LET IT ALL HANG OUT.
I'M BEGGING YOU, JUST LEAVE!!

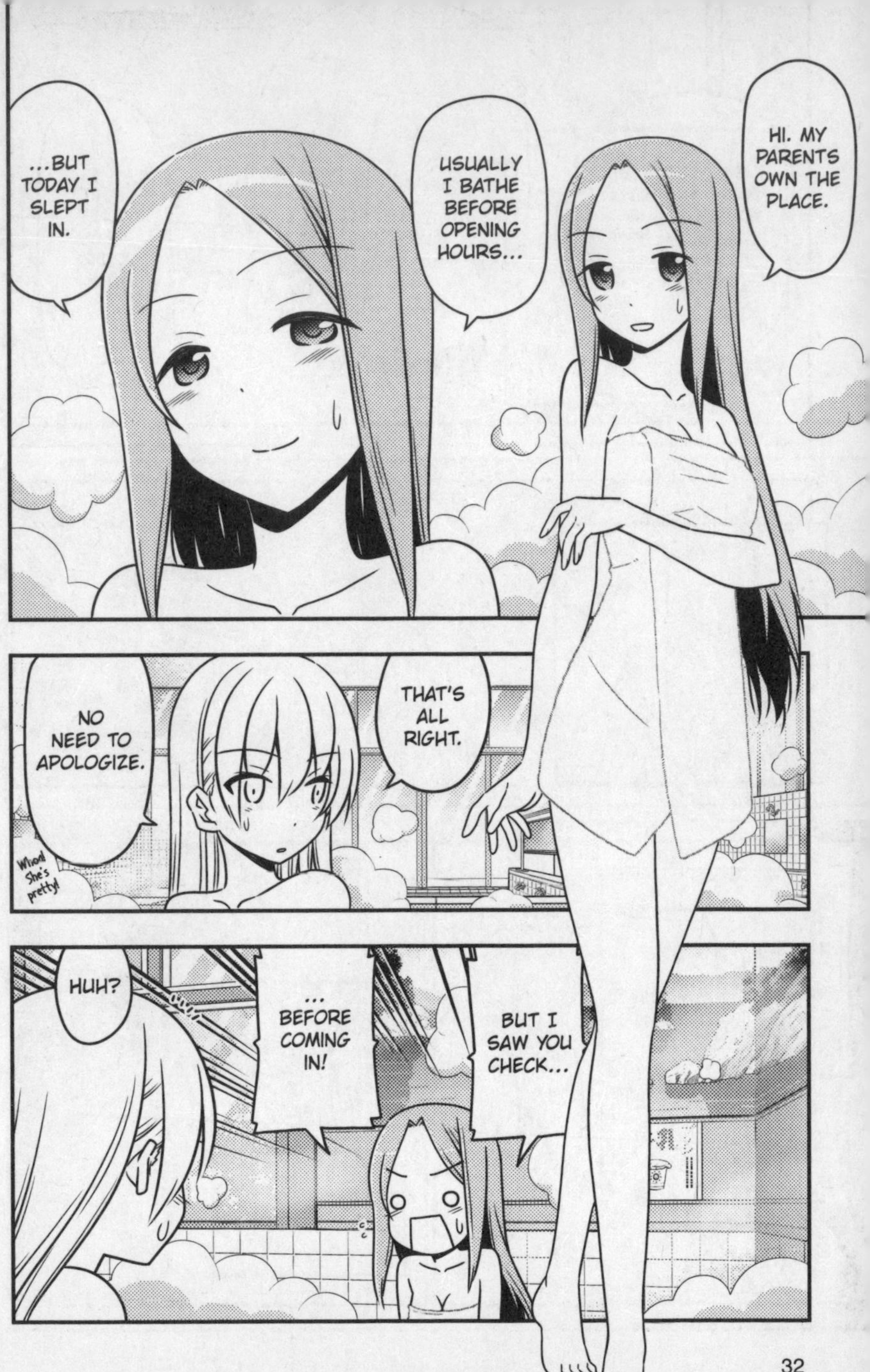
HI. MY PARENTS OWN THE PLACE.
USUALLY I BATHE BEFORE OPENING HOURS...
...BUT TODAY I SLEPT IN.
THAT'S ALL RIGHT.
NO NEED TO APOLOGIZE.
Whoa! She's pretty!
BUT I SAW YOU CHECK...
...BEFORE COMING IN!
HUH?

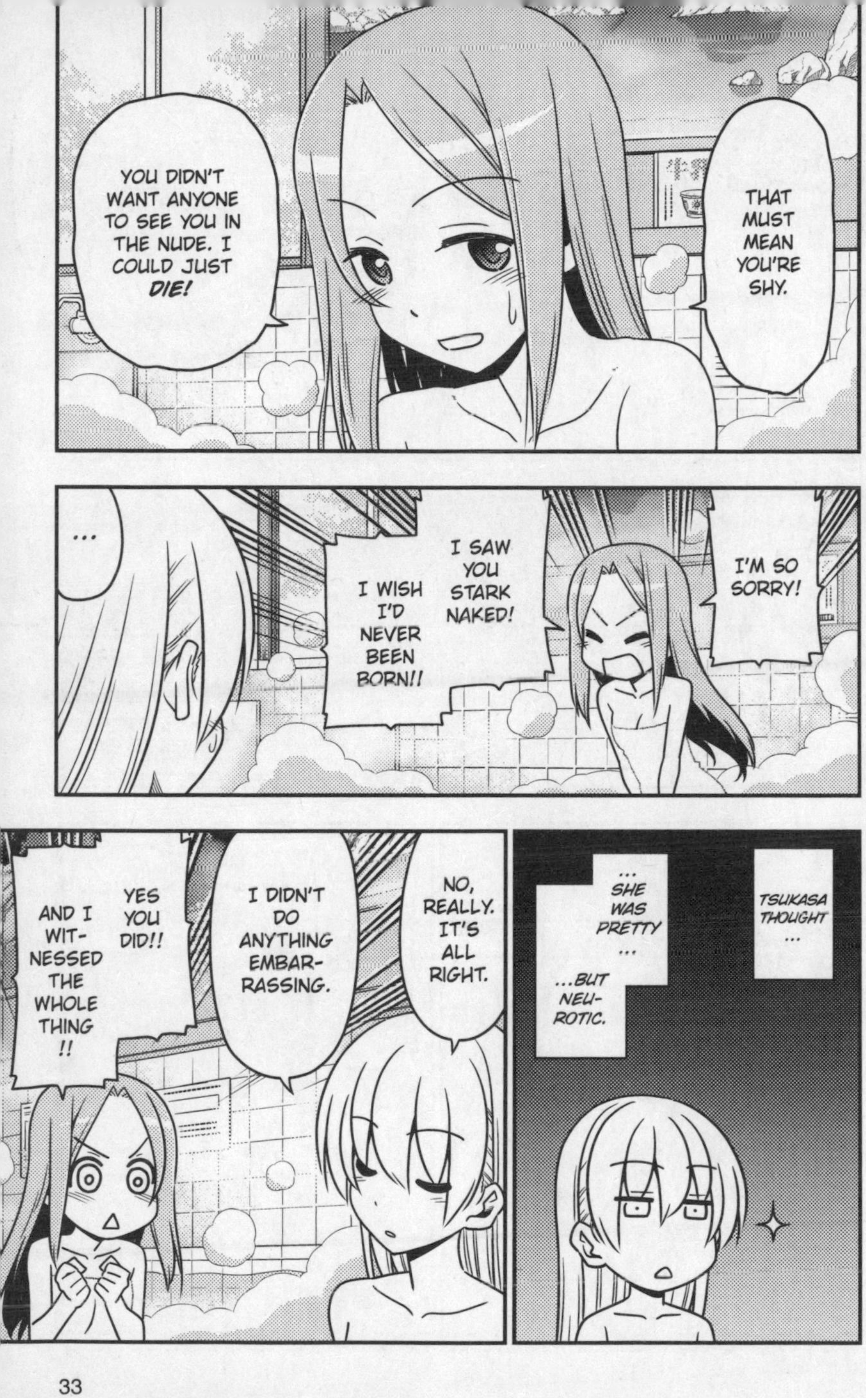
THAT MUST MEAN YOU'RE SHY.
YOU DIDN'T WANT ANYONE TO SEE YOU IN THE NUDE. I COULD JUST DIE!
I'M SO SORRY!
I SAW YOU STARK NAKED!
I WISH I'D NEVER BEEN BORN!!
...
TSUKASA THOUGHT ...
... SHE WAS PRETTY ...
...BUT NEU-ROTIC.
NO, REALLY. IT'S ALL RIGHT.
I DIDN'T DO ANYTHING EMBAR-RASSING.
YES YOU DID!!
AND I WIT-NESSED THE WHOLE THING!!

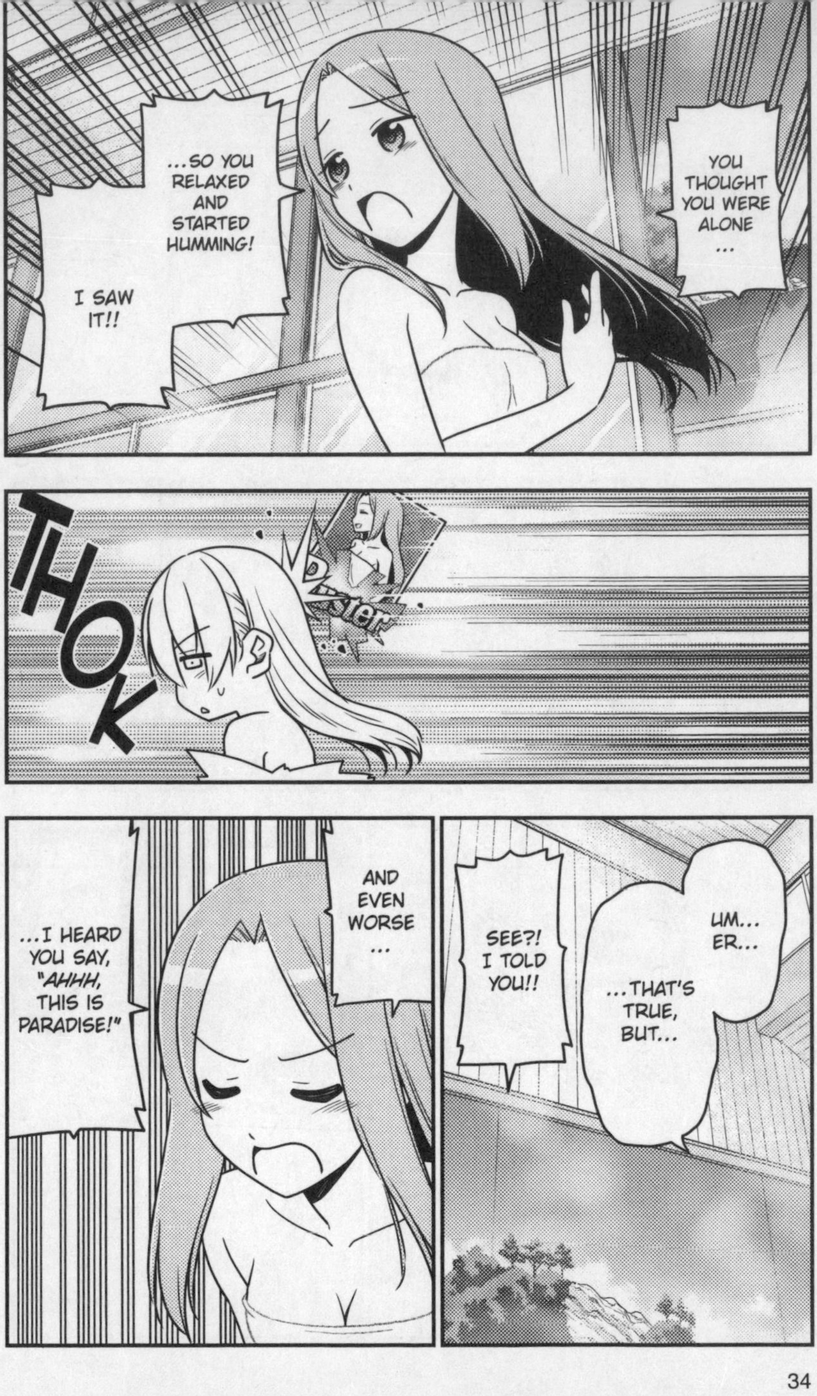
YOU THOUGHT YOU WERE ALONE ...
...SO YOU RELAXED AND STARTED HUMMING!
I SAW IT!!
THOK
UM... ER...
...THAT'S TRUE, BUT...
SEE?! I TOLD YOU!!
AND EVEN WORSE ...
...I HEARD YOU SAY, "AHHH, THIS IS PARADISE!"

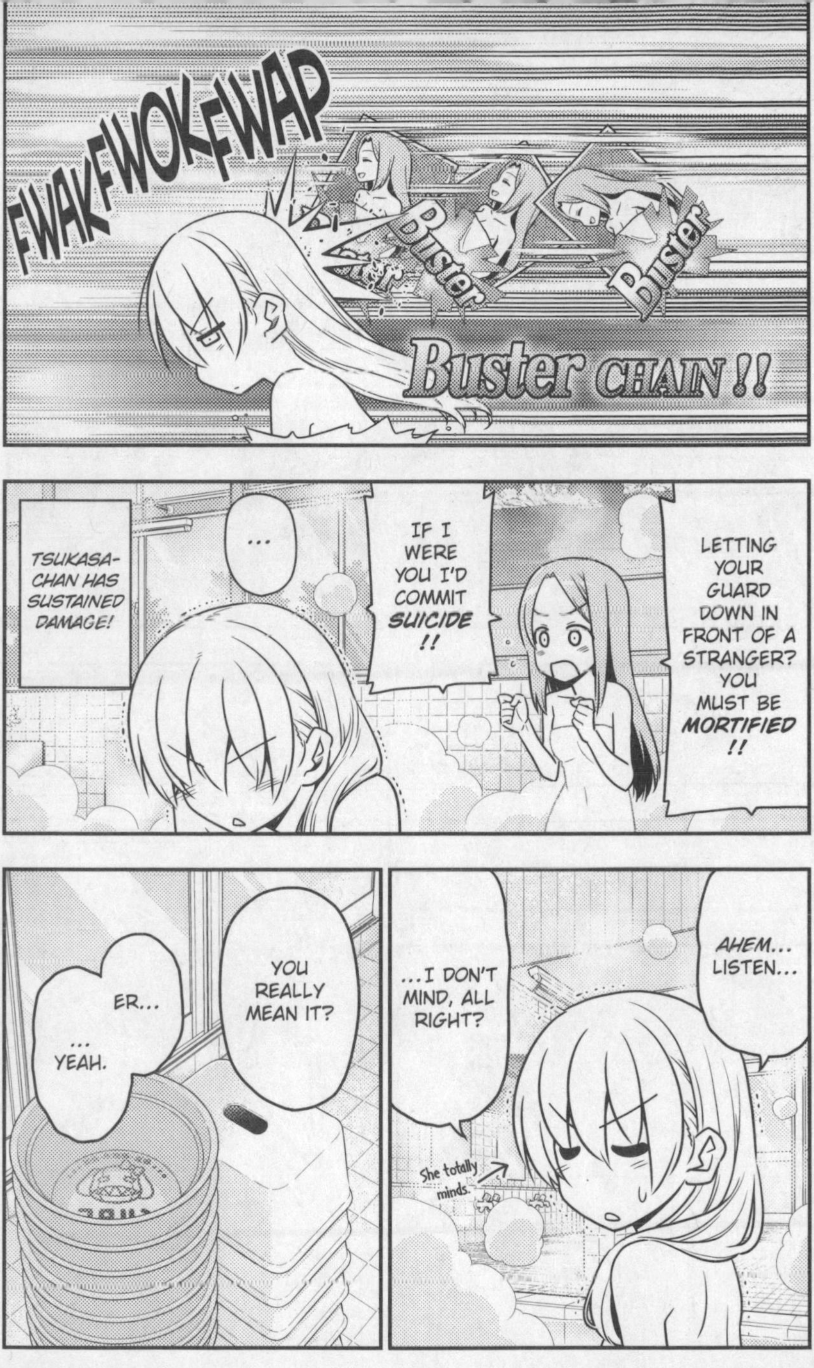
Buster
Buster
Buster CHAIN!!
FWAKFWOKFWAP
LETTING YOUR GUARD DOWN IN FRONT OF A STRANGER? YOU MUST BE MORTIFIED!!
IF I WERE YOU I'D COMMIT SUICIDE!!
...
TSUKASA-CHAN HAS SUSTAINED DAMAGE!
AHEM... LISTEN...
...I DON'T MIND, ALL RIGHT?
She totally minds.
YOU REALLY MEAN IT?
ER... ...YEAH.

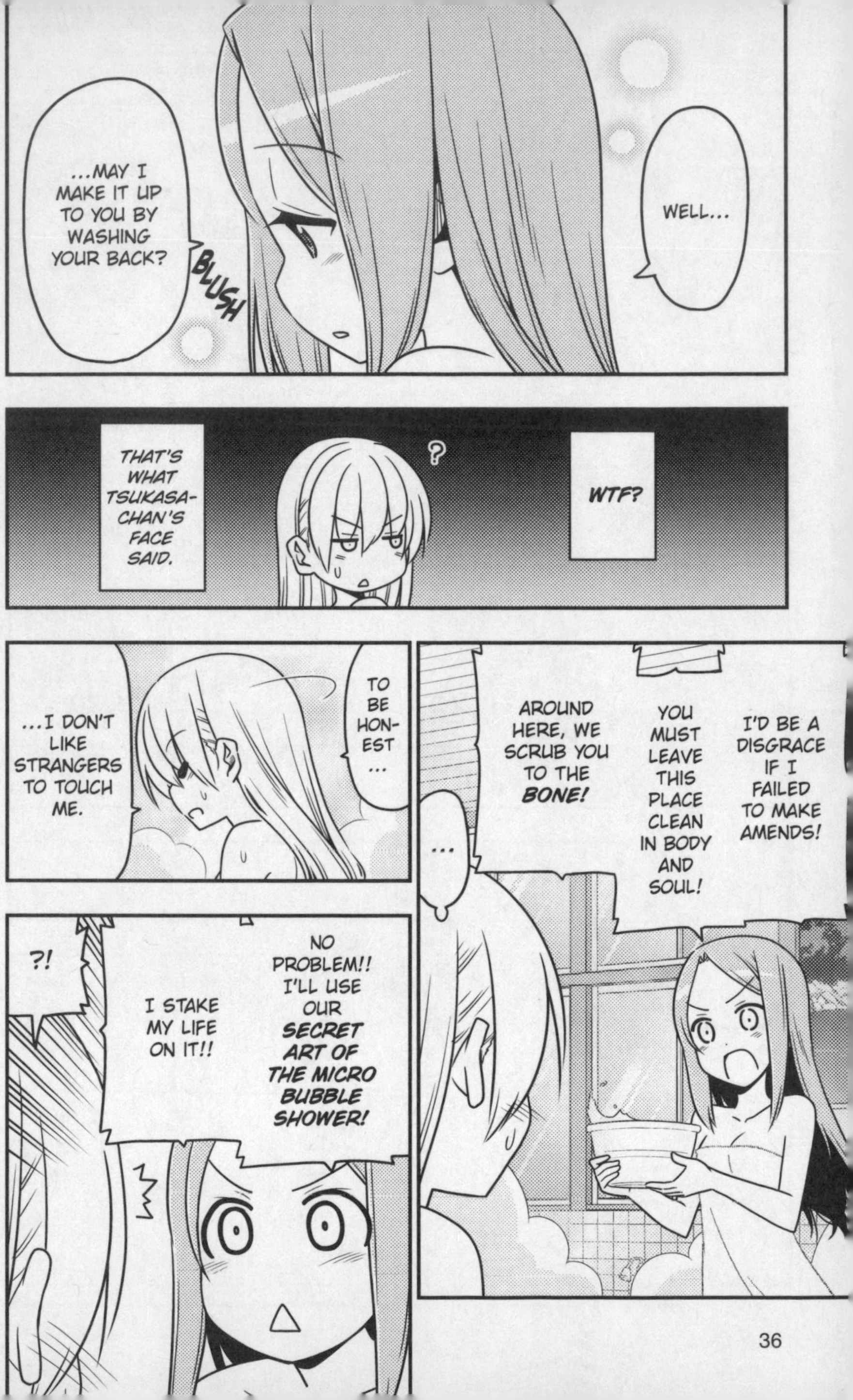
WELL...
...MAY I MAKE IT UP TO YOU BY WASHING YOUR BACK?
BLUSH
WTF?
?
THAT'S WHAT TSUKASA-CHAN'S FACE SAID.
I'D BE A DISGRACE IF I FAILED TO MAKE AMENDS!
YOU MUST LEAVE THIS PLACE CLEAN IN BODY AND SOUL!
AROUND HERE, WE SCRUB YOU TO THE BONE!
...
TO BE HON-EST...
...I DON'T LIKE STRANGERS TO TOUCH ME.
NO PROBLEM!! I'LL USE OUR SECRET ART OF THE MICRO BUBBLE SHOWER!
I STAKE MY LIFE ON IT!!
?!

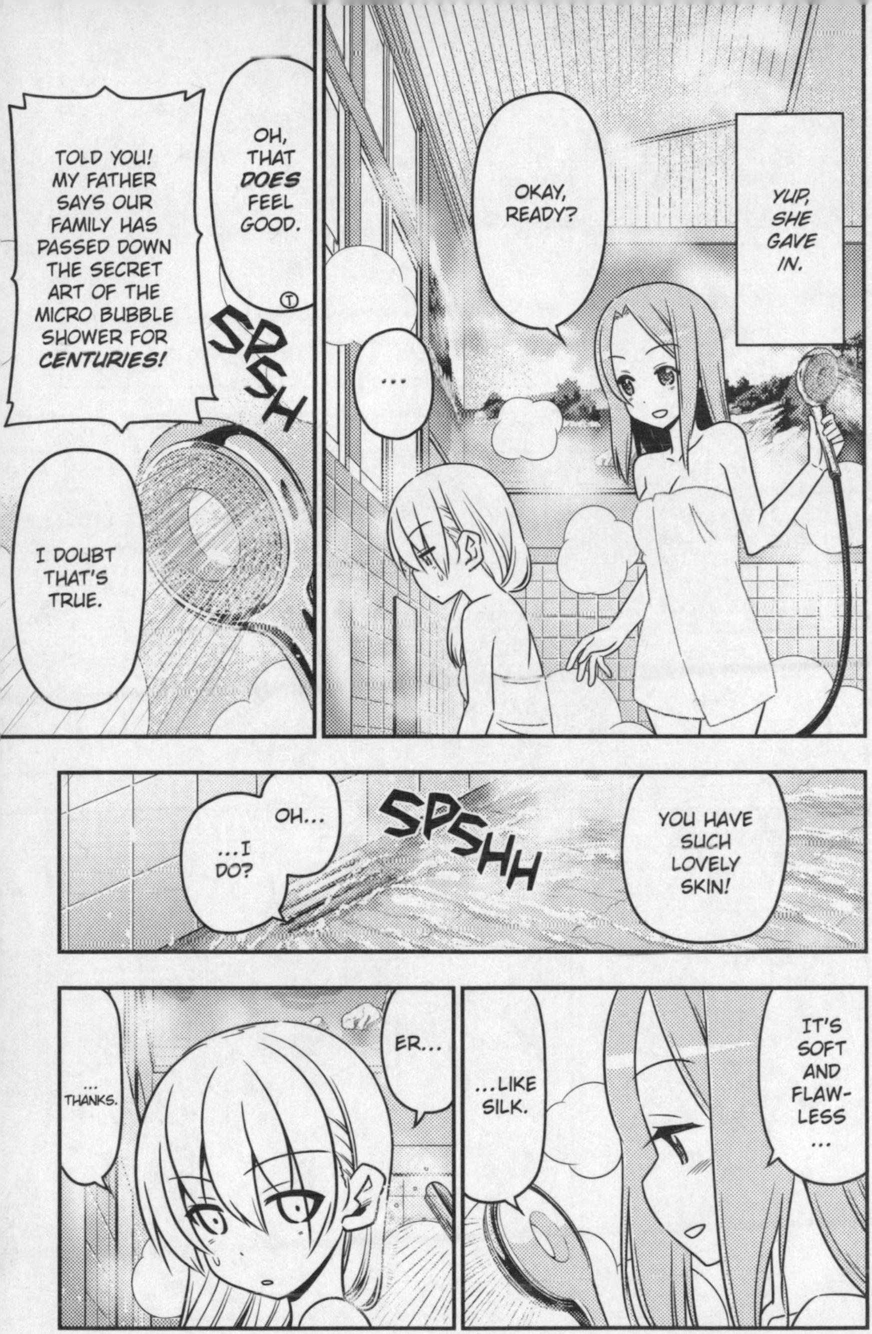
YUP, SHE GAVE IN.
OKAY, READY?
...
OH, THAT DOES FEEL GOOD.
TOLD YOU! MY FATHER SAYS OUR FAMILY HAS PASSED DOWN THE SECRET ART OF THE MICRO BUBBLE SHOWER FOR CENTURIES!
SPSH
I DOUBT THAT'S TRUE.
YOU HAVE SUCH LOVELY SKIN!
SPSHH
OH...
...I DO?
IT'S SOFT AND FLAW-LESS...
...LIKE SILK.
ER...
...THANKS.

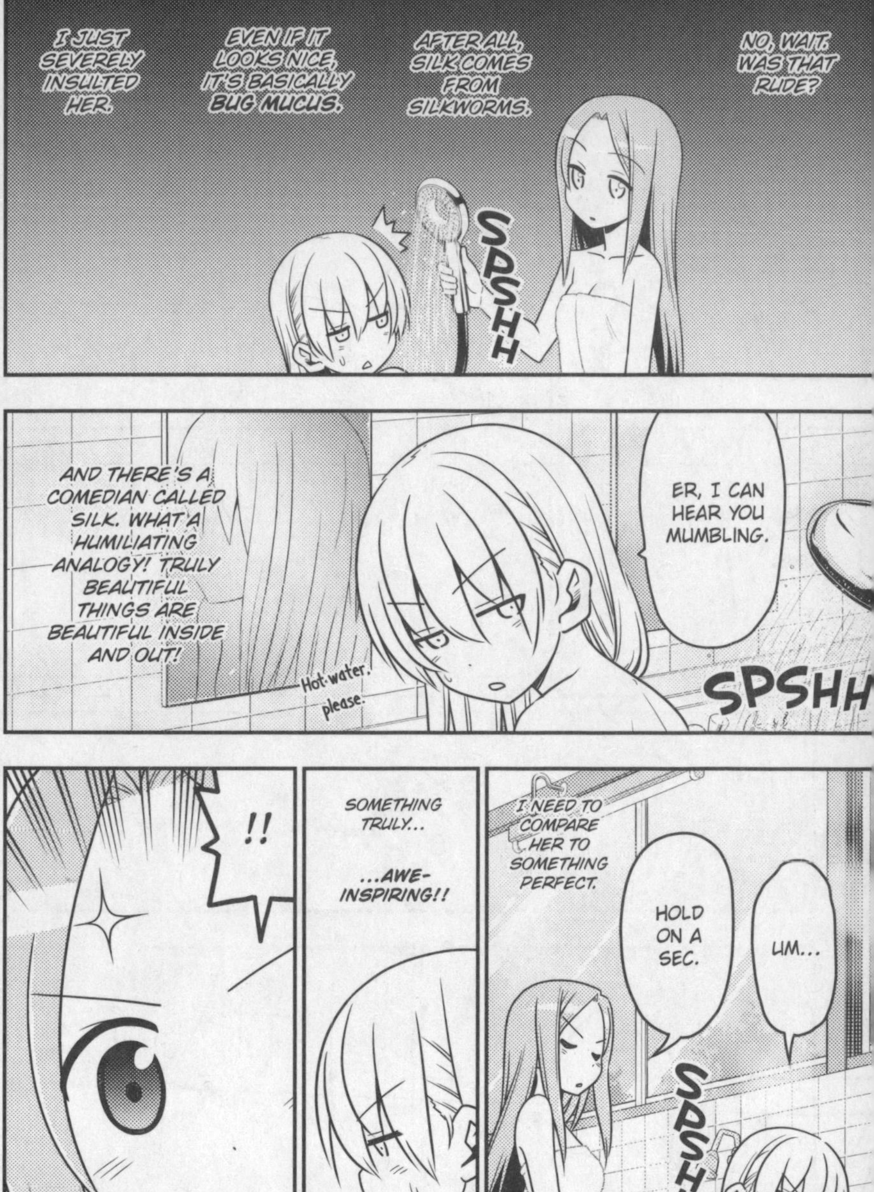
NO, WAIT. WAS THAT RUDE?
AFTER ALL, SILK COMES FROM SILKWORMS.
EVEN IF IT LOOKS NICE, IT'S BASICALLY BUG MUCUS.
I JUST SEVERELY INSULTED HER.
SPSHH
SPSHH
ER, I CAN HEAR YOU MUMBLING.
AND THERE'S A COMEDIAN CALLED SILK. WHAT A HUMILIATING ANALOGY! TRULY BEAUTIFUL THINGS ARE BEAUTIFUL INSIDE AND OUT!
Hot water, please.
UM...
HOLD ON A SEC.
I NEED TO COMPARE HER TO SOMETHING PERFECT.
SPSHH
SOMETHING TRULY...
...AWE-INSPIRING!!
!!

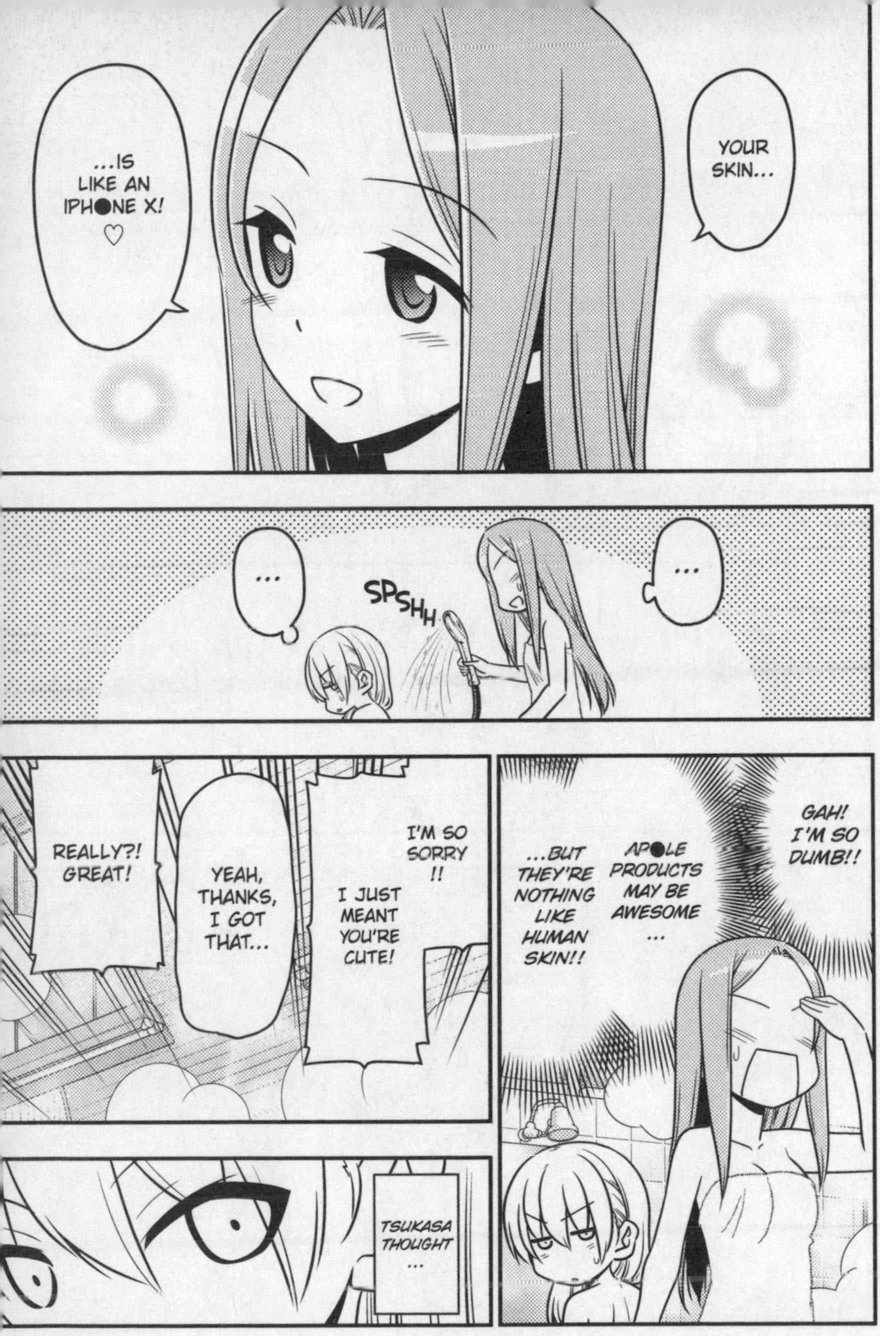
YOUR SKIN...
...IS LIKE AN IPH●NE X! ♡
...
SPSHH
...
GAH! I'M SO DUMB!!
AP●LE PRODUCTS MAY BE AWESOME...
...BUT THEY'RE NOTHING LIKE HUMAN SKIN!!
I'M SO SORRY!!
I JUST MEANT YOU'RE CUTE!
YEAH, THANKS, I GOT THAT...
REALLY?! GREAT!
TSUKASA THOUGHT...

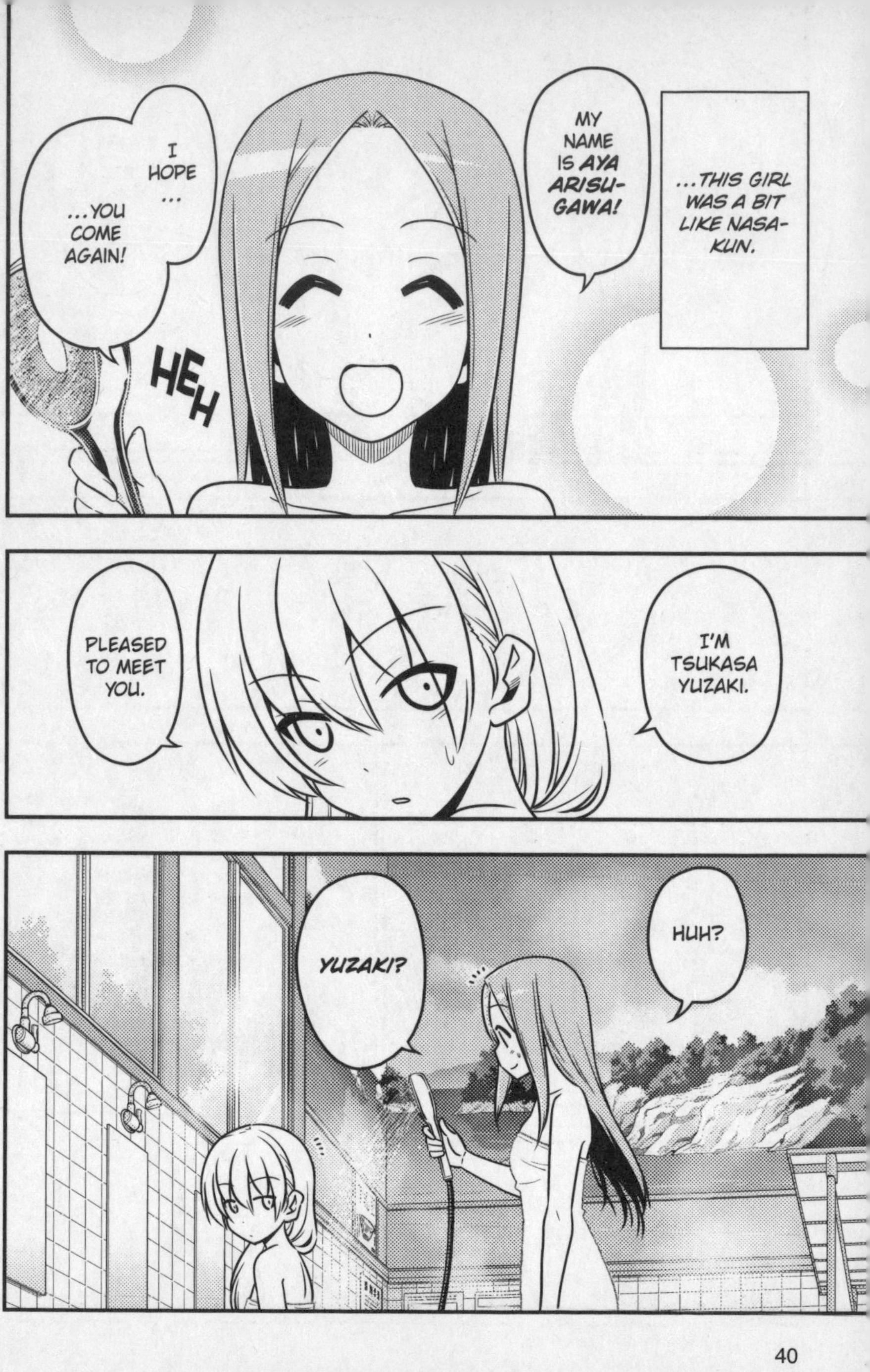
...THIS GIRL WAS A BIT LIKE NASA-KUN.
MY NAME IS *AYA ARISUGAWA!*
HEH
I HOPE ...
...YOU COME AGAIN!
I'M TSUKASA YUZAKI.
PLEASED TO MEET YOU.
HUH?
YUZAKI?

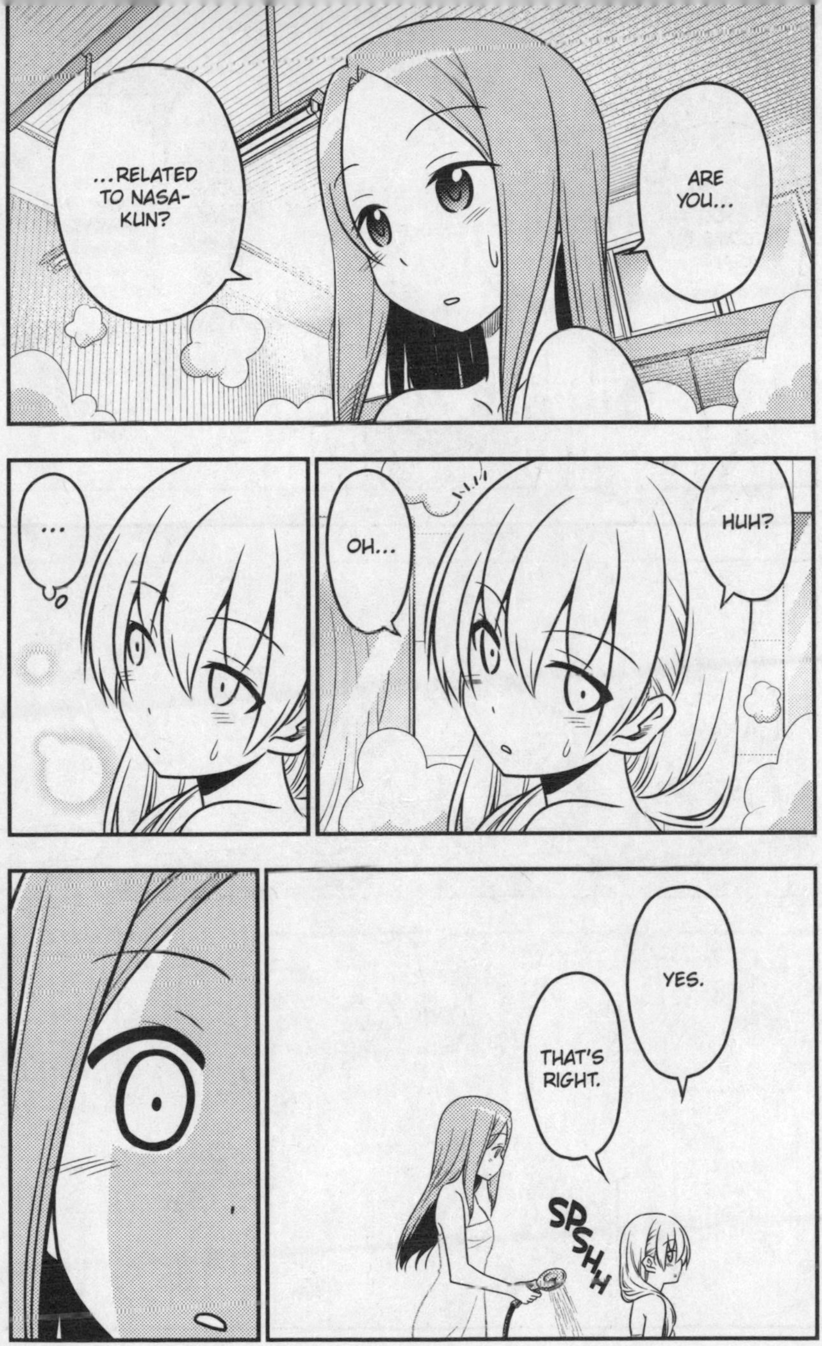
ARE YOU...
...RELATED TO NASA-KUN?
HUH?
OH...
...
YES.
THAT'S RIGHT.
SPSHH

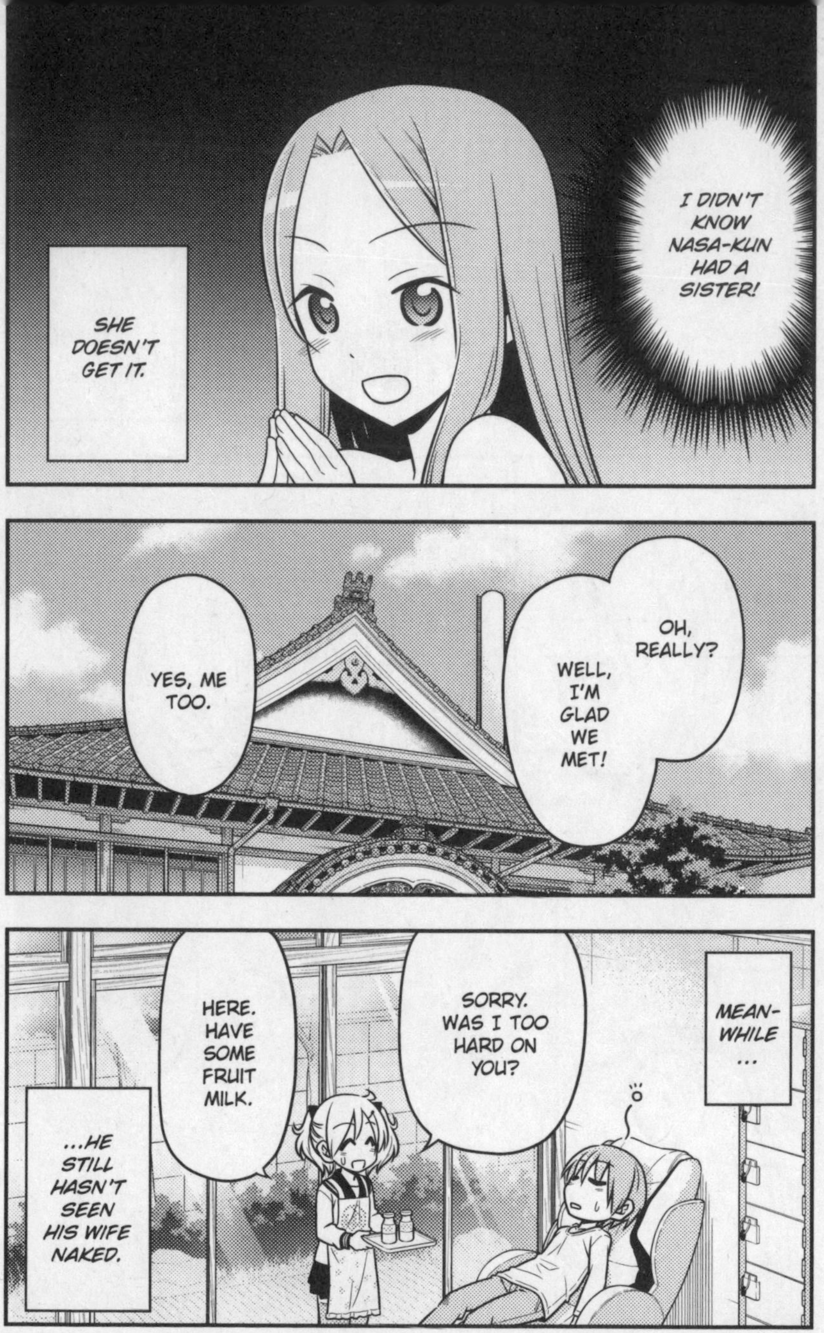
I DIDN'T KNOW NASA-KUN HAD A SISTER!
SHE DOESN'T GET IT.
OH, REALLY?
WELL, I'M GLAD WE MET!
YES, ME TOO.
MEAN-WHILE...
SORRY. WAS I TOO HARD ON YOU?
HERE. HAVE SOME FRUIT MILK.
...HE STILL HASN'T SEEN HIS WIFE NAKED.

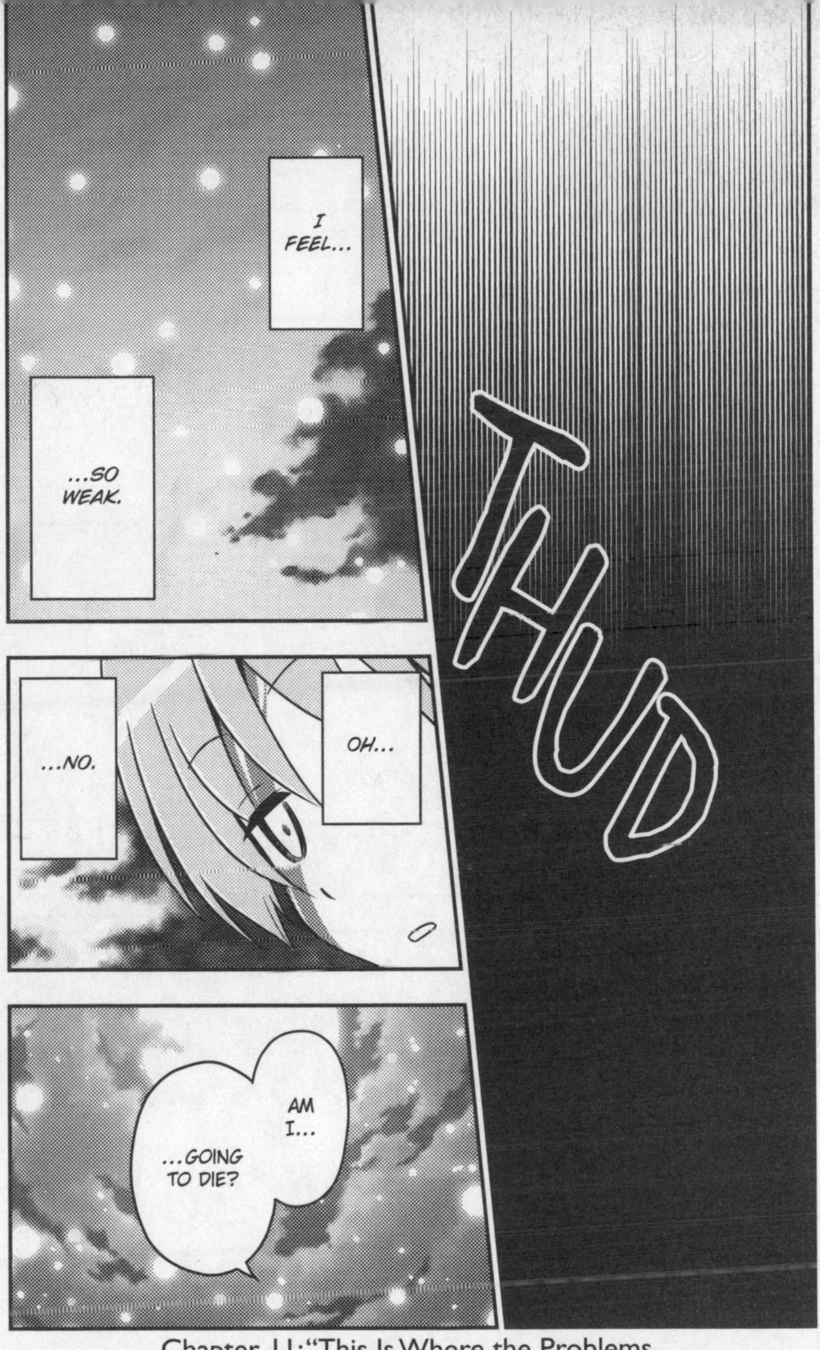
THUD
I FEEL...
...SO WEAK.
OH...
...NO.
AM I...
...GOING TO DIE?

Chapter 11: "This Is Where the Problems Between Men and Women Begin"

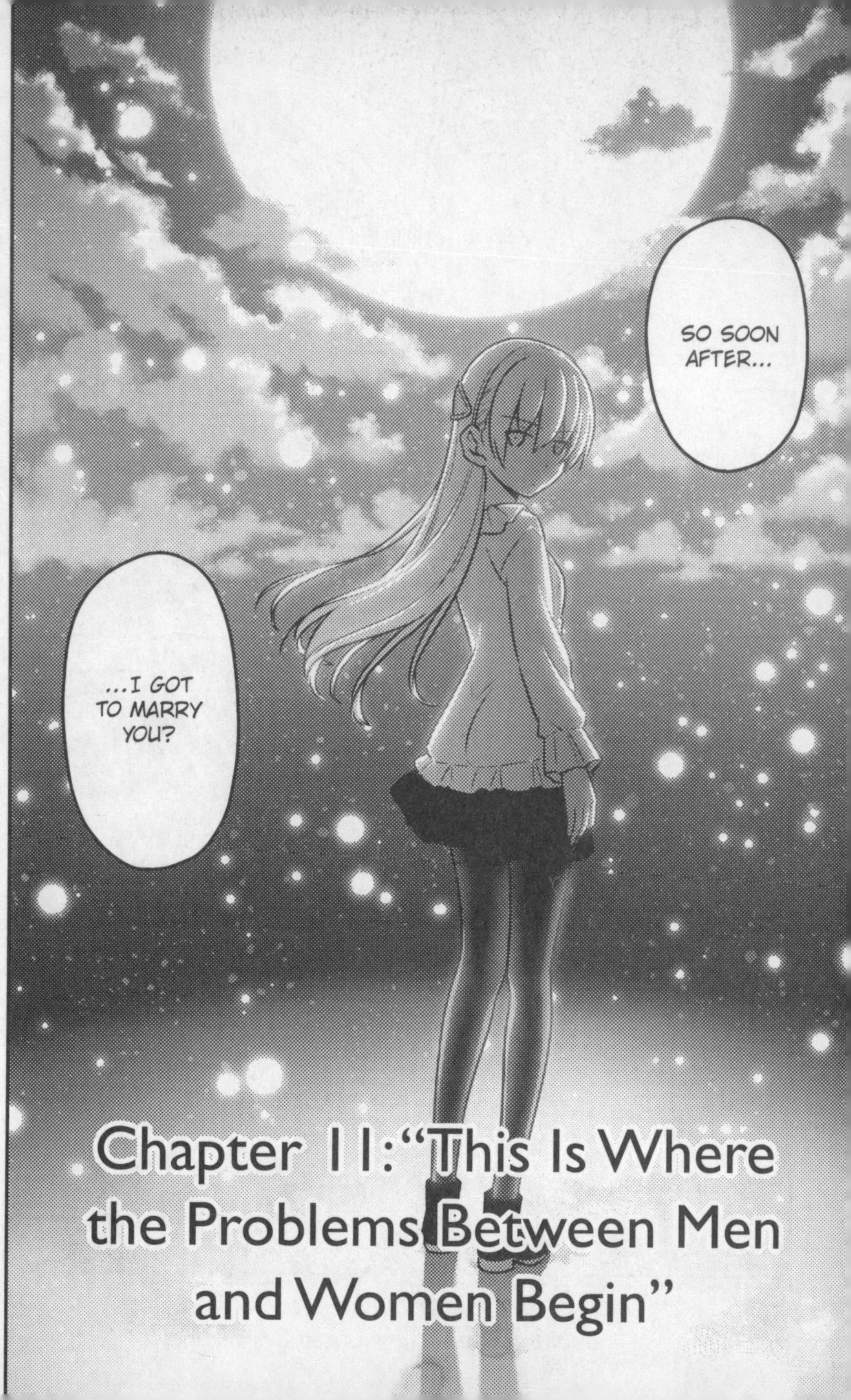
SO SOON AFTER...
...I GOT TO MARRY YOU?

Chapter 11: "This Is Where the Problems Between Men and Women Begin"

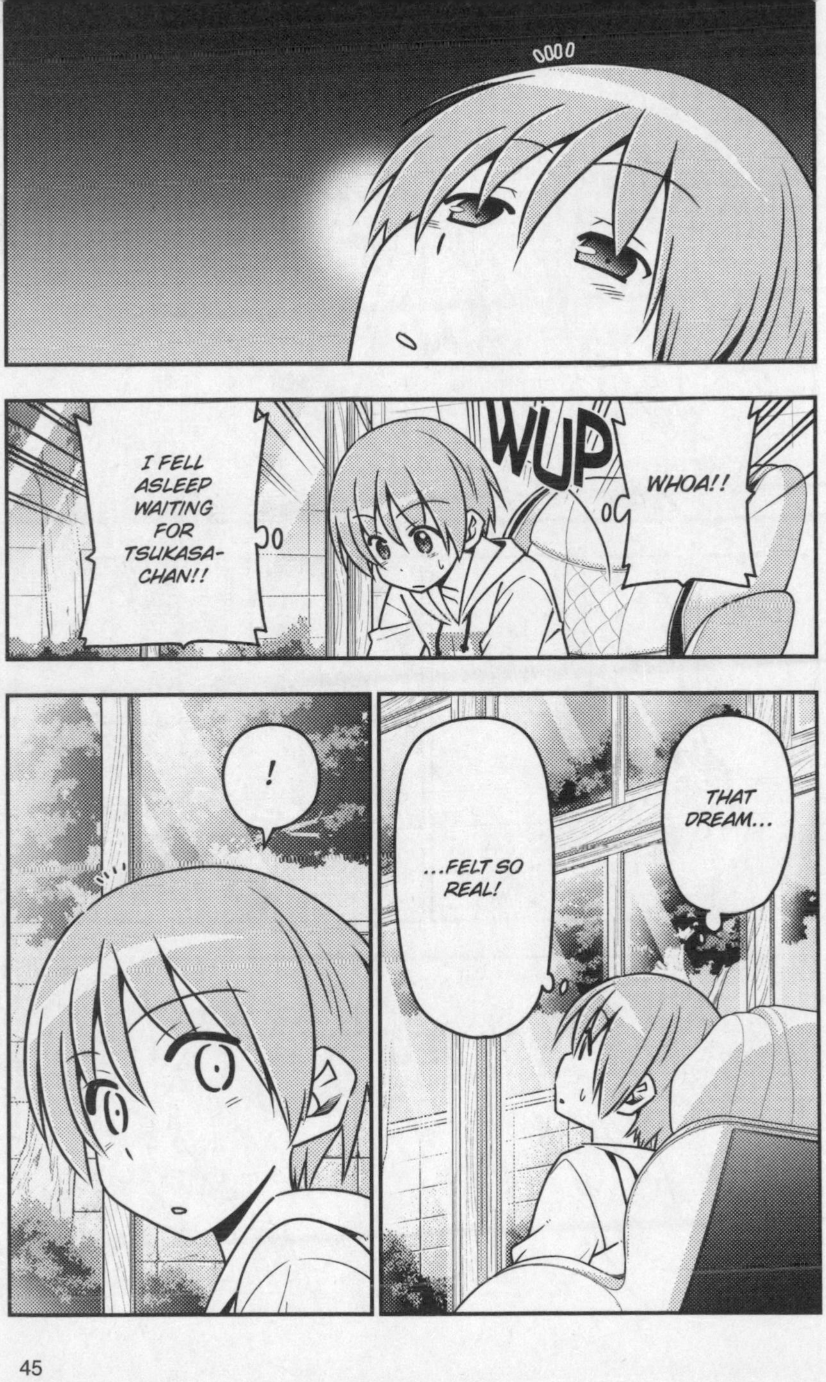
OOOO
WUP
WHOA!!
I FELL ASLEEP WAITING FOR TSUKASA-CHAN!!
THAT DREAM...
...FELT SO REAL!
!

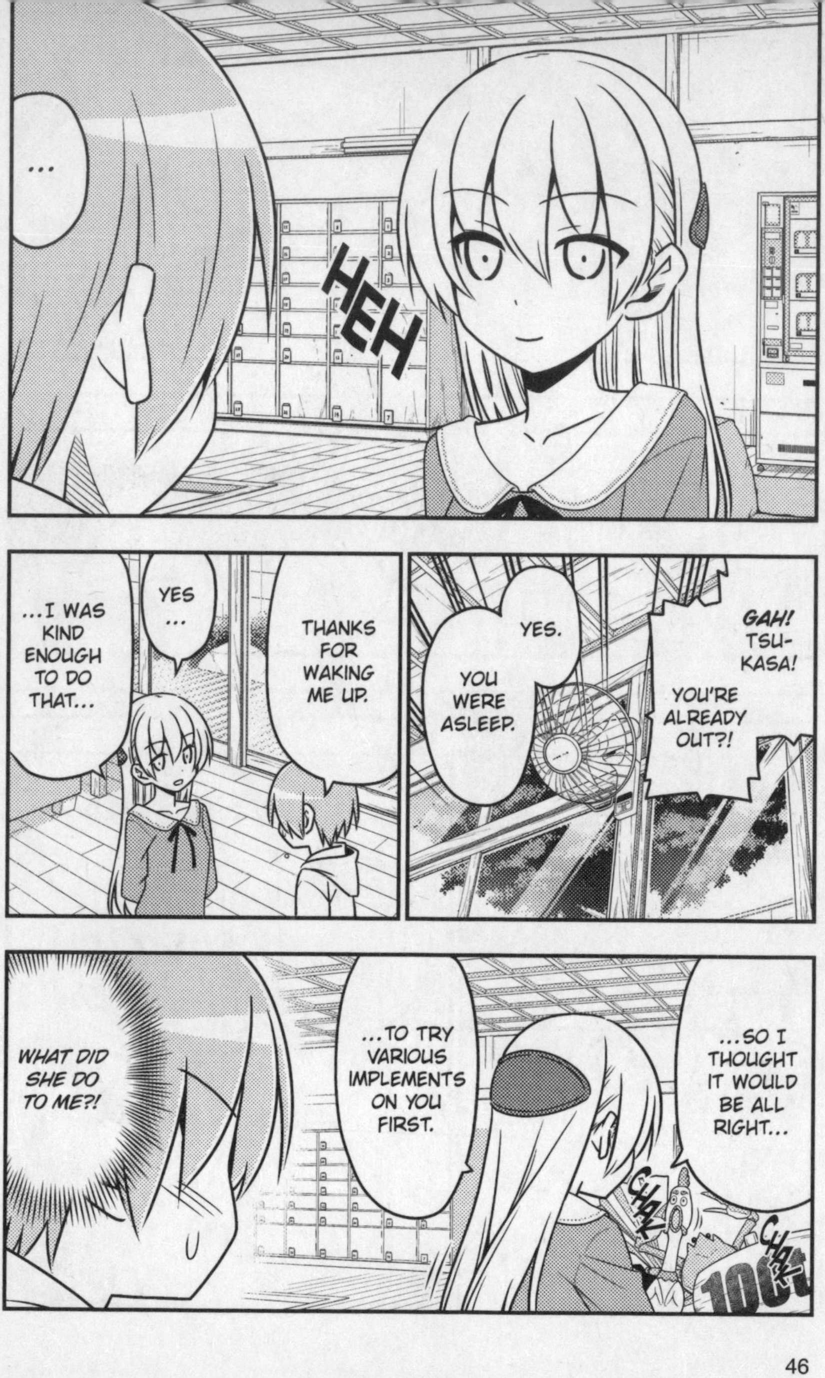
...
HEH
GAH! TSU-KASA!
YOU'RE ALREADY OUT?!
YES.
YOU WERE ASLEEP.
THANKS FOR WAKING ME UP.
YES ...
...I WAS KIND ENOUGH TO DO THAT...
...SO I THOUGHT IT WOULD BE ALL RIGHT...
...TO TRY VARIOUS IMPLEMENTS ON YOU FIRST.
CHAK
CHAK
WHAT DID SHE DO TO ME?!

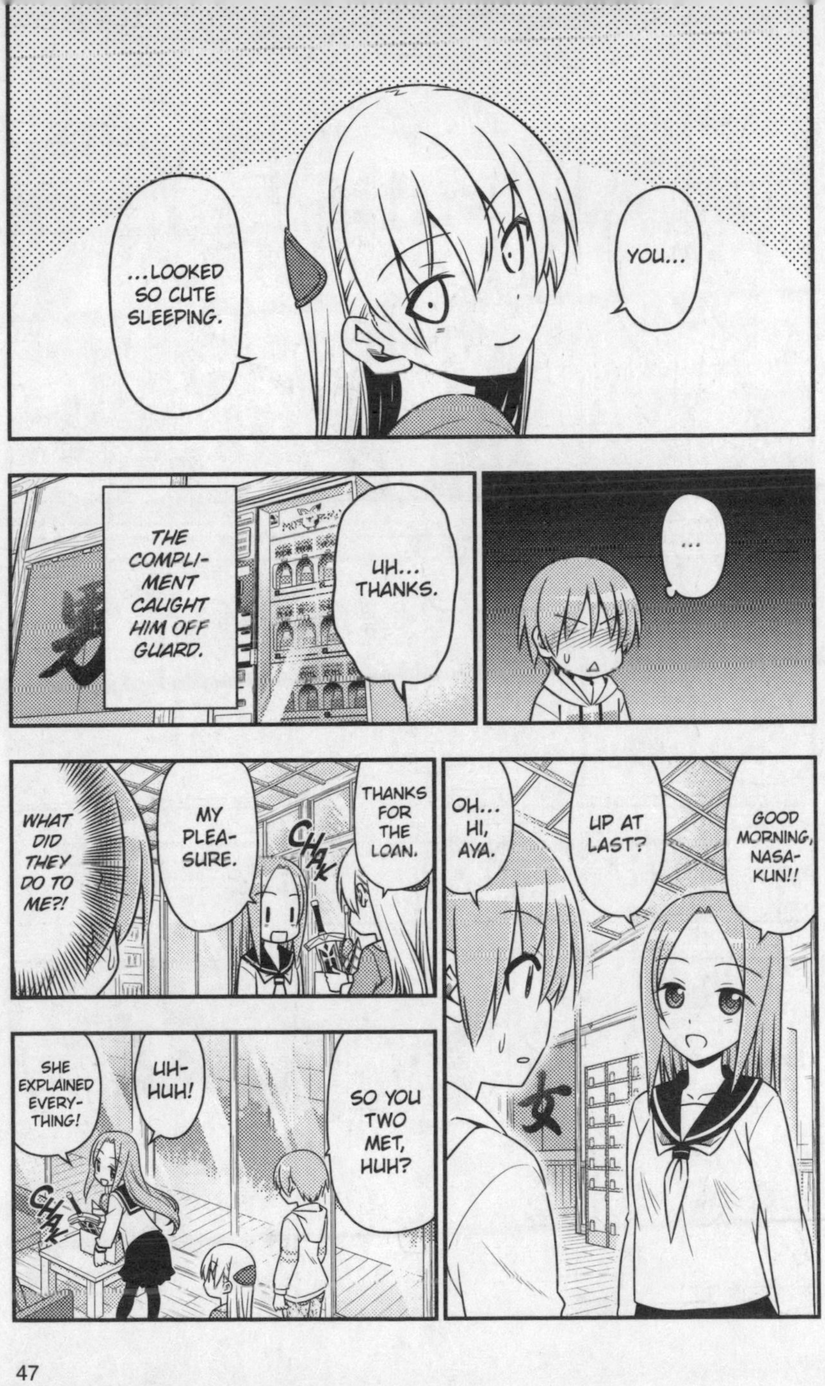
YOU...
...LOOKED SO CUTE SLEEPING.
...
UH... THANKS.
THE COMPLIMENT CAUGHT HIM OFF GUARD.
GOOD MORNING, NASA-KUN!!
UP AT LAST?
OH... HI, AYA.
女
THANKS FOR THE LOAN.
CHAK
MY PLEASURE.
WHAT DID THEY DO TO ME?!
SO YOU TWO MET, HUH?
UH-HUH!
SHE EXPLAINED EVERYTHING!
CHAK

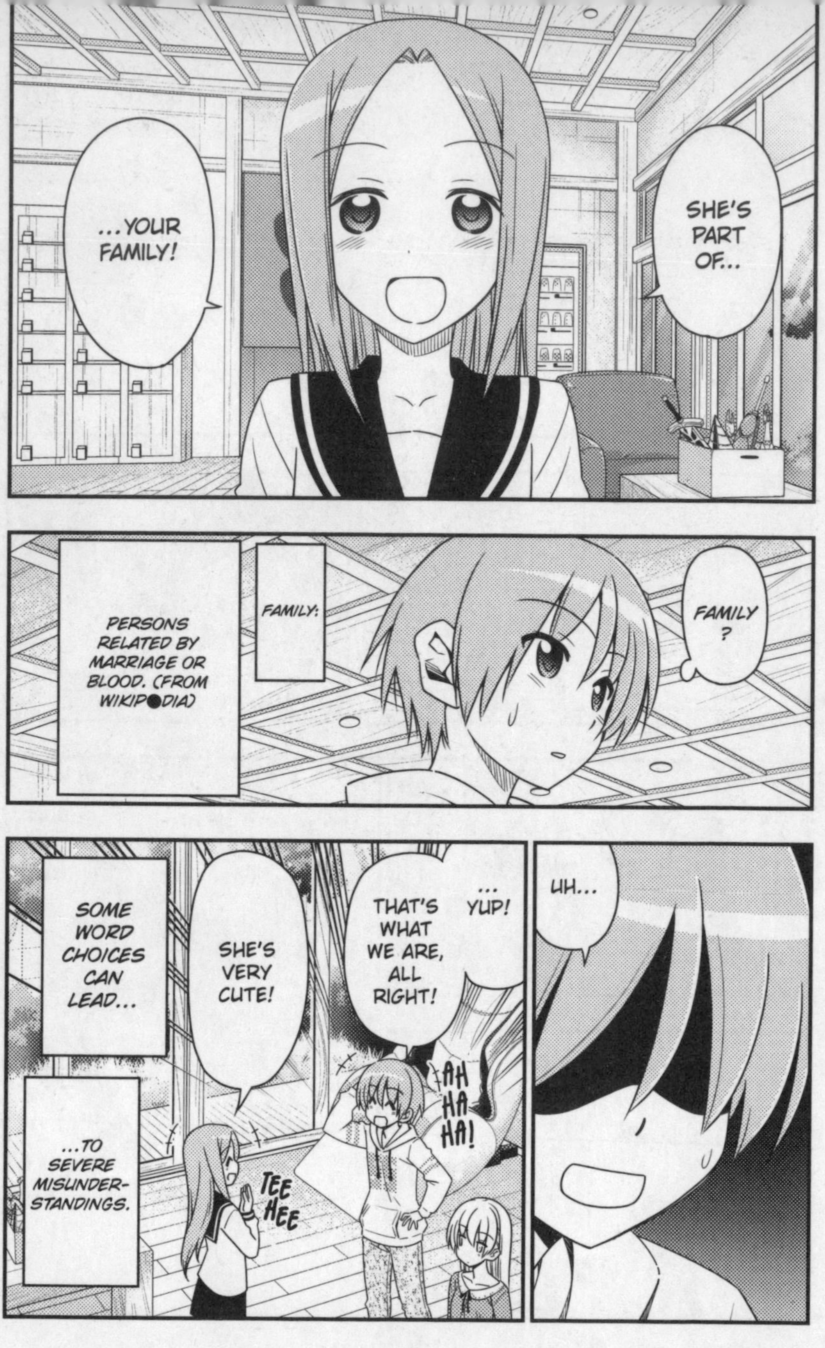
SHE'S PART OF...
...YOUR FAMILY!
FAMILY?
FAMILY:
PERSONS RELATED BY MARRIAGE OR BLOOD. (FROM WIKIP●DIA)
UH...
... YUP!
THAT'S WHAT WE ARE, ALL RIGHT!
AH HA HA!
SHE'S VERY CUTE!
TEE HEE
SOME WORD CHOICES CAN LEAD...
...TO SEVERE MISUNDERSTANDINGS.

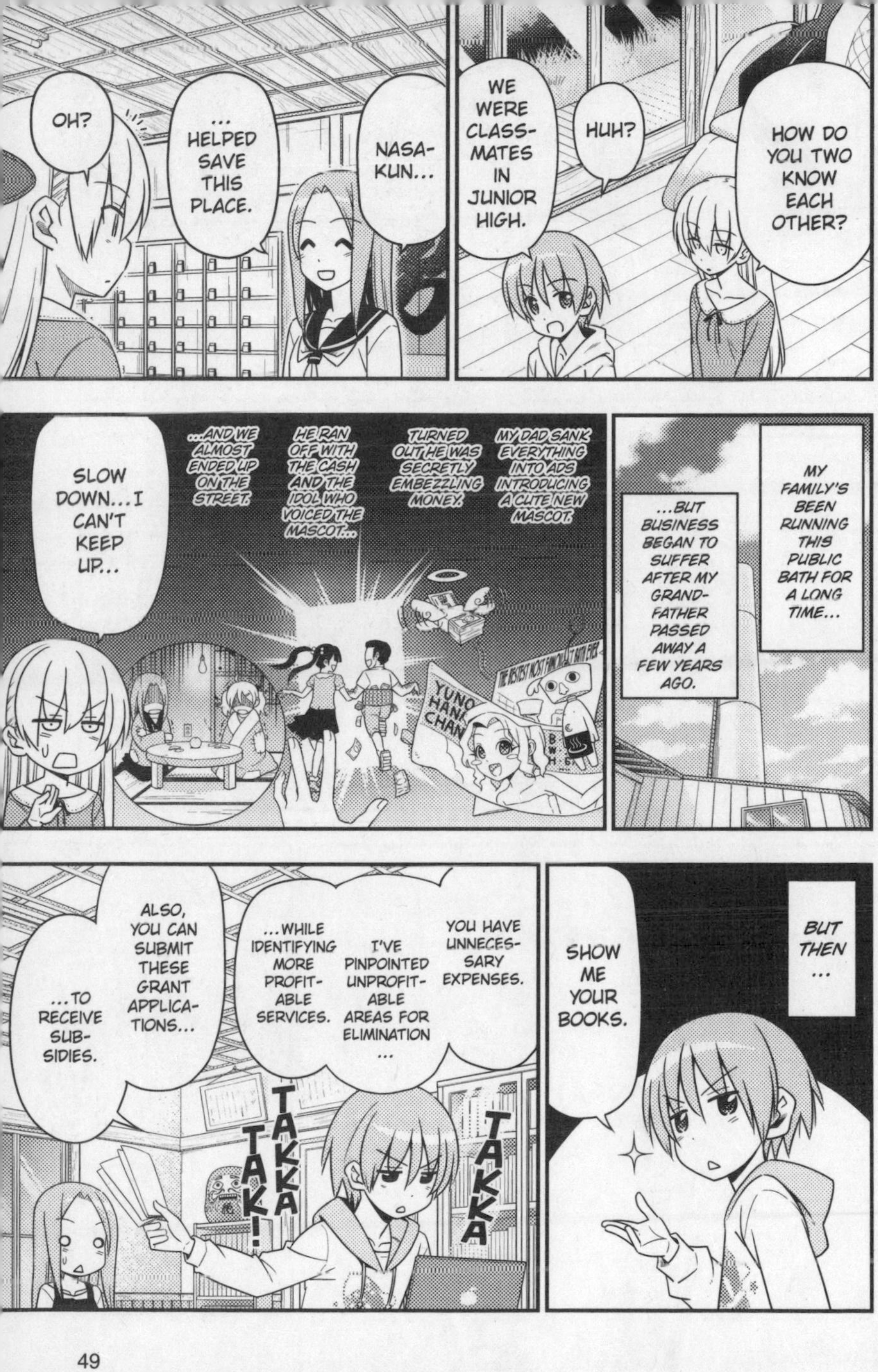
HOW DO YOU TWO KNOW EACH OTHER?
HUH?
WE WERE CLASS-MATES IN JUNIOR HIGH.
NASA-KUN...
...HELPED SAVE THIS PLACE.
OH?
MY FAMILY'S BEEN RUNNING THIS PUBLIC BATH FOR A LONG TIME...
...BUT BUSINESS BEGAN TO SUFFER AFTER MY GRAND-FATHER PASSED AWAY A FEW YEARS AGO.
MY DAD SANK EVERYTHING INTO ADS INTRODUCING A CUTE NEW MASCOT.
TURNED OUT HE WAS SECRETLY EMBEZZLING MONEY.
HE RAN OFF WITH THE CASH AND THE IDOL WHO VOICED THE MASCOT...
...AND WE ALMOST ENDED UP ON THE STREET.
SLOW DOWN... I CAN'T KEEP UP...
BUT THEN...
SHOW ME YOUR BOOKS.
YOU HAVE UNNECES-SARY EXPENSES.
I'VE PINPOINTED UNPROFIT-ABLE AREAS FOR ELIMINATION...
...WHILE IDENTIFYING MORE PROFIT-ABLE SERVICES.
ALSO, YOU CAN SUBMIT THESE GRANT APPLICA-TIONS...
...TO RECEIVE SUB-SIDIES.
TAKKA
TAKKA
TAKA!

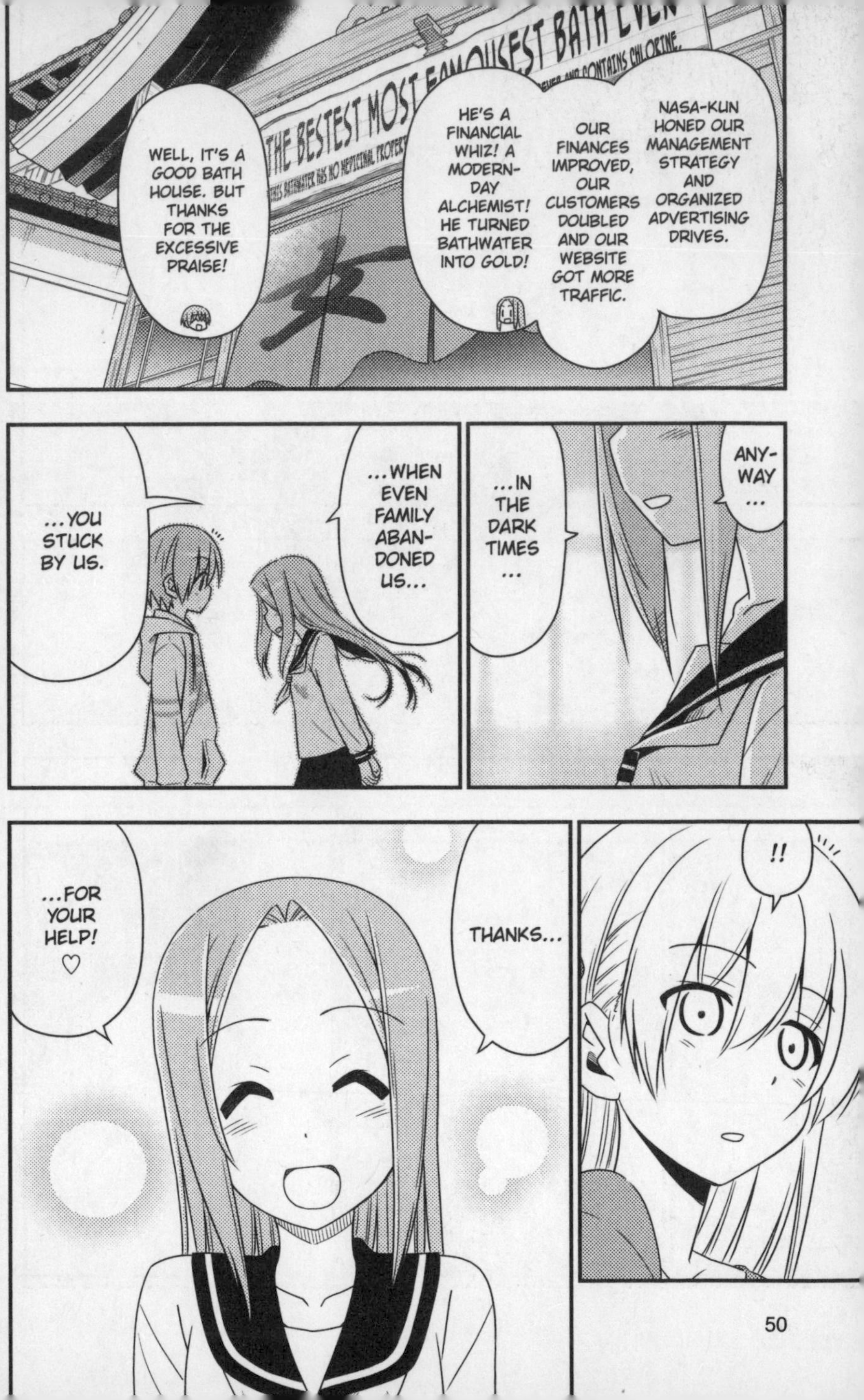
NASA-KUN HONED OUR MANAGEMENT STRATEGY AND ORGANIZED ADVERTISING DRIVES.
OUR FINANCES IMPROVED, OUR CUSTOMERS DOUBLED AND OUR WEBSITE GOT MORE TRAFFIC.
HE'S A FINANCIAL WHIZ! A MODERN-DAY ALCHEMIST! HE TURNED BATHWATER INTO GOLD!
WELL, IT'S A GOOD BATH HOUSE. BUT THANKS FOR THE EXCESSIVE PRAISE!
ANY-WAY...
...IN THE DARK TIMES...
...WHEN EVEN FAMILY ABAN-DONED US...
...YOU STUCK BY US.
!!
THANKS...
...FOR YOUR HELP! ♡

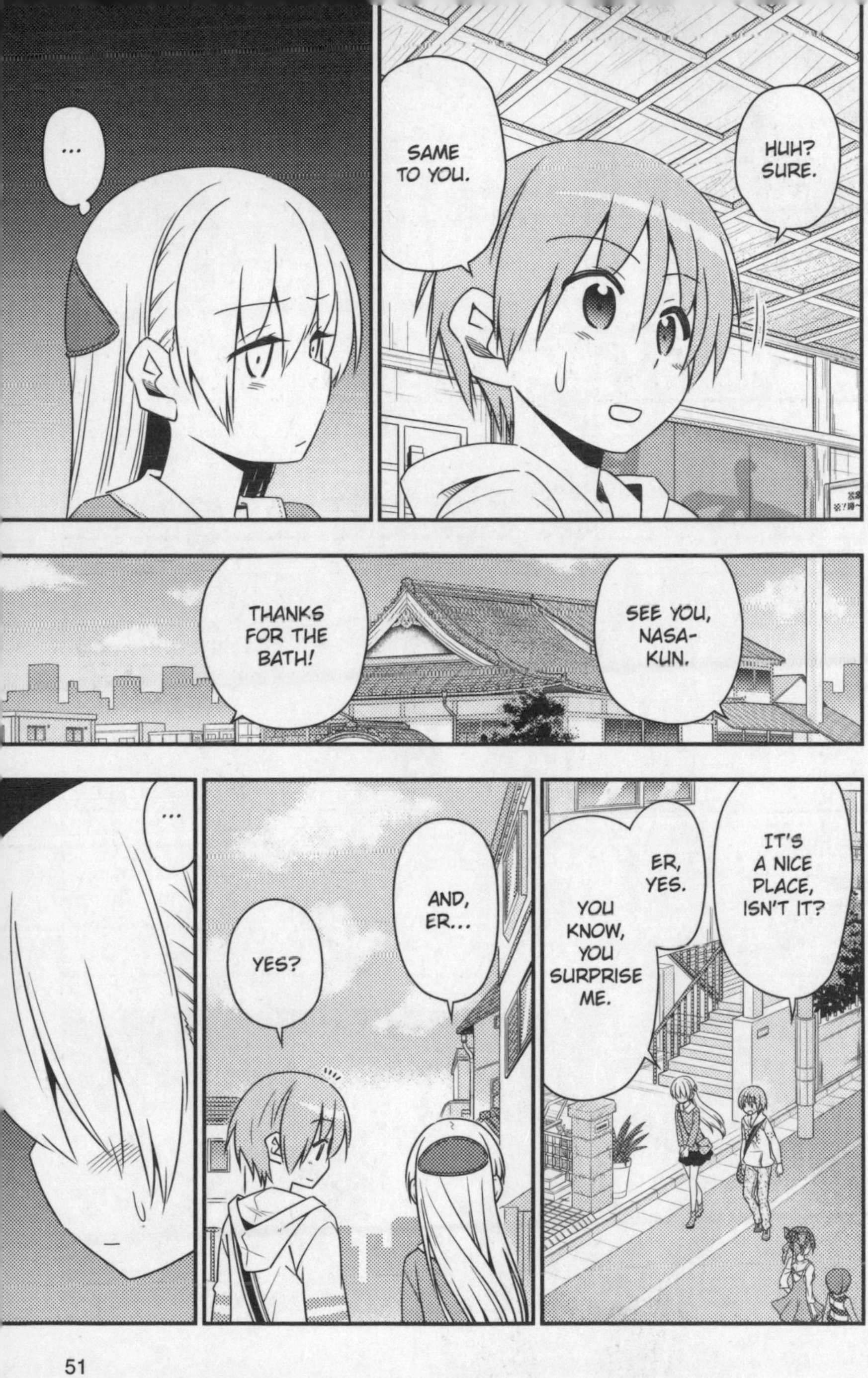
HUH? SURE.
SAME TO YOU.
...
SEE YOU, NASA-KUN.
THANKS FOR THE BATH!
IT'S A NICE PLACE, ISN'T IT?
ER, YES.
YOU KNOW, YOU SURPRISE ME.
AND, ER...
YES?
...

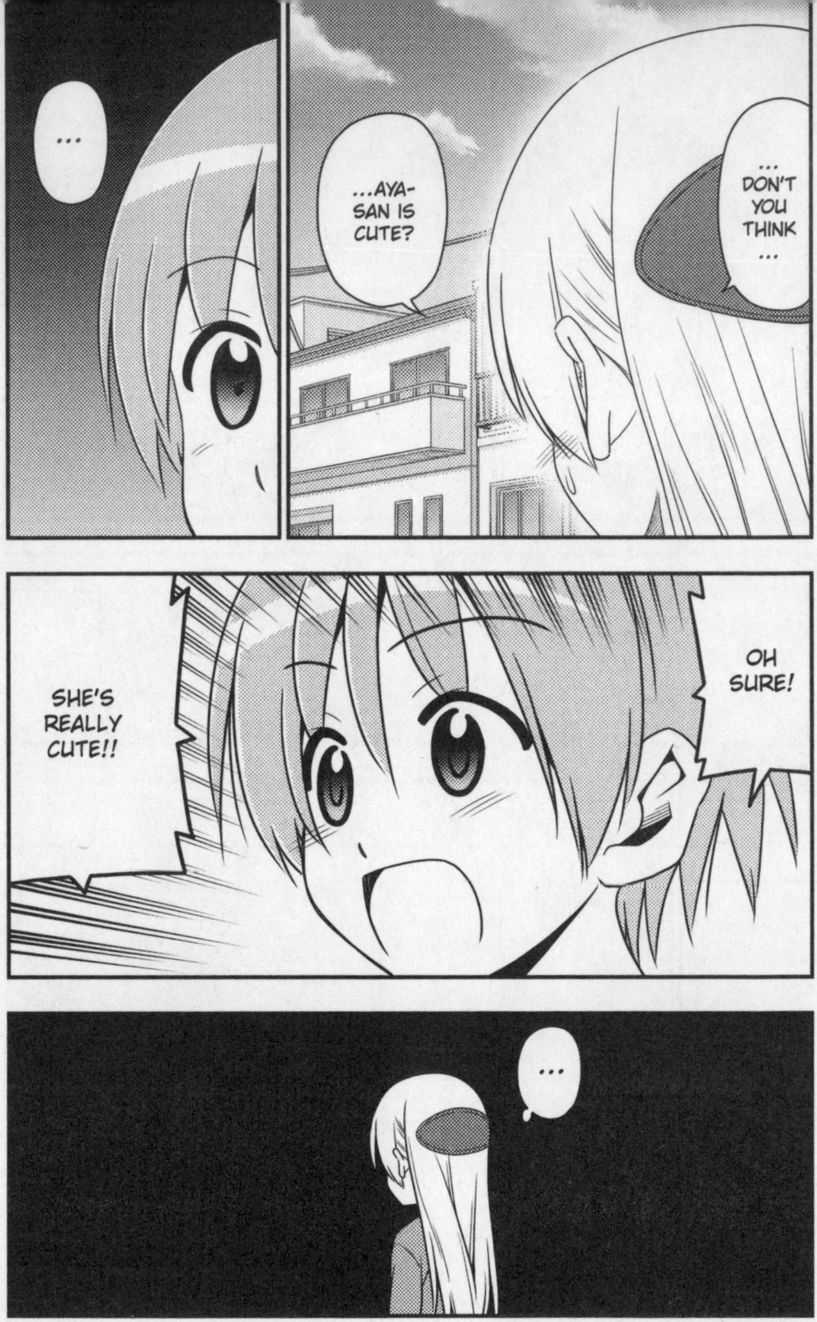
... DON'T YOU THINK ...
...AYA-SAN IS CUTE?
...
OH SURE!
SHE'S REALLY CUTE!!
...

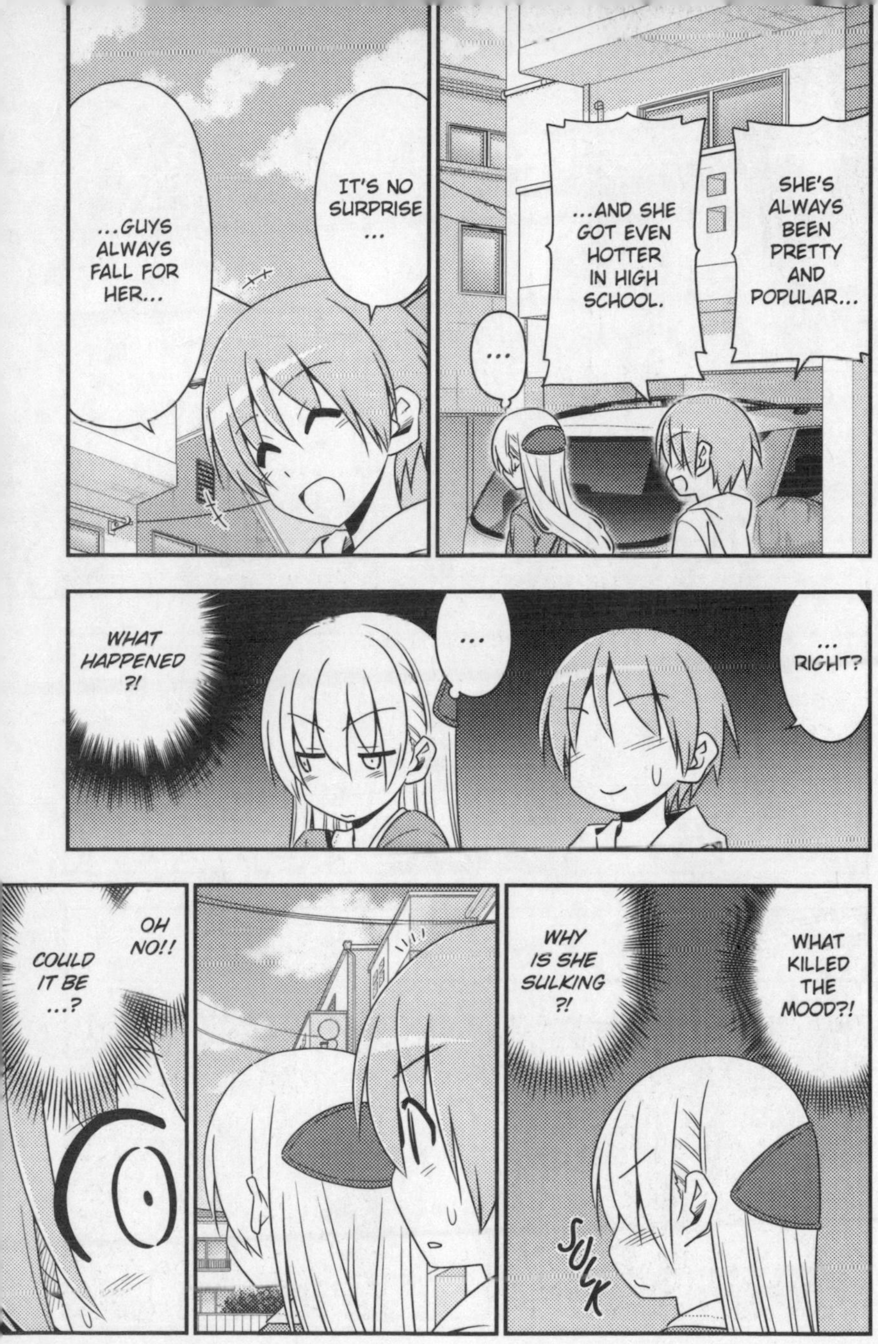
SHE'S ALWAYS BEEN PRETTY AND POPULAR...
...AND SHE GOT EVEN HOTTER IN HIGH SCHOOL.
...
IT'S NO SURPRISE ...
...GUYS ALWAYS FALL FOR HER...
... RIGHT?
...
WHAT HAPPENED ?!
WHAT KILLED THE MOOD?!
WHY IS SHE SULKING ?!
SULK
OH NO!!
COULD IT BE ...?

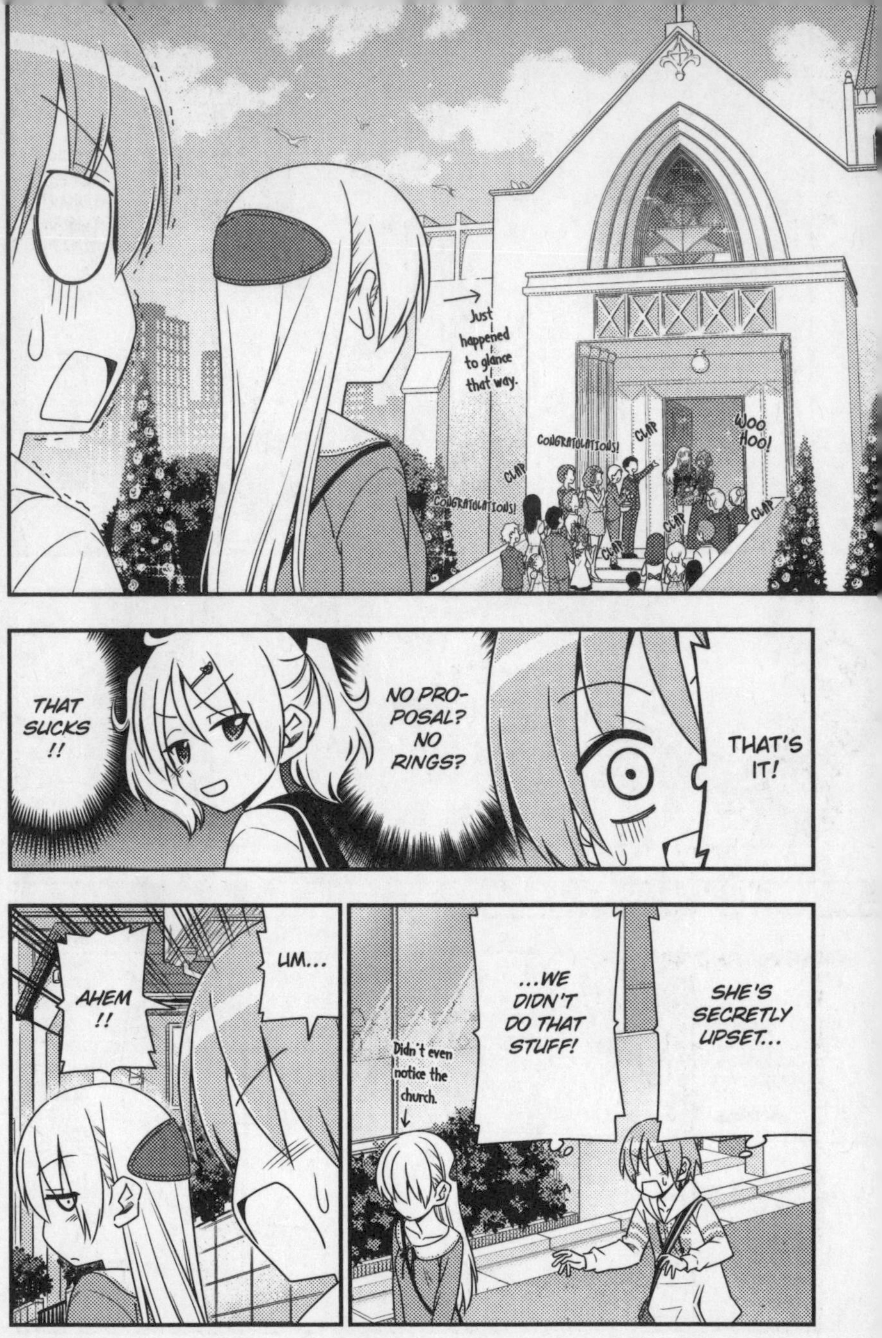
Just happened to glance that way.
WOO HOO!
CLAP
CONGRATULATIONS!
CLAP
CLAP
CLAP
CONGRATULATIONS!
CLAP
THAT'S IT!
NO PRO-POSAL? NO RINGS?
THAT SUCKS!!
SHE'S SECRETLY UPSET...
...WE DIDN'T DO THAT STUFF!
Didn't even notice the church.
UM...
AHEM!!

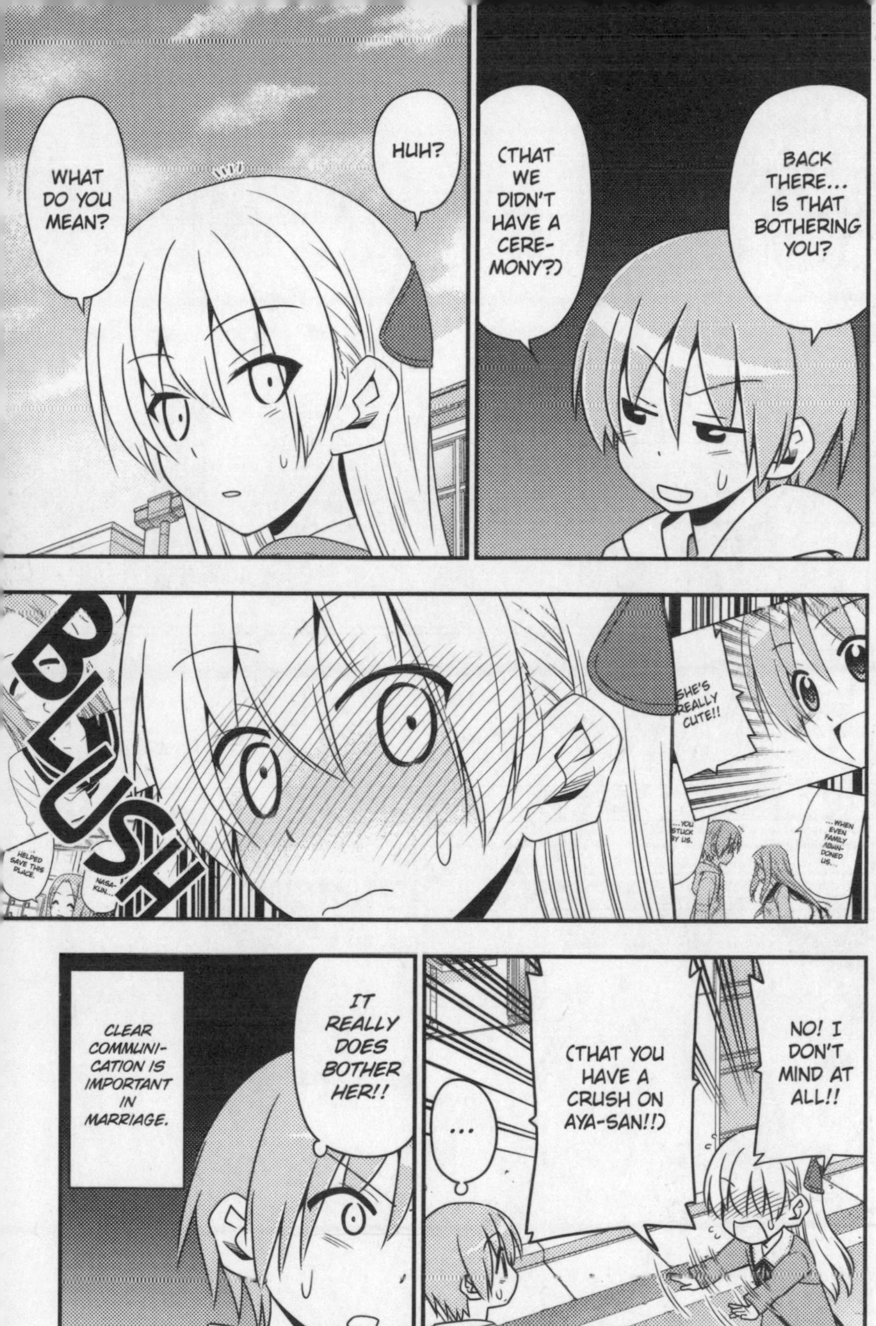
BACK THERE... IS THAT BOTHERING YOU?
(THAT WE DIDN'T HAVE A CERE-MONY?)
HUH?
WHAT DO YOU MEAN?
SHE'S REALLY CUTE!!
...WHEN EVEN FAMILY ABAN-DONED US...
...YOU STUCK BY US.
NASA-KUN...
HELPED SAVE THIS PLACE.
BLUSH
NO! I DON'T MIND AT ALL!!
(THAT YOU HAVE A CRUSH ON AYA-SAN!!)
...
IT REALLY DOES BOTHER HER!!
CLEAR COMMUNI-CATION IS IMPORTANT IN MARRIAGE.

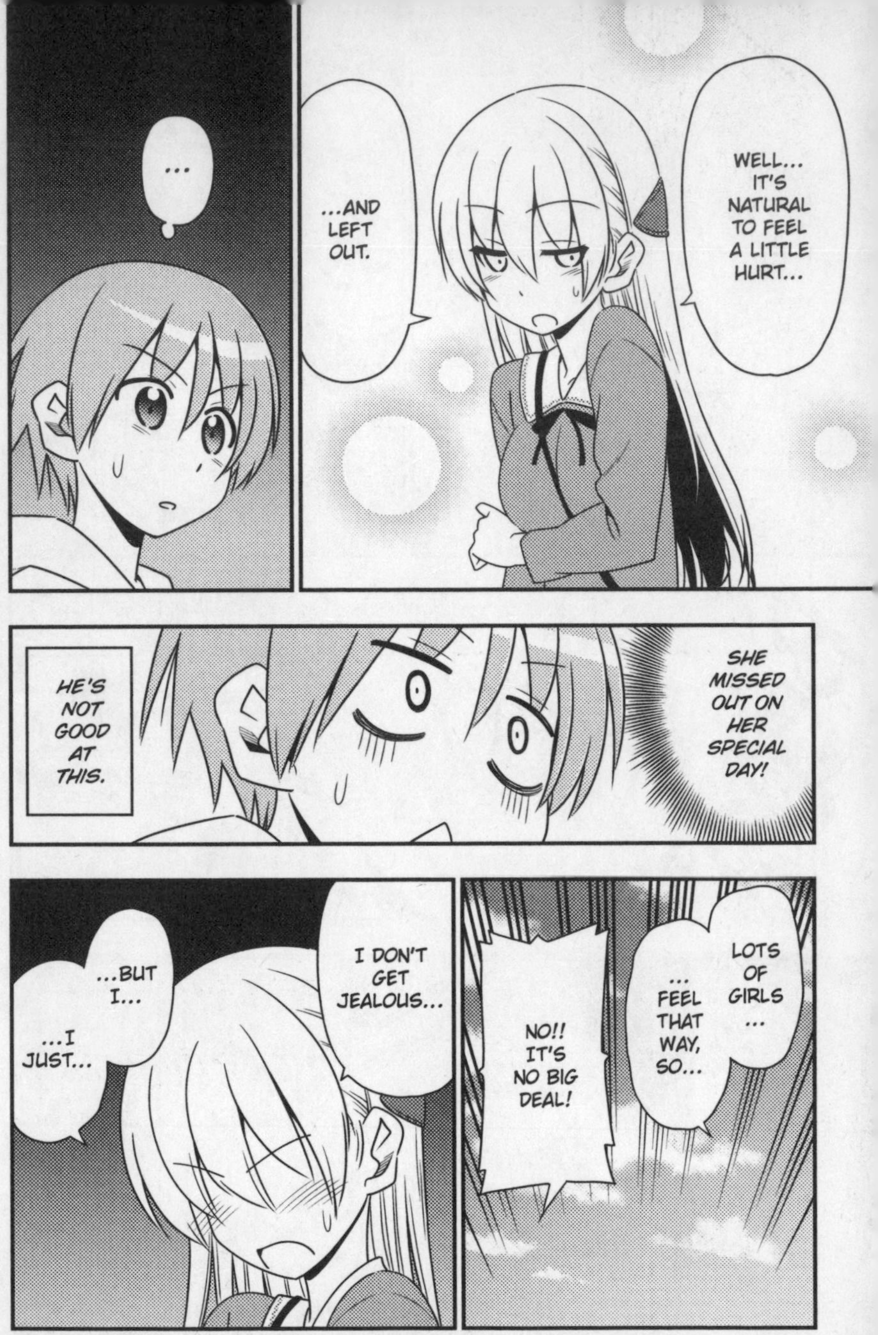
WELL... IT'S NATURAL TO FEEL A LITTLE HURT...
...AND LEFT OUT.
...
SHE MISSED OUT ON HER SPECIAL DAY!
HE'S NOT GOOD AT THIS.
LOTS OF GIRLS ...
... FEEL THAT WAY, SO...
NO!! IT'S NO BIG DEAL!
I DON'T GET JEALOUS...
...BUT I...
...I JUST...

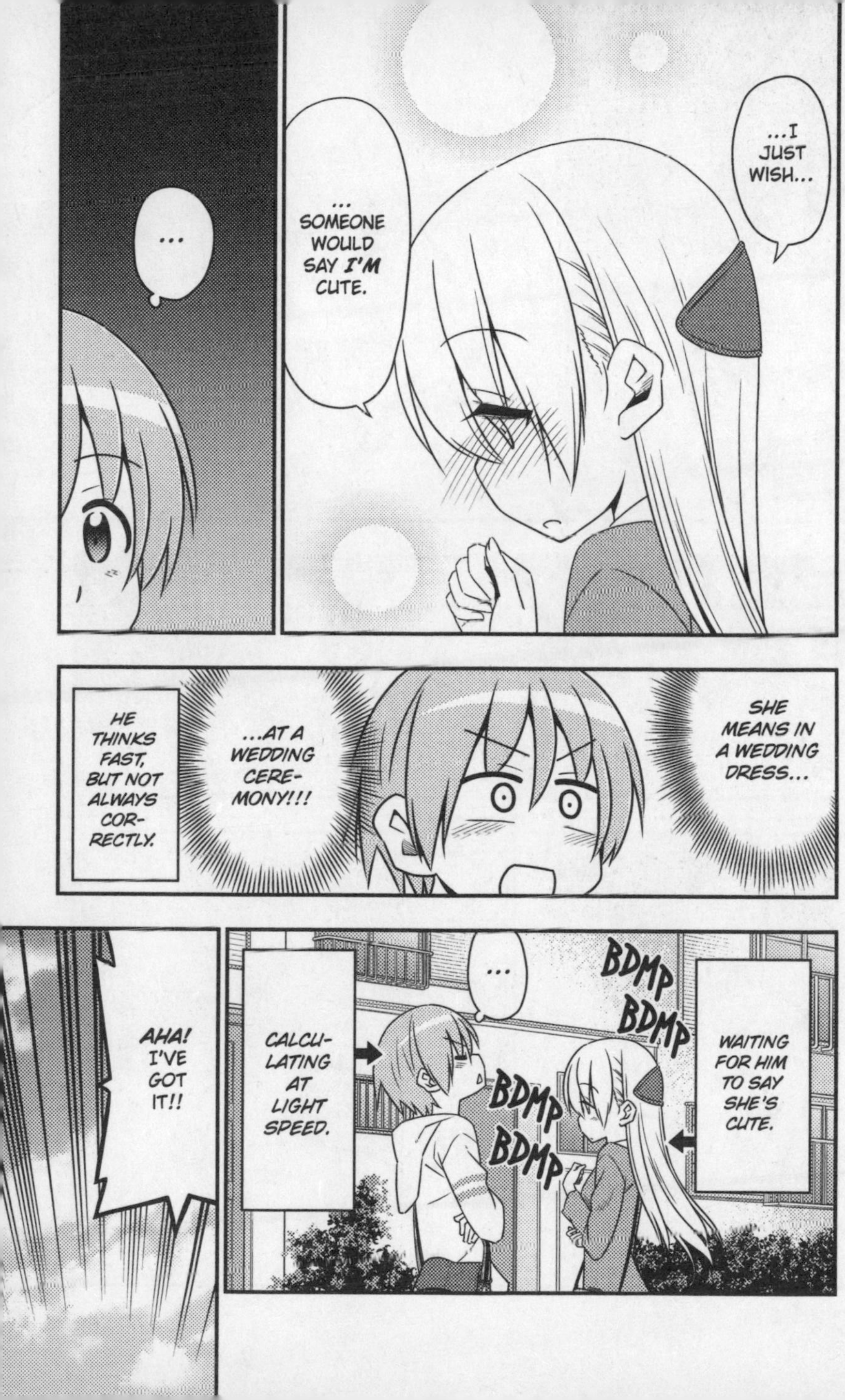
...I JUST WISH...
...SOMEONE WOULD SAY *I'M* CUTE.
...
SHE MEANS IN A WEDDING DRESS...
...AT A WEDDING CEREMONY!!!
HE THINKS FAST, BUT NOT ALWAYS CORRECTLY.
WAITING FOR HIM TO SAY SHE'S CUTE.
BDMP BDMP
...
BDMP BDMP
CALCULATING AT LIGHT SPEED.
AHA! I'VE GOT IT!!

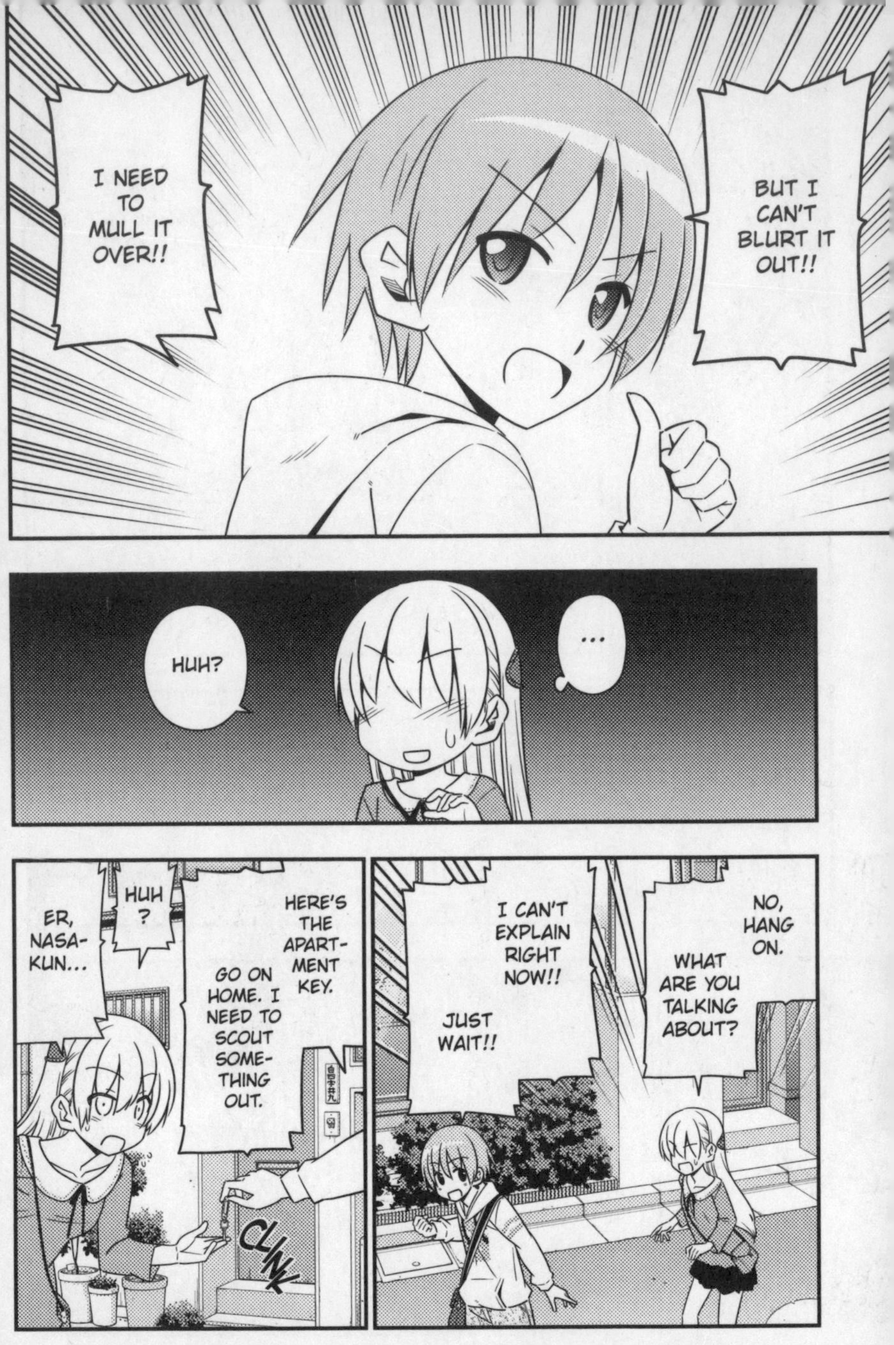
BUT I CAN'T BLURT IT OUT!!
I NEED TO MULL IT OVER!!
...
HUH?
NO, HANG ON.
WHAT ARE YOU TALKING ABOUT?
I CAN'T EXPLAIN RIGHT NOW!!
JUST WAIT!!
HERE'S THE APARTMENT KEY.
GO ON HOME. I NEED TO SCOUT SOMETHING OUT.
HUH?
ER, NASA-KUN...
CLINK

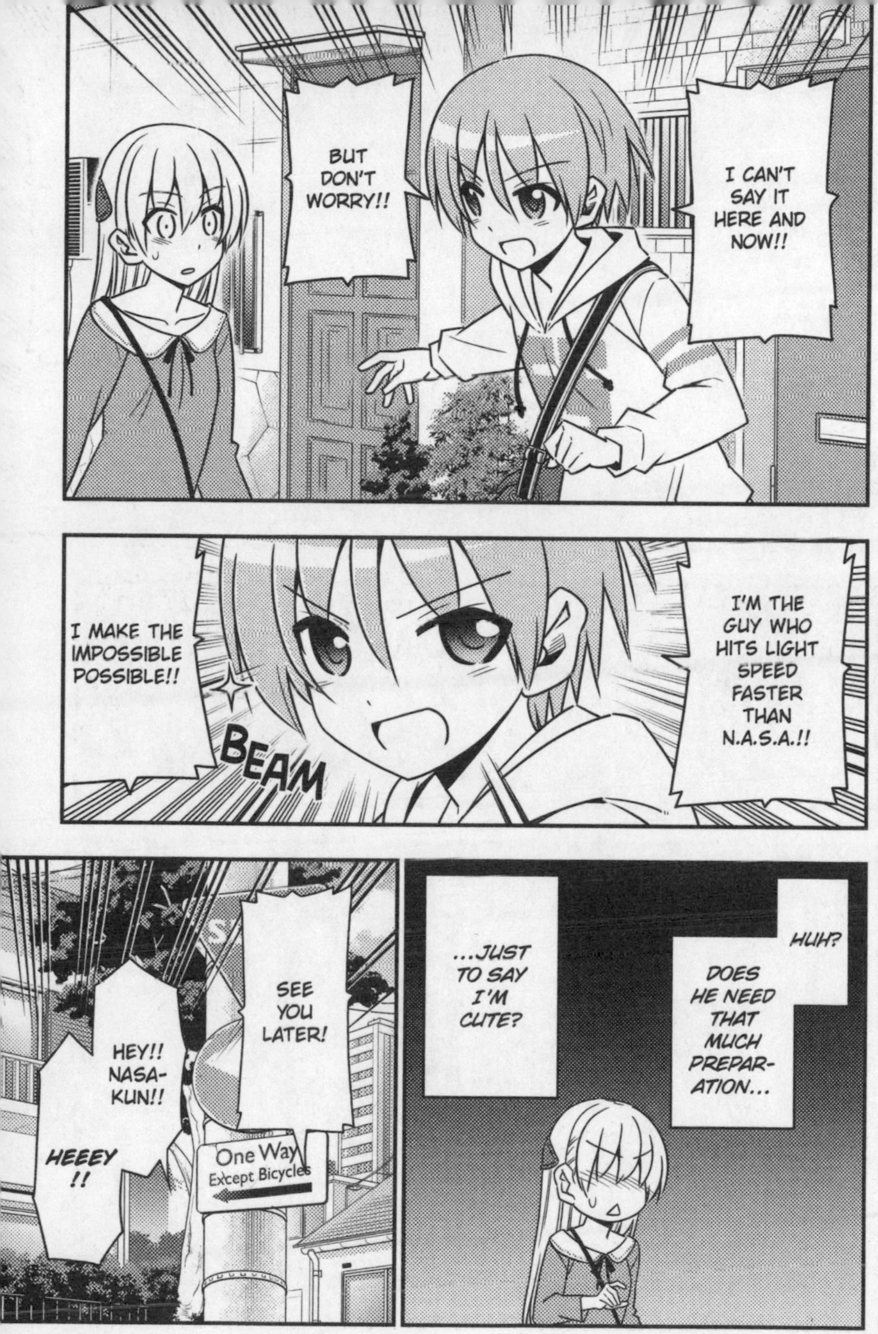
I CAN'T SAY IT HERE AND NOW!!
BUT DON'T WORRY!!
I'M THE GUY WHO HITS LIGHT SPEED FASTER THAN N.A.S.A.!!
I MAKE THE IMPOSSIBLE POSSIBLE!!
BEAM
HUH?
DOES HE NEED THAT MUCH PREPAR-ATION…
…JUST TO SAY I'M CUTE?
SEE YOU LATER!
HEY!! NASA-KUN!!
HEEEY!!
One Way
Except Bicycles

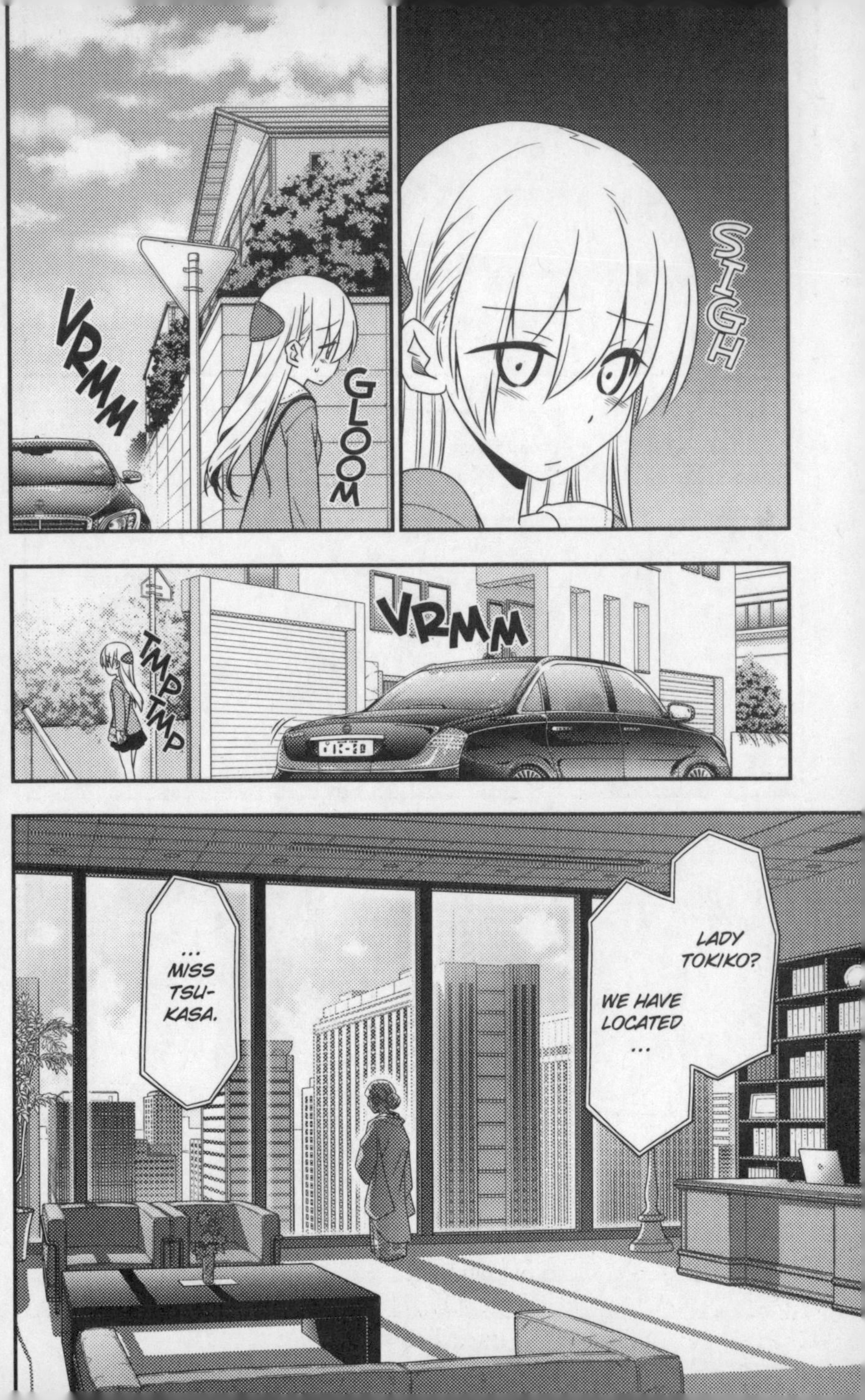
SIGH
VRMM
GLOOM
VRMM
TMP TMP
LADY TOKIKO?
WE HAVE LOCATED ...
... MISS TSU-KASA.

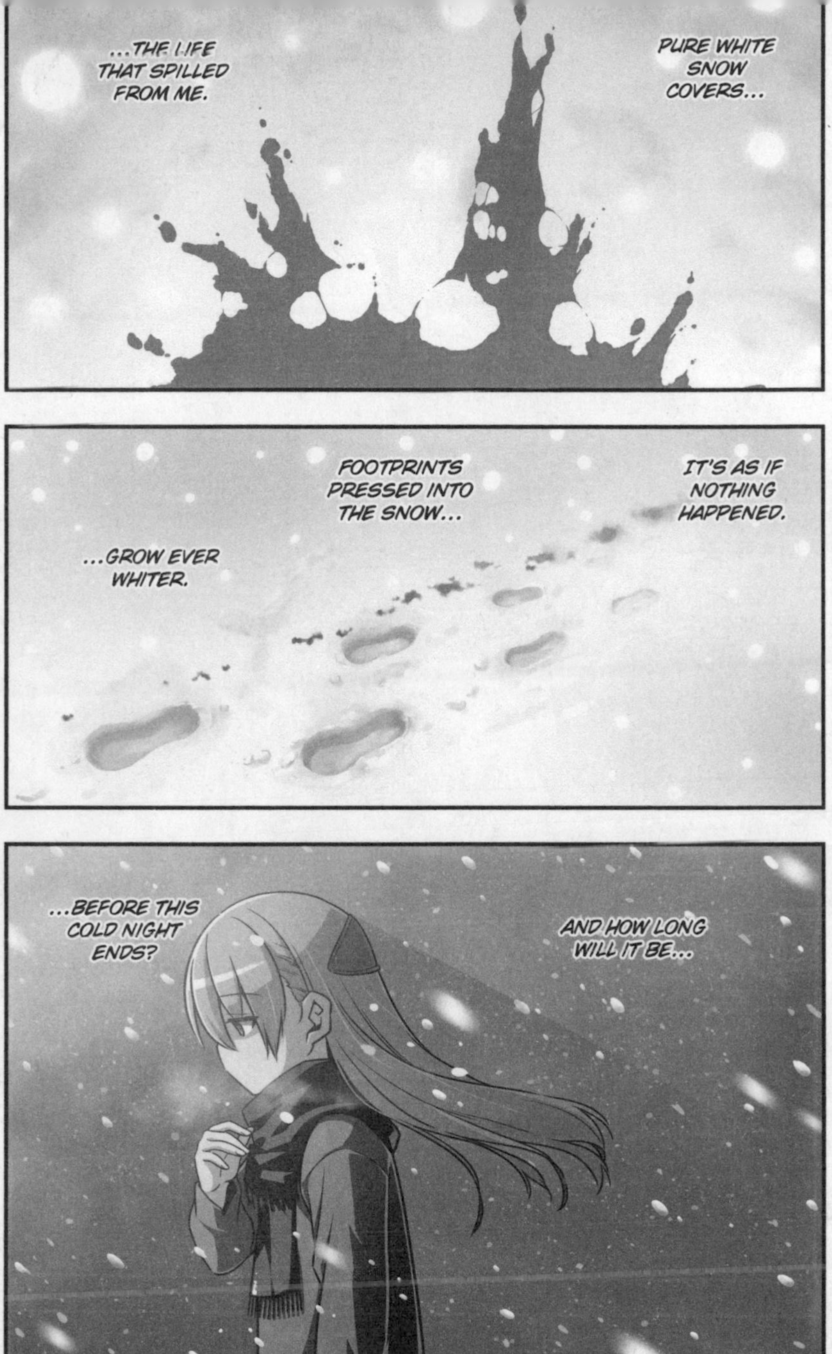
PURE WHITE SNOW COVERS...
...THE LIFE THAT SPILLED FROM ME.
IT'S AS IF NOTHING HAPPENED.
FOOTPRINTS PRESSED INTO THE SNOW...
...GROW EVER WHITER.
AND HOW LONG WILL IT BE...
...BEFORE THIS COLD NIGHT ENDS?

Chapter 12: "I Want to Go Back There Soon"

Chapter 12: "I Want to Go Back There Soon"

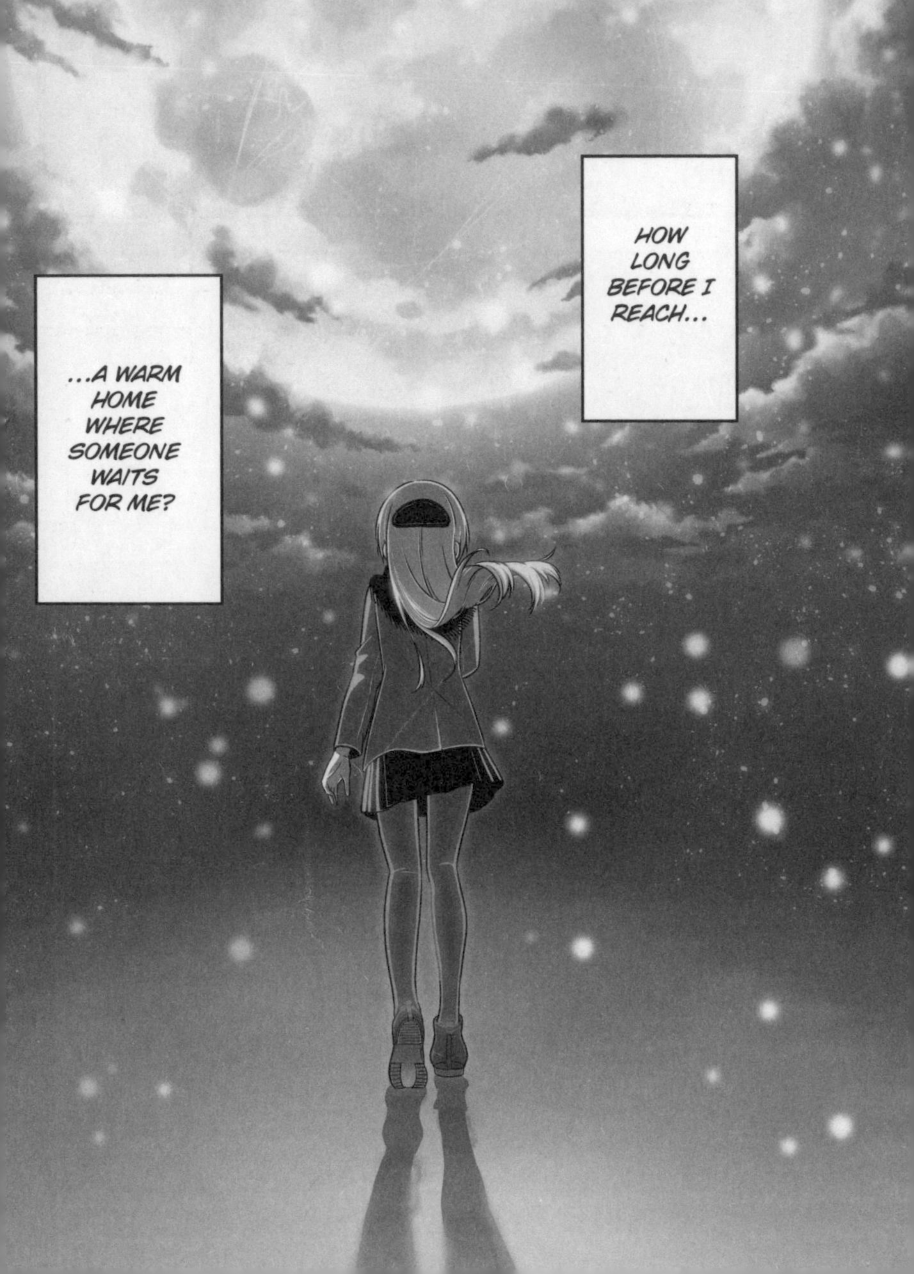
HOW LONG BEFORE I REACH...
...A WARM HOME WHERE SOMEONE WAITS FOR ME?

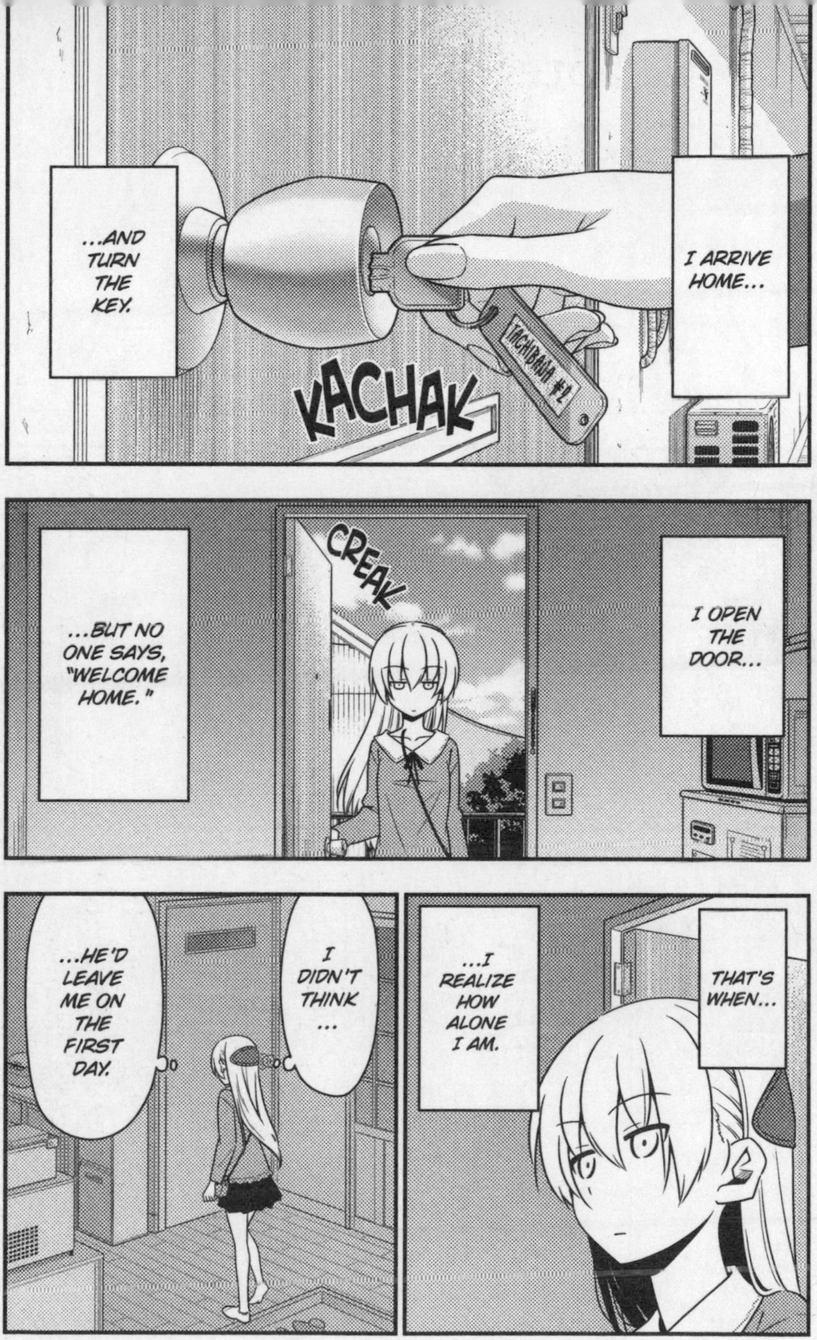
I ARRIVE HOME...
...AND TURN THE KEY.
KACHAK
I OPEN THE DOOR...
CREAK
...BUT NO ONE SAYS, "WELCOME HOME."
THAT'S WHEN...
...I REALIZE HOW ALONE I AM.
I DIDN'T THINK ...
...HE'D LEAVE ME ON THE FIRST DAY.

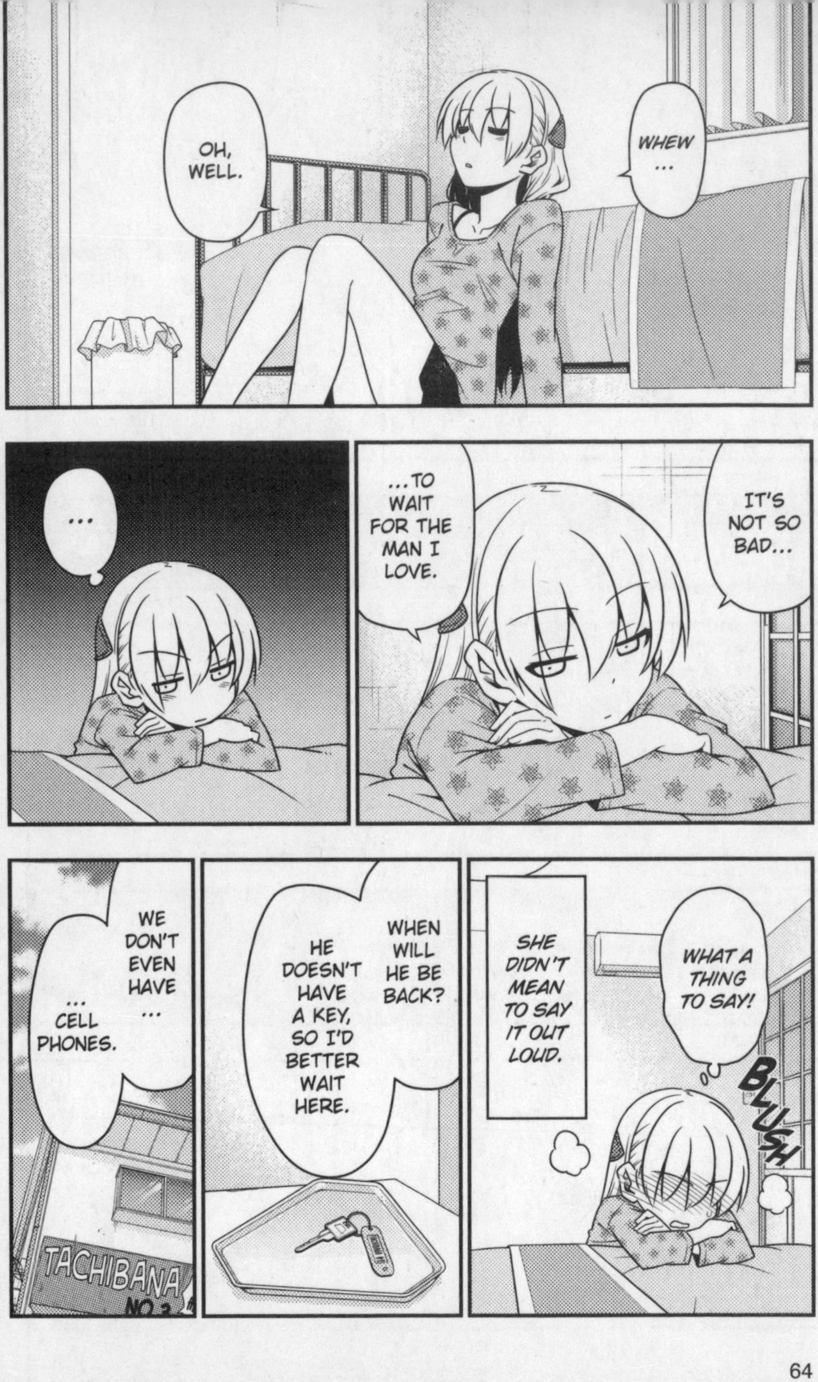
WHEW ...
OH, WELL.
IT'S NOT SO BAD...
...TO WAIT FOR THE MAN I LOVE.
...
WHAT A THING TO SAY!
SHE DIDN'T MEAN TO SAY IT OUT LOUD.
BLUSH
WHEN WILL HE BE BACK?
HE DOESN'T HAVE A KEY, SO I'D BETTER WAIT HERE.
WE DON'T EVEN HAVE ...
... CELL PHONES.
TACHIBANA

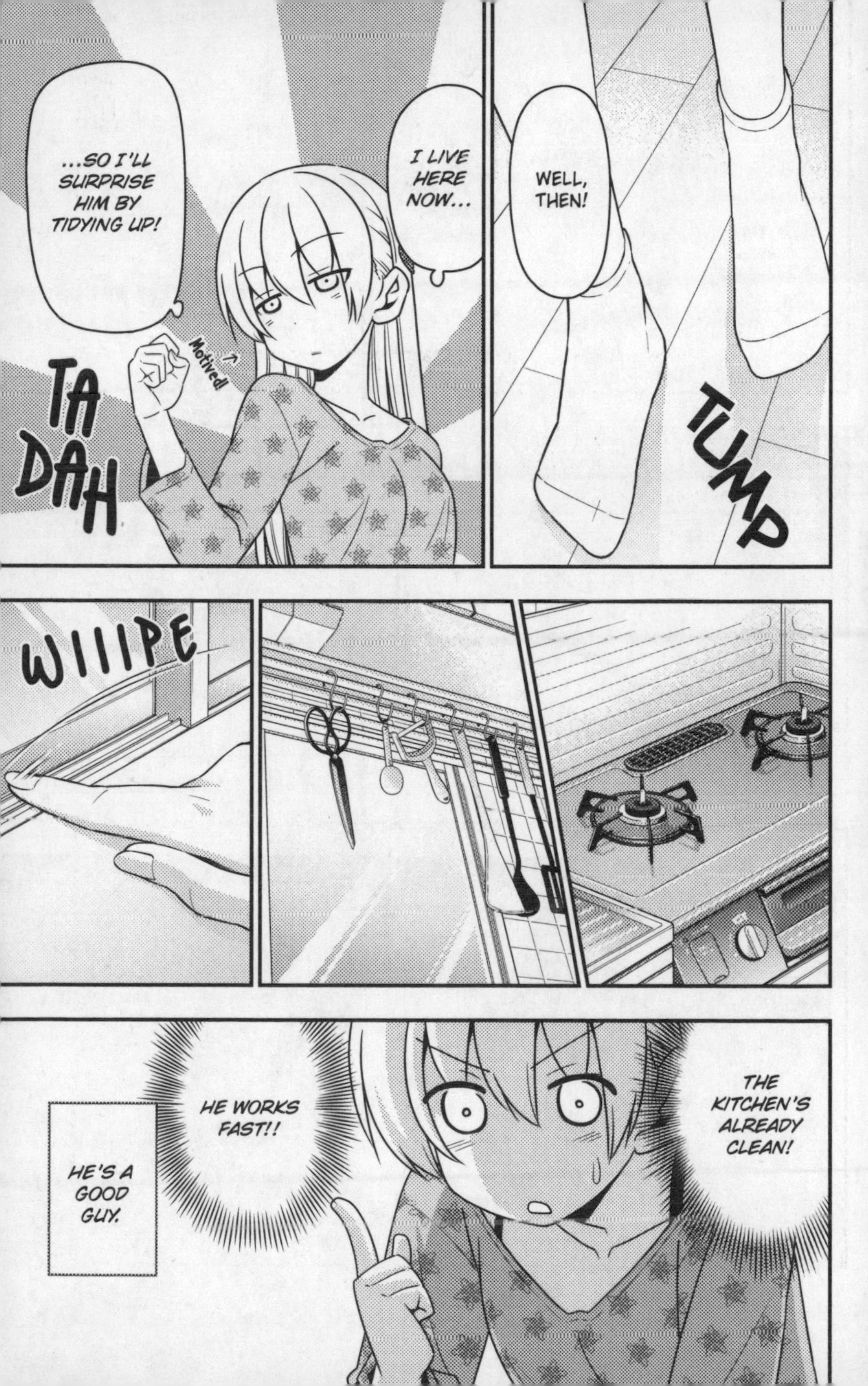
WELL, THEN!
TUMP
I LIVE HERE NOW...
...SO I'LL SURPRISE HIM BY TIDYING UP!
Motived!
TA DAH
WIIIPE
THE KITCHEN'S ALREADY CLEAN!
HE WORKS FAST!!
HE'S A GOOD GUY.

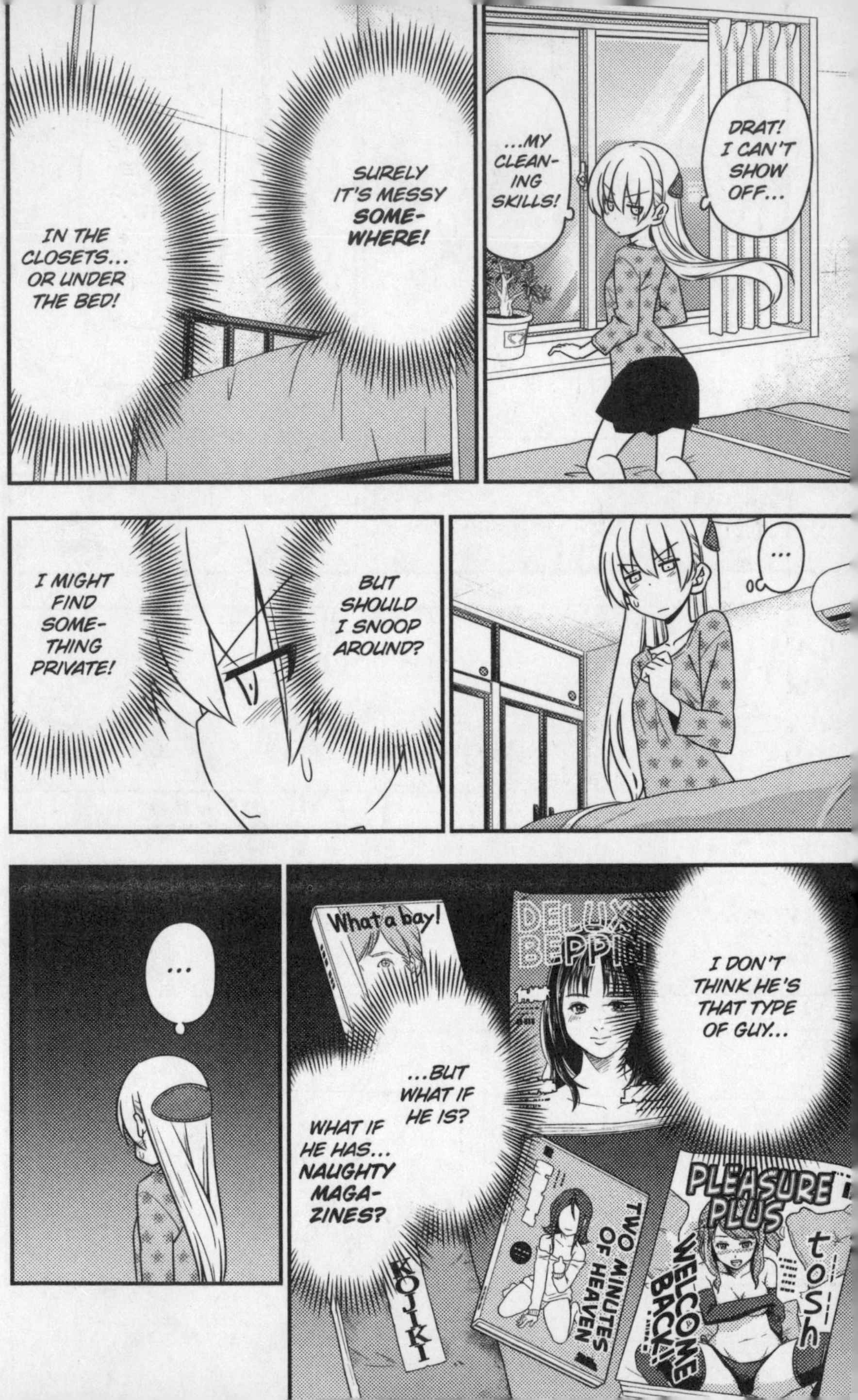
DRAT! I CAN'T SHOW OFF...
...MY CLEANING-ING SKILLS!
SURELY IT'S MESSY SOME-WHERE!
IN THE CLOSETS... OR UNDER THE BED!
...
BUT SHOULD I SNOOP AROUND?
I MIGHT FIND SOME-THING PRIVATE!
I DON'T THINK HE'S THAT TYPE OF GUY...
DELUX BEPPI
What a bay!
...BUT WHAT IF HE IS?
WHAT IF HE HAS... NAUGHTY MAGA-ZINES?
PLEASURE PLUS
WELCOME BACK!
tosh
TWO MINUTES OF HEAVEN
KOJIKI
...

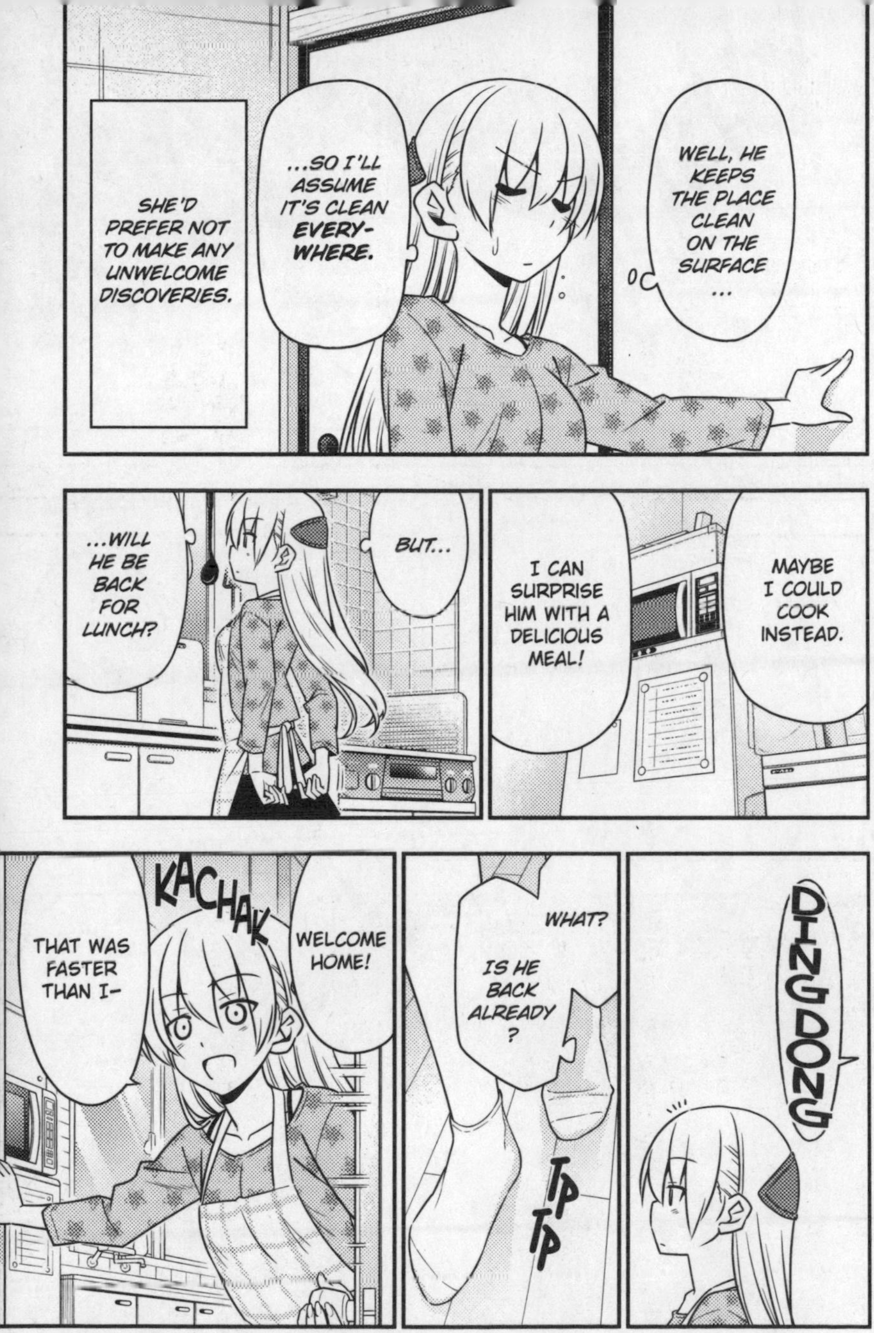
WELL, HE KEEPS THE PLACE CLEAN ON THE SURFACE...
...SO I'LL ASSUME IT'S CLEAN EVERY-WHERE.
SHE'D PREFER NOT TO MAKE ANY UNWELCOME DISCOVERIES.
MAYBE I COULD COOK INSTEAD.
I CAN SURPRISE HIM WITH A DELICIOUS MEAL!
BUT...
...WILL HE BE BACK FOR LUNCH?
DING DONG
WHAT?
IS HE BACK ALREADY?
TP TP
KACHAK
WELCOME HOME!
THAT WAS FASTER THAN I-

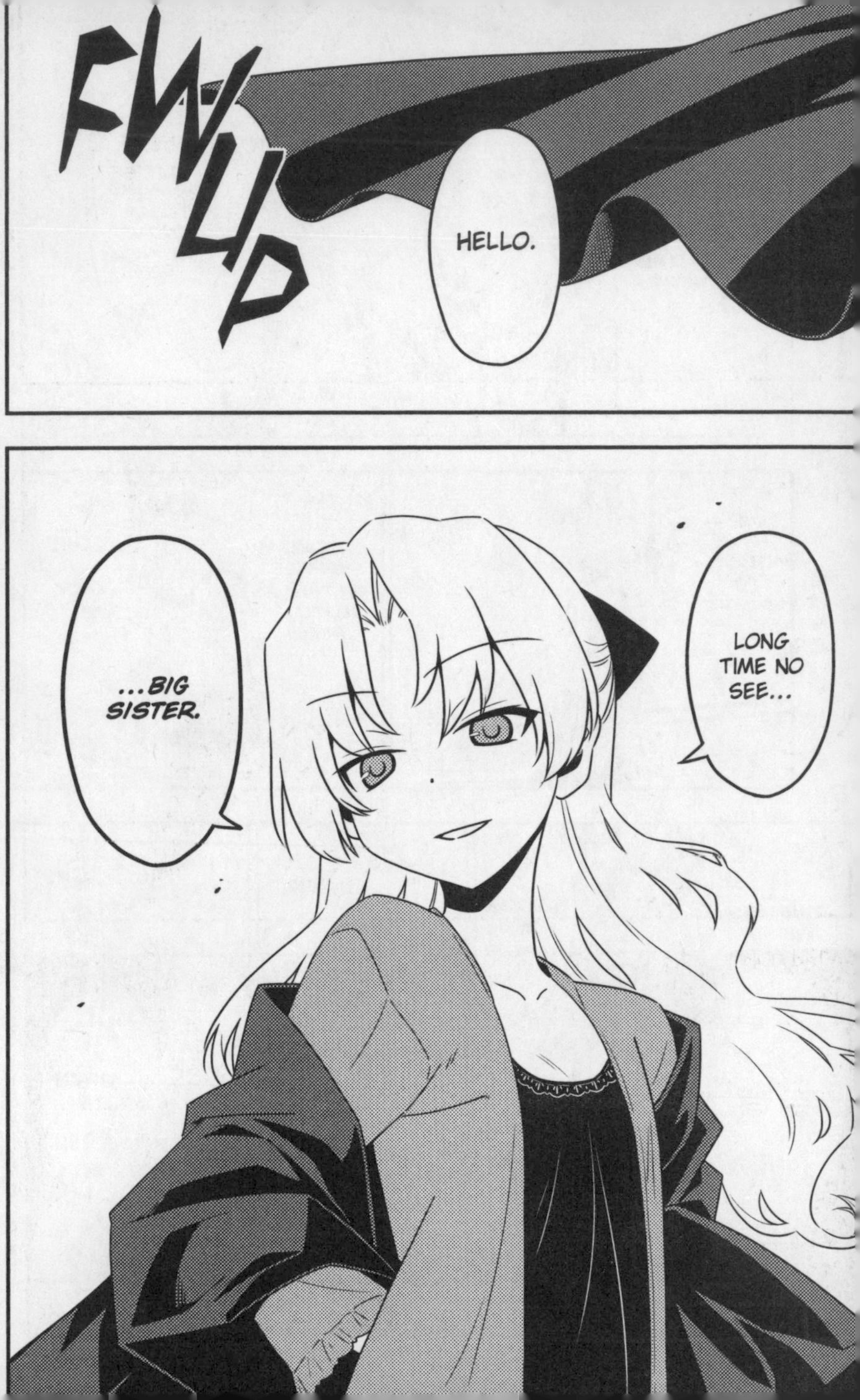
FWUP
HELLO.
LONG TIME NO SEE...
...BIG SISTER.

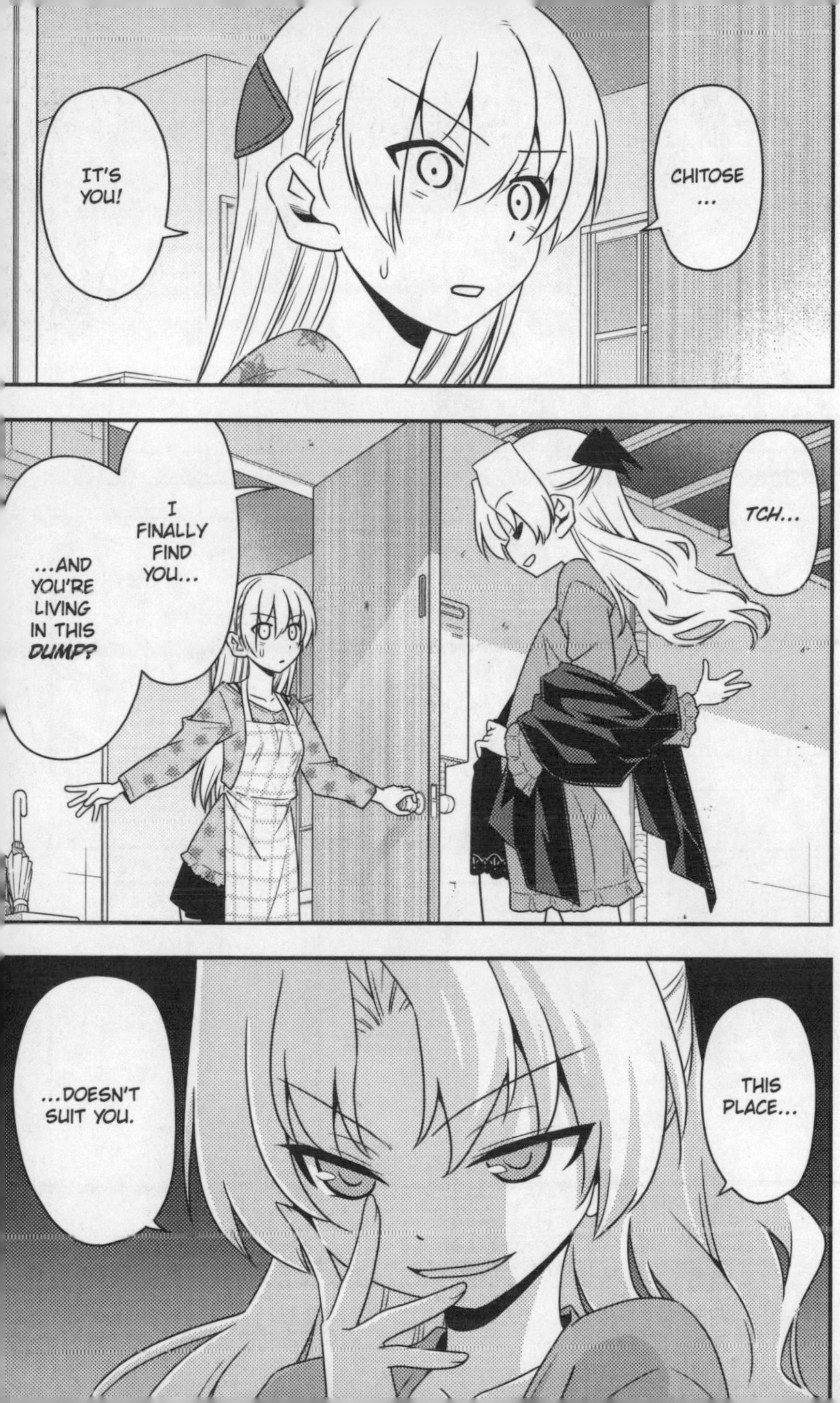
CHITOSE ...
IT'S YOU!
TCH...
I FINALLY FIND YOU...
...AND YOU'RE LIVING IN THIS *DUMP?*
THIS PLACE...
...DOESN'T SUIT YOU.

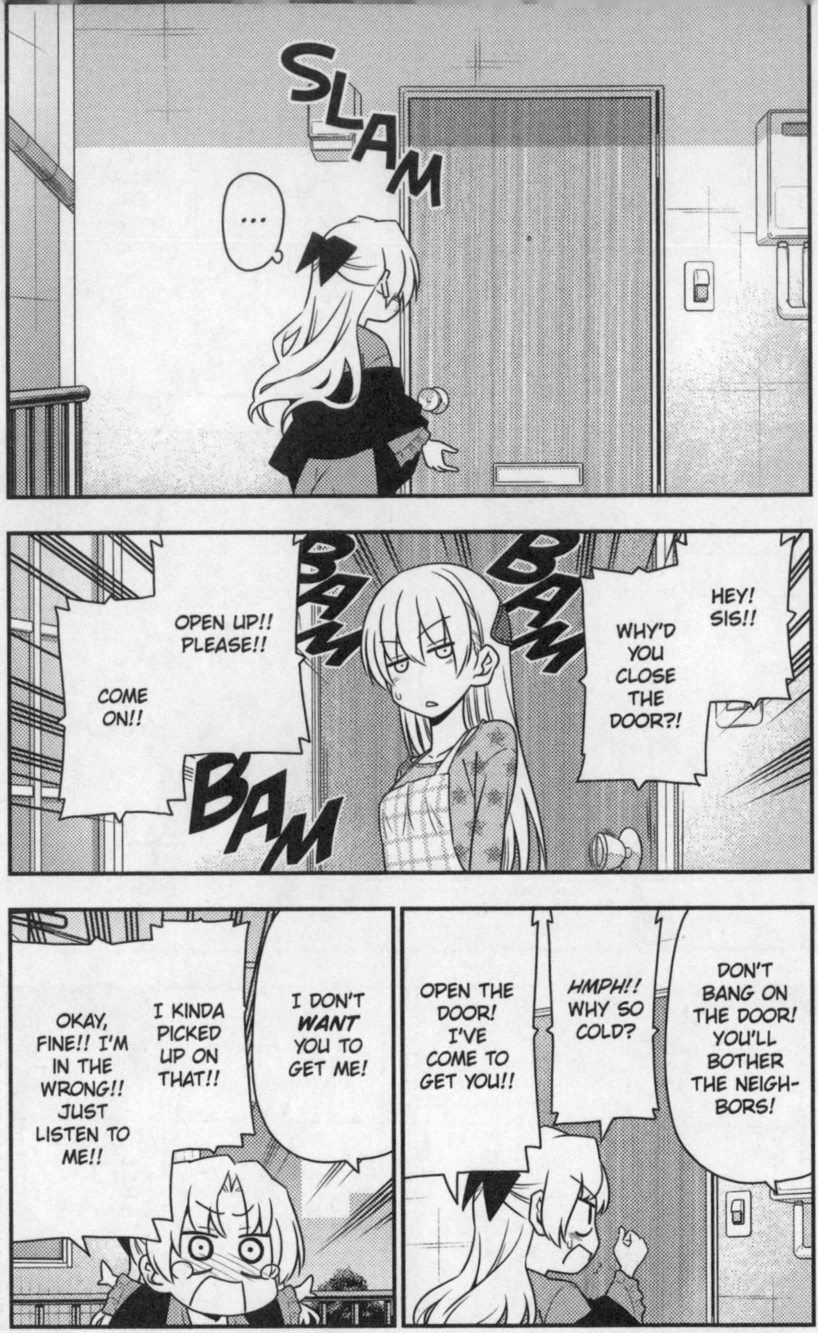
SLAM
...
HEY! SIS!!
WHY'D YOU CLOSE THE DOOR?!
BAM
BAM
OPEN UP!! PLEASE!!
COME ON!!
BAM
DON'T BANG ON THE DOOR! YOU'LL BOTHER THE NEIGH-BORS!
HMPH!! WHY SO COLD?
OPEN THE DOOR! I'VE COME TO GET YOU!!
I DON'T *WANT* YOU TO GET ME!
I KINDA PICKED UP ON THAT!!
OKAY, FINE!! I'M IN THE WRONG!! JUST LISTEN TO ME!!

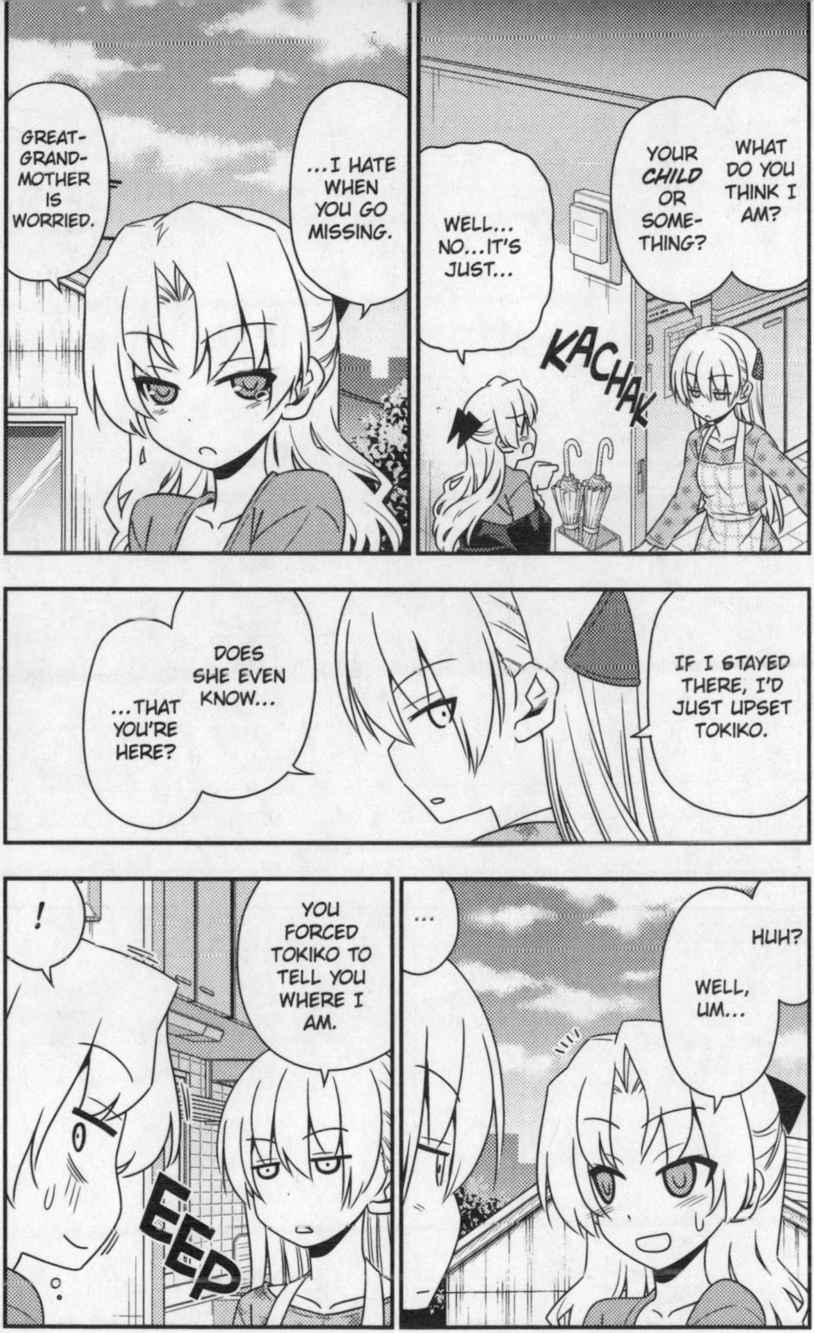
WHAT DO YOU THINK I AM?
YOUR *CHILD* OR SOMETHING?
KACHAK
WELL... NO...IT'S JUST...
...I HATE WHEN YOU GO MISSING.
GREAT-GRANDMOTHER IS WORRIED.
IF I STAYED THERE, I'D JUST UPSET TOKIKO.
DOES SHE EVEN KNOW...
...THAT YOU'RE HERE?
HUH?
WELL, UM...
...
YOU FORCED TOKIKO TO TELL YOU WHERE I AM.
!
EEP

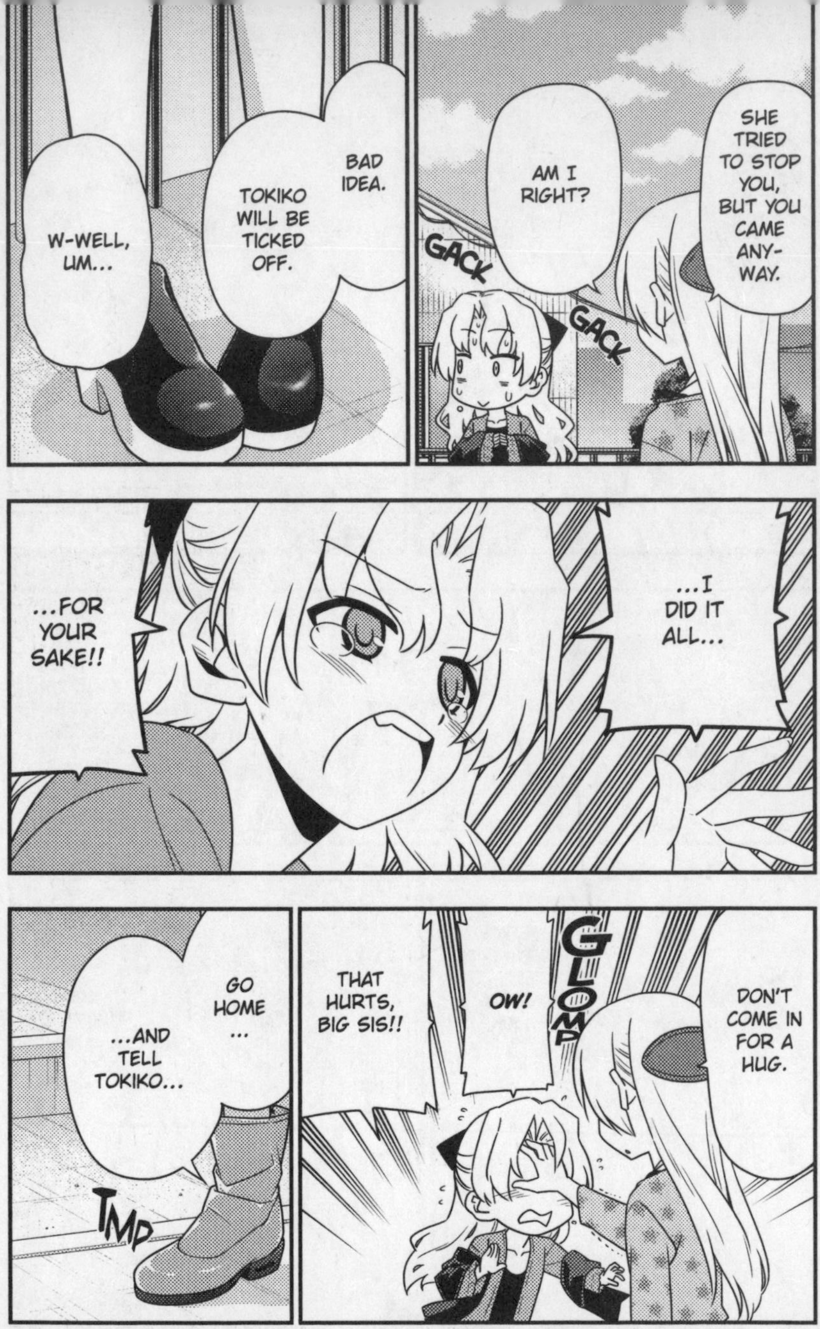
SHE TRIED TO STOP YOU, BUT YOU CAME ANY-WAY.
AM I RIGHT?
GACK
GACK
BAD IDEA.
TOKIKO WILL BE TICKED OFF.
W-WELL, UM...
...I DID IT ALL...
...FOR YOUR SAKE!!
DON'T COME IN FOR A HUG.
GLOMP
OW!
THAT HURTS, BIG SIS!!
GO HOME ...
...AND TELL TOKIKO...
TMP

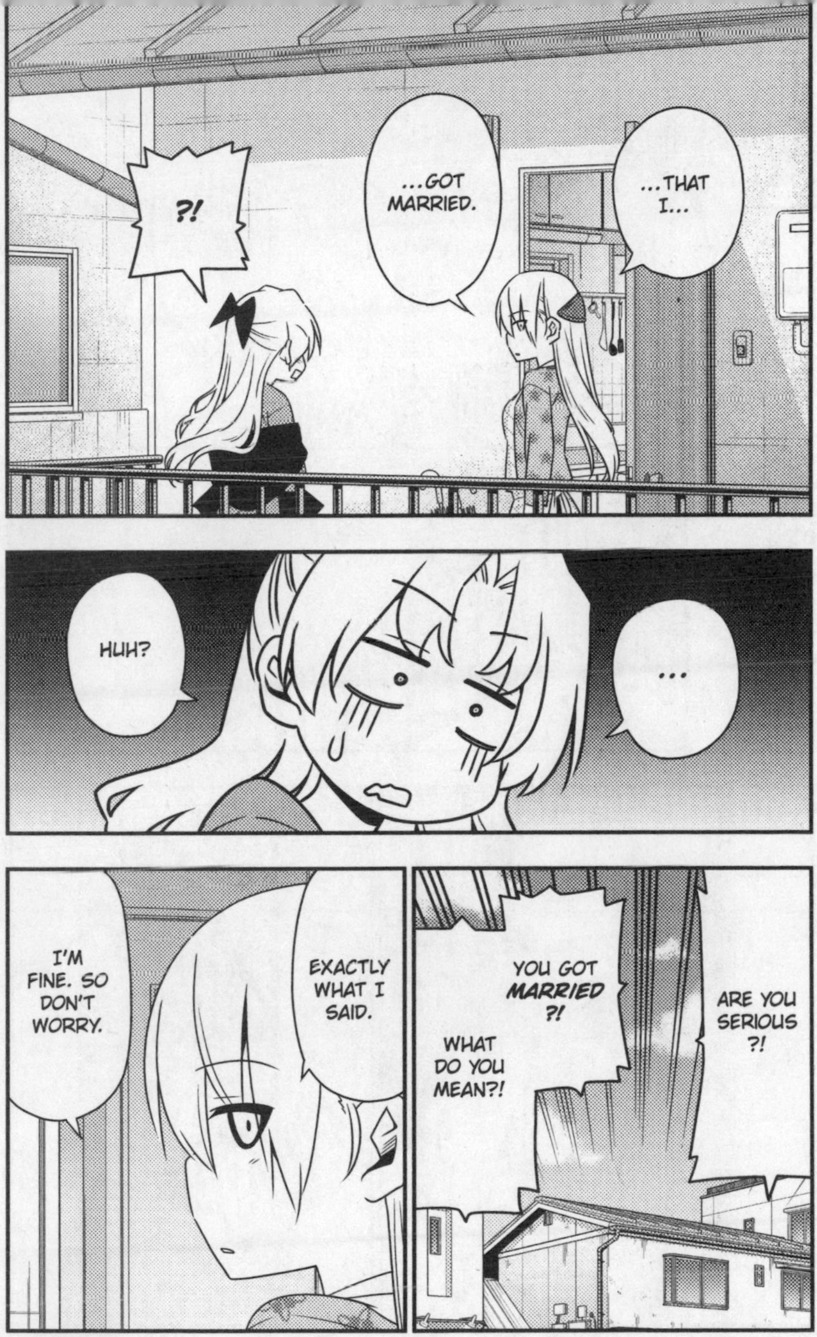
...THAT I...
...GOT MARRIED.
?!
...
HUH?
ARE YOU SERIOUS ?!
YOU GOT MARRIED ?!
WHAT DO YOU MEAN?!
EXACTLY WHAT I SAID.
I'M FINE. SO DON'T WORRY.

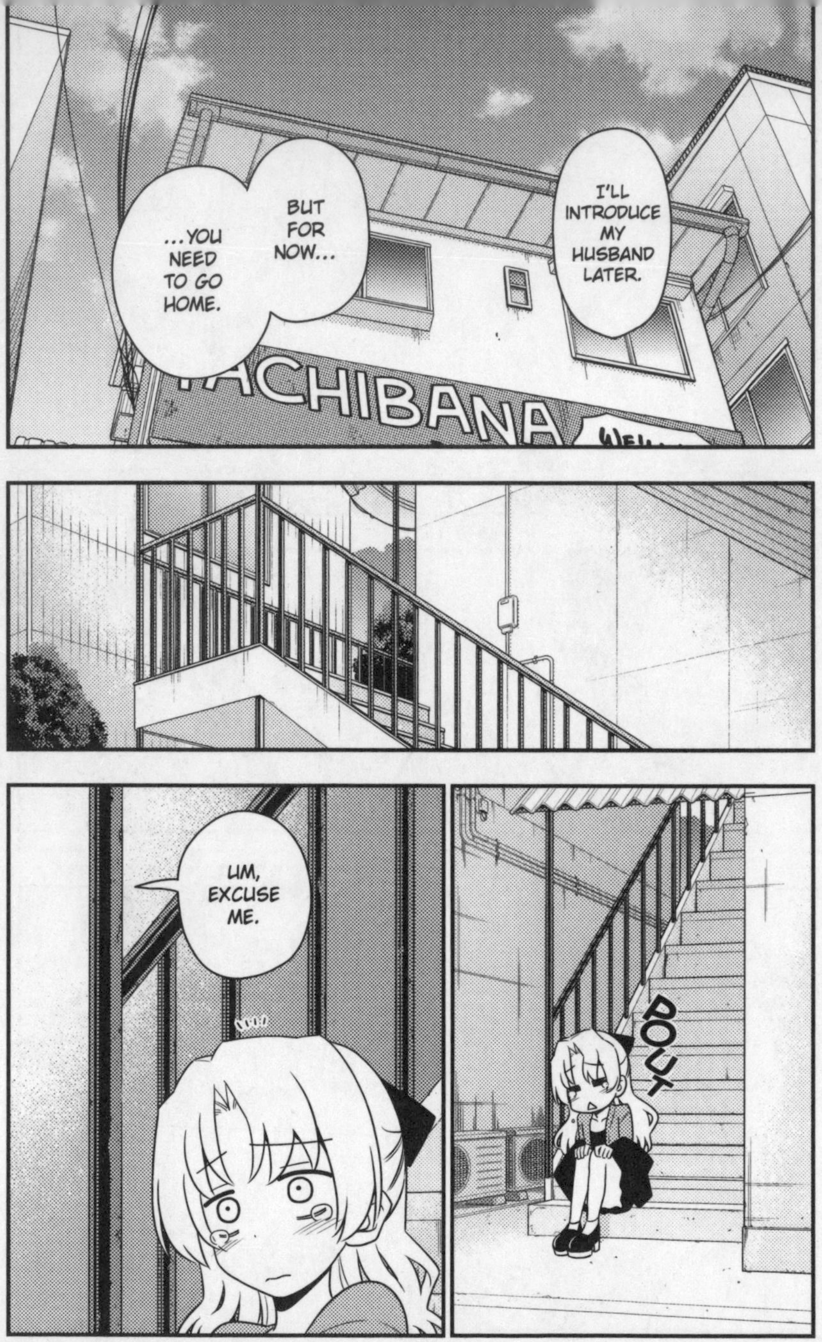
I'LL INTRODUCE MY HUSBAND LATER.
BUT FOR NOW...
...YOU NEED TO GO HOME.
POUT
UM, EXCUSE ME.

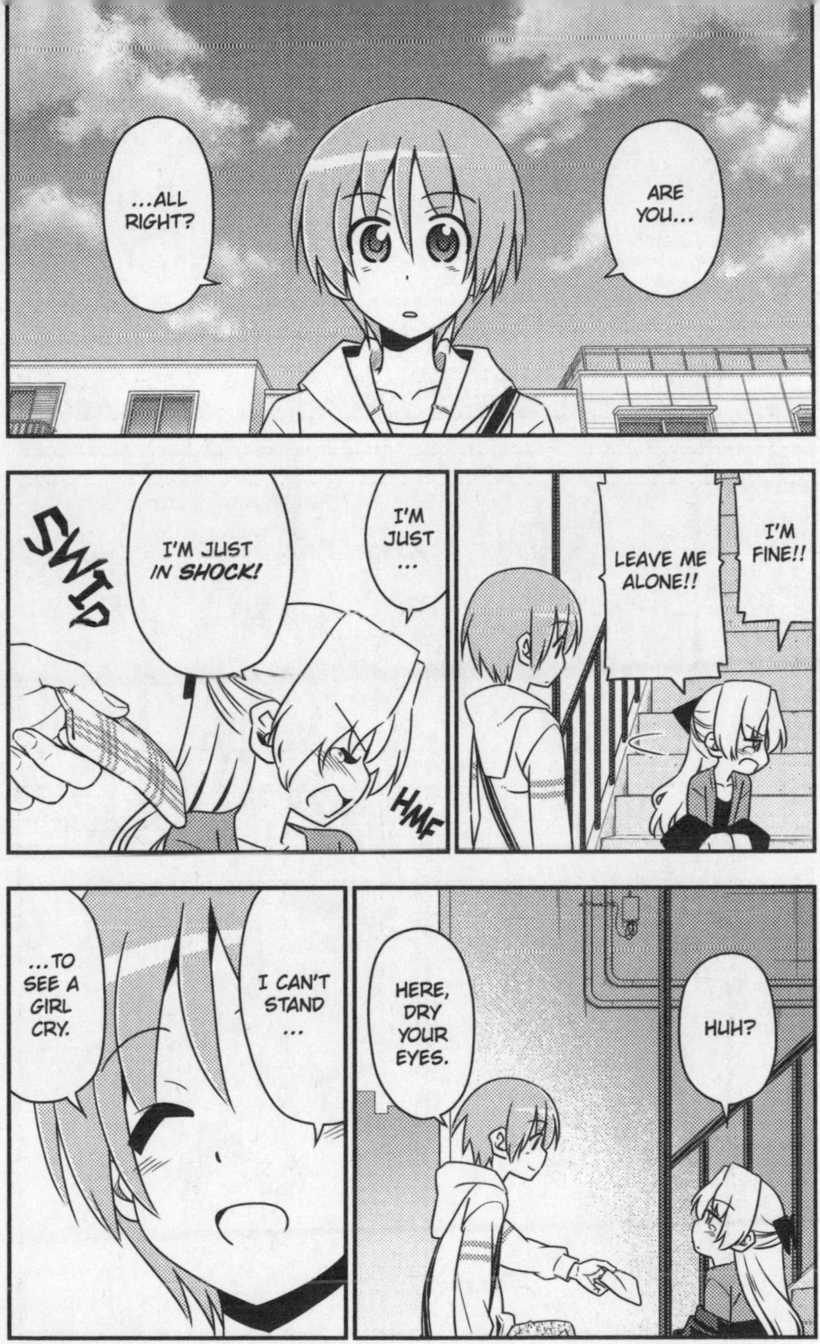
ARE YOU...
...ALL RIGHT?
I'M FINE!!
LEAVE ME ALONE!!
I'M JUST ...
I'M JUST IN SHOCK!
HMF
SWIP
HUH?
HERE, DRY YOUR EYES.
I CAN'T STAND ...
...TO SEE A GIRL CRY.

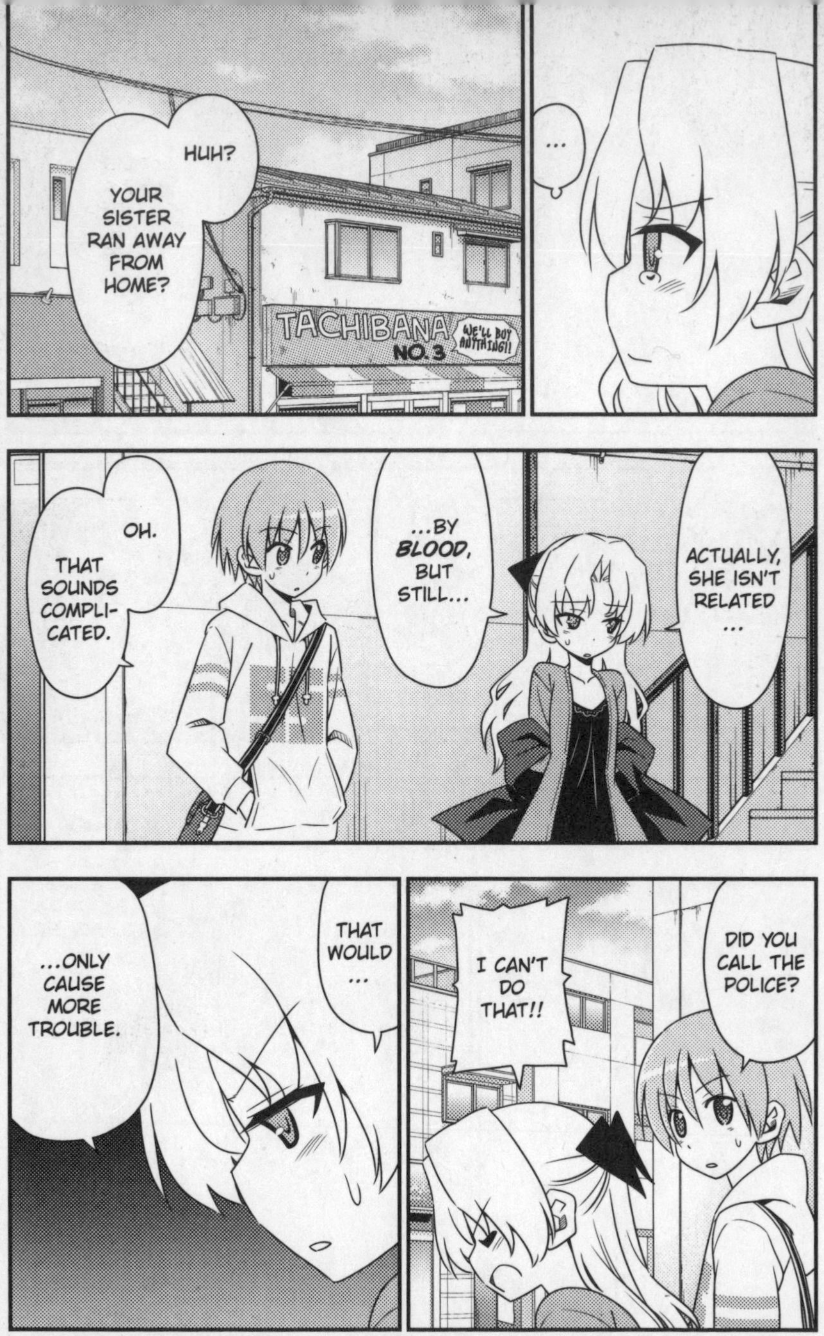
...
HUH? YOUR SISTER RAN AWAY FROM HOME?
TACHIBANA NO. 3
WE'LL BUY ANYTHING!!
ACTUALLY, SHE ISN'T RELATED ...
...BY BLOOD, BUT STILL...
OH. THAT SOUNDS COMPLICATED.
DID YOU CALL THE POLICE?
I CAN'T DO THAT!!
THAT WOULD ...
...ONLY CAUSE MORE TROUBLE.

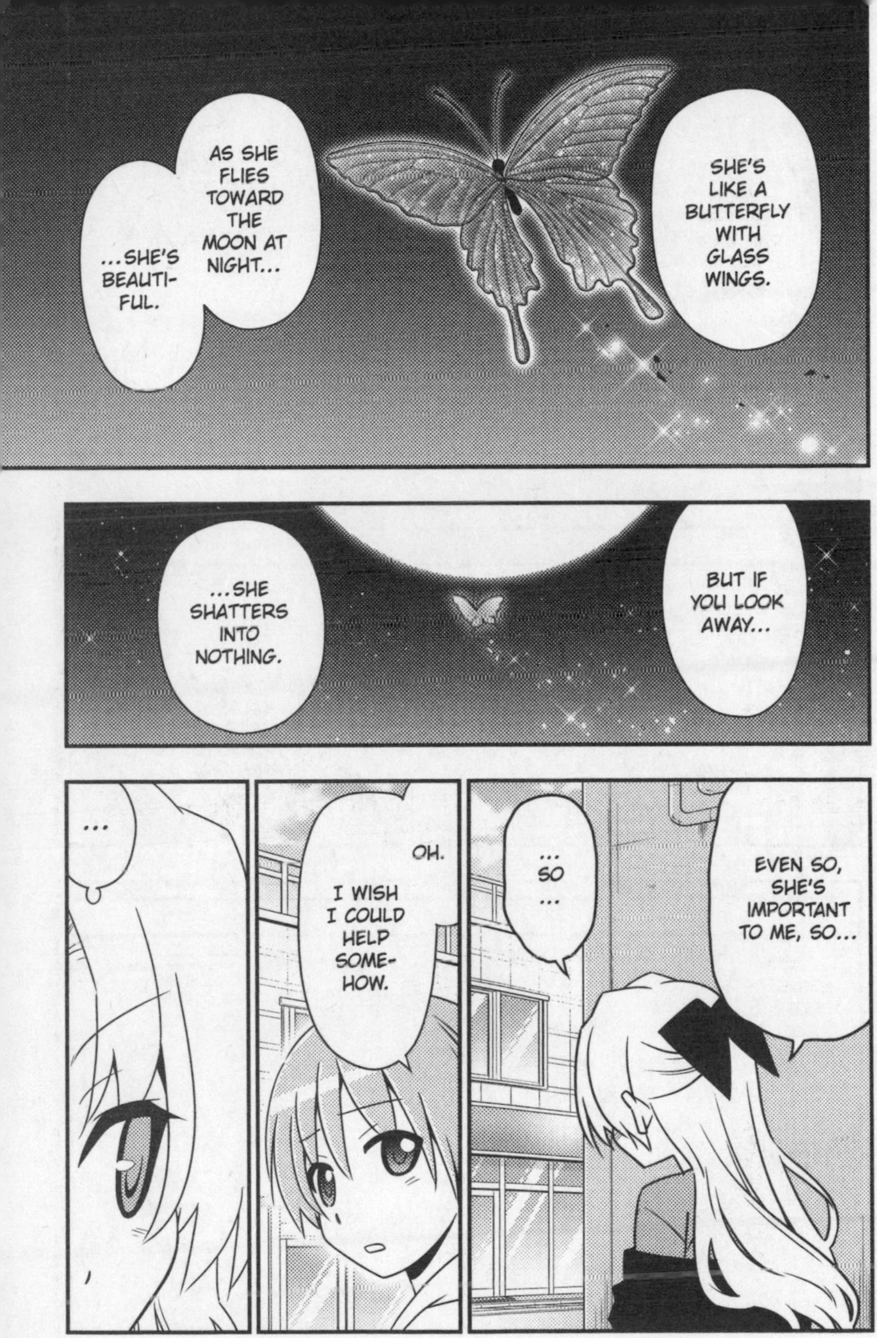
SHE'S LIKE A BUTTERFLY WITH GLASS WINGS.
AS SHE FLIES TOWARD THE MOON AT NIGHT...
...SHE'S BEAUTI-FUL.
BUT IF YOU LOOK AWAY...
...SHE SHATTERS INTO NOTHING.
EVEN SO, SHE'S IMPORTANT TO ME, SO...
...SO...
OH.
I WISH I COULD HELP SOME-HOW.
...

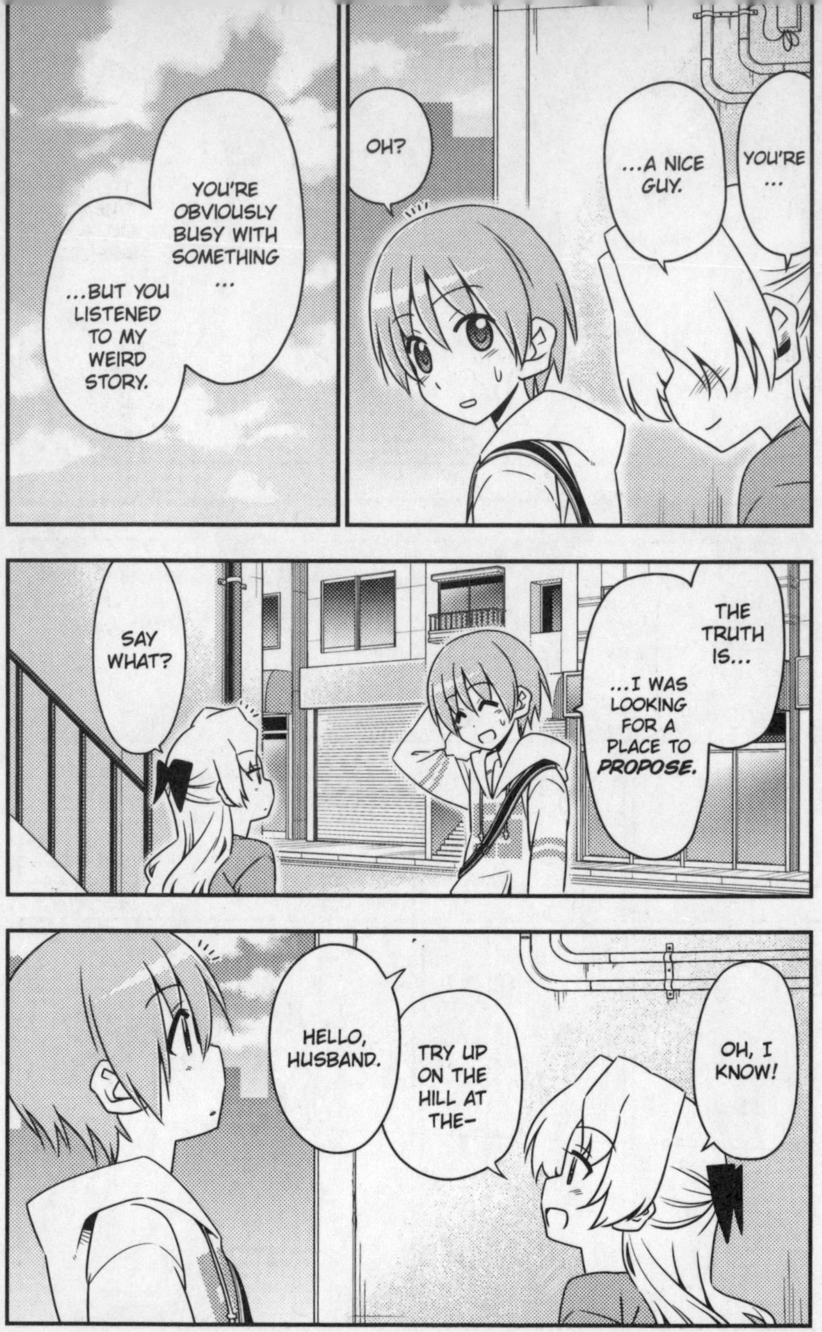
YOU'RE ...
...A NICE GUY.
OH?
YOU'RE OBVIOUSLY BUSY WITH SOMETHING ...
...BUT YOU LISTENED TO MY WEIRD STORY.
THE TRUTH IS...
...I WAS LOOKING FOR A PLACE TO *PROPOSE.*
SAY WHAT?
OH, I KNOW!
TRY UP ON THE HILL AT THE-
HELLO, HUSBAND.

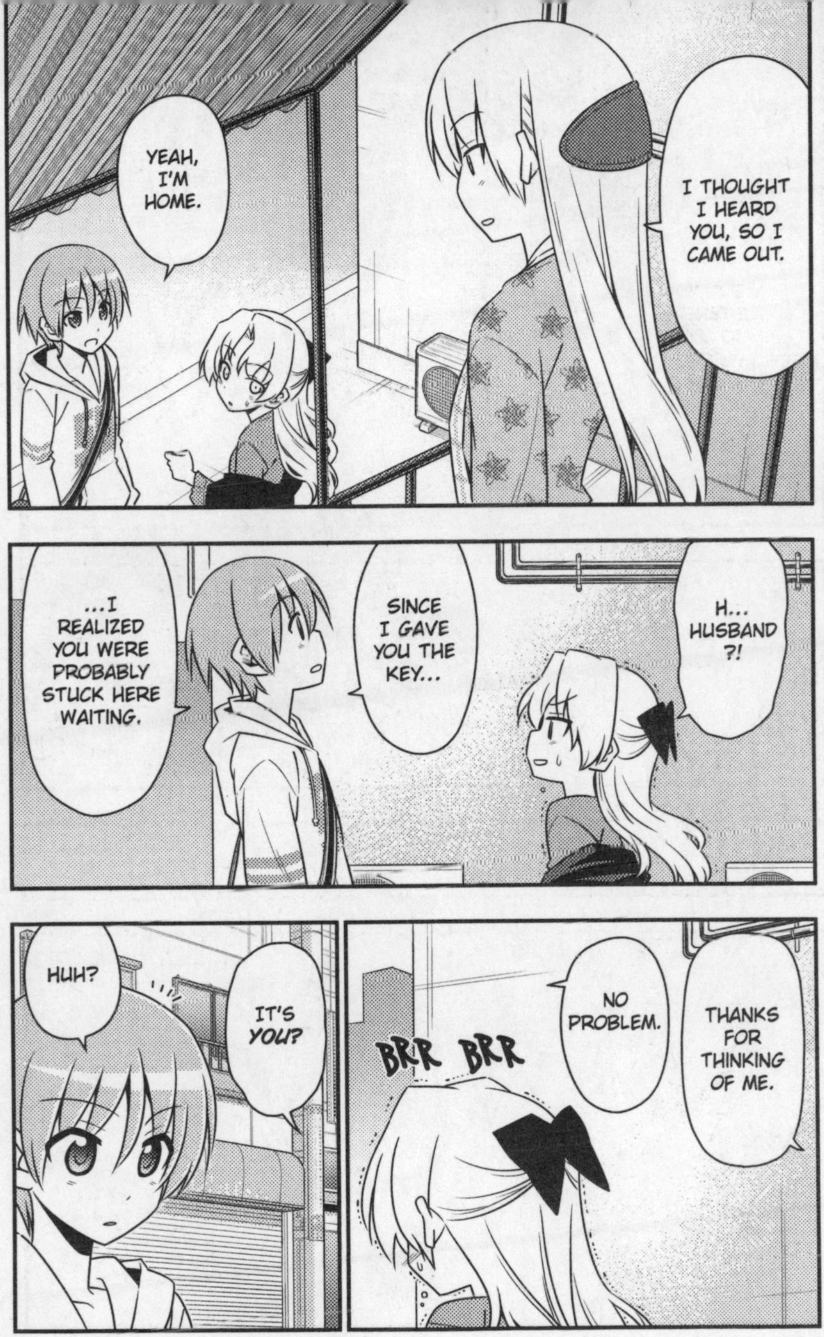
I THOUGHT I HEARD YOU, SO I CAME OUT.
YEAH, I'M HOME.
H... HUSBAND ?!
SINCE I GAVE YOU THE KEY...
...I REALIZED YOU WERE PROBABLY STUCK HERE WAITING.
THANKS FOR THINKING OF ME.
NO PROBLEM.
BRR BRR
HUH?
IT'S *YOU*?

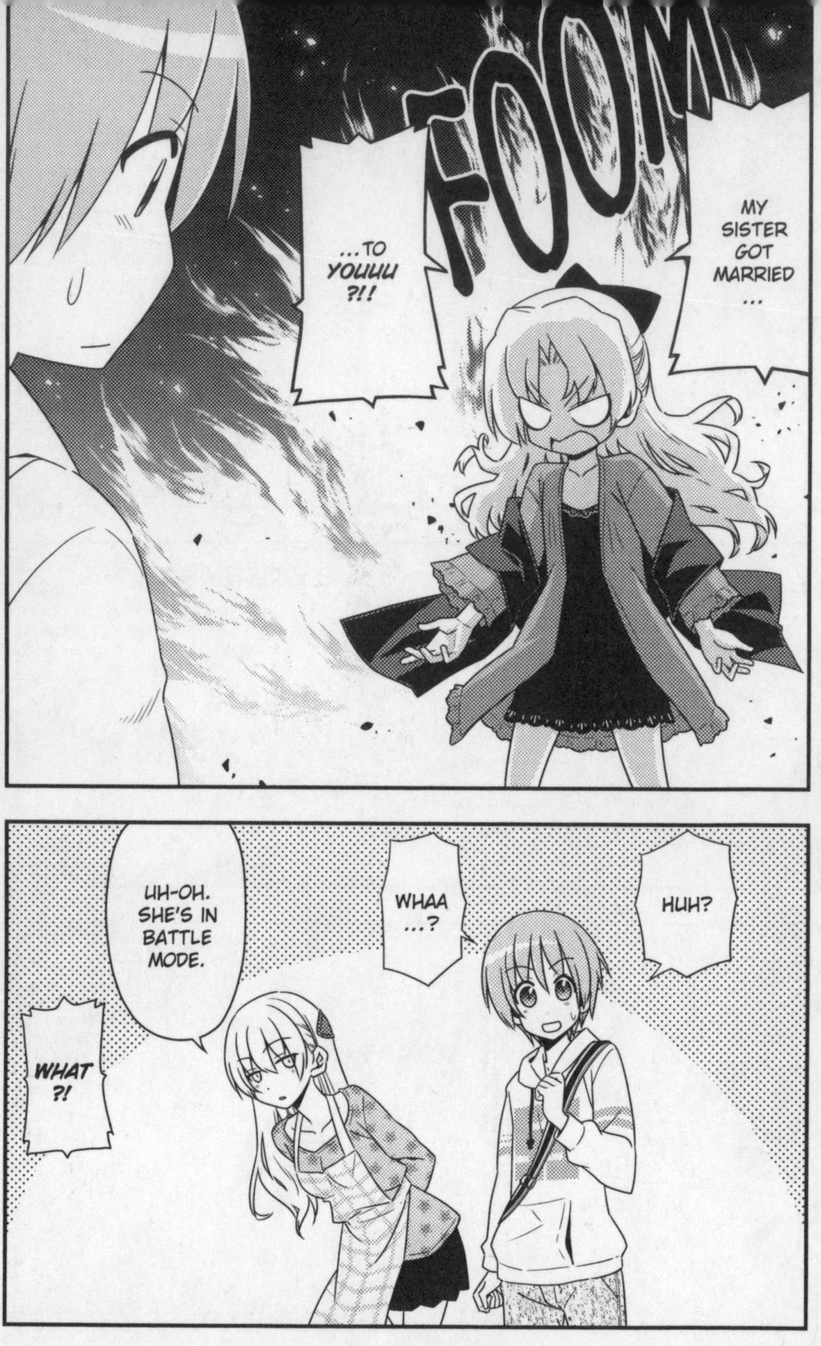
MY SISTER GOT MARRIED ...
FOOM
...TO YOUUU ?!!
HUH?
WHAA ...?
UH-OH. SHE'S IN BATTLE MODE.
WHAT ?!

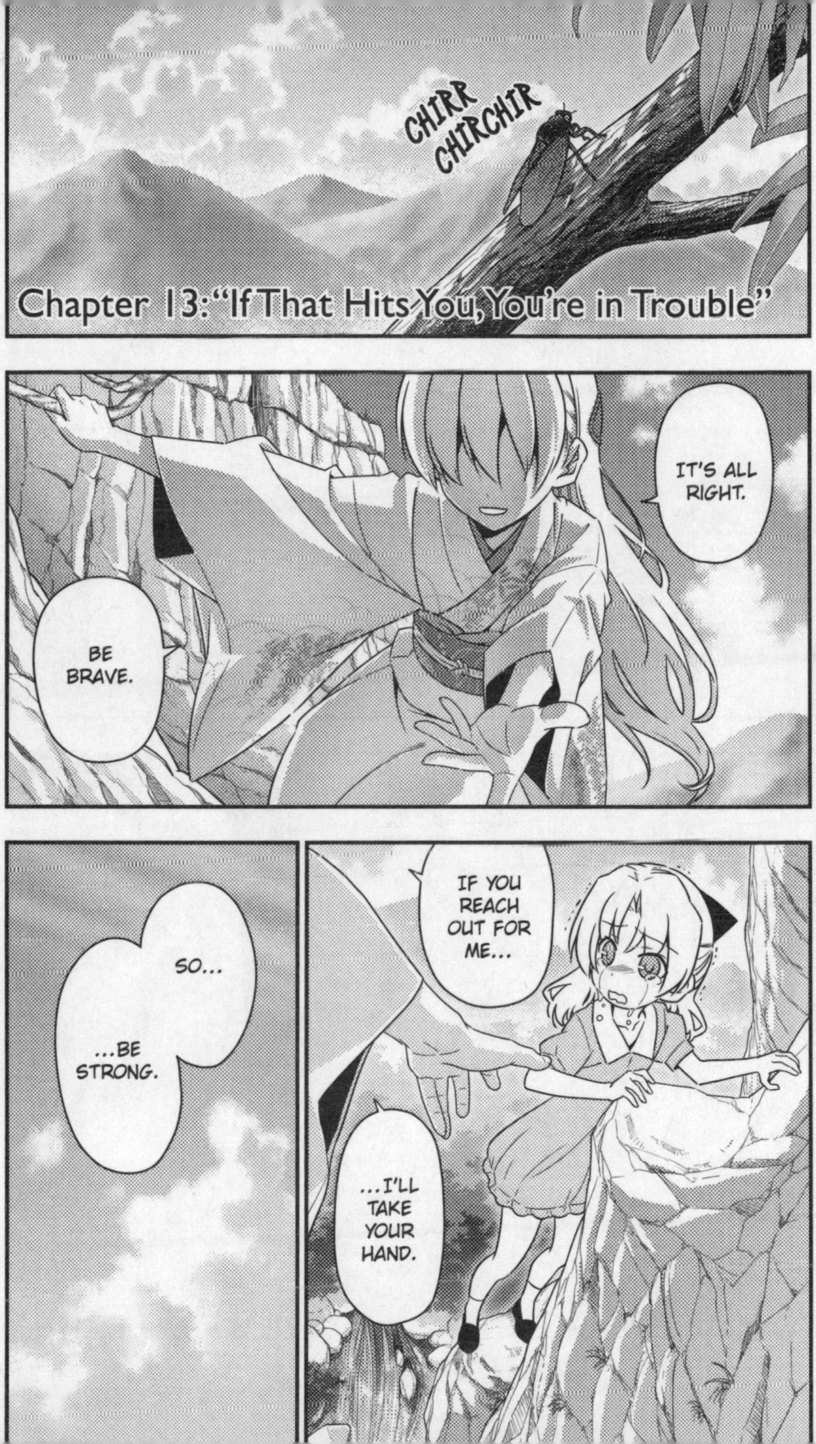
CHIRR CHIRCHIR
Chapter 13: "If That Hits You, You're in Trouble"
IT'S ALL RIGHT.
BE BRAVE.
IF YOU REACH OUT FOR ME...
...I'LL TAKE YOUR HAND.
SO...
...BE STRONG.

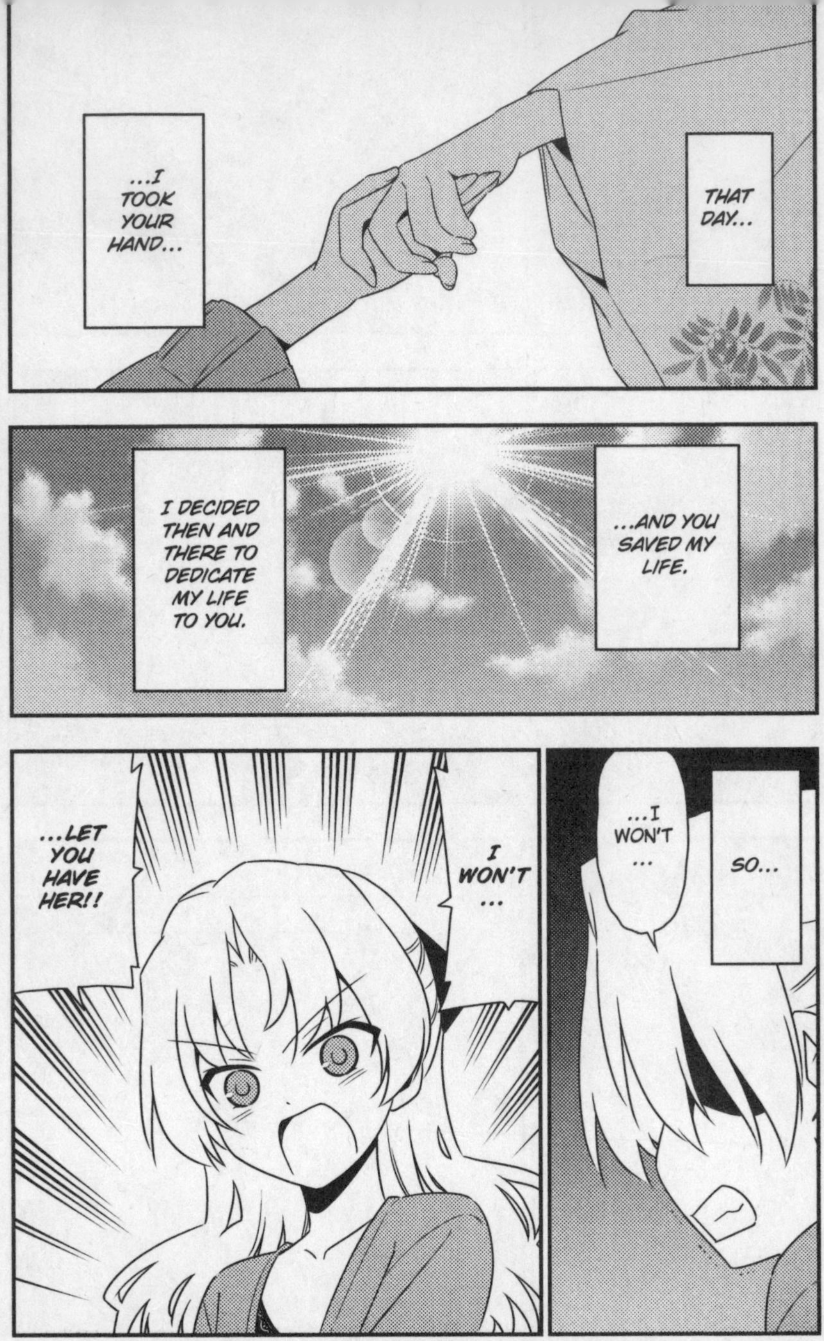
THAT DAY...
...I TOOK YOUR HAND...
...AND YOU SAVED MY LIFE.
I DECIDED THEN AND THERE TO DEDICATE MY LIFE TO YOU.
SO...
...I WON'T ...
I WON'T ...
...LET YOU HAVE HER!!

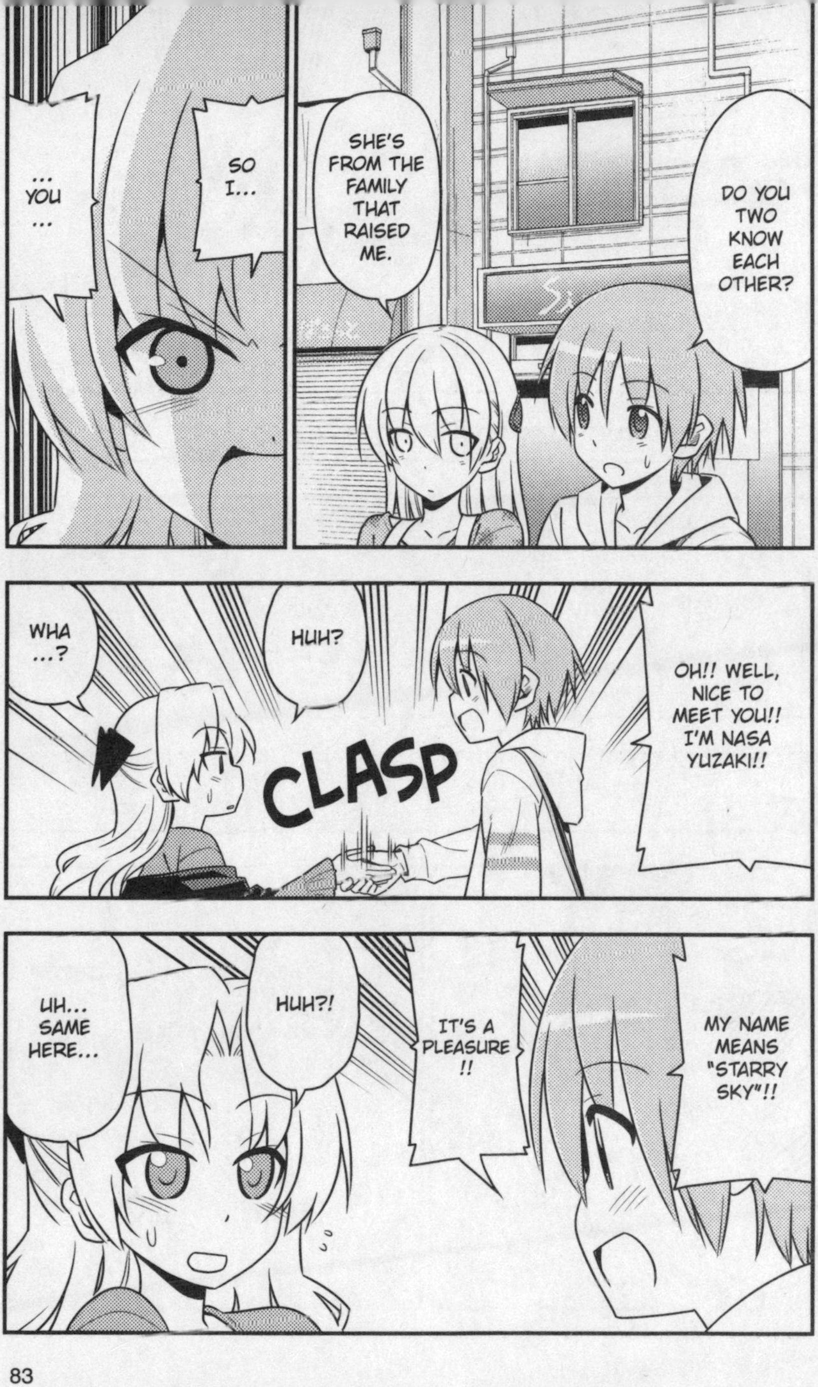
DO YOU TWO KNOW EACH OTHER?
SHE'S FROM THE FAMILY THAT RAISED ME.
SO I...
... YOU ...
OH!! WELL, NICE TO MEET YOU!! I'M NASA YUZAKI!!
CLASP
HUH?
WHA ...?
MY NAME MEANS "STARRY SKY"!!
IT'S A PLEASURE !!
HUH?!
UH... SAME HERE...

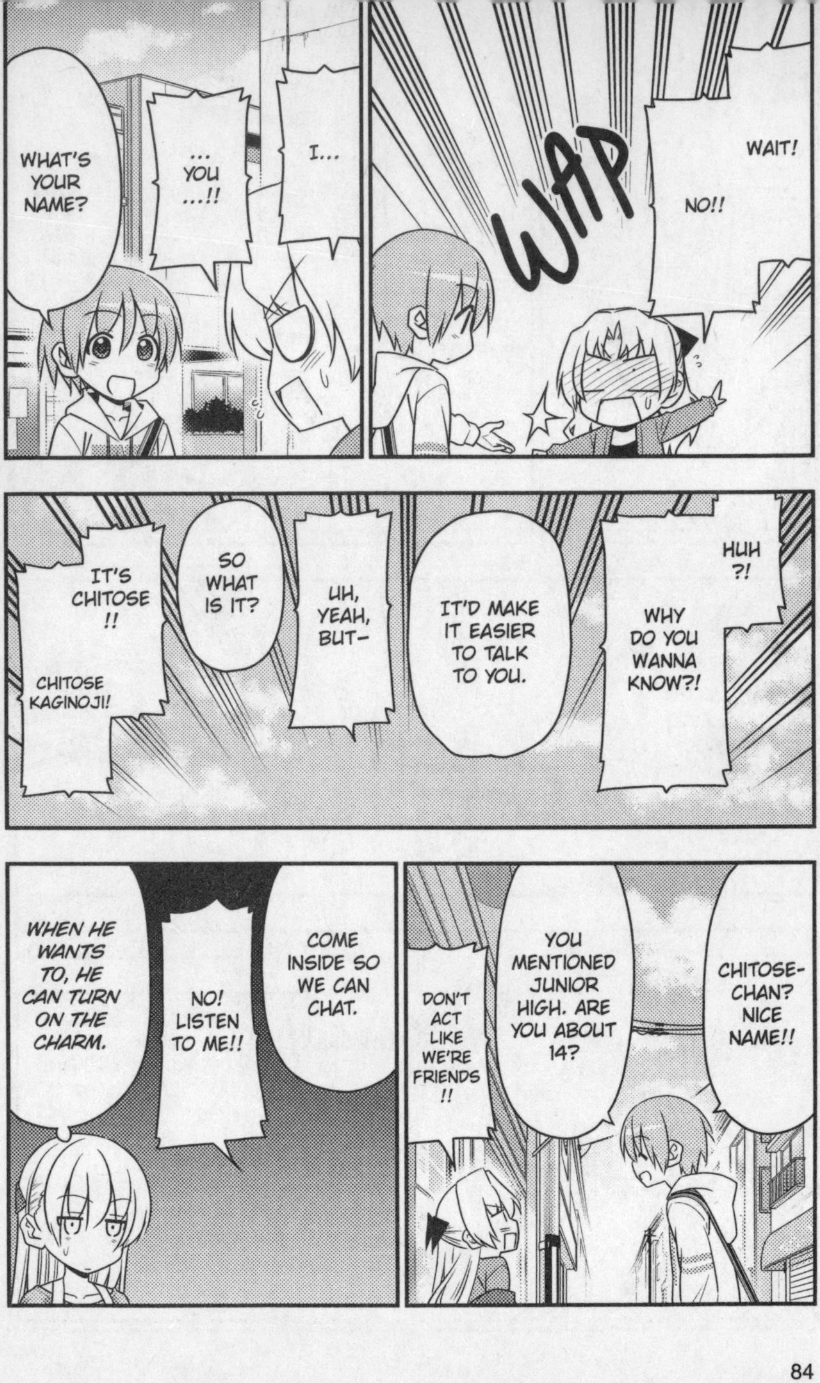

WAIT!
NO!!
WAP
I...
...YOU ...!!
WHAT'S YOUR NAME?
HUH?!
WHY DO YOU WANNA KNOW?!
IT'D MAKE IT EASIER TO TALK TO YOU.
UH, YEAH, BUT-
SO WHAT IS IT?
IT'S CHITOSE!!
CHITOSE KAGINOJI!
CHITOSE-CHAN? NICE NAME!!
YOU MENTIONED JUNIOR HIGH. ARE YOU ABOUT 14?
DON'T ACT LIKE WE'RE FRIENDS!!
COME INSIDE SO WE CAN CHAT.
NO! LISTEN TO ME!!
WHEN HE WANTS TO, HE CAN TURN ON THE CHARM.

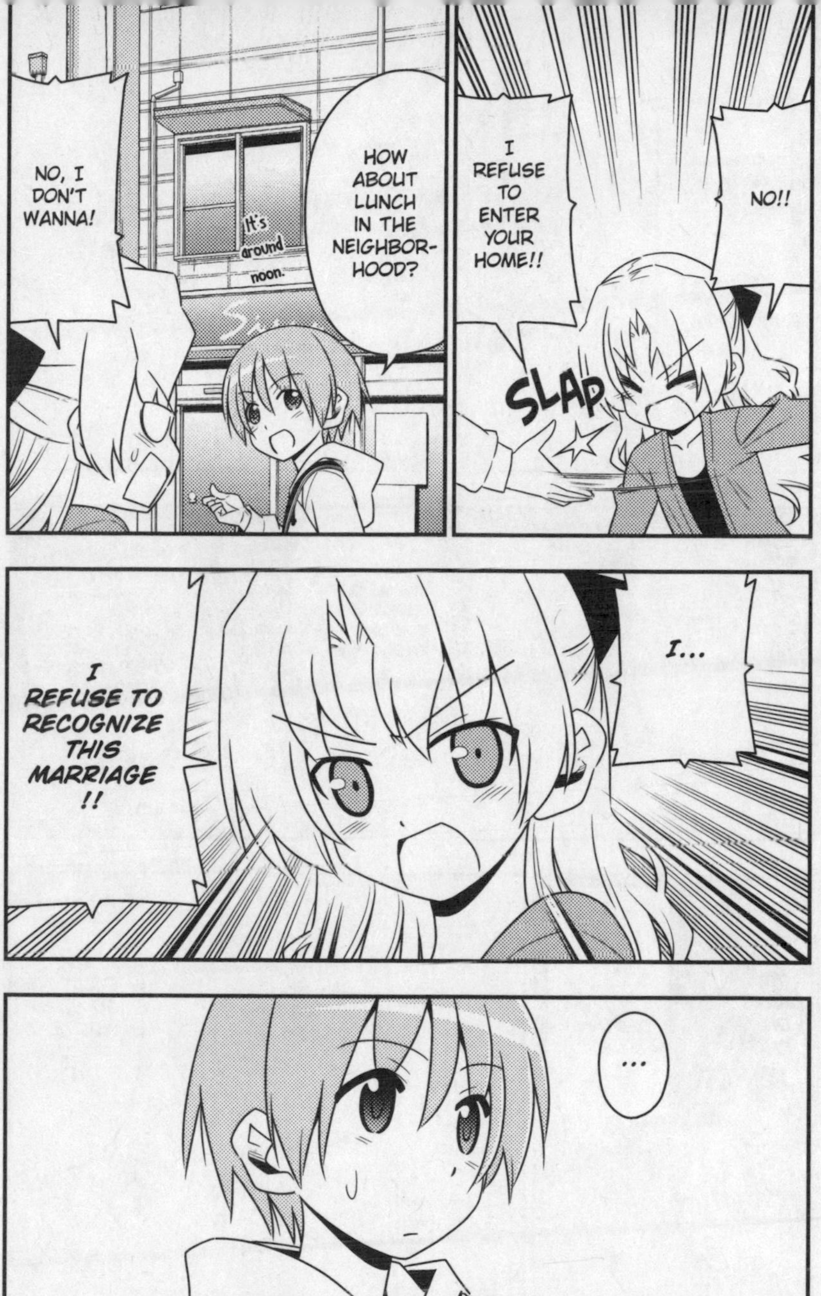
NO!!
I REFUSE TO ENTER YOUR HOME!!
SLAP
HOW ABOUT LUNCH IN THE NEIGHBOR-HOOD?
It's around noon.
NO, I DON'T WANNA!
I...
I REFUSE TO RECOGNIZE THIS MARRIAGE !!
...

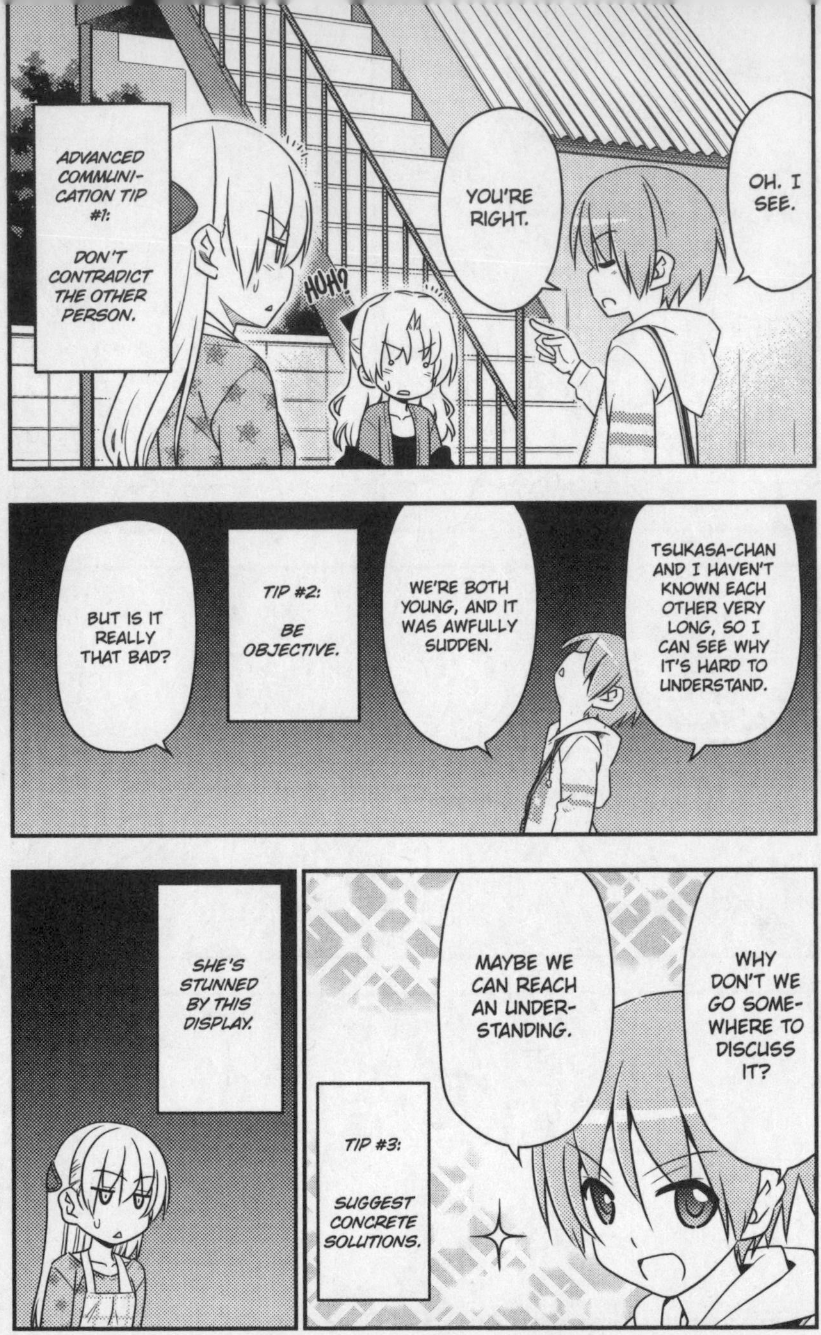
OH. I SEE.
YOU'RE RIGHT.
HUH?
ADVANCED COMMUNI-CATION TIP #1: DON'T CONTRADICT THE OTHER PERSON.
TSUKASA-CHAN AND I HAVEN'T KNOWN EACH OTHER VERY LONG, SO I CAN SEE WHY IT'S HARD TO UNDERSTAND.
WE'RE BOTH YOUNG, AND IT WAS AWFULLY SUDDEN.
TIP #2: BE OBJECTIVE.
BUT IS IT REALLY THAT BAD?
WHY DON'T WE GO SOME-WHERE TO DISCUSS IT?
MAYBE WE CAN REACH AN UNDER-STANDING.
TIP #3: SUGGEST CONCRETE SOLUTIONS.
SHE'S STUNNED BY THIS DISPLAY.

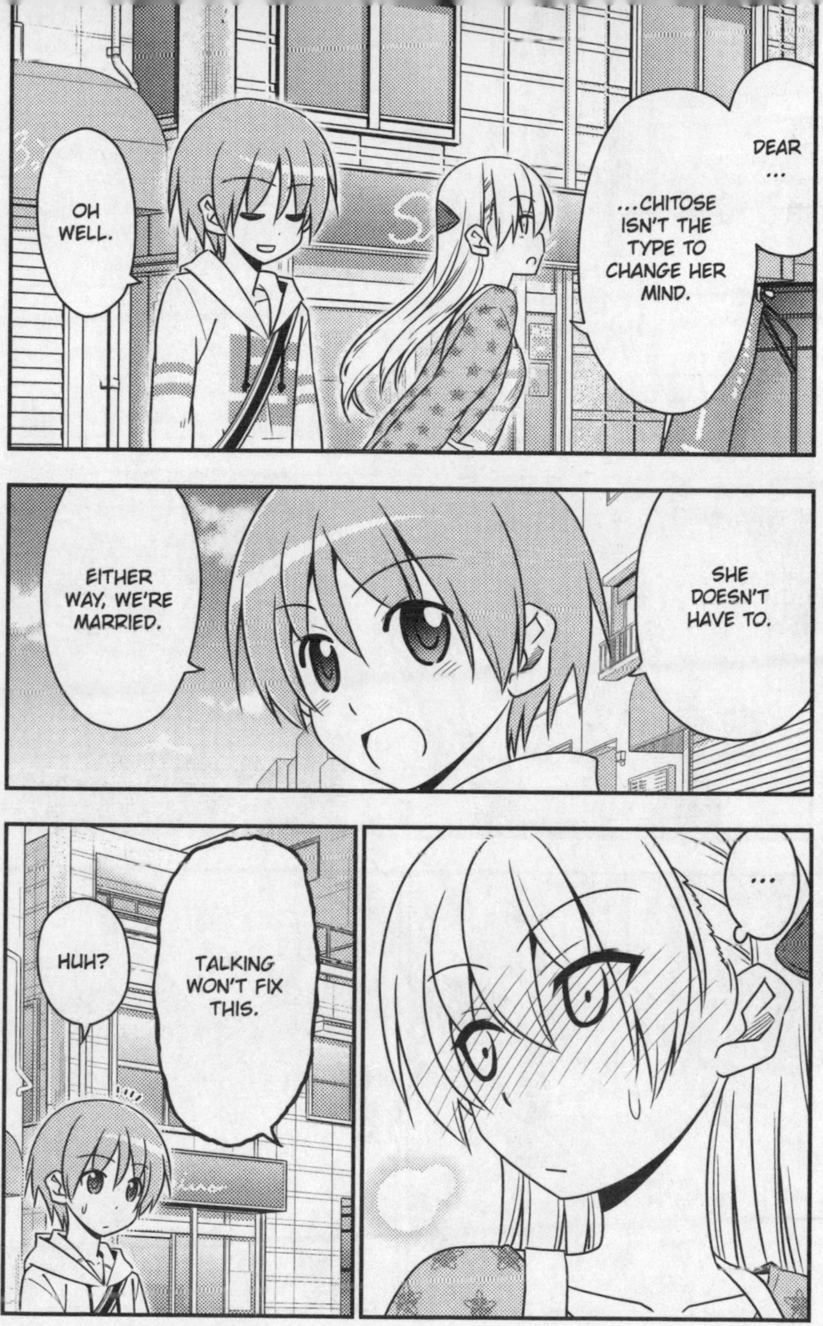
DEAR ...
...CHITOSE ISN'T THE TYPE TO CHANGE HER MIND.
OH WELL.
SHE DOESN'T HAVE TO.
EITHER WAY, WE'RE MARRIED.
...
TALKING WON'T FIX THIS.
HUH?

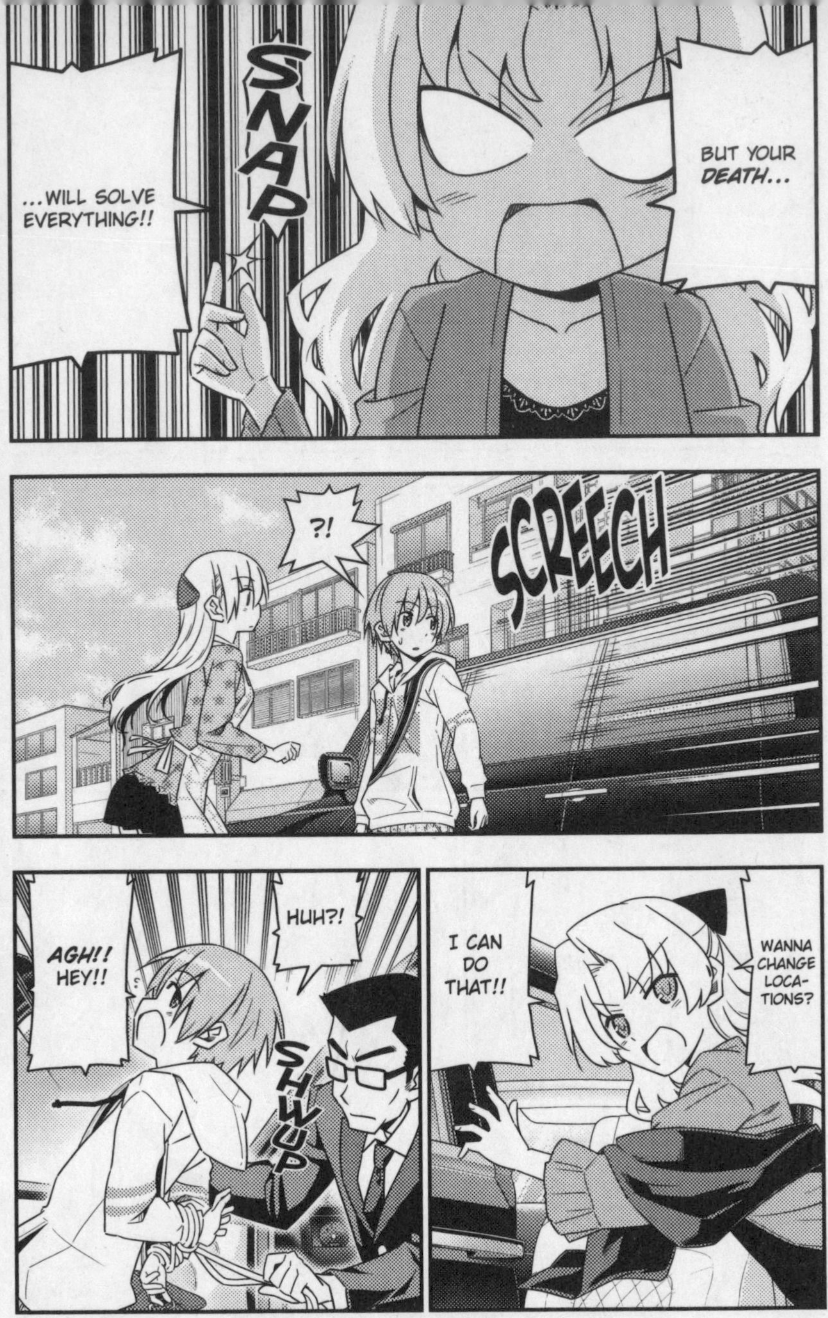
BUT YOUR DEATH...
SNAP
...WILL SOLVE EVERYTHING!!
SCREECH
?!
WANNA CHANGE LOCA-TIONS?
I CAN DO THAT!!
HUH?!
SHWUP
AGH!! HEY!!

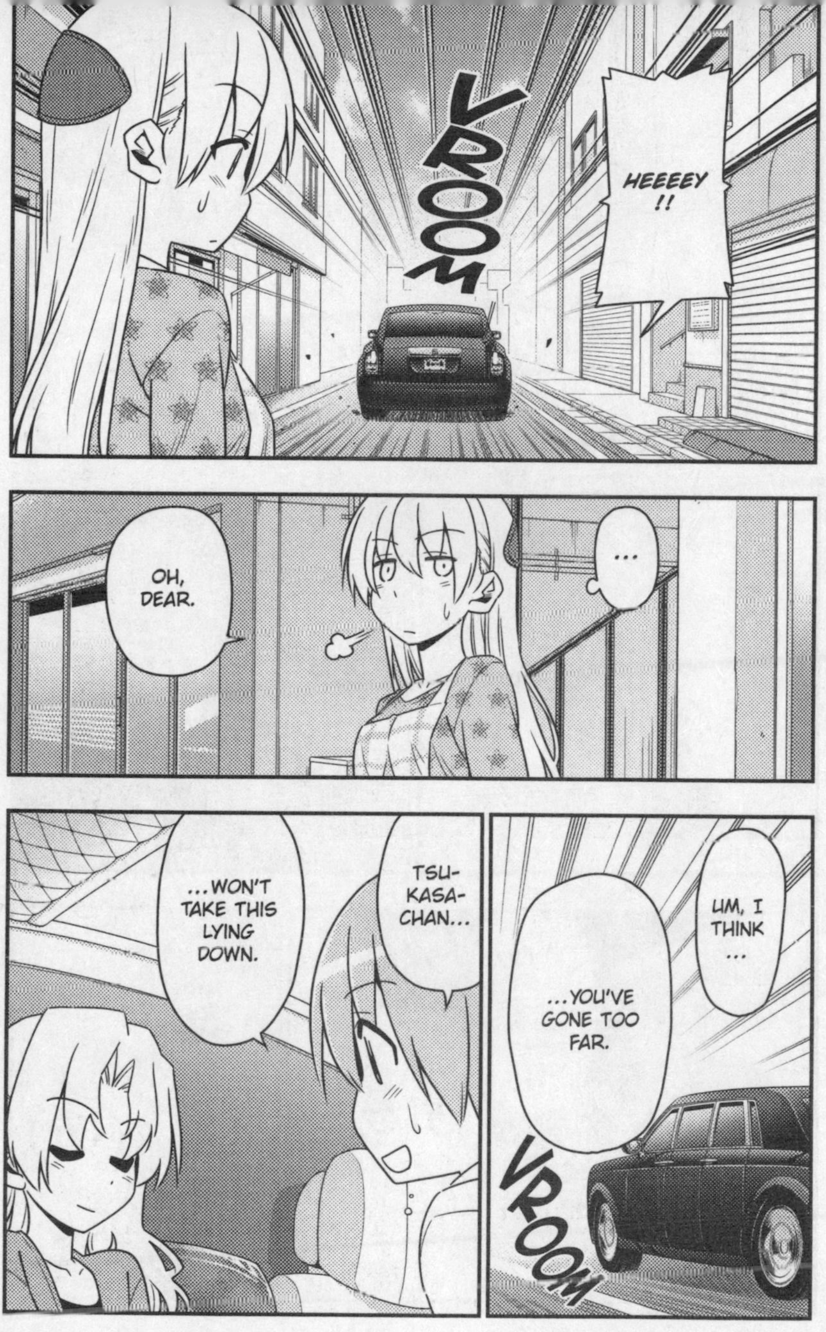
HEEEEY !!
VROOM
...
OH, DEAR.
UM, I THINK ...
...YOU'VE GONE TOO FAR.
VROOM
TSU-KASA-CHAN...
...WON'T TAKE THIS LYING DOWN.

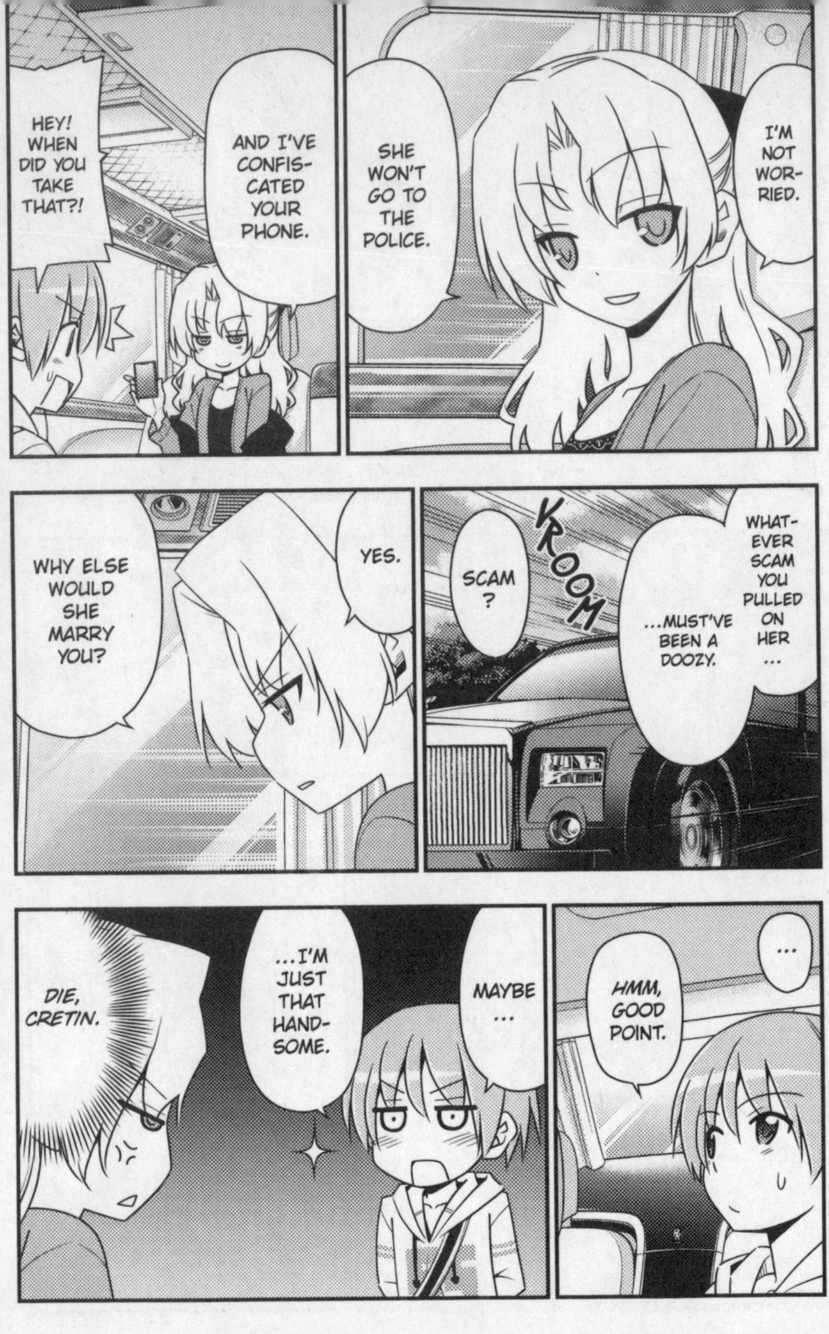
I'M NOT WORRIED.
SHE WON'T GO TO THE POLICE.
AND I'VE CONFISCATED YOUR PHONE.
HEY! WHEN DID YOU TAKE THAT?!
WHATEVER SCAM YOU PULLED ON HER...
...MUST'VE BEEN A DOOZY.
SCAM?
VROOM
YES.
WHY ELSE WOULD SHE MARRY YOU?
...
HMM, GOOD POINT.
MAYBE...
...I'M JUST THAT HANDSOME.
DIE, CRETIN.

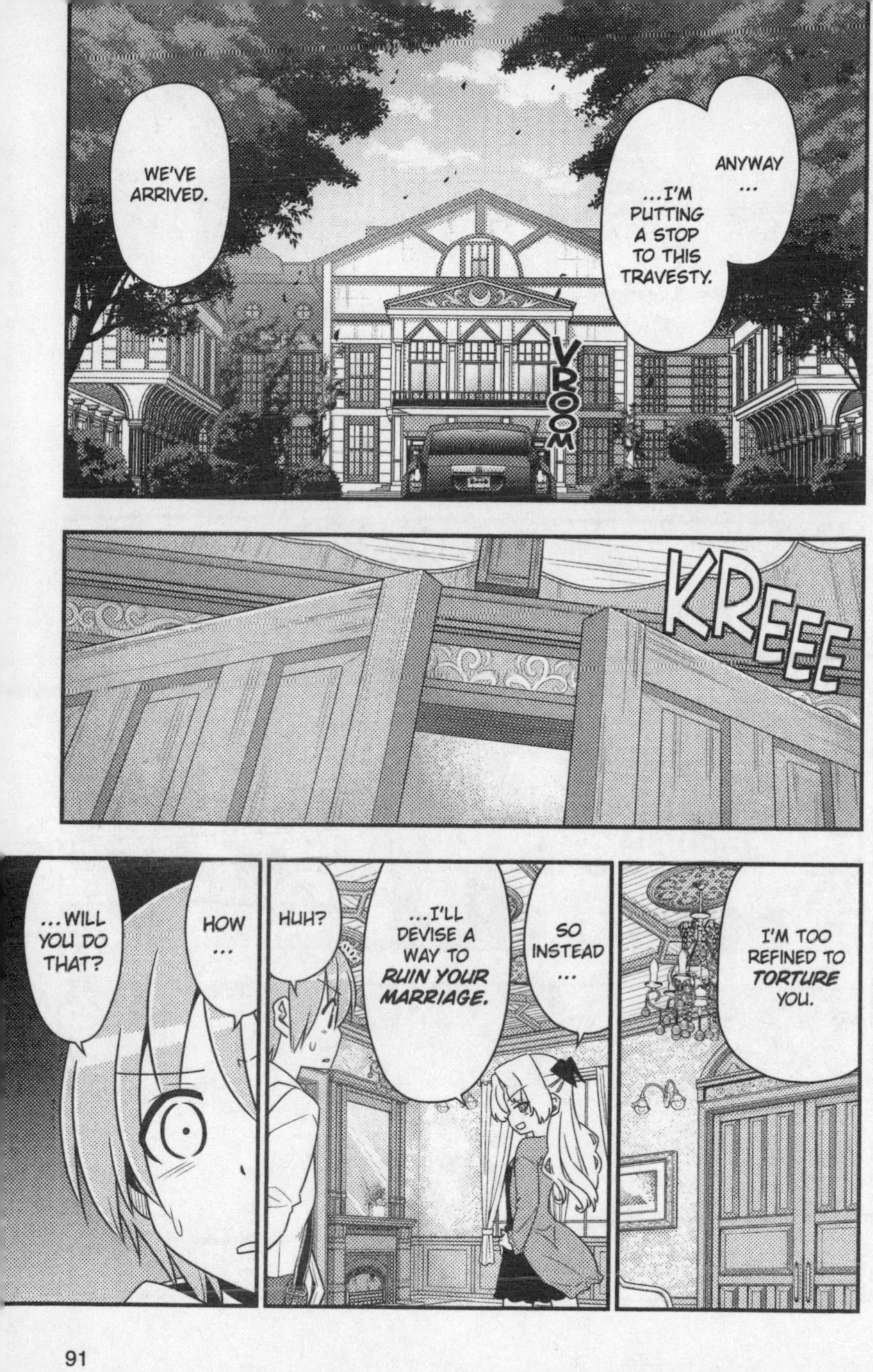
ANYWAY ...
...I'M PUTTING A STOP TO THIS TRAVESTY.
WE'VE ARRIVED.
VROOM
KREEEE
I'M TOO REFINED TO *TORTURE* YOU.
SO INSTEAD ...
...I'LL DEVISE A WAY TO ***RUIN YOUR MARRIAGE.***
HUH?
HOW ...
...WILL YOU DO THAT?

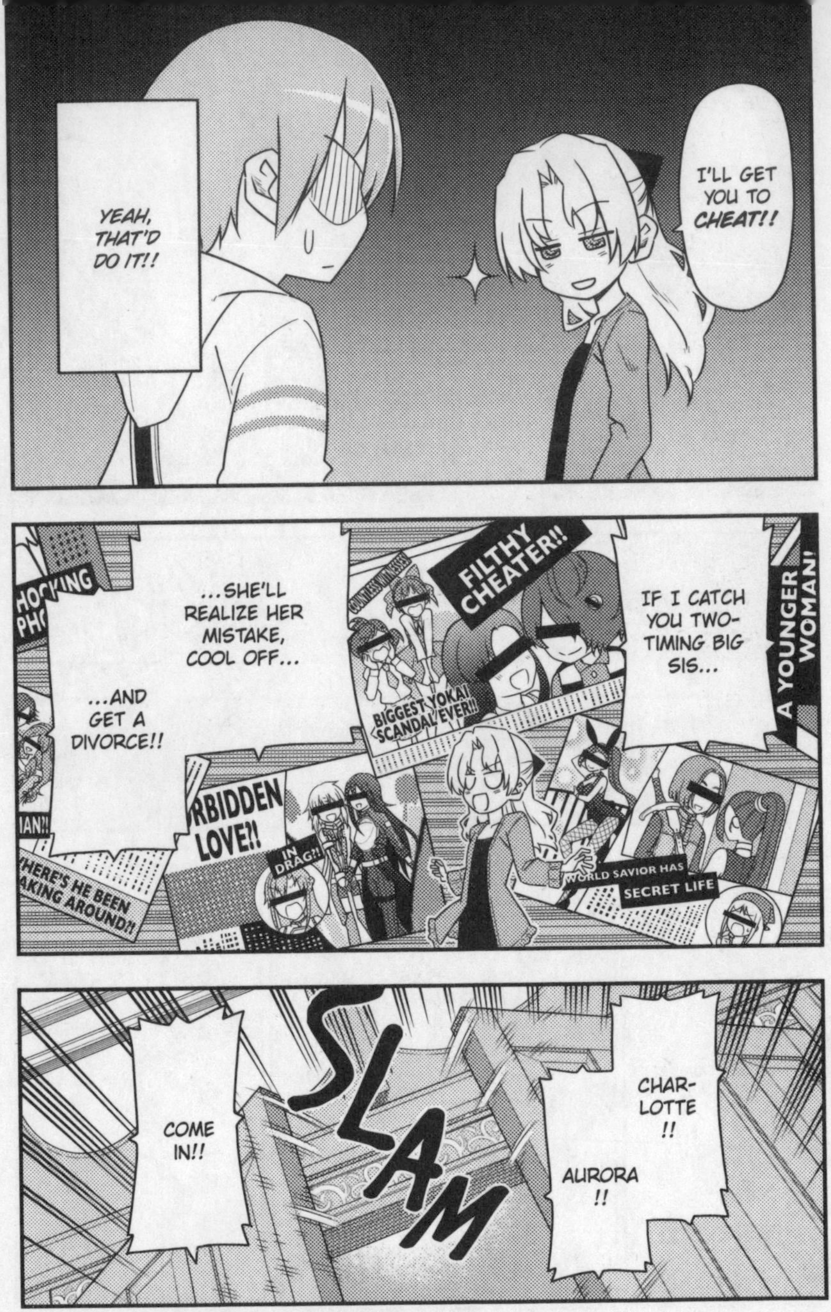
I'LL GET YOU TO CHEAT!!
YEAH, THAT'D DO IT!!
A YOUNGER WOMAN!
IF I CATCH YOU TWO-TIMING BIG SIS...
FILTHY CHEATER!!
BIGGEST YOKAI SCANDAL EVER!!
...SHE'LL REALIZE HER MISTAKE, COOL OFF...
...AND GET A DIVORCE!!
WORLD SAVIOR HAS SECRET LIFE
IN DRAG?!
CHAR-LOTTE!!
AURORA!!
SLAM
COME IN!!

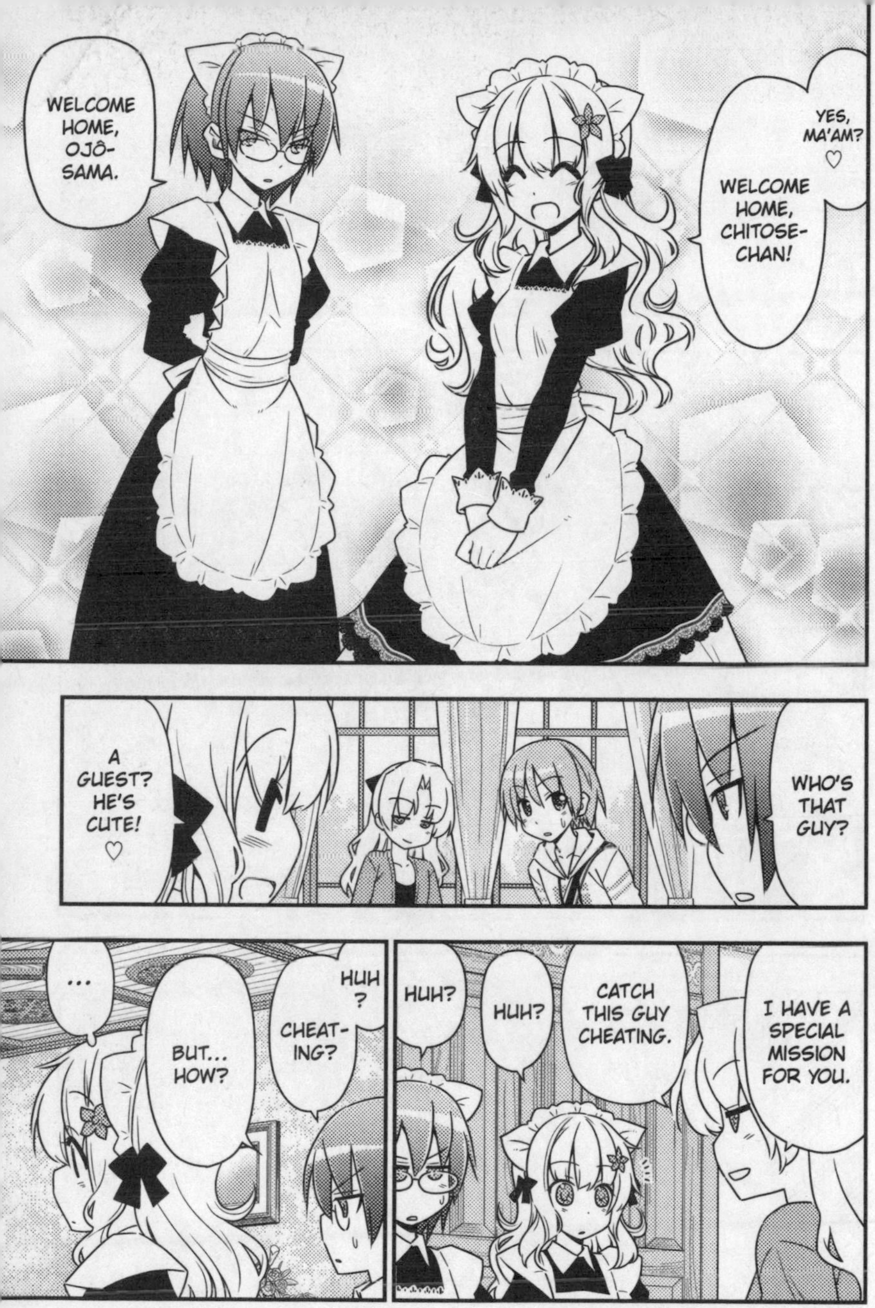
YES, MA'AM? ♡
WELCOME HOME, CHITOSE-CHAN!
WELCOME HOME, OJÔ-SAMA.
WHO'S THAT GUY?
A GUEST? HE'S CUTE! ♡
I HAVE A SPECIAL MISSION FOR YOU.
CATCH THIS GUY CHEATING.
HUH?
HUH?
HUH? CHEATING?
BUT... HOW?
...

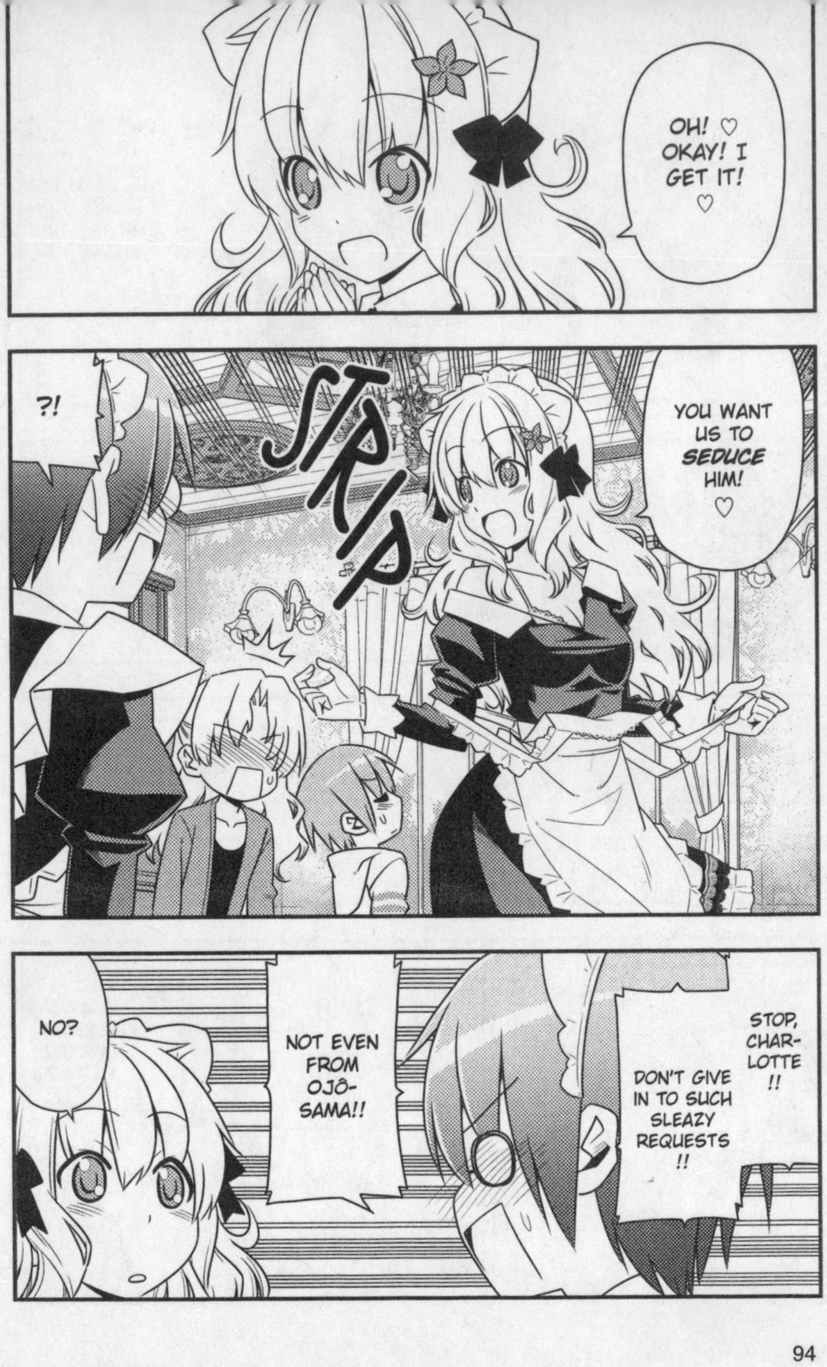
OH! ♡ OKAY! I GET IT! ♡
YOU WANT US TO *SEDUCE* HIM! ♡
STRIP
?!
STOP, CHARLOTTE!!
DON'T GIVE IN TO SUCH SLEAZY REQUESTS!!
NOT EVEN FROM OJÔ-SAMA!!
NO?

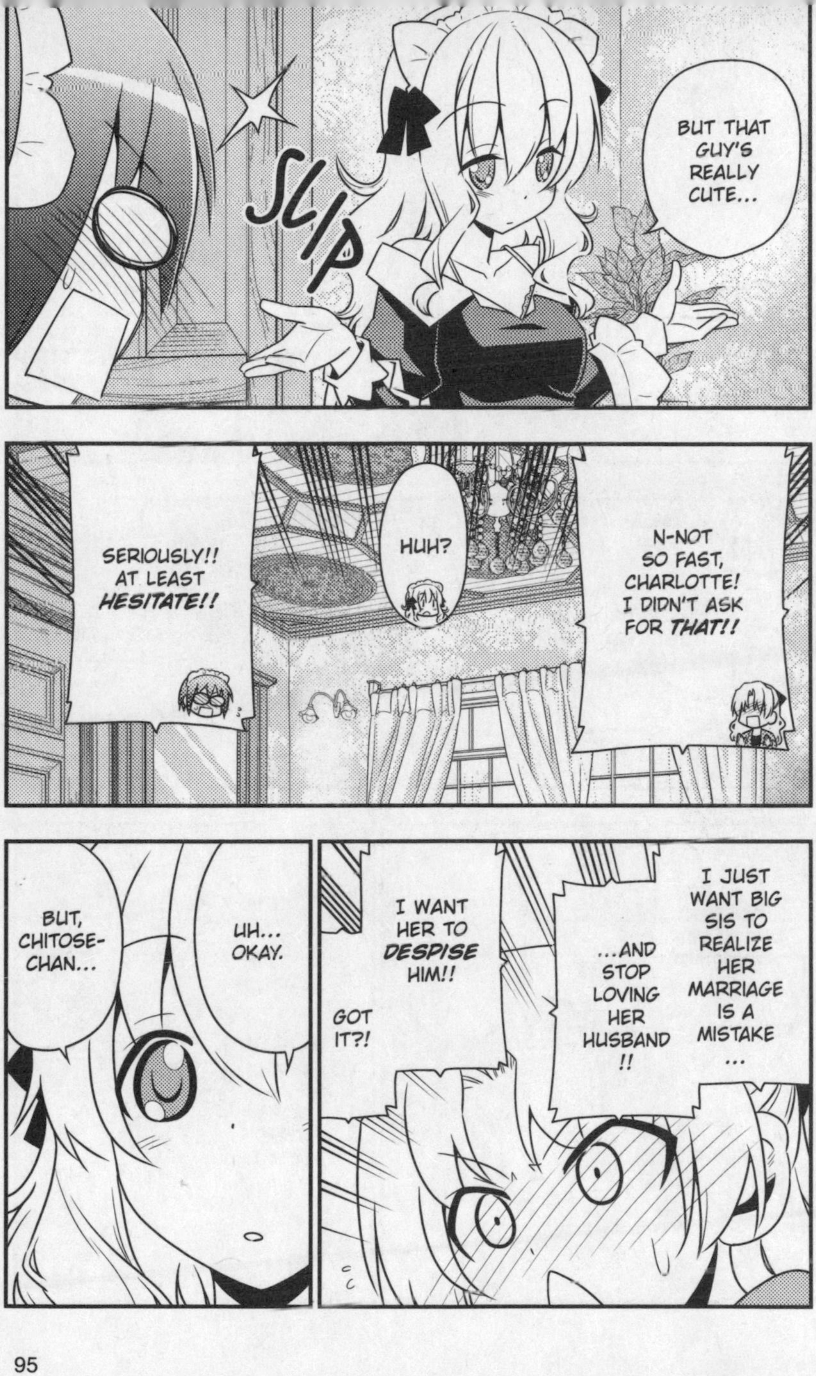
BUT THAT GUY'S REALLY CUTE...
SLIP
N-NOT SO FAST, CHARLOTTE! I DIDN'T ASK FOR *THAT!!*
HUH?
SERIOUSLY!! AT LEAST *HESITATE!!*
I JUST WANT BIG SIS TO REALIZE HER MARRIAGE IS A MISTAKE...
...AND STOP LOVING HER HUSBAND!!
I WANT HER TO *DESPISE* HIM!!
GOT IT?!
UH... OKAY.
BUT, CHITOSE-CHAN...

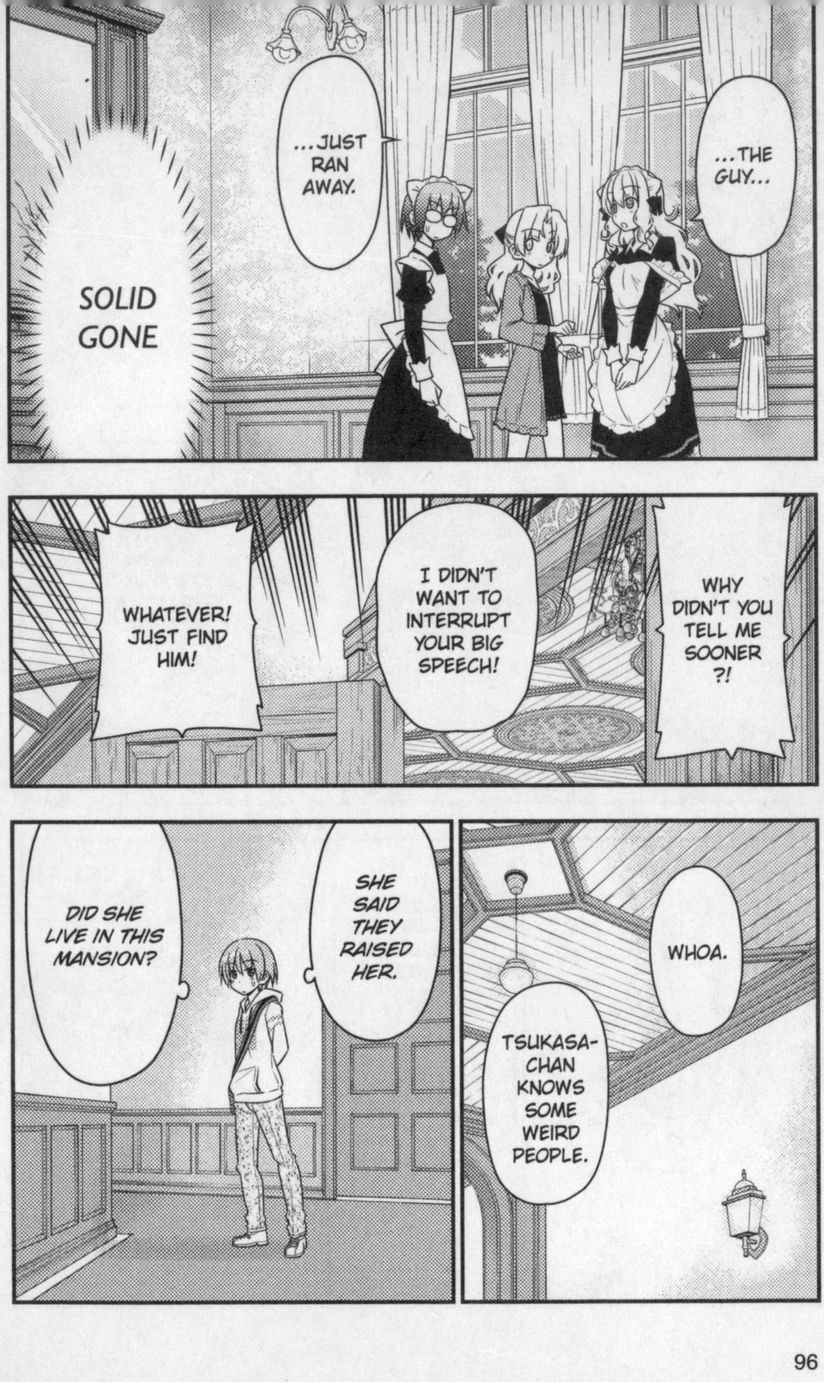
...THE GUY...
...JUST RAN AWAY.
SOLID GONE
WHY DIDN'T YOU TELL ME SOONER ?!
I DIDN'T WANT TO INTERRUPT YOUR BIG SPEECH!
WHATEVER! JUST FIND HIM!
WHOA.
TSUKASA-CHAN KNOWS SOME WEIRD PEOPLE.
SHE SAID THEY RAISED HER.
DID SHE LIVE IN THIS MANSION?

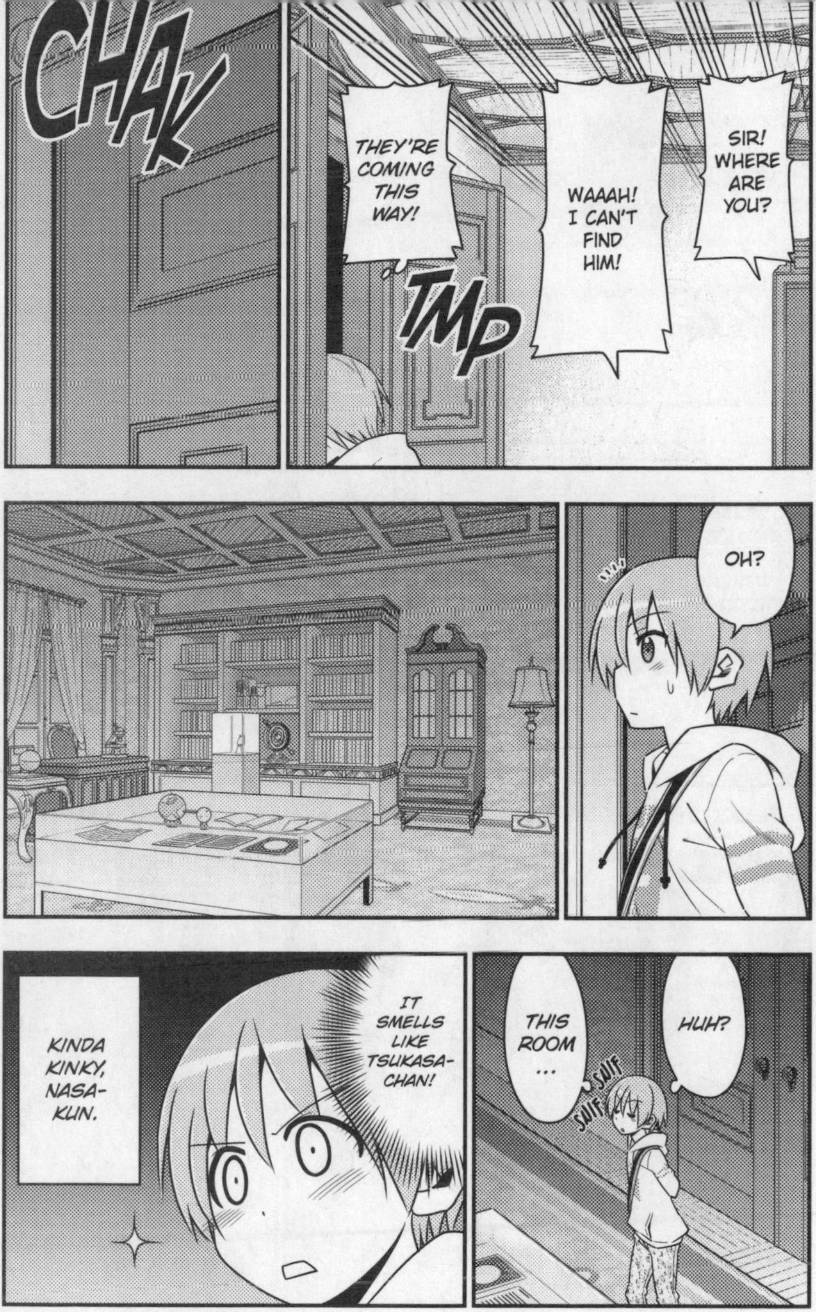
SIR! WHERE ARE YOU?
WAAAH! I CAN'T FIND HIM!
THEY'RE COMING THIS WAY!
TMP
CHAK
OH?
HUH?
THIS ROOM ...
SNIF SNIF
IT SMELLS LIKE TSUKASA-CHAN!
KINDA KINKY, NASA-KUN.

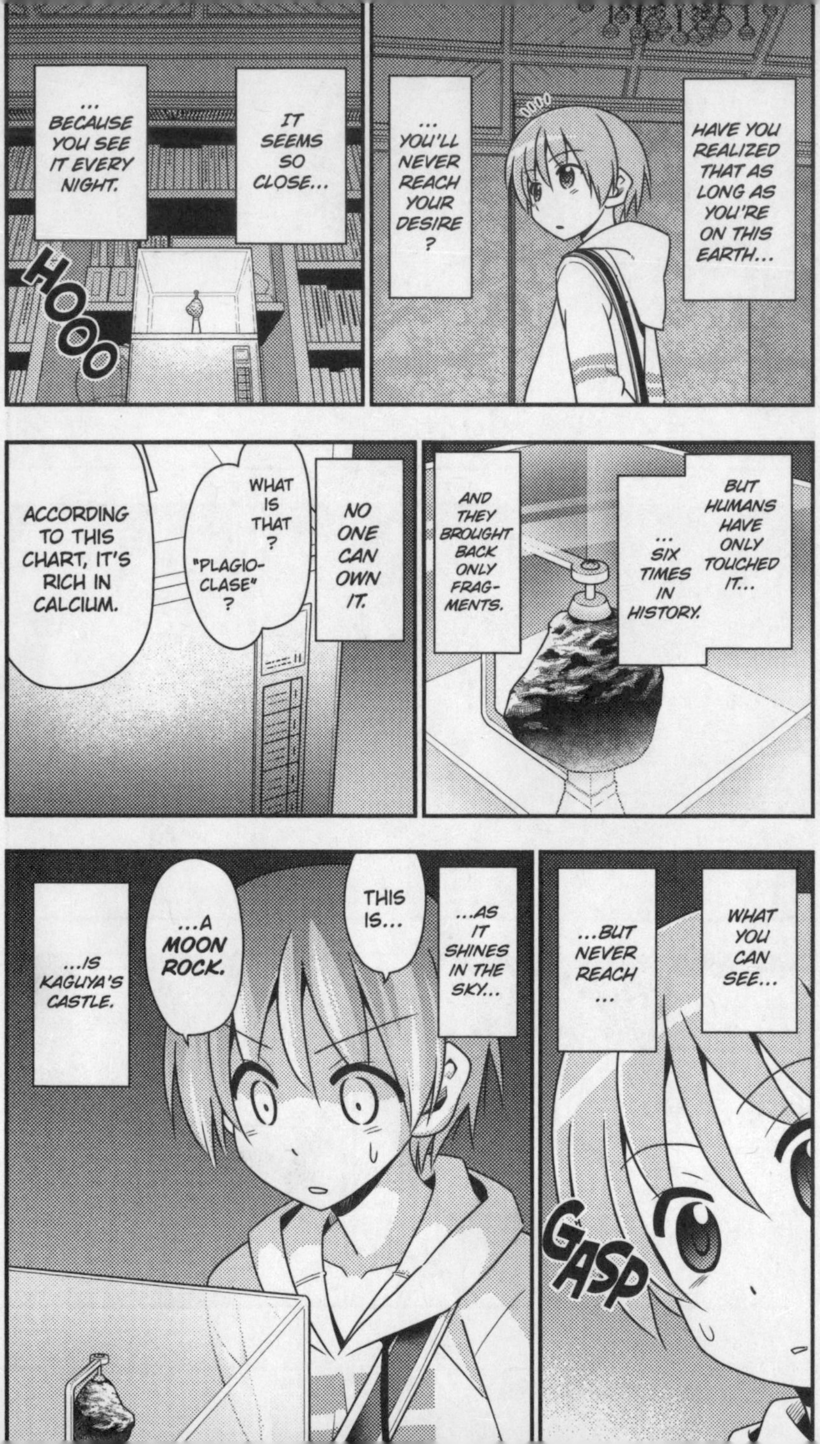
HAVE YOU REALIZED THAT AS LONG AS YOU'RE ON THIS EARTH...
...YOU'LL NEVER REACH YOUR DESIRE?
IT SEEMS SO CLOSE...
...BECAUSE YOU SEE IT EVERY NIGHT.
HOOO
BUT HUMANS HAVE ONLY TOUCHED IT...
...SIX TIMES IN HISTORY.
AND THEY BROUGHT BACK ONLY FRAGMENTS.
NO ONE CAN OWN IT.
WHAT IS THAT? "PLAGIOCLASE"?
ACCORDING TO THIS CHART, IT'S RICH IN CALCIUM.
WHAT YOU CAN SEE...
...BUT NEVER REACH...
GASP
...AS IT SHINES IN THE SKY...
THIS IS...
...A MOON ROCK.
...IS KAGUYA'S CASTLE.

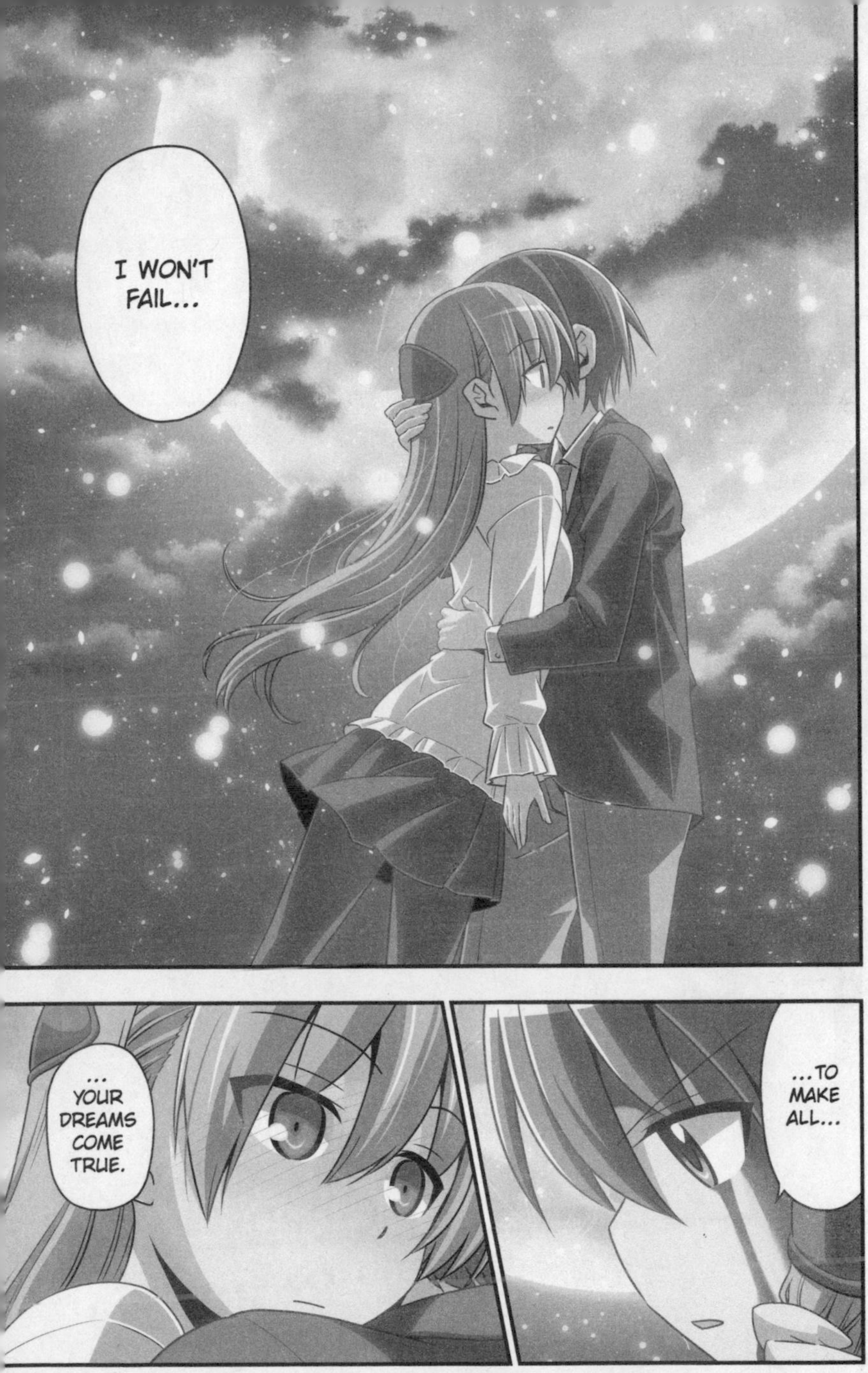
I WON'T FAIL...
...TO MAKE ALL...
... YOUR DREAMS COME TRUE.

Chapter 14: "Promise"

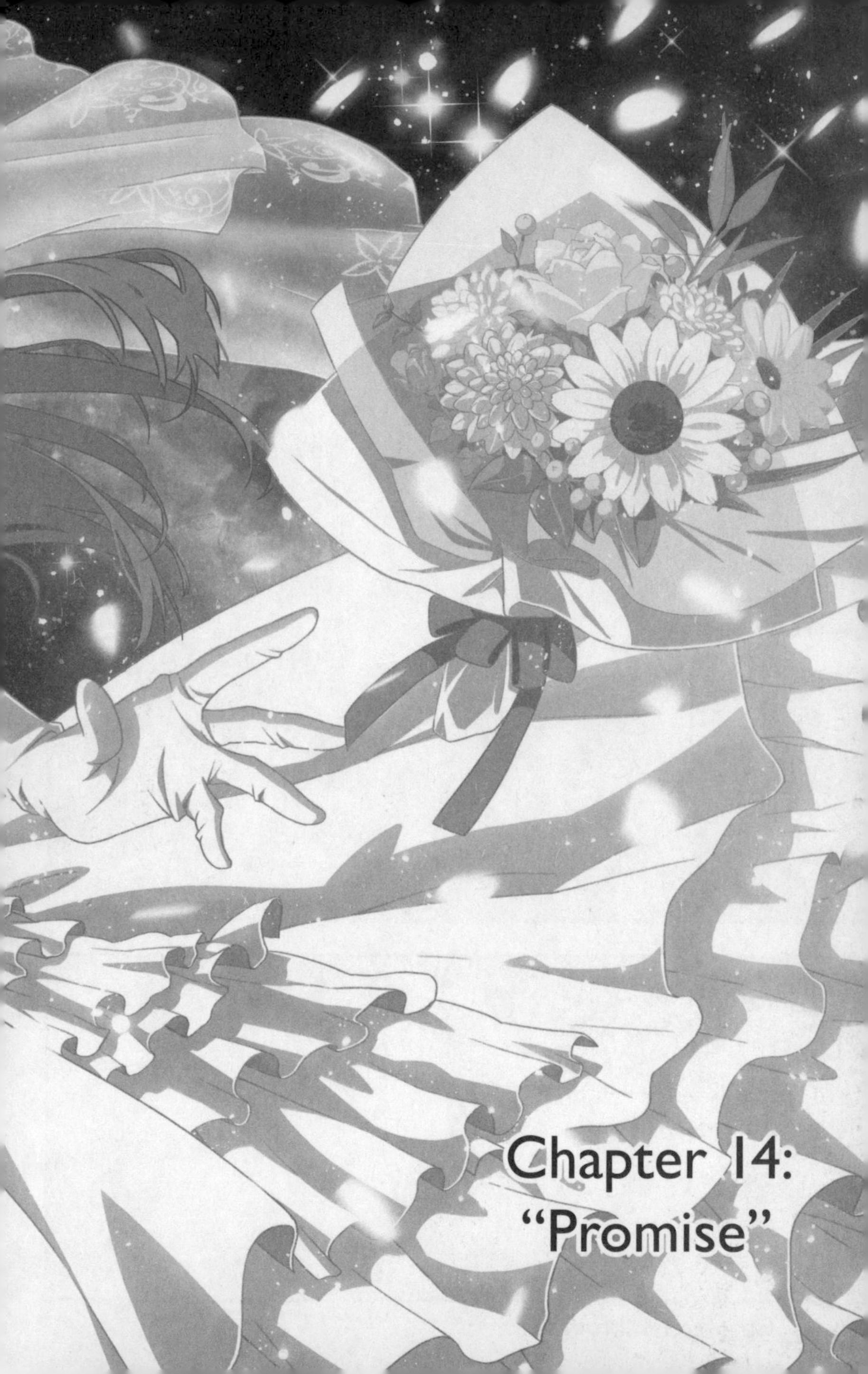
Chapter 14:
"Promise"

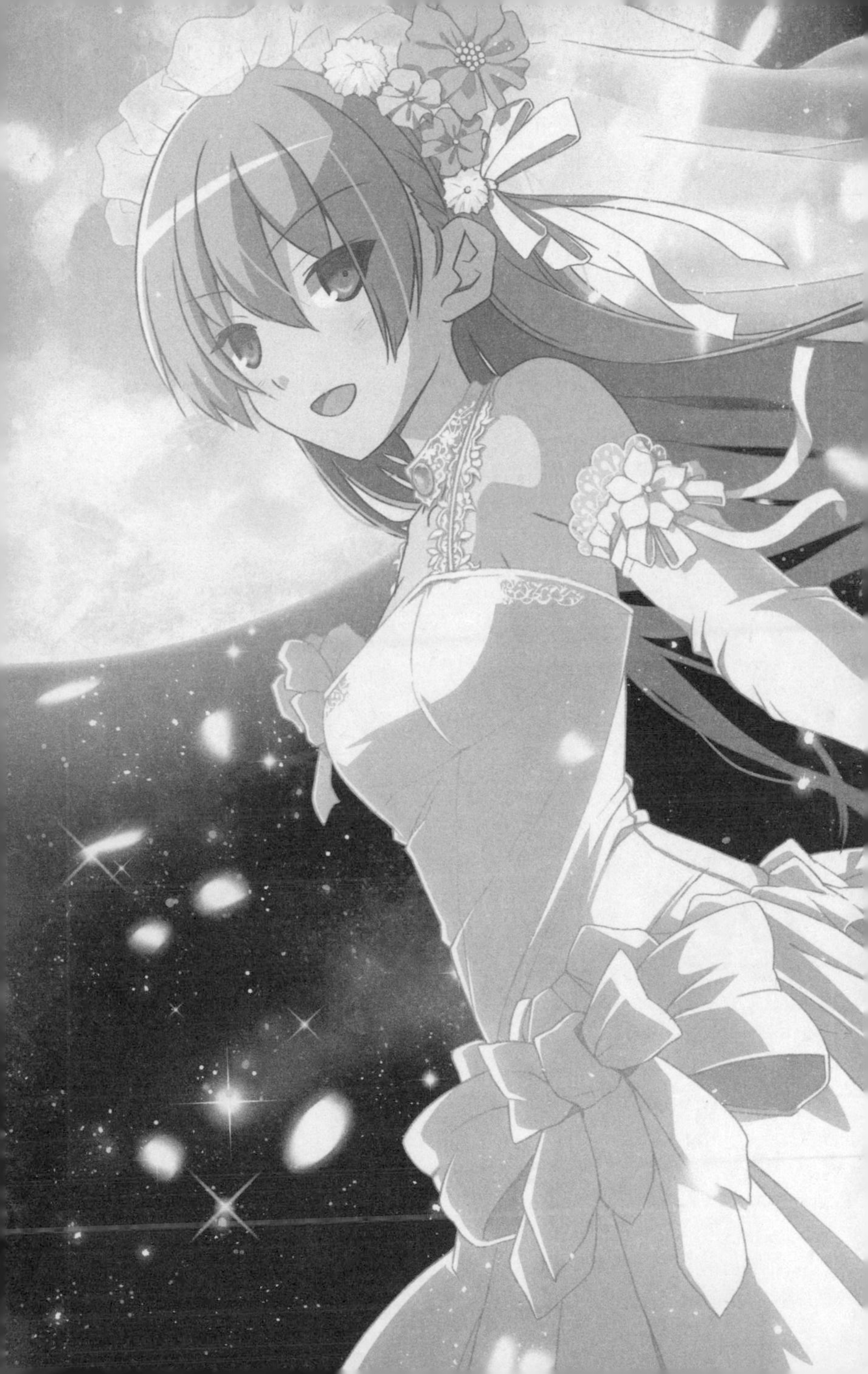

FLY ME TO THE MOON

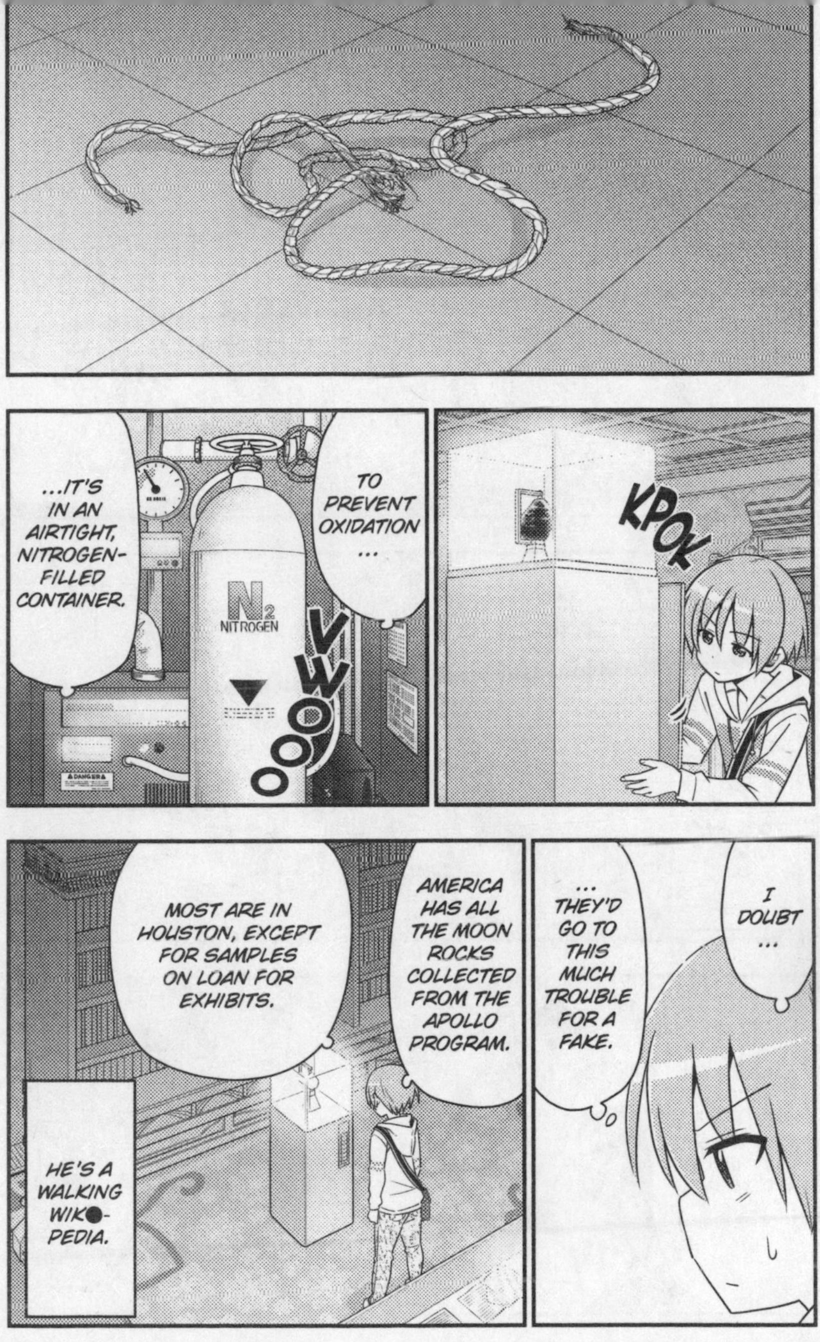
KPOK
TO PREVENT OXIDATION ...
...IT'S IN AN AIRTIGHT, NITROGEN-FILLED CONTAINER.
N2 NITROGEN
VWOOOO
I DOUBT ...
... THEY'D GO TO THIS MUCH TROUBLE FOR A FAKE.
AMERICA HAS ALL THE MOON ROCKS COLLECTED FROM THE APOLLO PROGRAM.
MOST ARE IN HOUSTON, EXCEPT FOR SAMPLES ON LOAN FOR EXHIBITS.
HE'S A WALKING WIK●-PEDIA.

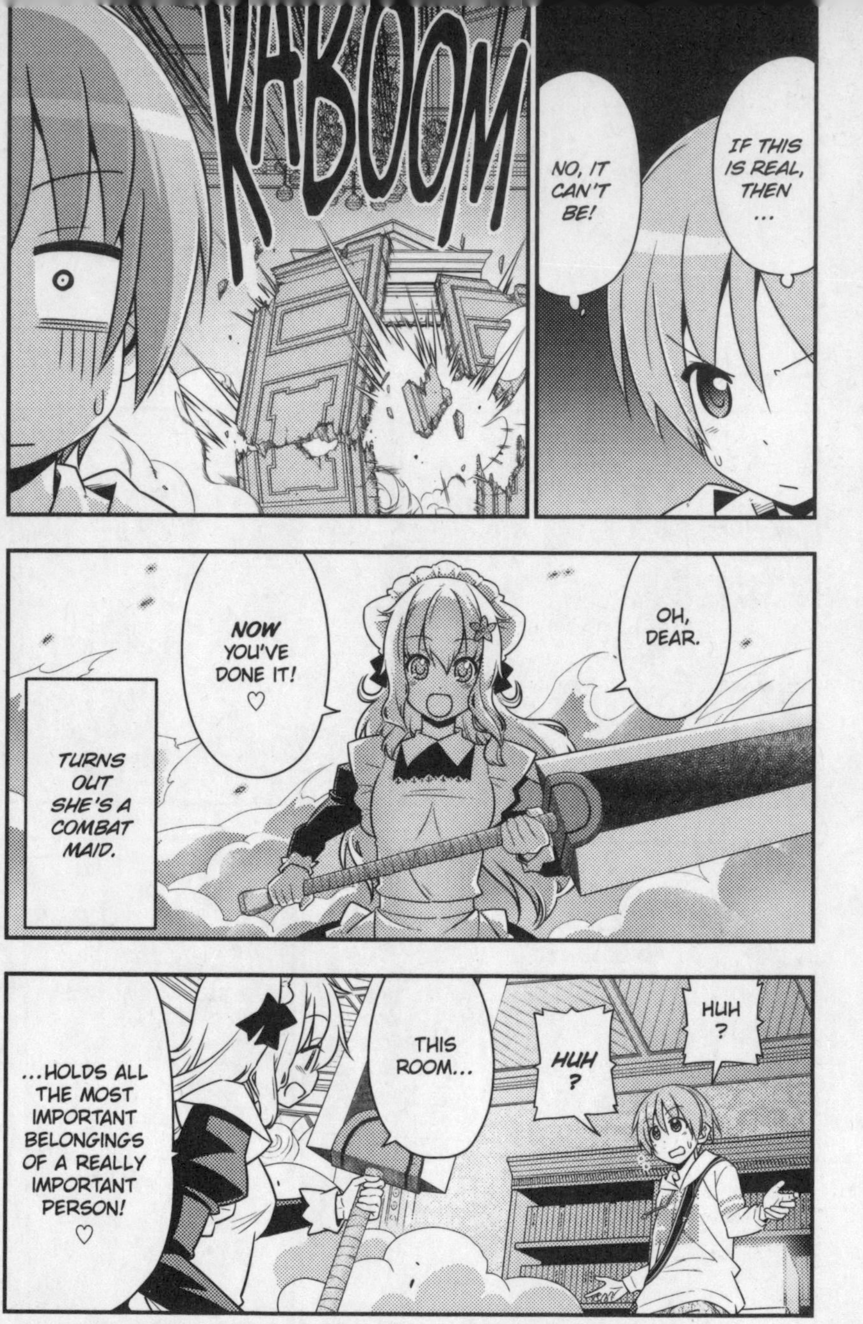
IF THIS IS REAL, THEN ...
NO, IT CAN'T BE!
KABOOM
OH, DEAR.
NOW YOU'VE DONE IT! ♡
TURNS OUT SHE'S A COMBAT MAID.
HUH?
HUH?
THIS ROOM...
...HOLDS ALL THE MOST IMPORTANT BELONGINGS OF A REALLY IMPORTANT PERSON! ♡

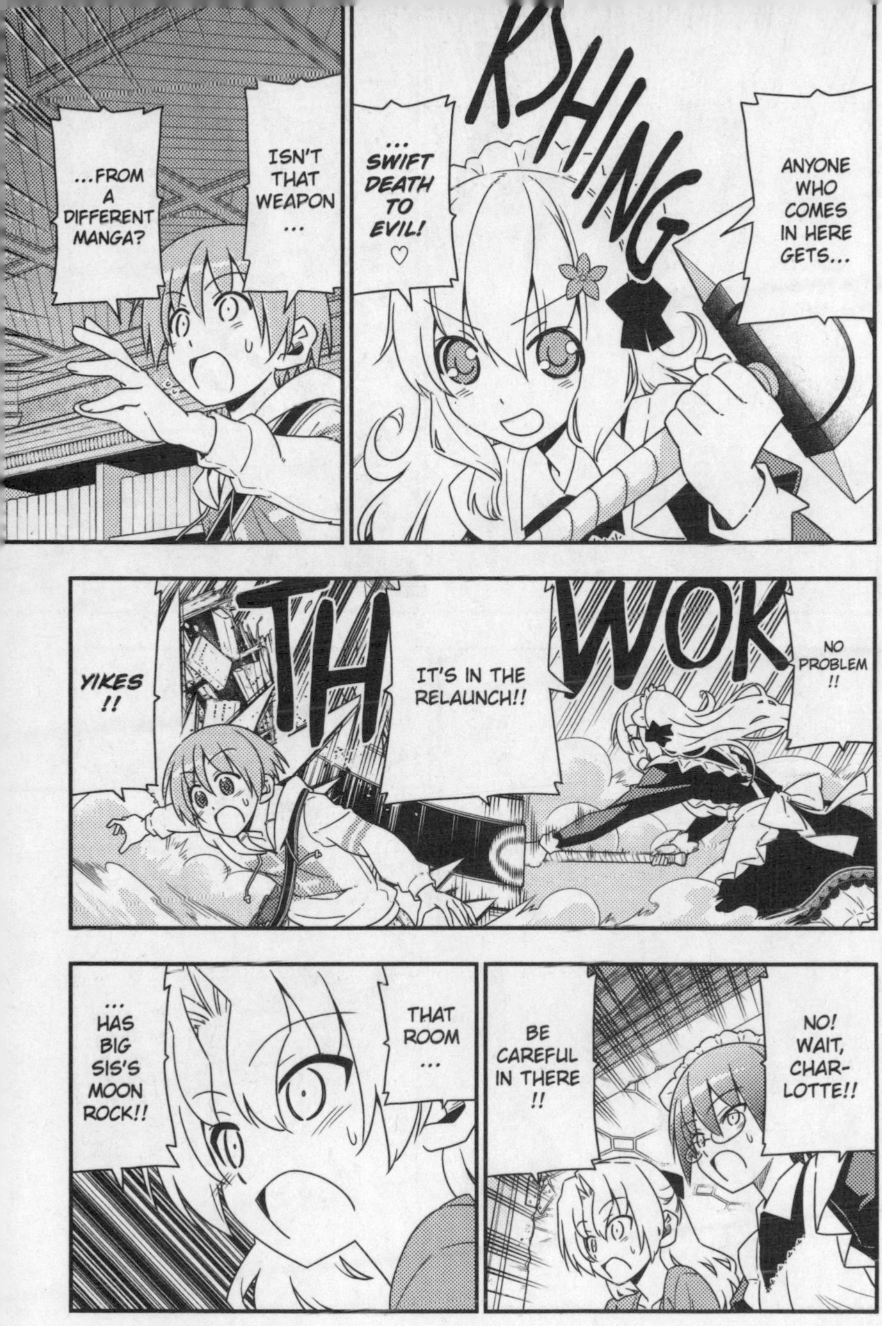

ANYONE WHO COMES IN HERE GETS...
KSHING
... SWIFT DEATH TO EVIL! ♡
ISN'T THAT WEAPON ...
...FROM A DIFFERENT MANGA?
NO PROBLEM !!
TH WOK
IT'S IN THE RELAUNCH!!
YIKES !!
NO! WAIT, CHAR-LOTTE!!
BE CAREFUL IN THERE !!
THAT ROOM ...
... HAS BIG SIS'S MOON ROCK!!

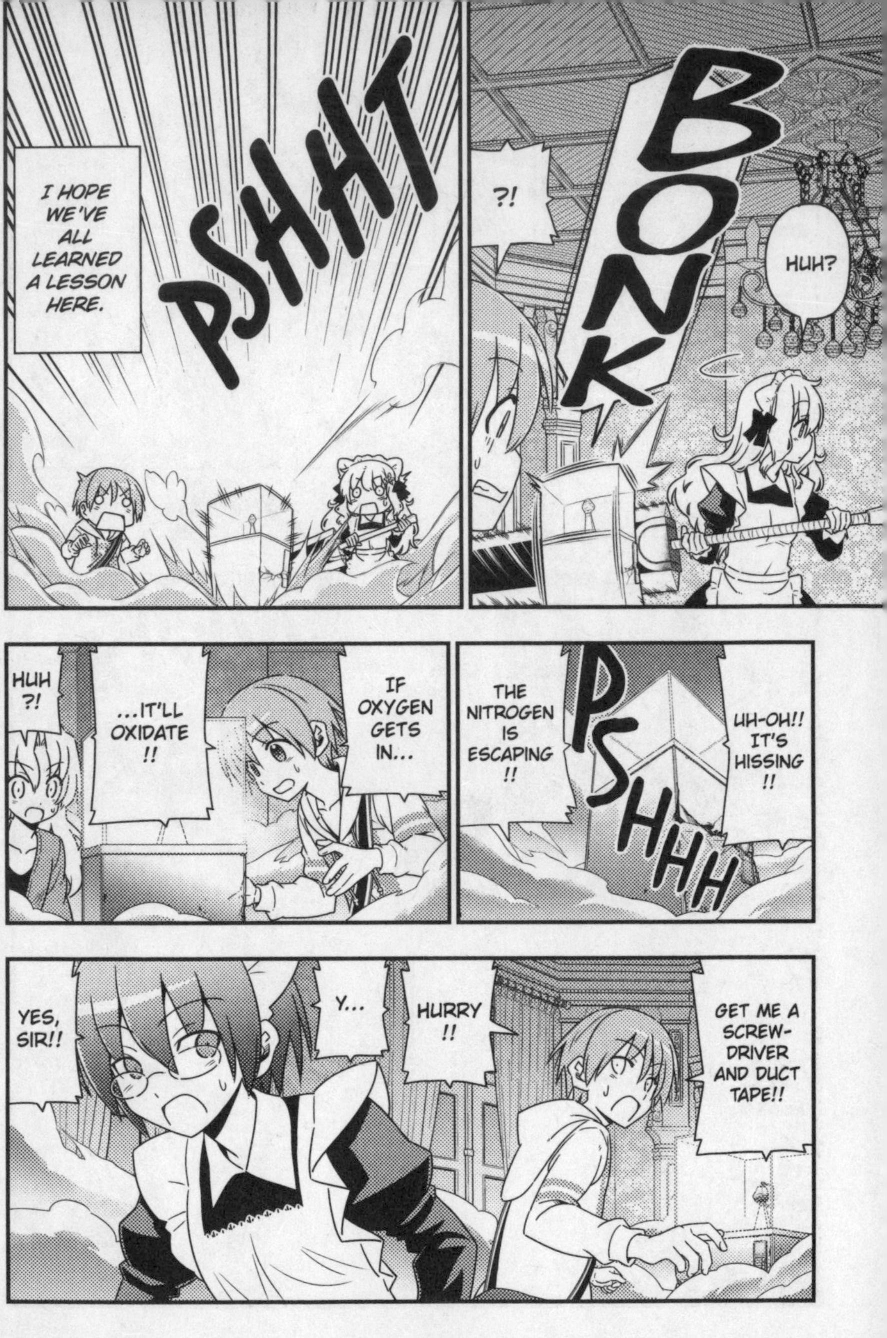
HUH?
BONK
?!
PSHHT
I HOPE WE'VE ALL LEARNED A LESSON HERE.
UH-OH!! IT'S HISSING!!
PSHHH
THE NITROGEN IS ESCAPING!!
IF OXYGEN GETS IN...
...IT'LL OXIDATE!!
HUH?!
GET ME A SCREW-DRIVER AND DUCT TAPE!!
HURRY!!
Y...
YES, SIR!!

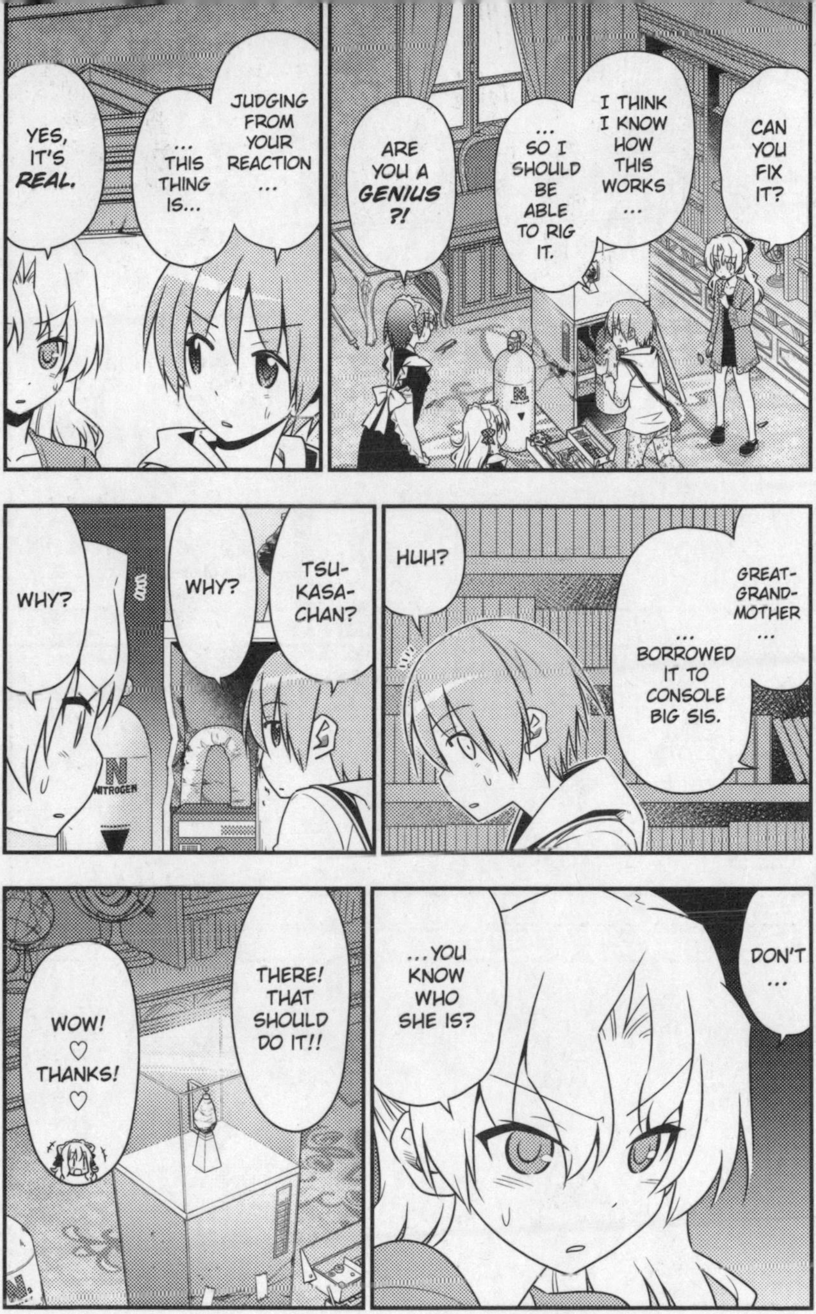
CAN YOU FIX IT?
I THINK I KNOW HOW THIS WORKS...
... SO I SHOULD BE ABLE TO RIG IT.
ARE YOU A *GENIUS*?!
JUDGING FROM YOUR REACTION...
... THIS THING IS...
YES, IT'S *REAL.*
GREAT-GRANDMOTHER...
... BORROWED IT TO CONSOLE BIG SIS.
HUH?
TSU-KASA-CHAN?
WHY?
NITROGEN
WHY?
DON'T...
...YOU KNOW WHO SHE IS?
THERE! THAT SHOULD DO IT!!
WOW! ♡ THANKS! ♡

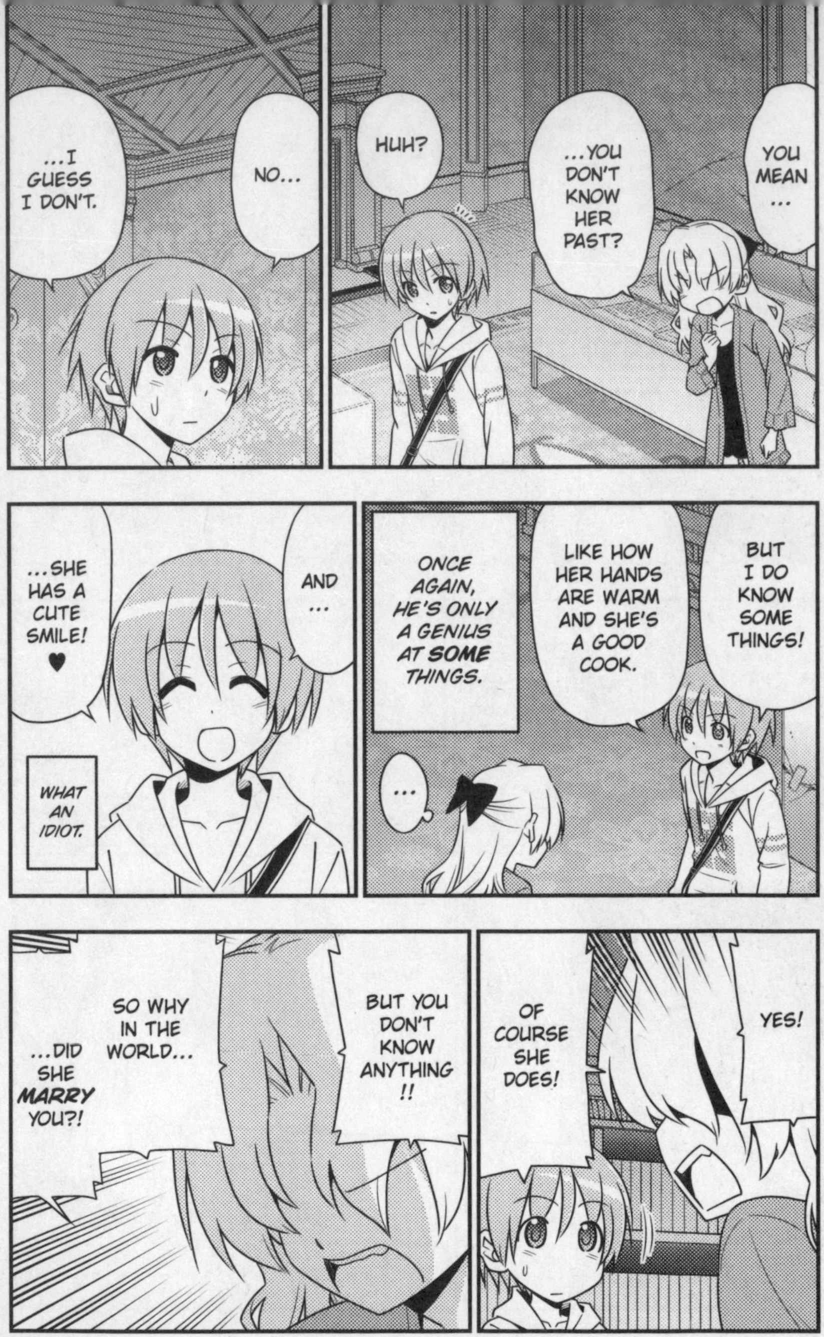
YOU MEAN ...
...YOU DON'T KNOW HER PAST?
HUH?
NO...
...I GUESS I DON'T.
BUT I DO KNOW SOME THINGS!
LIKE HOW HER HANDS ARE WARM AND SHE'S A GOOD COOK.
ONCE AGAIN, HE'S ONLY A GENIUS AT SOME THINGS.
...
AND ...
...SHE HAS A CUTE SMILE! ♥
WHAT AN IDIOT.
YES!
OF COURSE SHE DOES!
BUT YOU DON'T KNOW ANYTHING !!
SO WHY IN THE WORLD...
...DID SHE MARRY YOU?!

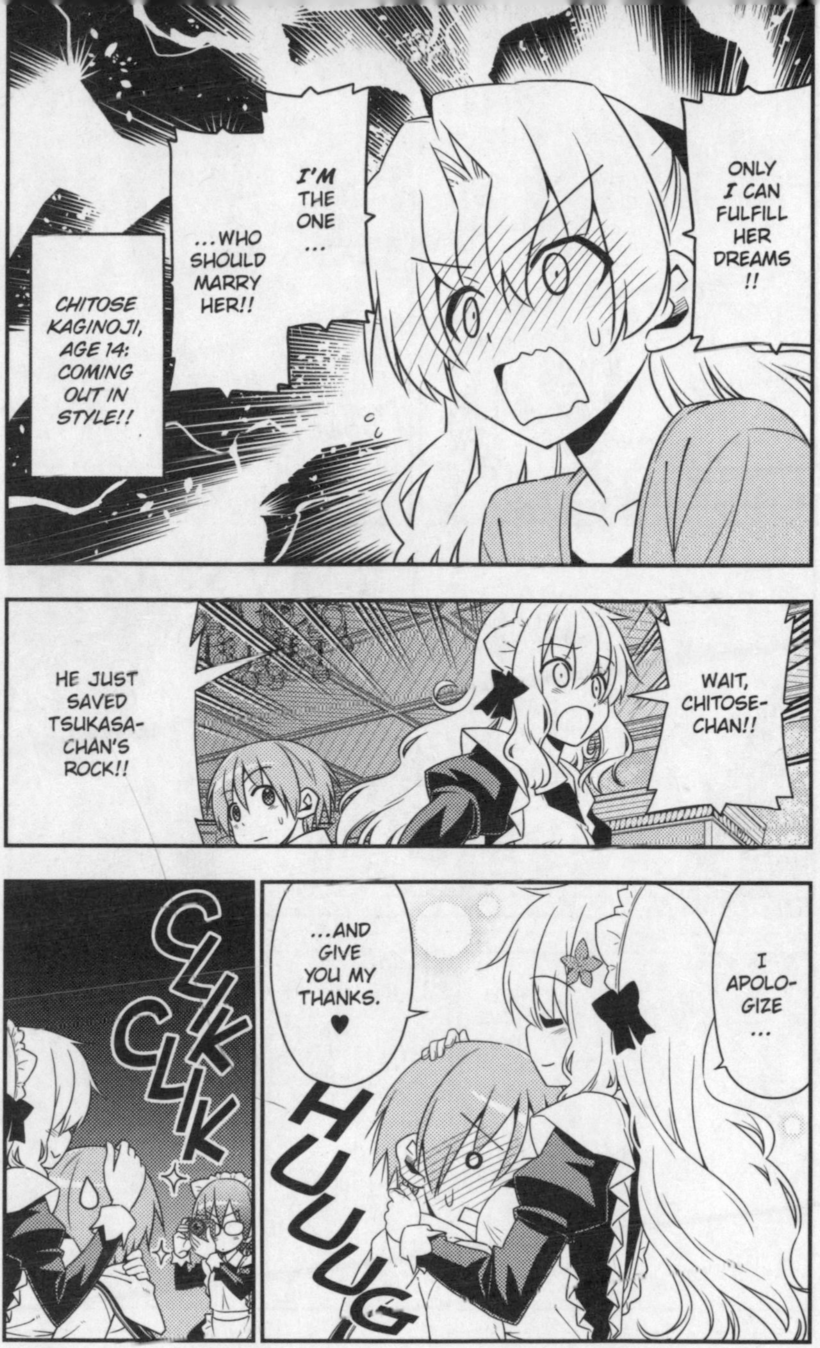
ONLY I CAN FULFILL HER DREAMS!!
I'M THE ONE ...
...WHO SHOULD MARRY HER!!
CHITOSE KAGINOJI, AGE 14: COMING OUT IN STYLE!!
WAIT, CHITOSE-CHAN!!
HE JUST SAVED TSUKASA-CHAN'S ROCK!!
I APOLOGIZE ...
...AND GIVE YOU MY THANKS. ♥
HUUUG
CLIK CLIK

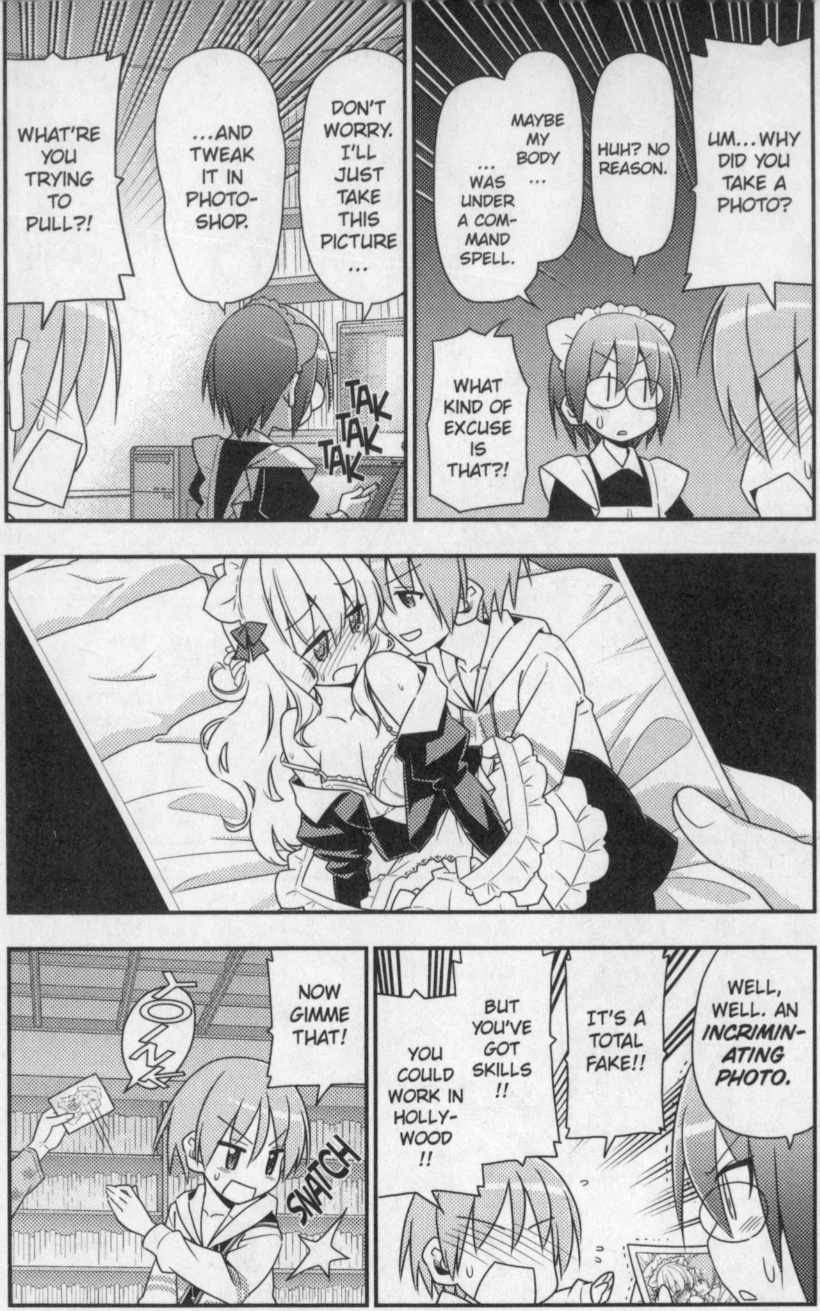
UM...WHY DID YOU TAKE A PHOTO?
HUH? NO REASON.
MAYBE MY BODY ...
... WAS UNDER A COMMAND SPELL.
WHAT KIND OF EXCUSE IS THAT?!
DON'T WORRY. I'LL JUST TAKE THIS PICTURE ...
...AND TWEAK IT IN PHOTOSHOP.
WHAT'RE YOU TRYING TO PULL?!
TAK TAK TAK
WELL, WELL. AN *INCRIMINATING PHOTO.*
IT'S A TOTAL FAKE!!
BUT YOU'VE GOT SKILLS !!
YOU COULD WORK IN HOLLYWOOD !!
NOW GIMME THAT!
YOINK
SNATCH

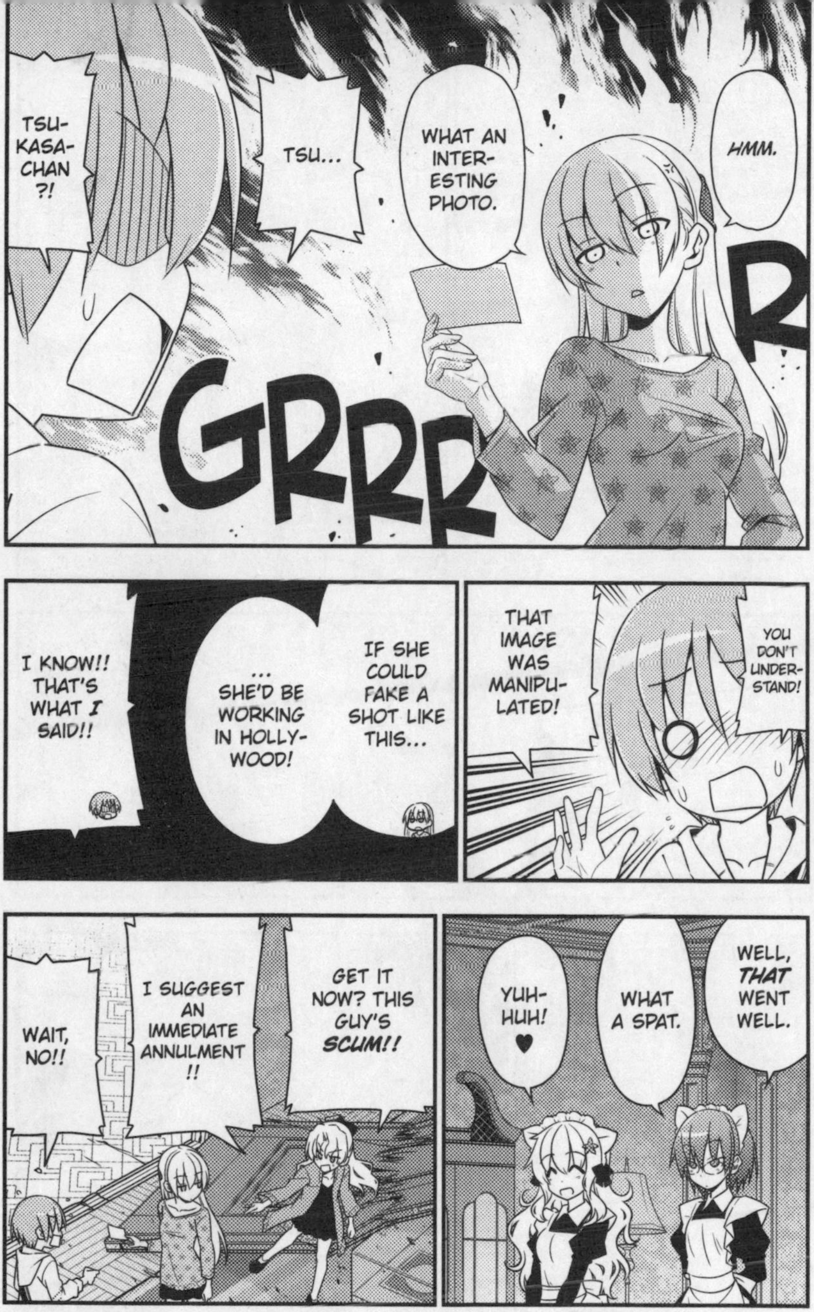
HMM.
WHAT AN INTERESTING PHOTO.
TSU...
TSU-KASA-CHAN?!
GRRR
YOU DON'T UNDERSTAND!
THAT IMAGE WAS MANIPULATED!
IF SHE COULD FAKE A SHOT LIKE THIS...
...SHE'D BE WORKING IN HOLLYWOOD!
I KNOW!! THAT'S WHAT *I* SAID!!
WELL, *THAT* WENT WELL.
WHAT A SPAT.
YUH-HUH! ♥
GET IT NOW? THIS GUY'S *SCUM!!*
I SUGGEST AN IMMEDIATE ANNULMENT!!
WAIT, NO!!

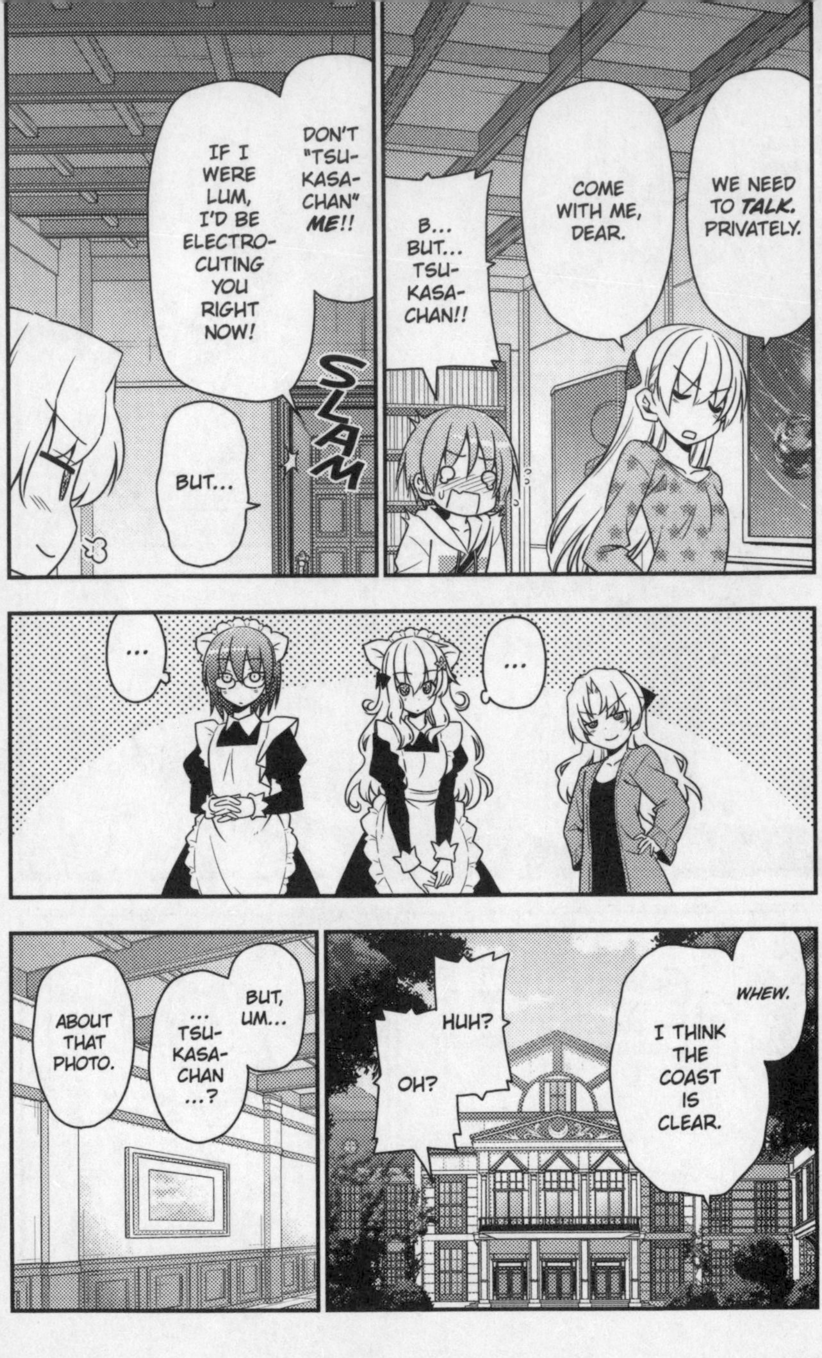
WE NEED TO TALK. PRIVATELY.
COME WITH ME, DEAR.
B… BUT… TSU-KASA-CHAN!!
DON'T "TSU-KASA-CHAN" ME!!
IF I WERE LUM, I'D BE ELECTRO-CUTING YOU RIGHT NOW!
SLAM
BUT…
…
…
WHEW.
I THINK THE COAST IS CLEAR.
HUH?
OH?
BUT, UM…
…TSU-KASA-CHAN…?
ABOUT THAT PHOTO.

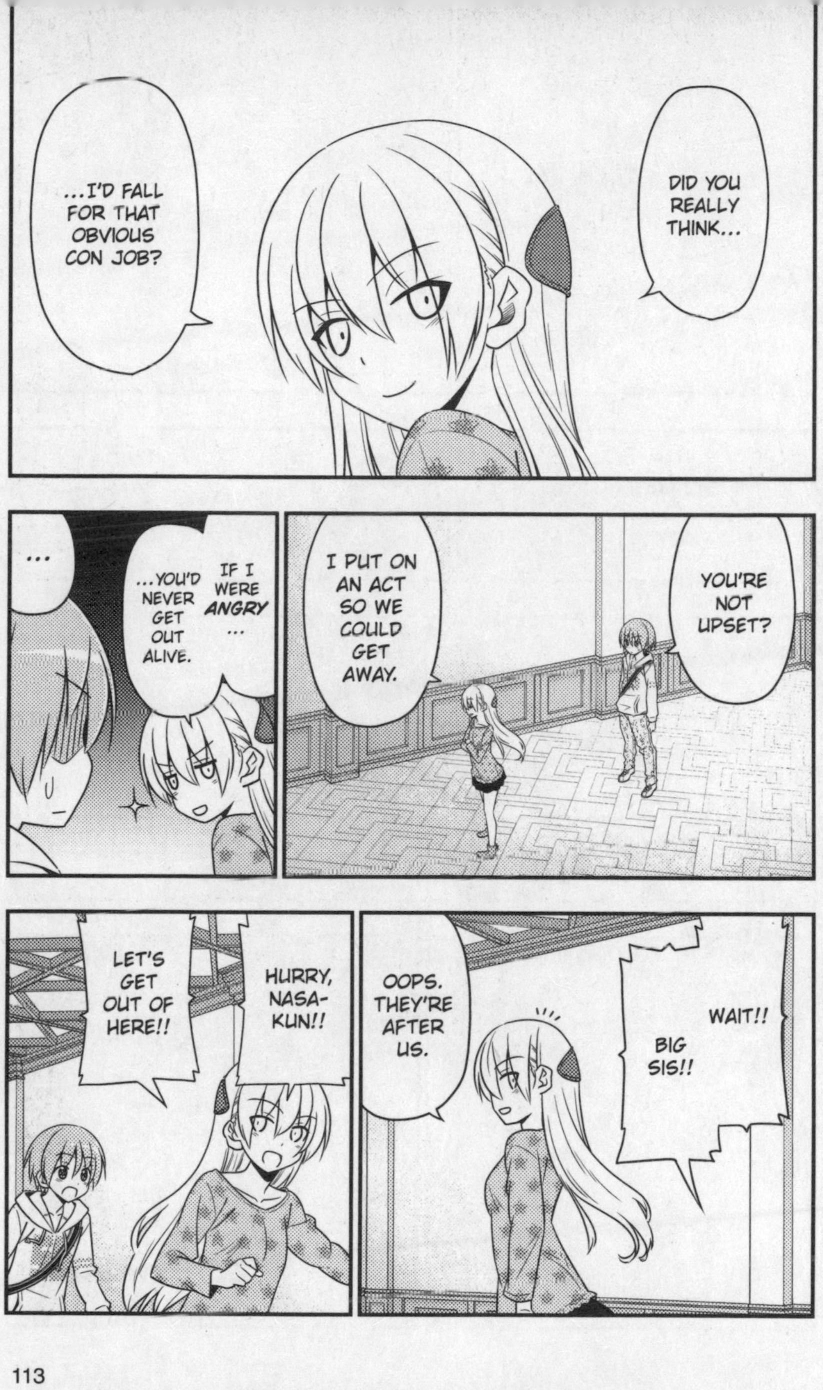
DID YOU REALLY THINK...
...I'D FALL FOR THAT OBVIOUS CON JOB?
YOU'RE NOT UPSET?
I PUT ON AN ACT SO WE COULD GET AWAY.
IF I WERE ANGRY...
...YOU'D NEVER GET OUT ALIVE.
...
WAIT!!
BIG SIS!!
OOPS. THEY'RE AFTER US.
HURRY, NASA-KUN!!
LET'S GET OUT OF HERE!!

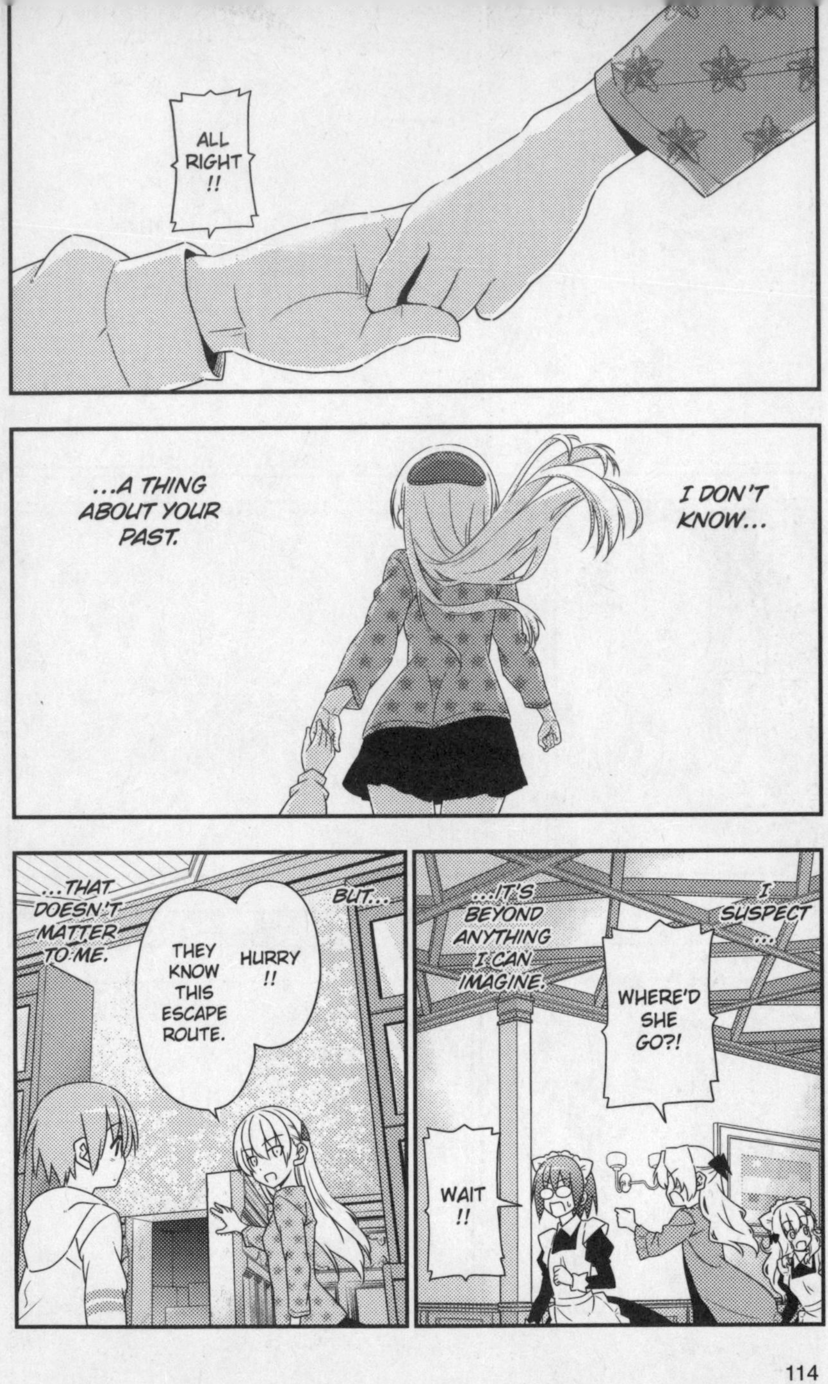
ALL RIGHT !!
I DON'T KNOW...
...A THING ABOUT YOUR PAST.
I SUSPECT ...
...IT'S BEYOND ANYTHING I CAN IMAGINE.
WHERE'D SHE GO?!
WAIT !!
BUT...
...THAT DOESN'T MATTER TO ME.
HURRY !!
THEY KNOW THIS ESCAPE ROUTE.

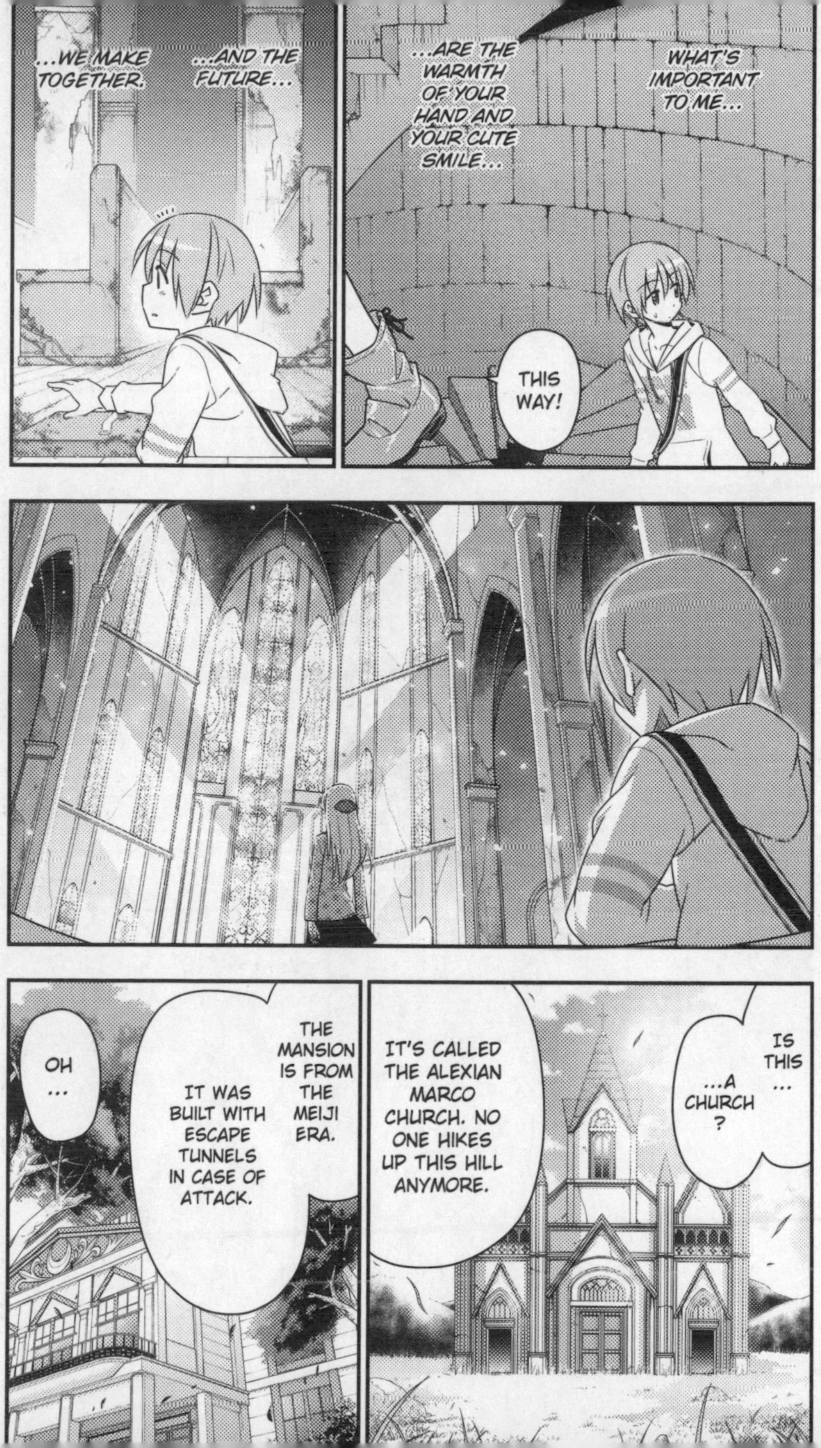
WHAT'S IMPORTANT TO ME...
...ARE THE WARMTH OF YOUR HAND AND YOUR CUTE SMILE...
THIS WAY!
...AND THE FUTURE...
...WE MAKE TOGETHER.
IS THIS ...
...A CHURCH ?
IT'S CALLED THE ALEXIAN MARCO CHURCH. NO ONE HIKES UP THIS HILL ANYMORE.
THE MANSION IS FROM THE MEIJI ERA.
IT WAS BUILT WITH ESCAPE TUNNELS IN CASE OF ATTACK.
OH ...

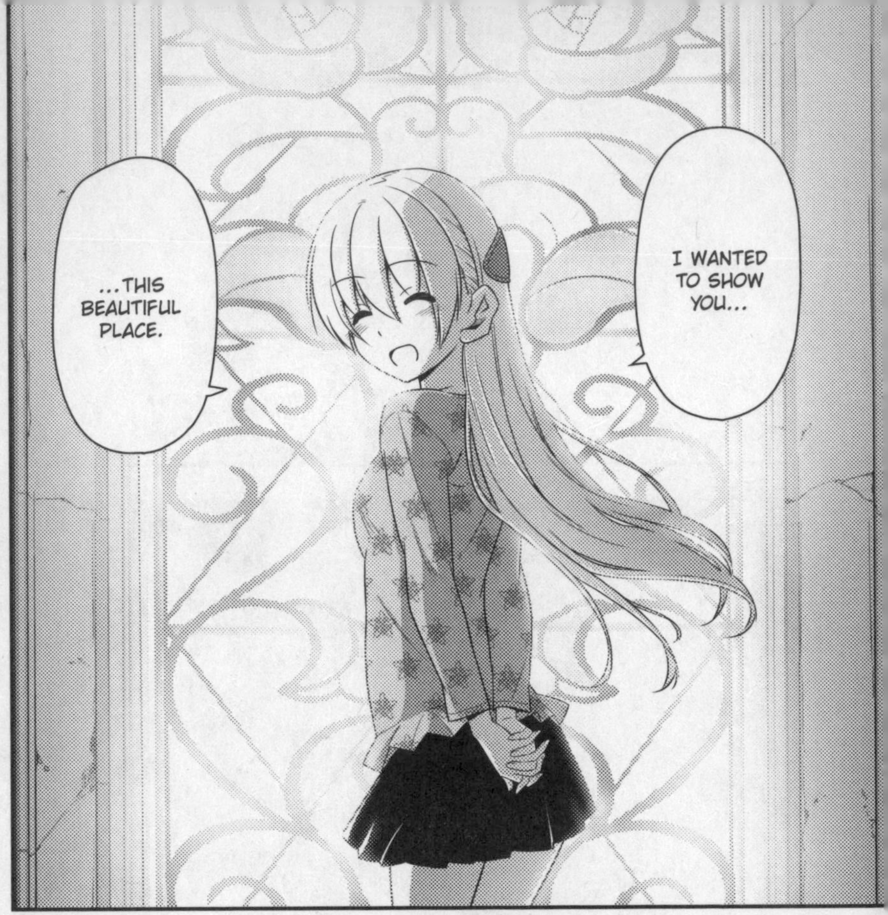
I WANTED TO SHOW YOU...
...THIS BEAUTIFUL PLACE.

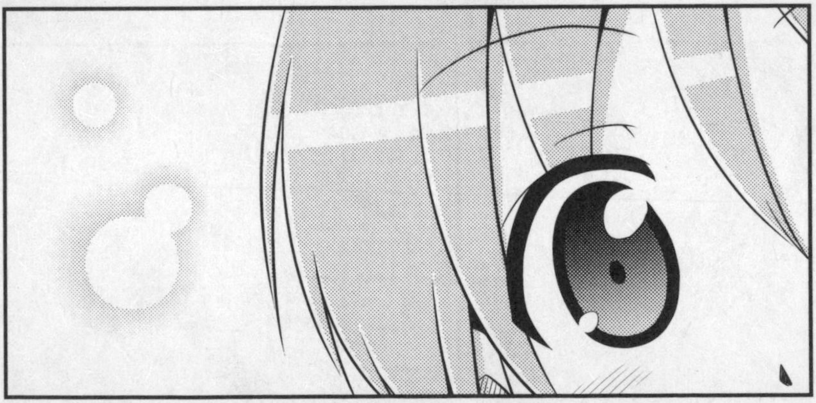

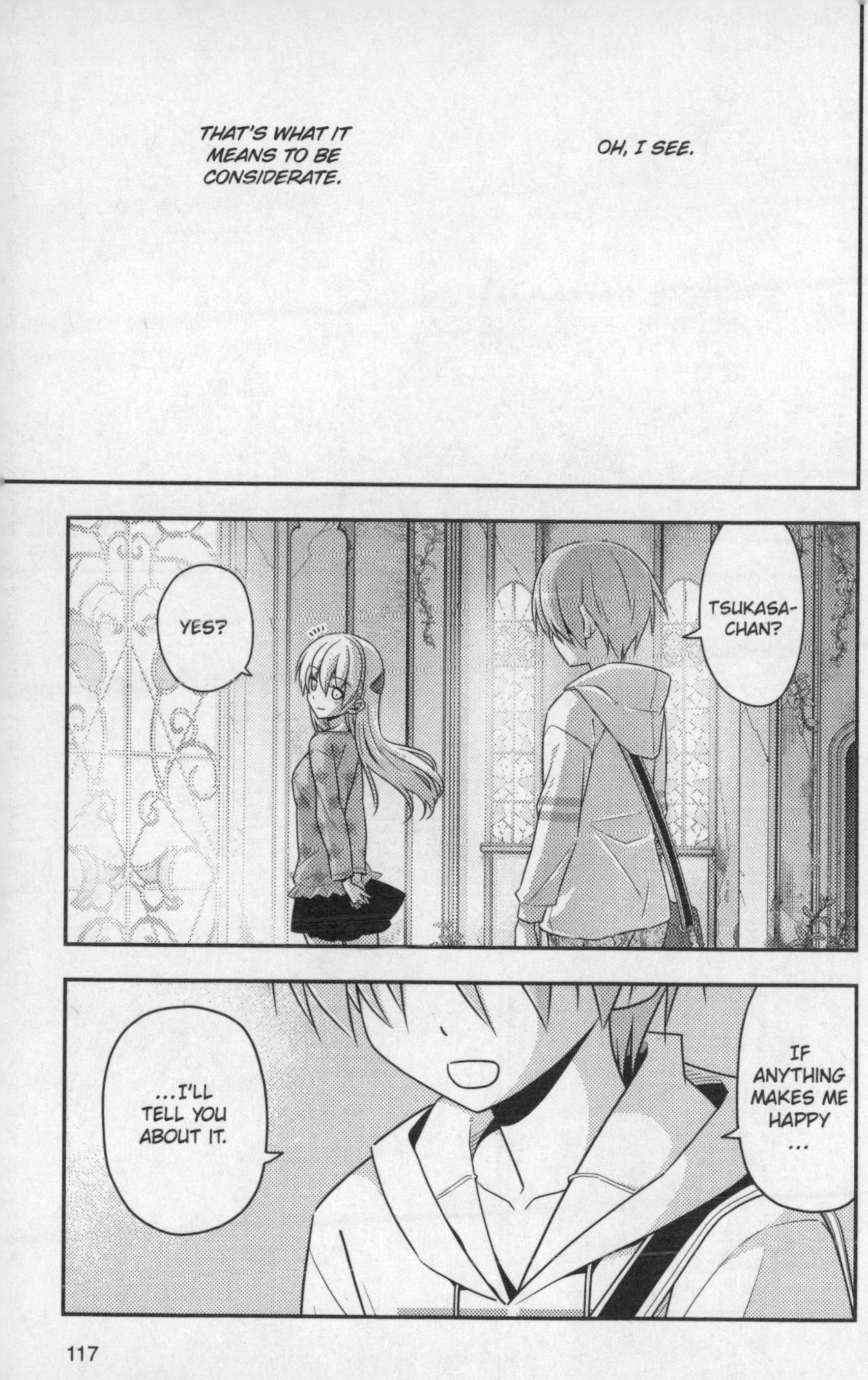
OH, I SEE.
THAT'S WHAT IT MEANS TO BE CONSIDERATE.
TSUKASA-CHAN?
YES?
IF ANYTHING MAKES ME HAPPY ...
...I'LL TELL YOU ABOUT IT.

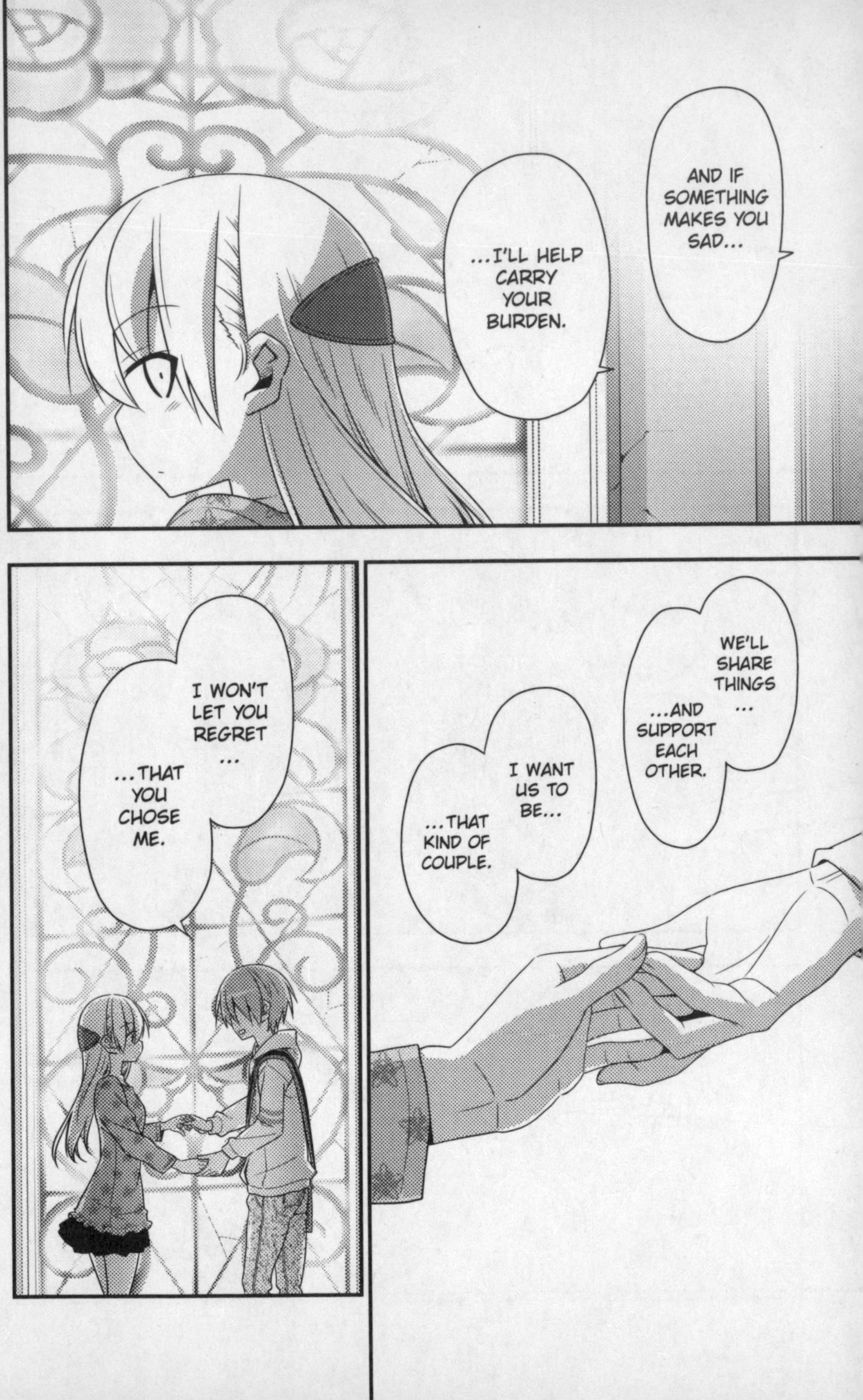
AND IF SOMETHING MAKES YOU SAD...
...I'LL HELP CARRY YOUR BURDEN.
WE'LL SHARE THINGS...
...AND SUPPORT EACH OTHER.
I WANT US TO BE...
...THAT KIND OF COUPLE.
I WON'T LET YOU REGRET...
...THAT YOU CHOSE ME.

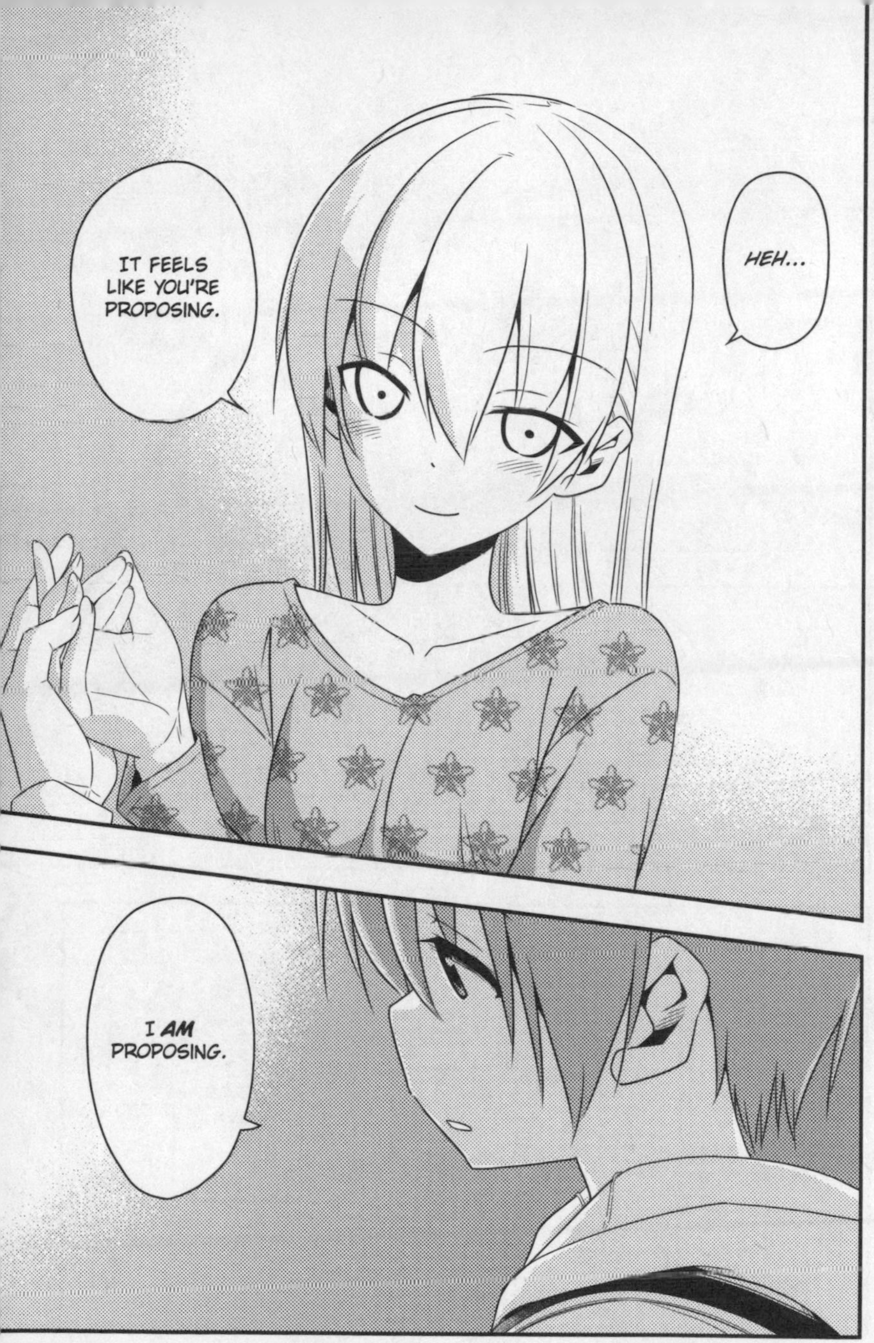
HEH...
IT FEELS LIKE YOU'RE PROPOSING.
I *AM* PROPOSING.

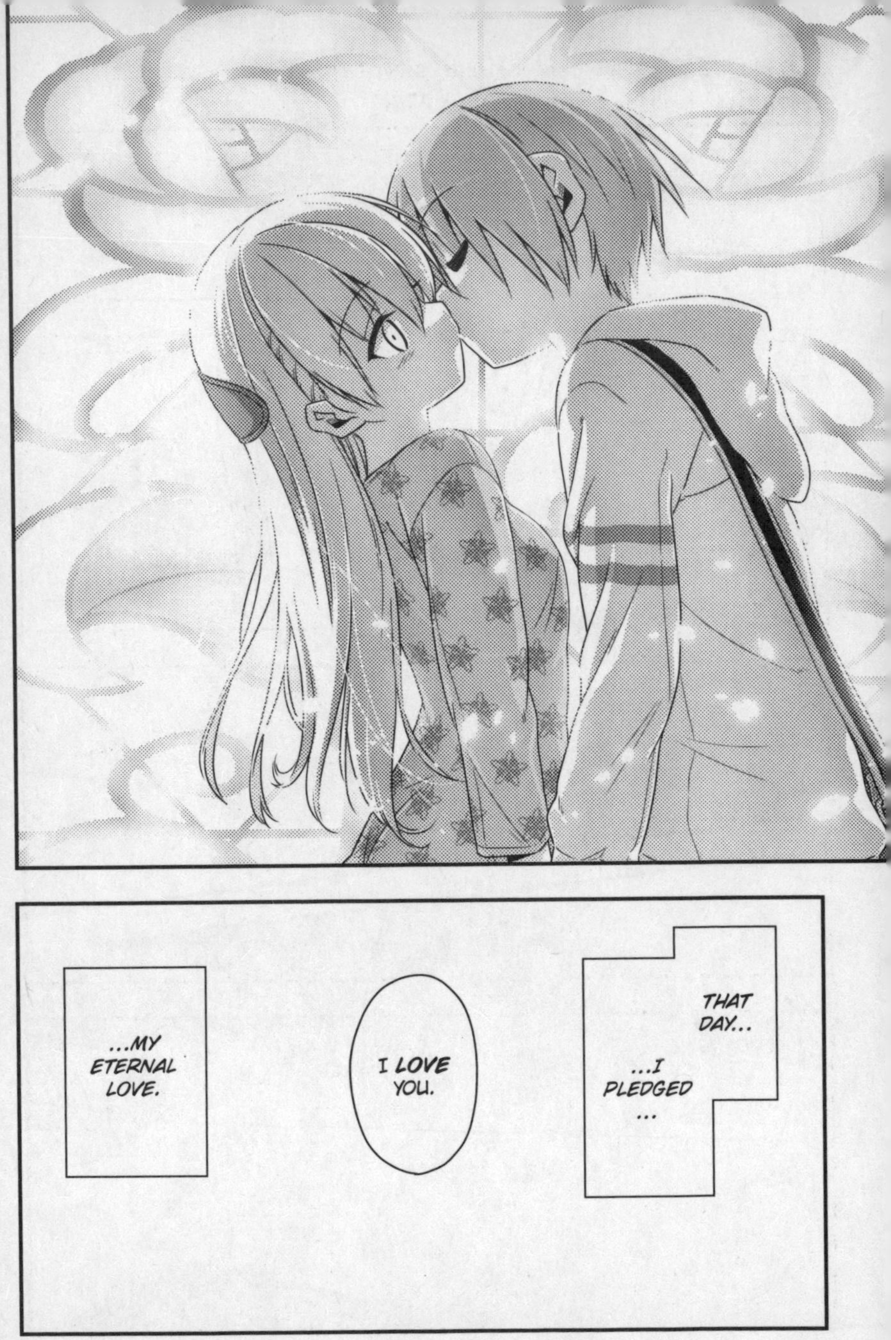
THAT DAY...
...I PLEDGED ...
I LOVE YOU.
...MY ETERNAL LOVE.

Chapter 15: "I Was Under Orders Not to Stop, So I Kept Going and Drew This"

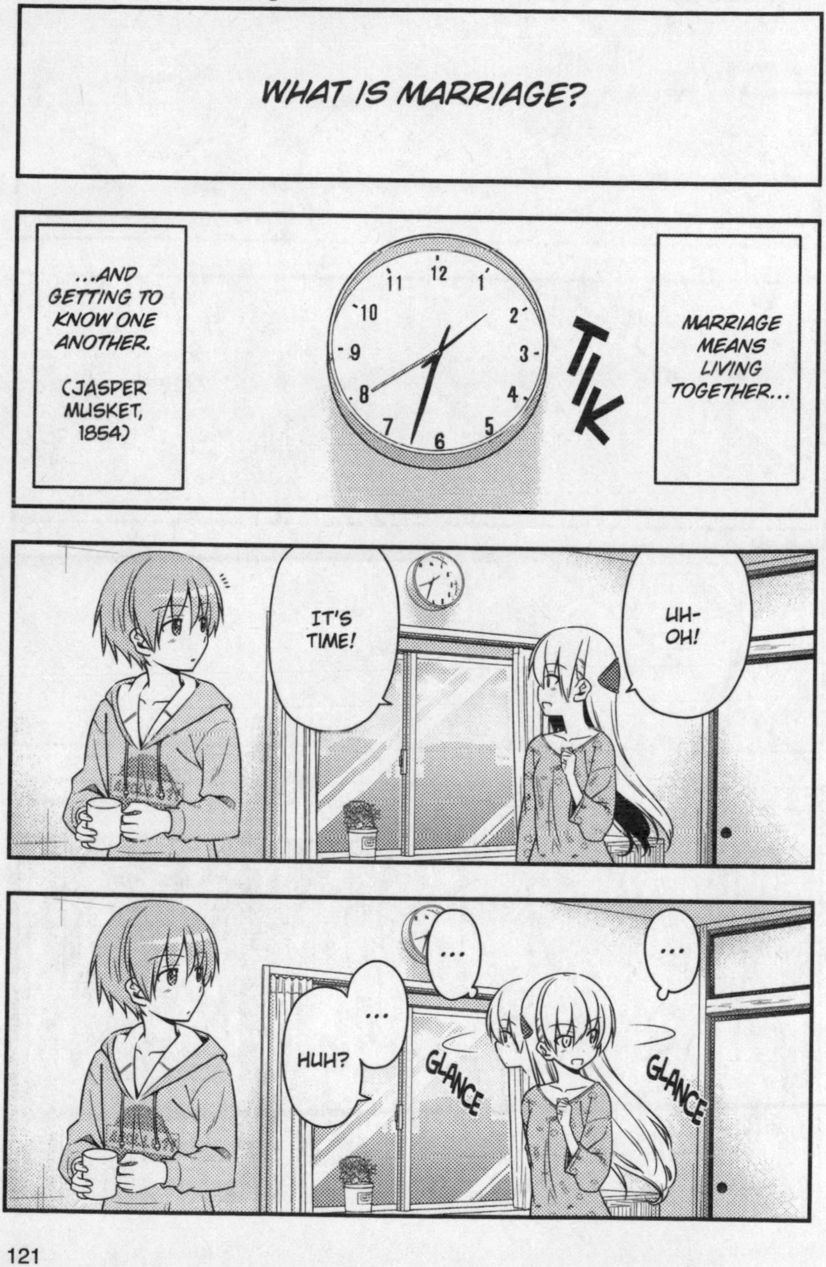
WHAT IS MARRIAGE?
MARRIAGE MEANS LIVING TOGETHER...
TIK
...AND GETTING TO KNOW ONE ANOTHER.
(JASPER MUSKET, 1854)
UH-OH!
IT'S TIME!
...
...
GLANCE
... HUH?
GLANCE

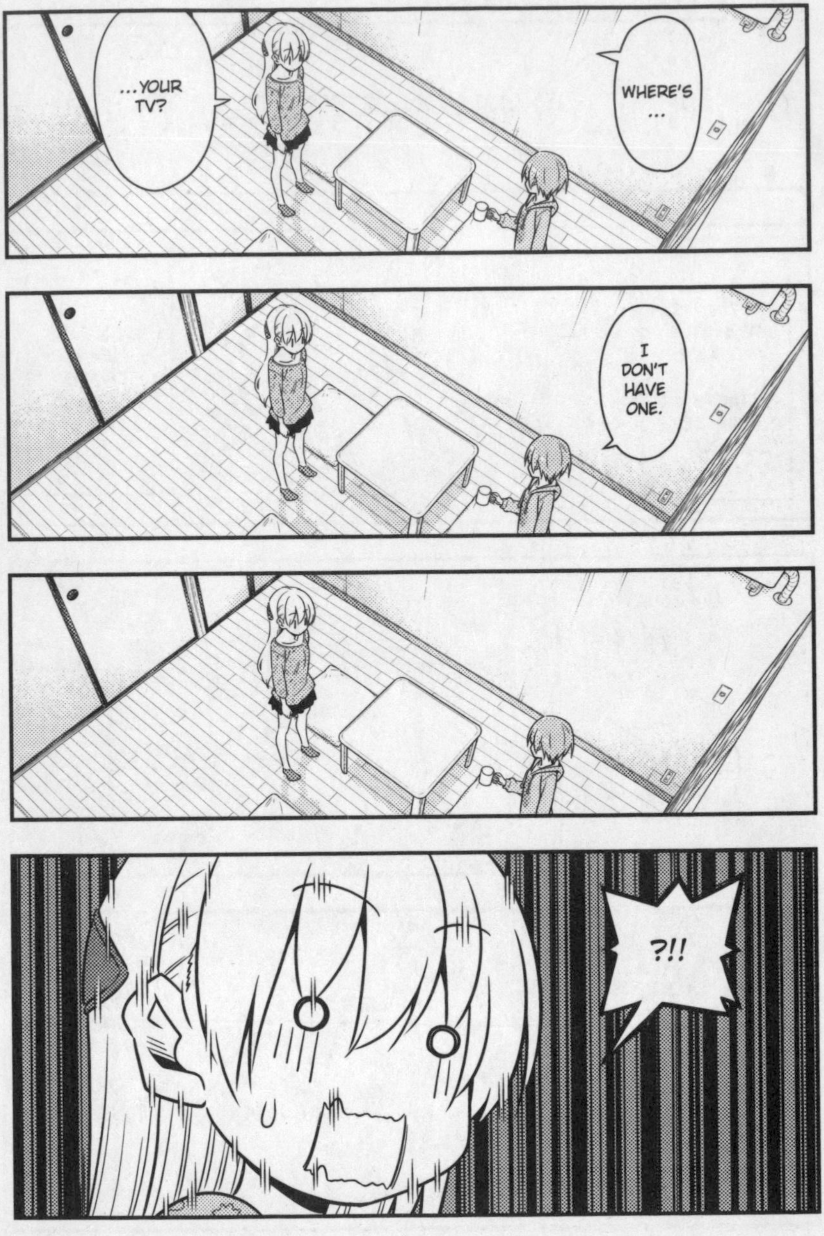
WHERE'S ...
...YOUR TV?
I DON'T HAVE ONE.
?!!

Chapter 15: "I Was Under Orders Not to Stop, So I Kept Going and Drew This"

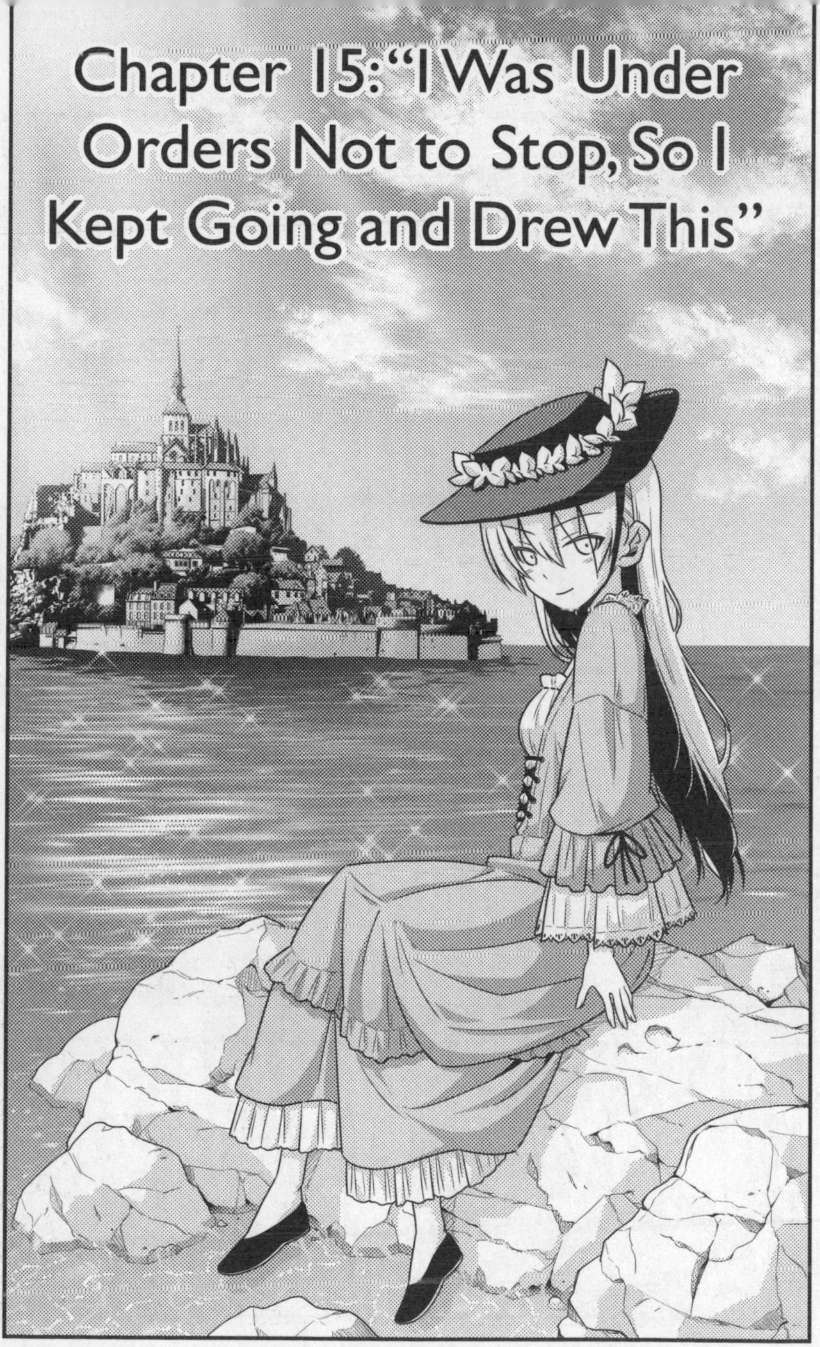

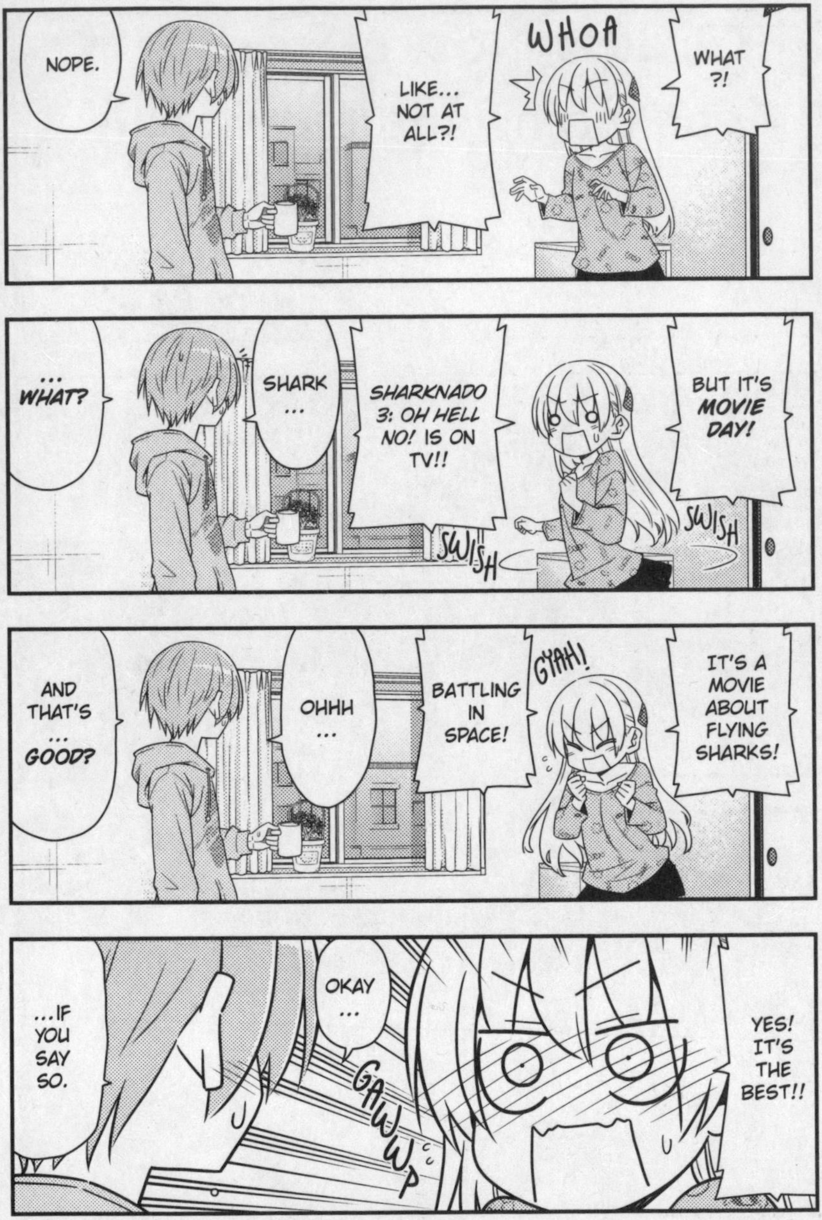
WHAT?!
WHOA
LIKE... NOT AT ALL?!
NOPE.
BUT IT'S MOVIE DAY!
SWISH
SHARKNADO 3: OH HELL NO! IS ON TV!!
SWISH
SHARK...
...WHAT?
IT'S A MOVIE ABOUT FLYING SHARKS!
GYAH!
BATTLING IN SPACE!
OHHH...
AND THAT'S... GOOD?
YES! IT'S THE BEST!!
GAWWP
OKAY...
...IF YOU SAY SO.

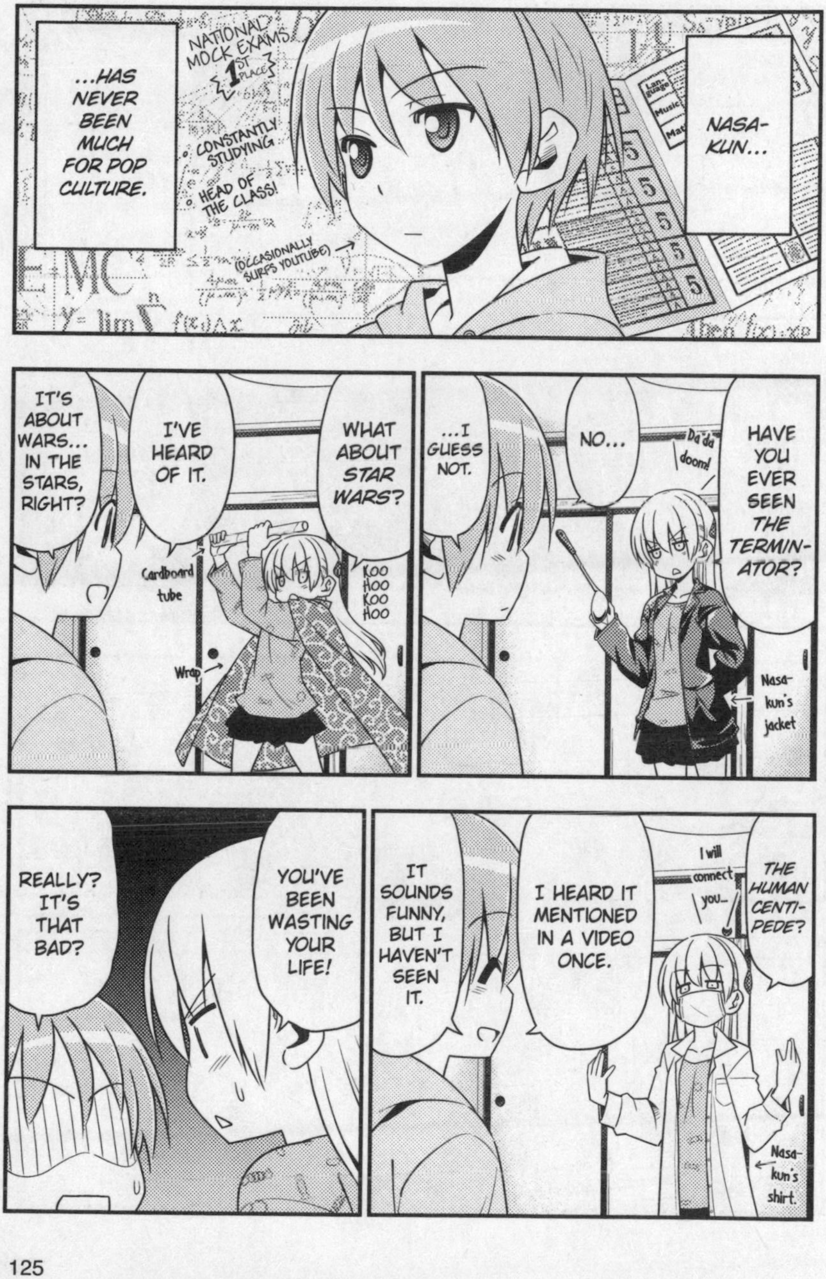
NASA-KUN...
NATIONAL MOCK EXAMS 1ST PLACE
CONSTANTLY STUDYING
HEAD OF THE CLASS!
(OCCASIONALLY SURFS YOUTUBE)
Language
Music
...HAS NEVER BEEN MUCH FOR POP CULTURE.
HAVE YOU EVER SEEN THE TERMINATOR?
Da'da doom!
NO...
...I GUESS NOT.
Nasa-kun's jacket
WHAT ABOUT STAR WARS?
KOO HOO KOO HOO
I'VE HEARD OF IT.
IT'S ABOUT WARS... IN THE STARS, RIGHT?
Cardboard tube
Wrap
THE HUMAN CENTIPEDE?
I will connect you...
I HEARD IT MENTIONED IN A VIDEO ONCE.
IT SOUNDS FUNNY, BUT I HAVEN'T SEEN IT.
Nasa-kun's shirt.
YOU'VE BEEN WASTING YOUR LIFE!
REALLY? IT'S THAT BAD?

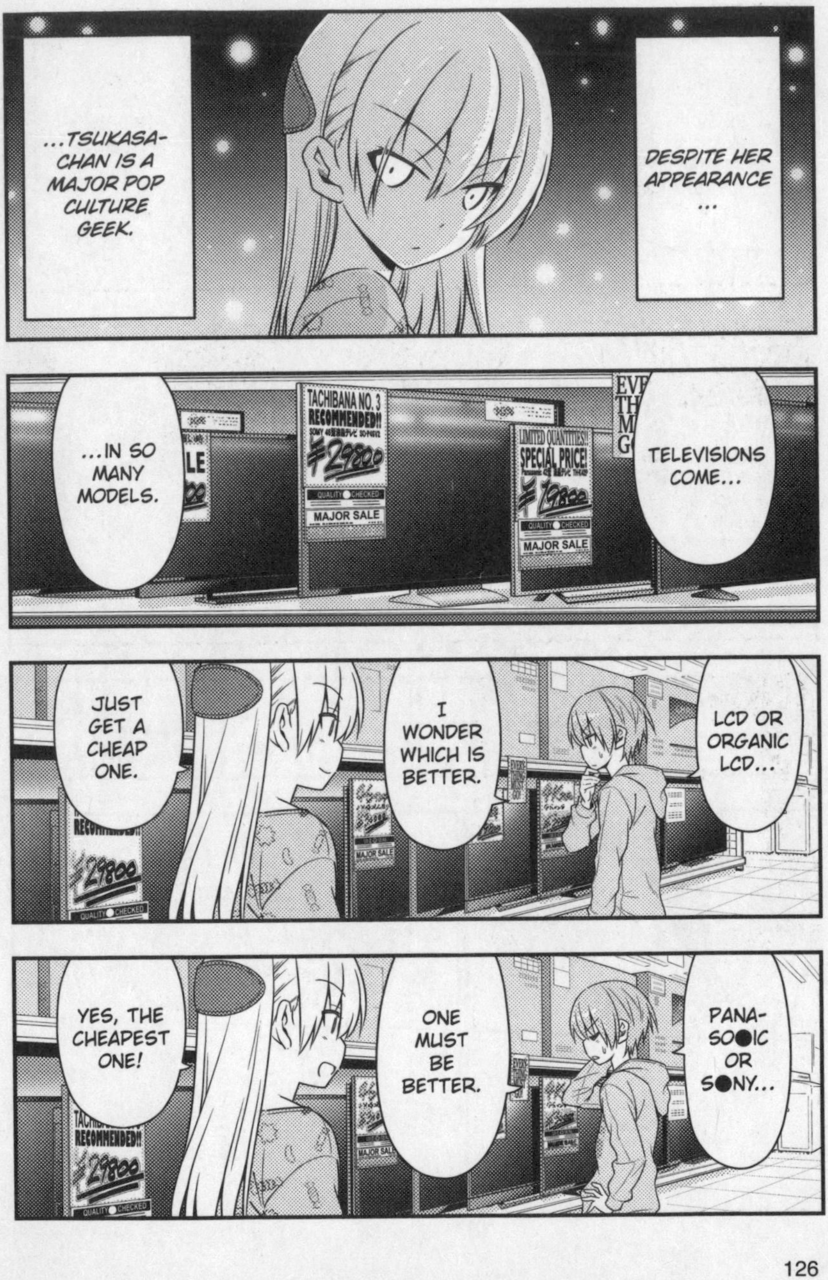
DESPITE HER APPEARANCE ...
...TSUKASA-CHAN IS A MAJOR POP CULTURE GEEK.
TELEVISIONS COME...
...IN SO MANY MODELS.
TACHIBANA NO. 3 RECOMMENDED!!
¥29800
QUALITY CHECKED
MAJOR SALE
LIMITED QUANTITIES!! SPECIAL PRICE!
LCD OR ORGANIC LCD...
I WONDER WHICH IS BETTER.
JUST GET A CHEAP ONE.
PANA-SO●IC OR S●NY...
ONE MUST BE BETTER.
YES, THE CHEAPEST ONE!

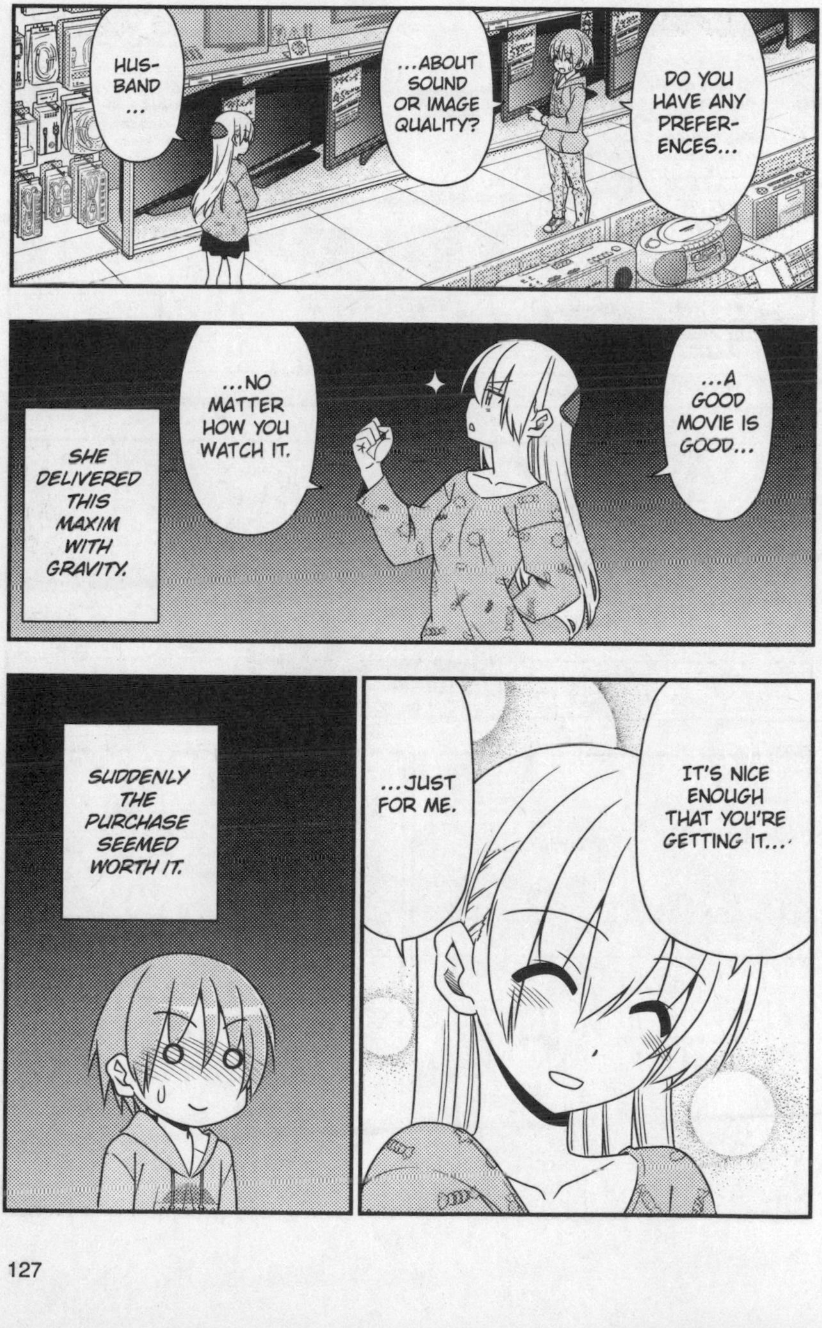
DO YOU HAVE ANY PREFER-ENCES...
...ABOUT SOUND OR IMAGE QUALITY?
HUS-BAND...
...A GOOD MOVIE IS GOOD...
...NO MATTER HOW YOU WATCH IT.
SHE DELIVERED THIS MAXIM WITH GRAVITY.
IT'S NICE ENOUGH THAT YOU'RE GETTING IT...
...JUST FOR ME.
SUDDENLY THE PURCHASE SEEMED WORTH IT.

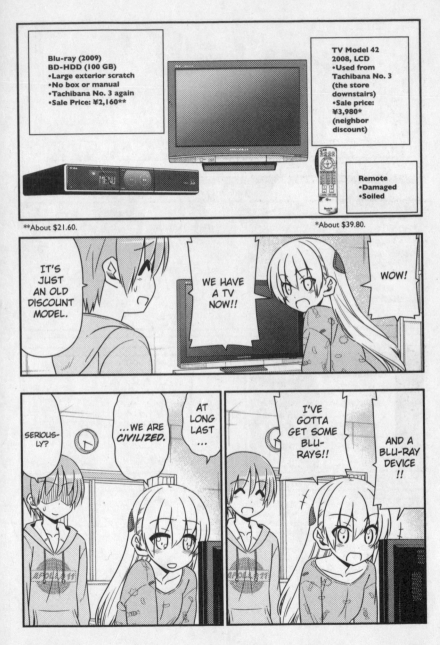

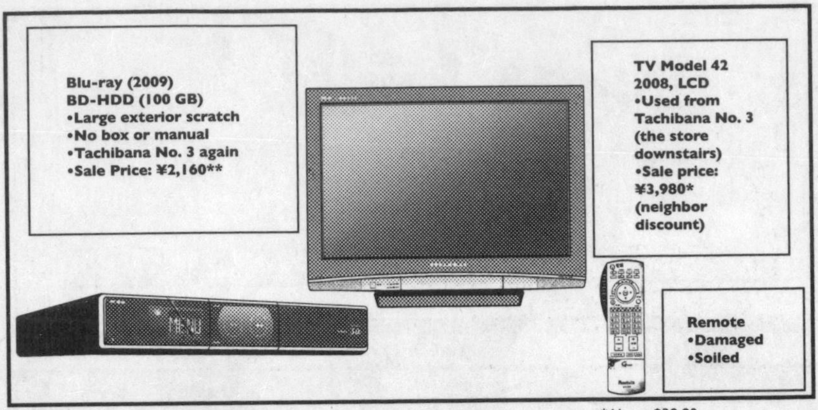
TV Model 42
2008, LCD
•Used from Tachibana No. 3 (the store downstairs)
•Sale price: ¥3,980*
(neighbor discount)
Remote
•Damaged
•Soiled
Blu-ray (2009)
BD-HDD (100 GB)
•Large exterior scratch
•No box or manual
•Tachibana No. 3 again
•Sale Price: ¥2,160**

*About $39.80.

**About $21.60.

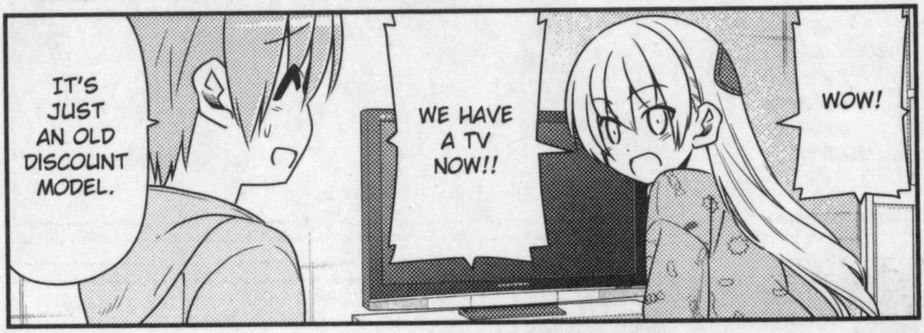
WOW!
WE HAVE A TV NOW!!
IT'S JUST AN OLD DISCOUNT MODEL.

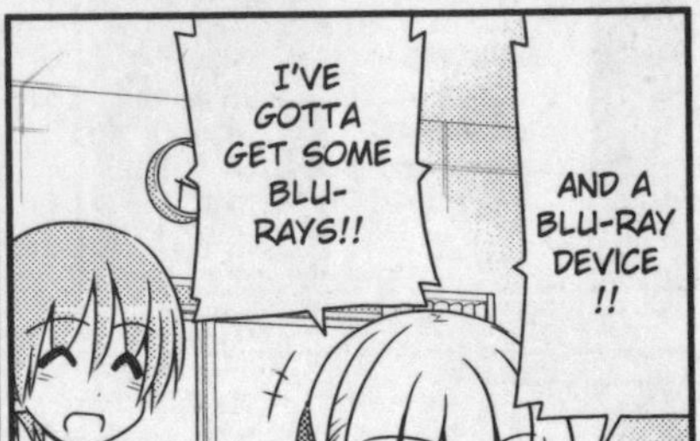
AND A BLU-RAY DEVICE !!
I'VE GOTTA GET SOME BLU-RAYS!!

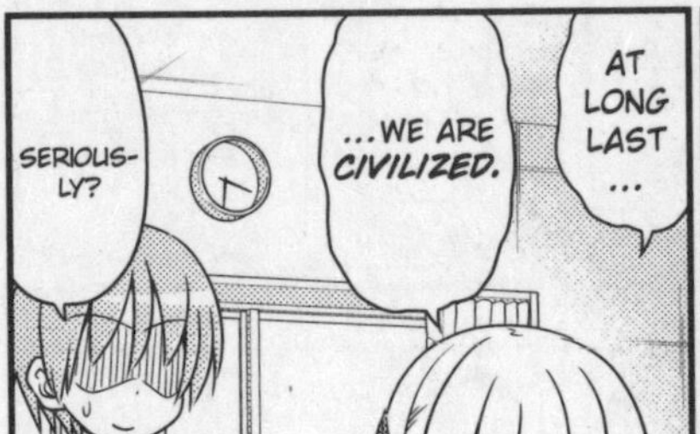
AT LONG LAST ...
...WE ARE *CIVILIZED.*
SERIOUS-LY?

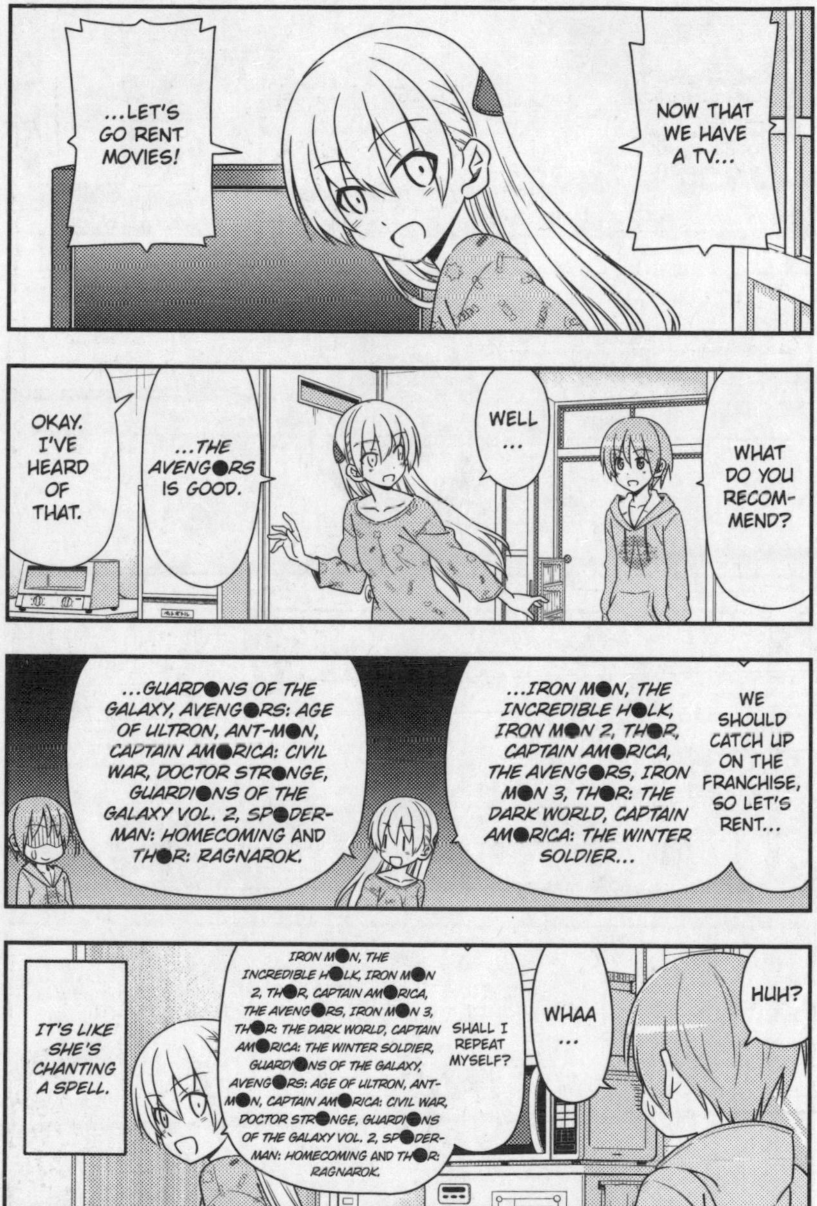
NOW THAT WE HAVE A TV...
...LET'S GO RENT MOVIES!
WHAT DO YOU RECOM-MEND?
WELL ...
...THE AVENG●RS IS GOOD.
OKAY. I'VE HEARD OF THAT.
WE SHOULD CATCH UP ON THE FRANCHISE, SO LET'S RENT...
...IRON M●N, THE INCREDIBLE H●LK, IRON M●N 2, TH●R, CAPTAIN AM●RICA, THE AVENG●RS, IRON M●N 3, TH●R: THE DARK WORLD, CAPTAIN AM●RICA: THE WINTER SOLDIER...
...GUARD●NS OF THE GALAXY, AVENG●RS: AGE OF ULTRON, ANT-M●N, CAPTAIN AM●RICA: CIVIL WAR, DOCTOR STR●NGE, GUARDI●NS OF THE GALAXY VOL. 2, SP●DER-MAN: HOMECOMING AND TH●R: RAGNAROK.
HUH?
WHAA ...
SHALL I REPEAT MYSELF?
IRON M●N, THE INCREDIBLE H●LK, IRON M●N 2, TH●R, CAPTAIN AM●RICA, THE AVENG●RS, IRON M●N 3, TH●R: THE DARK WORLD, CAPTAIN AM●RICA: THE WINTER SOLDIER, GUARDI●NS OF THE GALAXY, AVENG●RS: AGE OF ULTRON, ANT-M●N, CAPTAIN AM●RICA: CIVIL WAR, DOCTOR STR●NGE, GUARDI●NS OF THE GALAXY VOL. 2, SP●DER-MAN: HOMECOMING AND TH●R: RAGNAROK.
IT'S LIKE SHE'S CHANTING A SPELL.

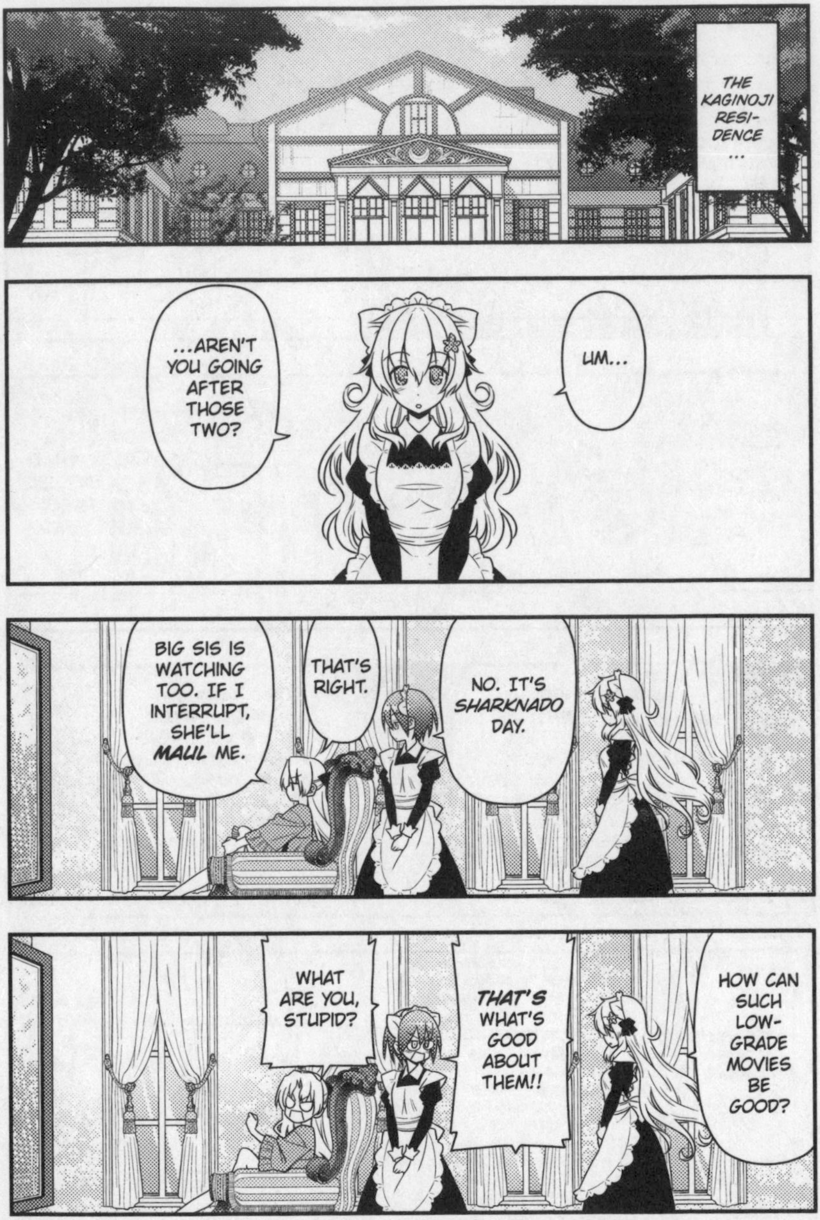
THE KAGINOJI RESI-DENCE ...
UM...
...AREN'T YOU GOING AFTER THOSE TWO?
NO. IT'S SHARKNADO DAY.
THAT'S RIGHT.
BIG SIS IS WATCHING TOO. IF I INTERRUPT, SHE'LL MAUL ME.
HOW CAN SUCH LOW-GRADE MOVIES BE GOOD?
THAT'S WHAT'S GOOD ABOUT THEM!!
WHAT ARE YOU, STUPID?

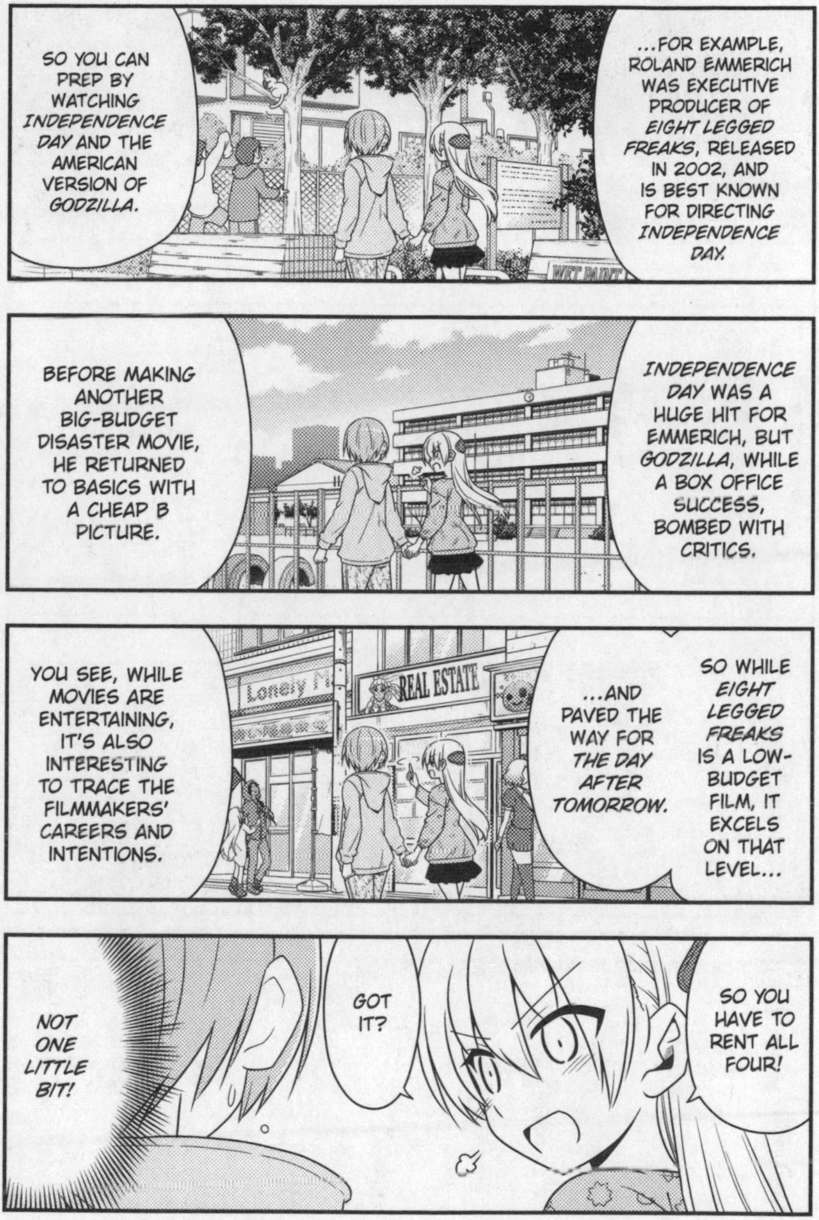
...FOR EXAMPLE, ROLAND EMMERICH WAS EXECUTIVE PRODUCER OF *EIGHT LEGGED FREAKS*, RELEASED IN 2002, AND IS BEST KNOWN FOR DIRECTING *INDEPENDENCE DAY*.
WET PAINT
SO YOU CAN PREP BY WATCHING *INDEPENDENCE DAY* AND THE AMERICAN VERSION OF *GODZILLA*.
INDEPENDENCE DAY WAS A HUGE HIT FOR EMMERICH, BUT *GODZILLA*, WHILE A BOX OFFICE SUCCESS, BOMBED WITH CRITICS.
BEFORE MAKING ANOTHER BIG-BUDGET DISASTER MOVIE, HE RETURNED TO BASICS WITH A CHEAP B PICTURE.
SO WHILE *EIGHT LEGGED FREAKS* IS A LOW-BUDGET FILM, IT EXCELS ON THAT LEVEL...
...AND PAVED THE WAY FOR *THE DAY AFTER TOMORROW*.
REAL ESTATE
YOU SEE, WHILE MOVIES ARE ENTERTAINING, IT'S ALSO INTERESTING TO TRACE THE FILMMAKERS' CAREERS AND INTENTIONS.
SO YOU HAVE TO RENT ALL FOUR!
GOT IT?
NOT ONE LITTLE BIT!

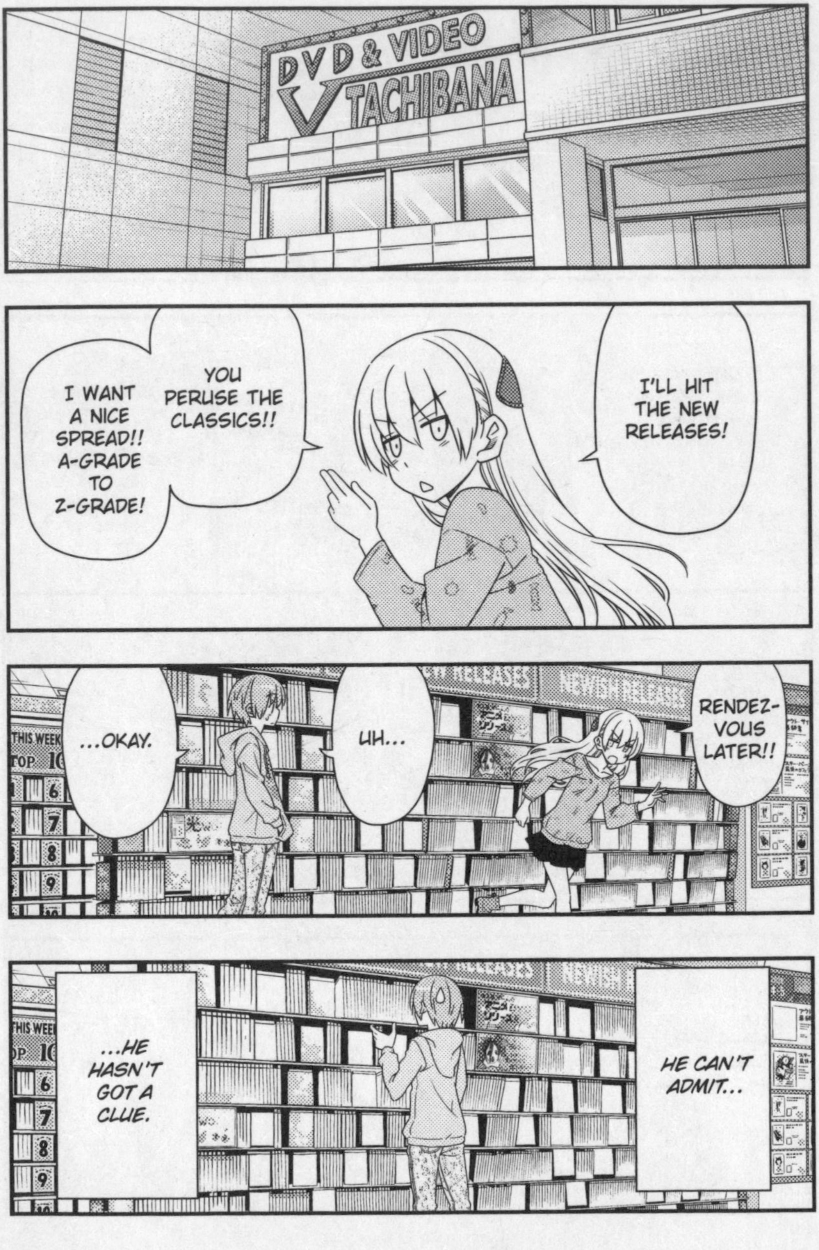
DVD & VIDEO
TACHIBANA
I'LL HIT THE NEW RELEASES!
YOU PERUSE THE CLASSICS!!
I WANT A NICE SPREAD!! A-GRADE TO Z-GRADE!
NEWISH RELEASES
RENDEZ-VOUS LATER!!
UH...
...OKAY.
HE CAN'T ADMIT...
...HE HASN'T GOT A CLUE.

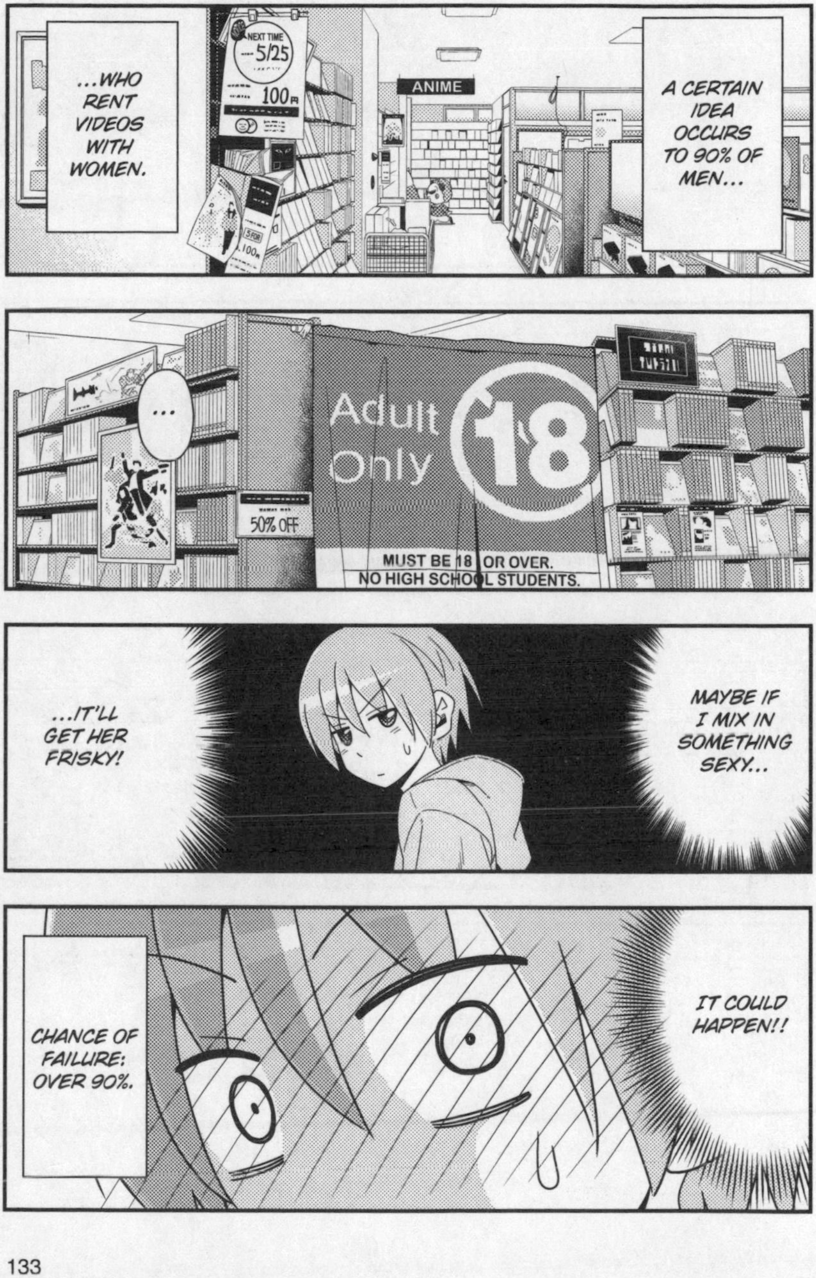
A CERTAIN IDEA OCCURS TO 90% OF MEN...
ANIME
NEXT TIME
5/25
100円
5 FOR
100円
...WHO RENT VIDEOS WITH WOMEN.
Adult Only 18
MUST BE 18 OR OVER.
NO HIGH SCHOOL STUDENTS.
50% OFF
...
MAYBE IF I MIX IN SOMETHING SEXY...
...IT'LL GET HER FRISKY!
IT COULD HAPPEN!!
CHANCE OF FAILURE: OVER 90%.

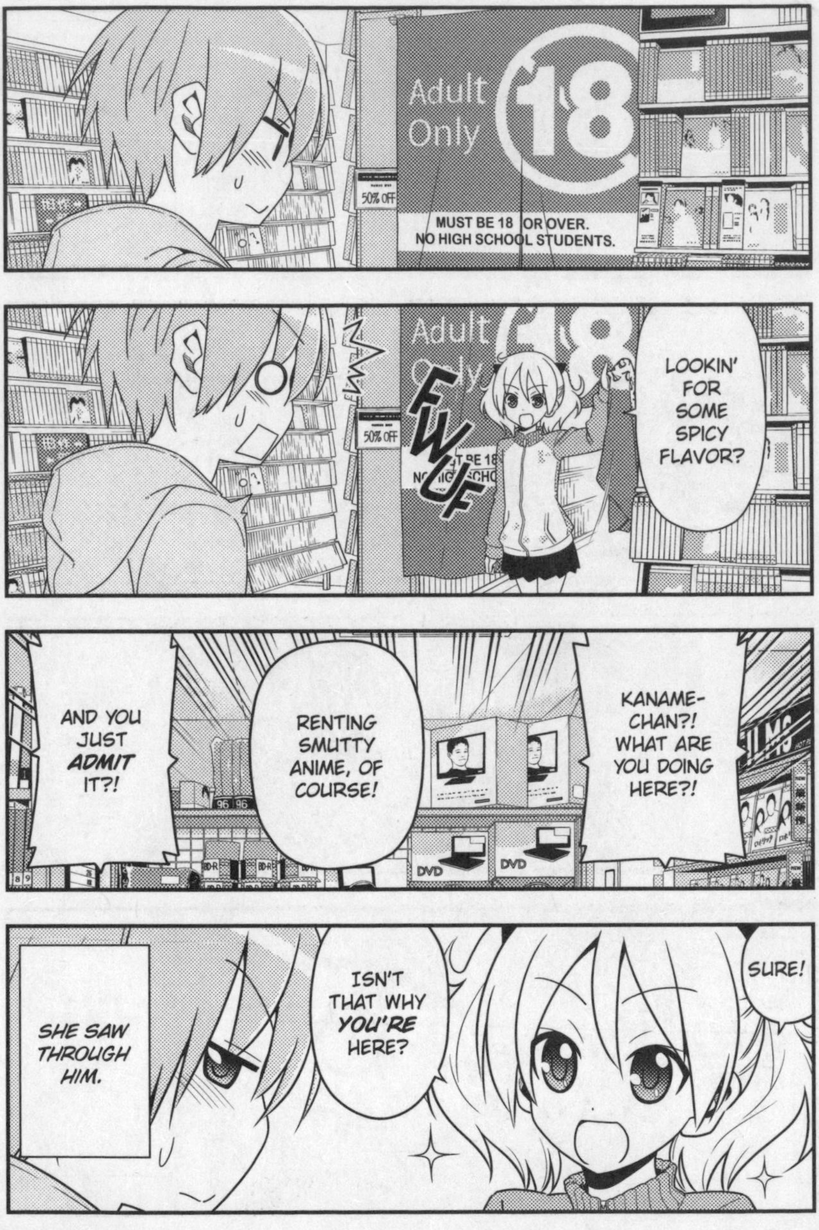
Adult Only 18
MUST BE 18 OR OVER. NO HIGH SCHOOL STUDENTS.
50% OFF
LOOKIN' FOR SOME SPICY FLAVOR?
FWUF
KANAME-CHAN?! WHAT ARE YOU DOING HERE?!
RENTING SMUTTY ANIME, OF COURSE!
AND YOU JUST *ADMIT* IT?!
DVD
DVD
SURE!
ISN'T THAT WHY *YOU'RE* HERE?
SHE SAW THROUGH HIM.

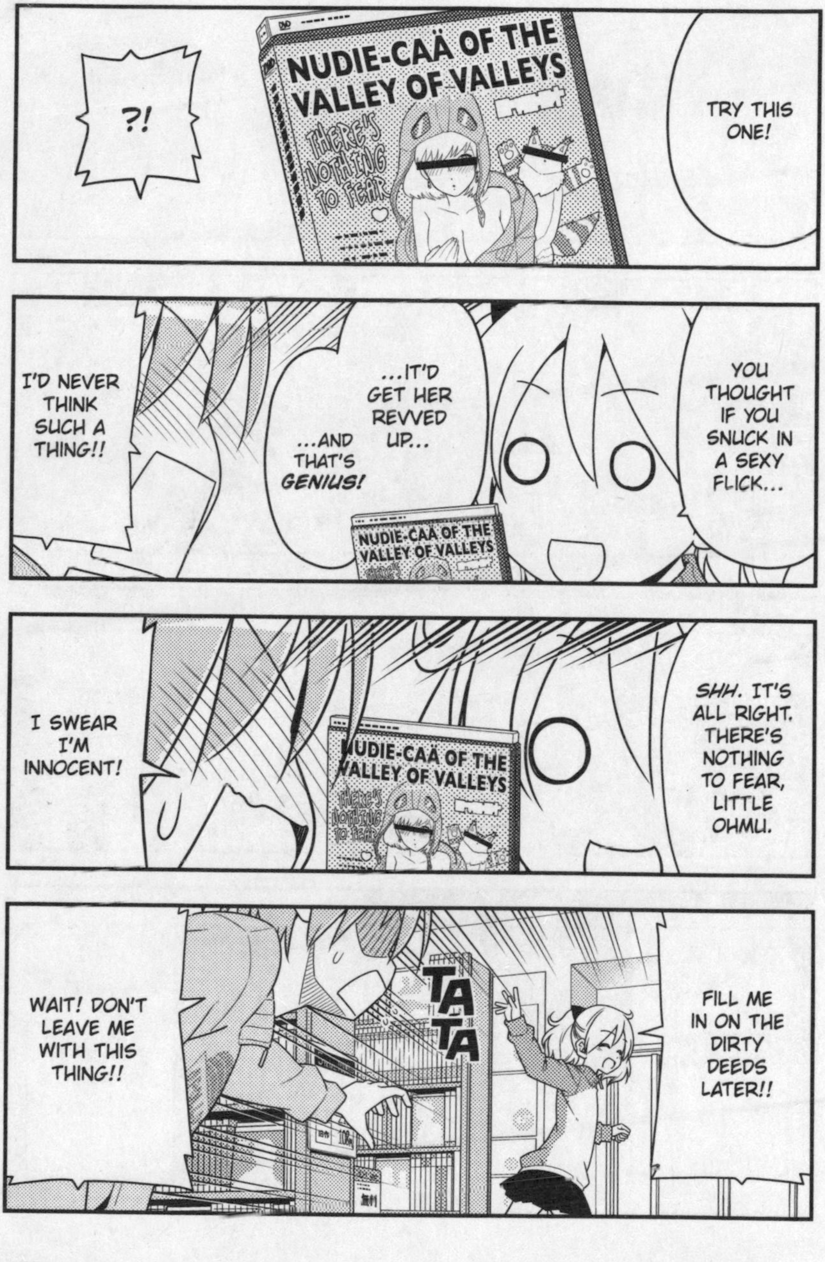
TRY THIS ONE!
NUDIE-CAÄ OF THE VALLEY OF VALLEYS
THERE'S NOTHING TO FEAR
?!
YOU THOUGHT IF YOU SNUCK IN A SEXY FLICK...
...IT'D GET HER REVVED UP...
...AND THAT'S *GENIUS!*
NUDIE-CAA OF THE VALLEY OF VALLEYS
I'D NEVER THINK SUCH A THING!!
SHH. IT'S ALL RIGHT. THERE'S NOTHING TO FEAR, LITTLE OHMU.
NUDIE-CAÄ OF THE VALLEY OF VALLEYS
THERE'S NOTHING TO FEAR
I SWEAR I'M INNOCENT!
FILL ME IN ON THE DIRTY DEEDS LATER!!
TATA
WAIT! DON'T LEAVE ME WITH THIS THING!!

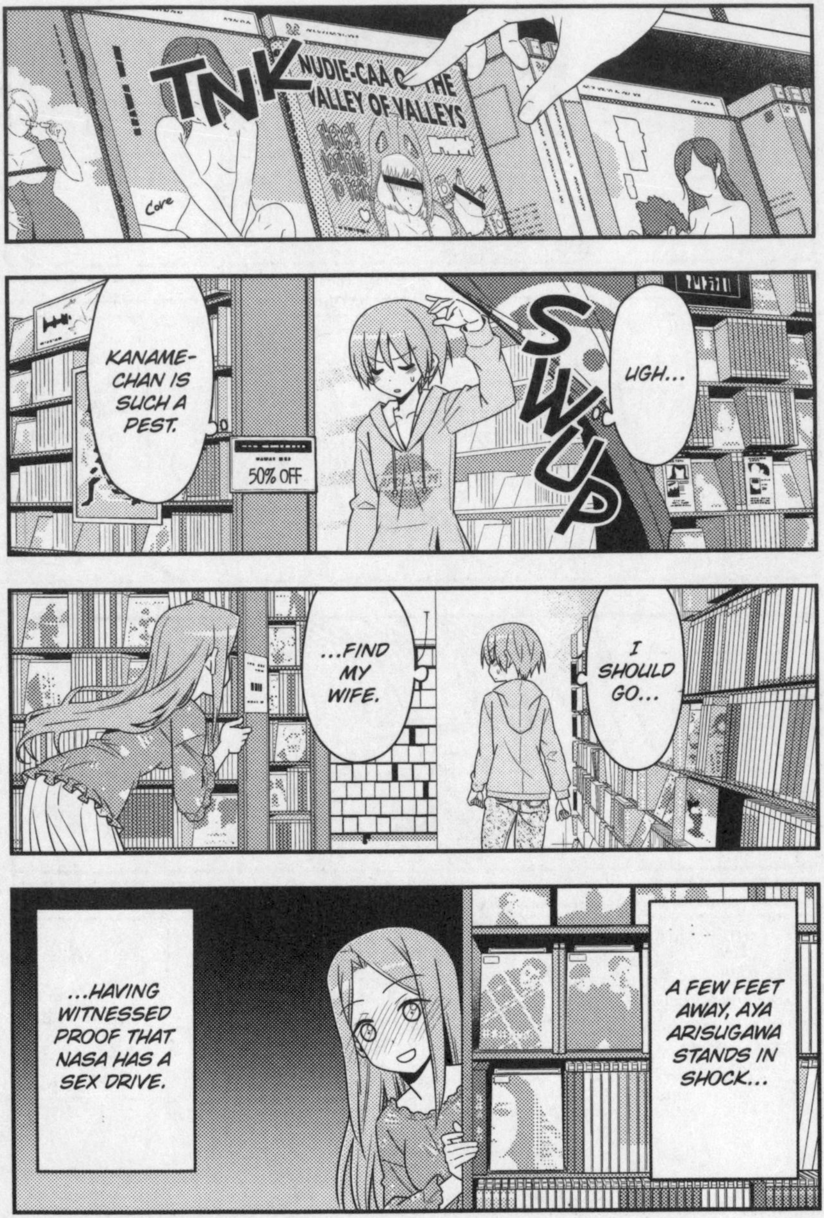
TNK
NUDIE-CAA
THE
VALLEY OF VALLEYS
UGH...
SWUP
50% OFF
KANAME-CHAN IS SUCH A PEST.
I SHOULD GO...
...FIND MY WIFE.
A FEW FEET AWAY, AYA ARISUGAWA STANDS IN SHOCK...
...HAVING WITNESSED PROOF THAT NASA HAS A SEX DRIVE.

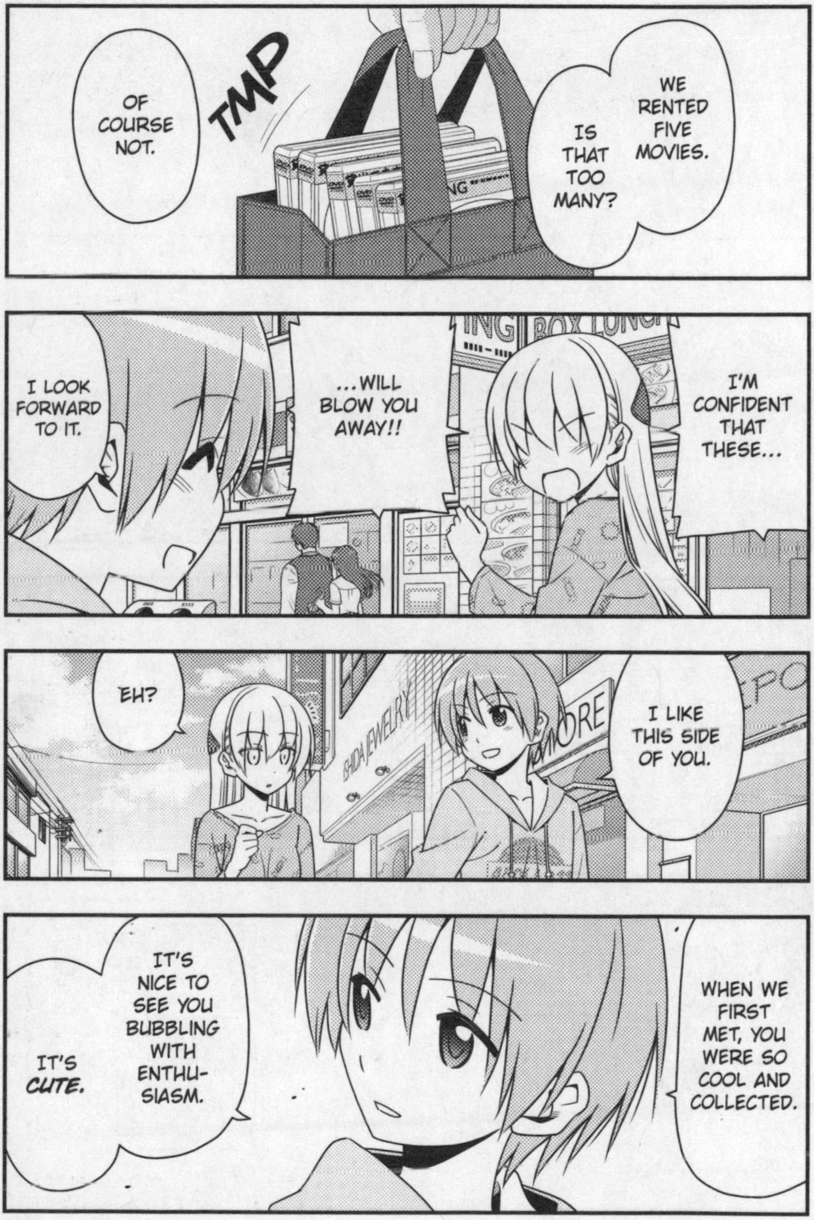
WE RENTED FIVE MOVIES.
IS THAT TOO MANY?
TMP
OF COURSE NOT.
I'M CONFIDENT THAT THESE...
...WILL BLOW YOU AWAY!!
I LOOK FORWARD TO IT.
I LIKE THIS SIDE OF YOU.
ISHIDA JEWELRY
EH?
WHEN WE FIRST MET, YOU WERE SO COOL AND COLLECTED.
IT'S NICE TO SEE YOU BUBBLING WITH ENTHUSIASM.
IT'S *CUTE.*

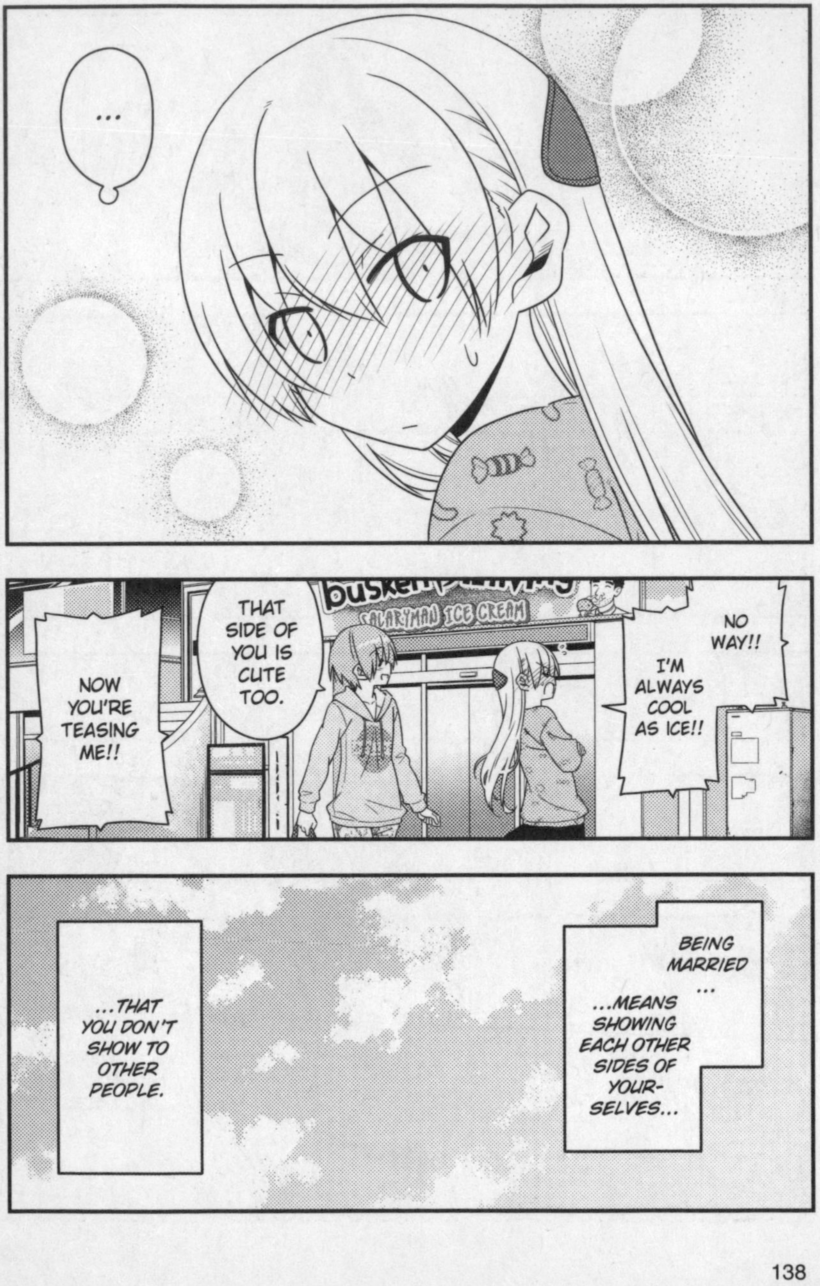
...
NO WAY!! I'M ALWAYS COOL AS ICE!!
SALARYMAN ICE CREAM
THAT SIDE OF YOU IS CUTE TOO.
NOW YOU'RE TEASING ME!!
BEING MARRIED... ...MEANS SHOWING EACH OTHER SIDES OF YOURSELVES...
...THAT YOU DON'T SHOW TO OTHER PEOPLE.

Chapter 16: "A Chapter So Sweet You Can't Help Picturing Dark Alternate Timelines"

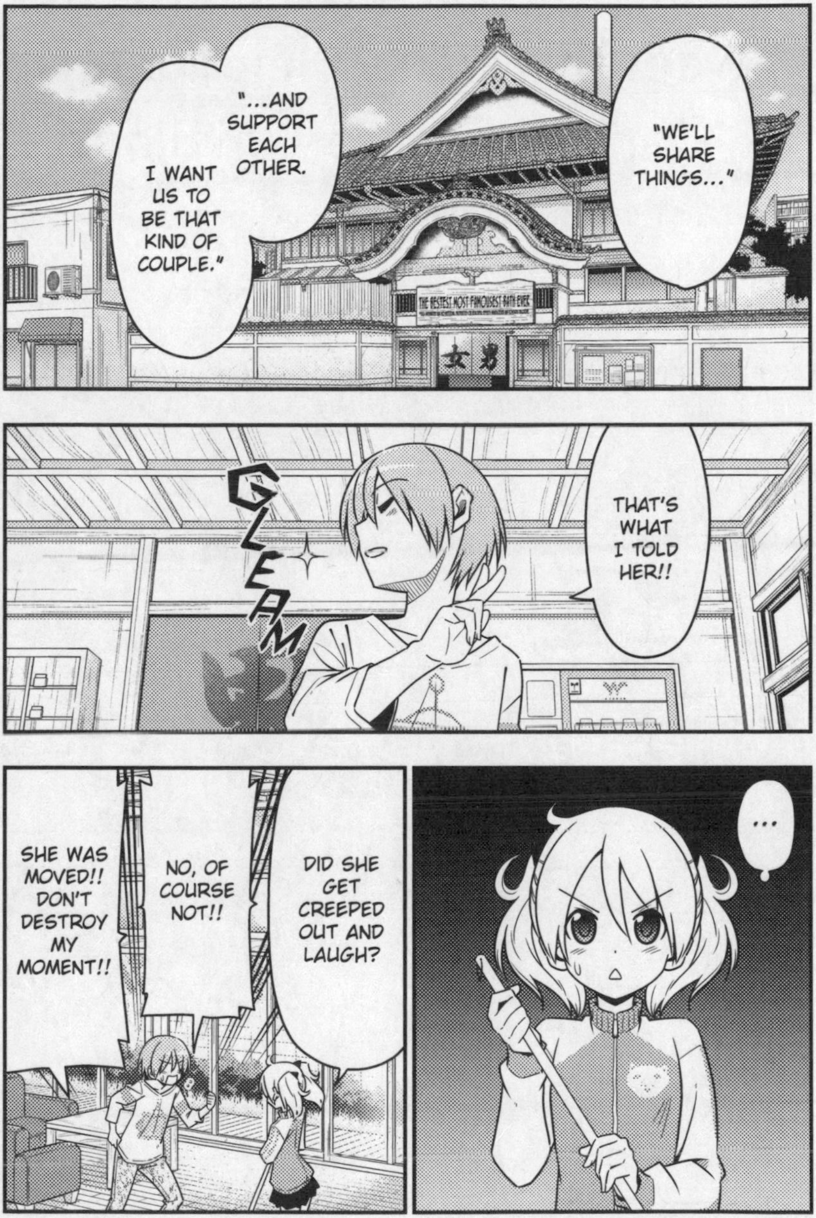
"WE'LL SHARE THINGS..."
"...AND SUPPORT EACH OTHER.
I WANT US TO BE THAT KIND OF COUPLE."
THE BESTEST MOST FAMOUSEST BATH EVER
女 男
GLEAM
THAT'S WHAT I TOLD HER!!
...
DID SHE GET CREEPED OUT AND LAUGH?
NO, OF COURSE NOT!!
SHE WAS MOVED!! DON'T DESTROY MY MOMENT!!

Chapter 16: "A Chapter So Sweet You Can't Help Picturing Dark Alternate Timelines"

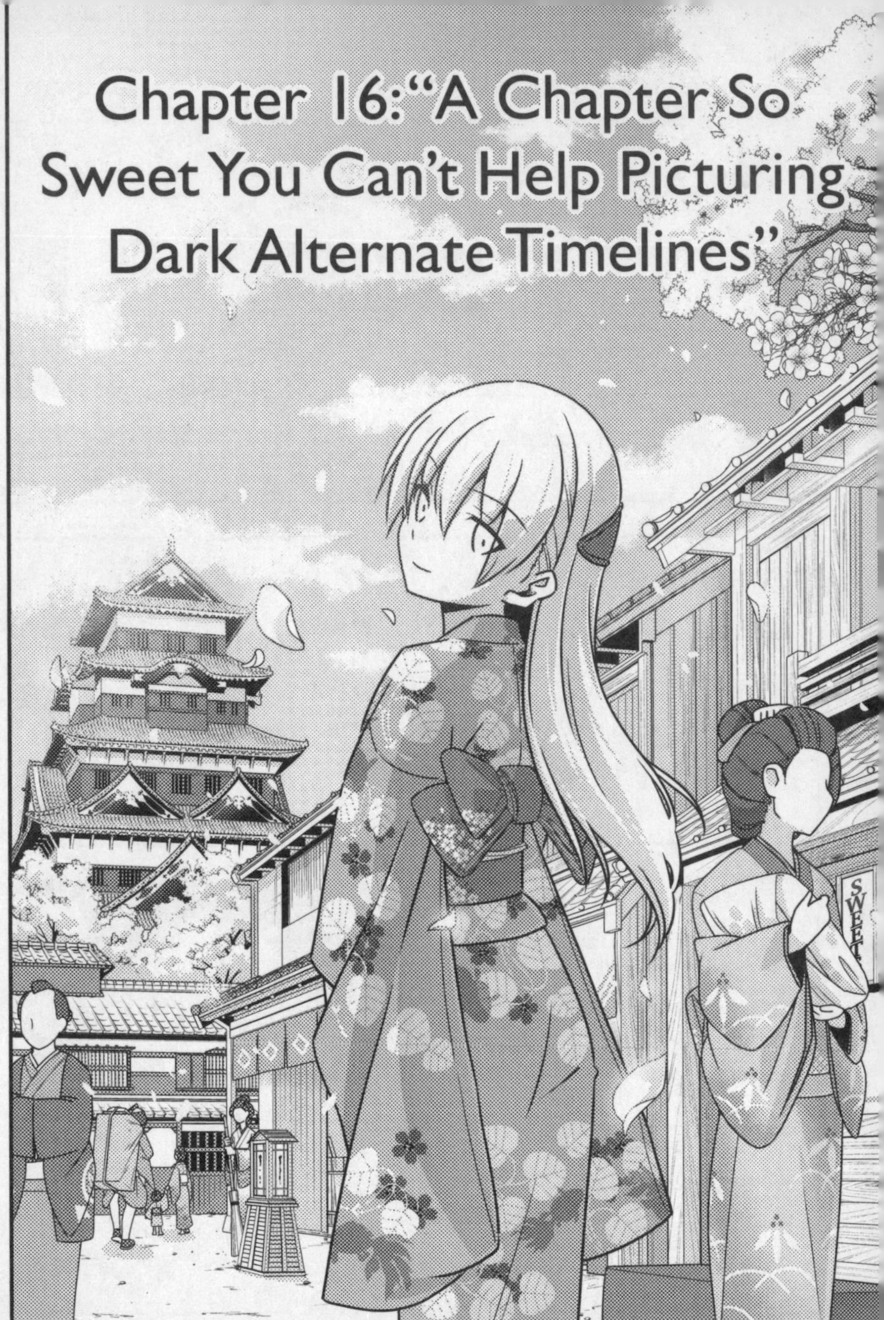
SWEET

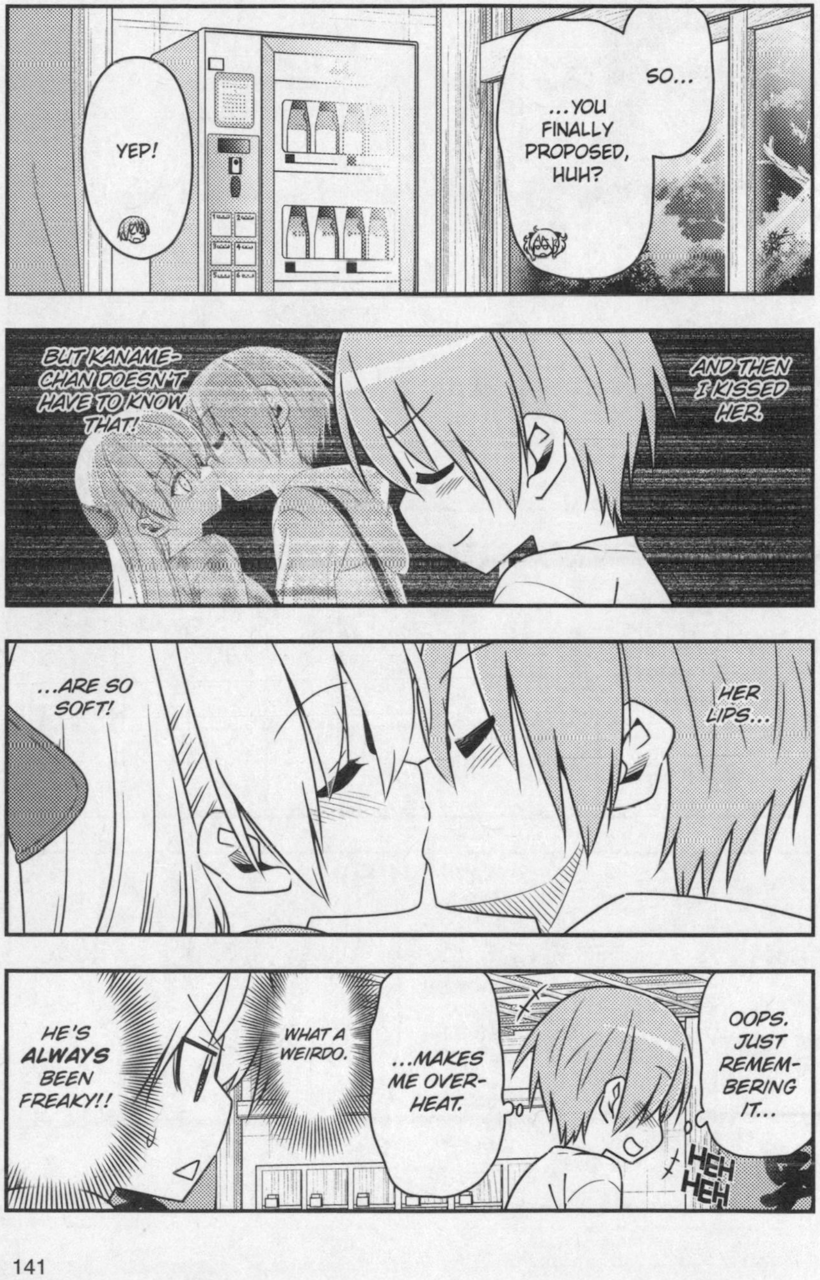
SO...
...YOU FINALLY PROPOSED, HUH?
YEP!
AND THEN I KISSED HER.
BUT KANAME-CHAN DOESN'T HAVE TO KNOW THAT!
HER LIPS...
...ARE SO SOFT!
OOPS. JUST REMEM-BERING IT...
HEH HEH
...MAKES ME OVER-HEAT.
WHAT A WEIRDO.
HE'S **ALWAYS** BEEN FREAKY!!

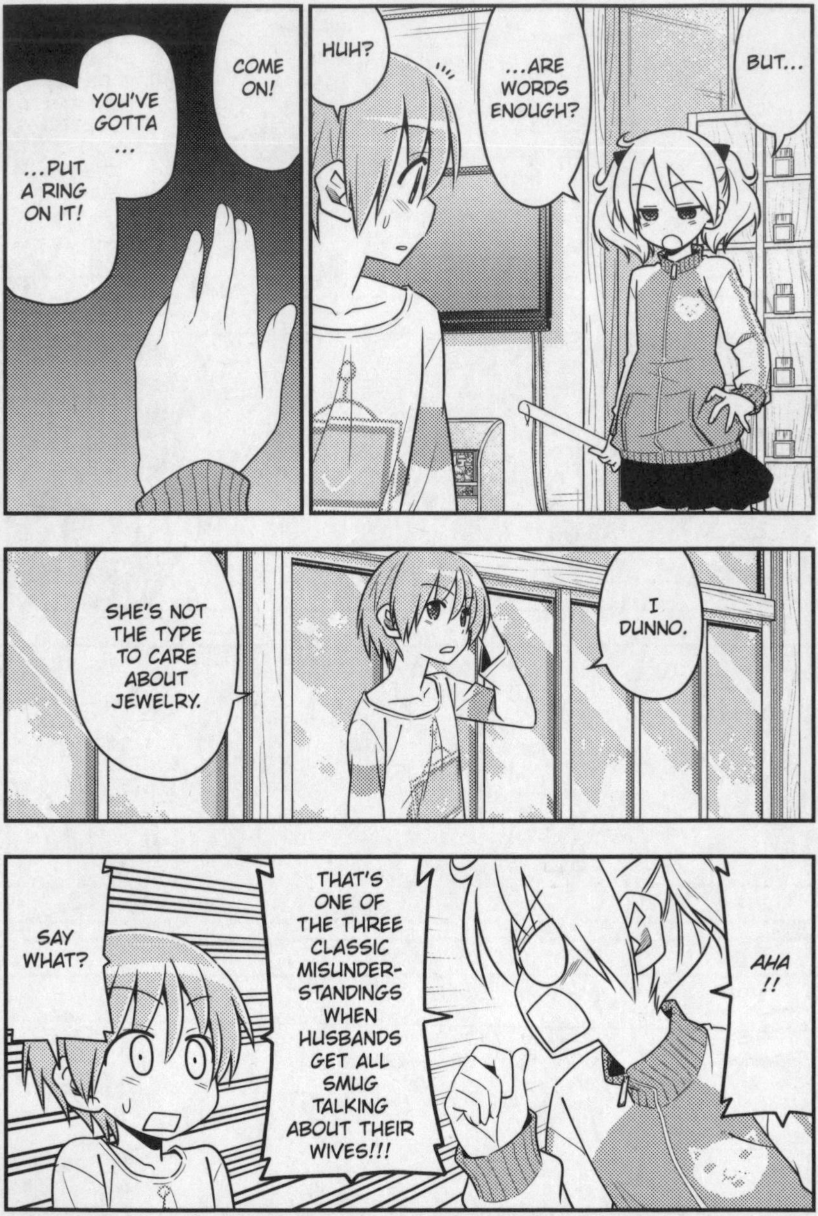
BUT...
...ARE WORDS ENOUGH?
HUH?
COME ON!
YOU'VE GOTTA ...
...PUT A RING ON IT!
I DUNNO.
SHE'S NOT THE TYPE TO CARE ABOUT JEWELRY.
AHA !!
THAT'S ONE OF THE THREE CLASSIC MISUNDER-STANDINGS WHEN HUSBANDS GET ALL SMUG TALKING ABOUT THEIR WIVES!!!
SAY WHAT?

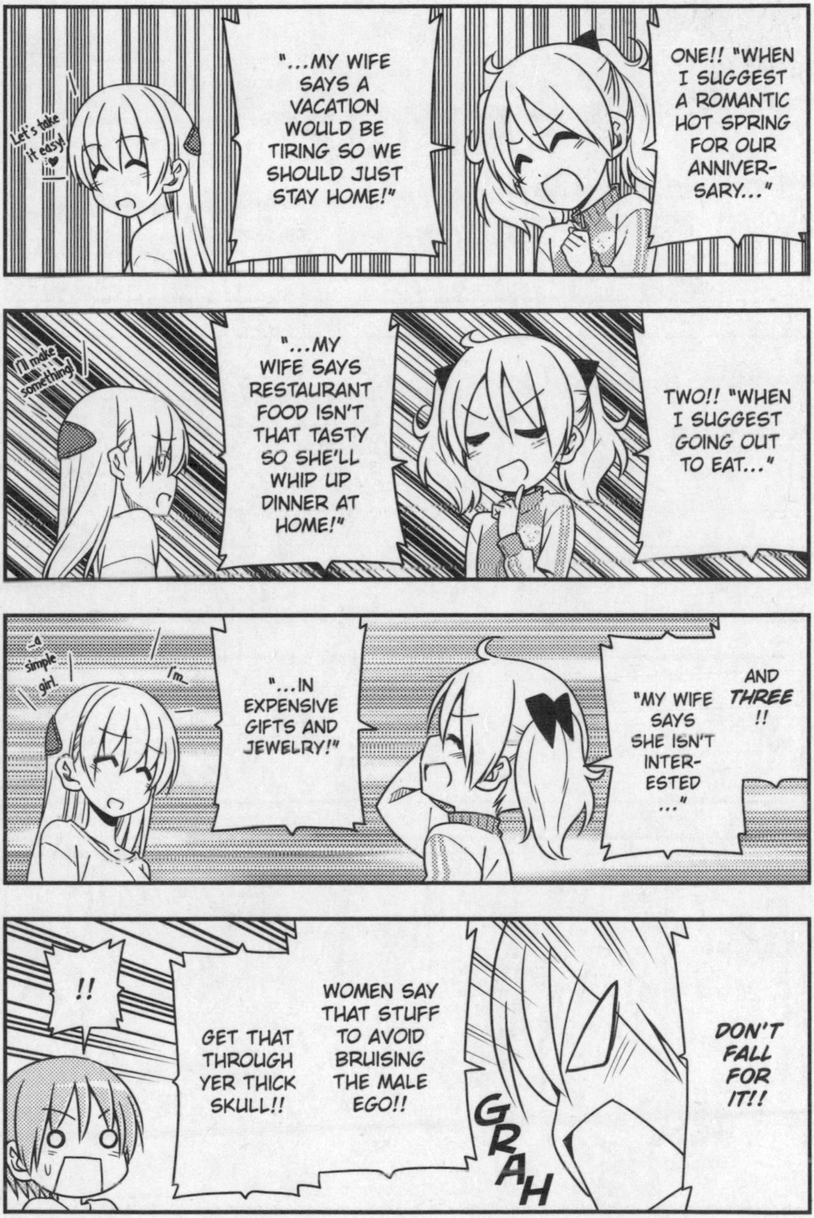
ONE!! "WHEN I SUGGEST A ROMANTIC HOT SPRING FOR OUR ANNIVERSARY..."
"...MY WIFE SAYS A VACATION WOULD BE TIRING SO WE SHOULD JUST STAY HOME!"
Let's take it easy! ♥
TWO!! "WHEN I SUGGEST GOING OUT TO EAT..."
"...MY WIFE SAYS RESTAURANT FOOD ISN'T THAT TASTY SO SHE'LL WHIP UP DINNER AT HOME!"
I'll make something!
AND THREE!!
"MY WIFE SAYS SHE ISN'T INTERESTED..."
"...IN EXPENSIVE GIFTS AND JEWELRY!"
I'm...
...a simple girl.
DON'T FALL FOR IT!!
GRAH
WOMEN SAY THAT STUFF TO AVOID BRUISING THE MALE EGO!!
GET THAT THROUGH YER THICK SKULL!!
!!

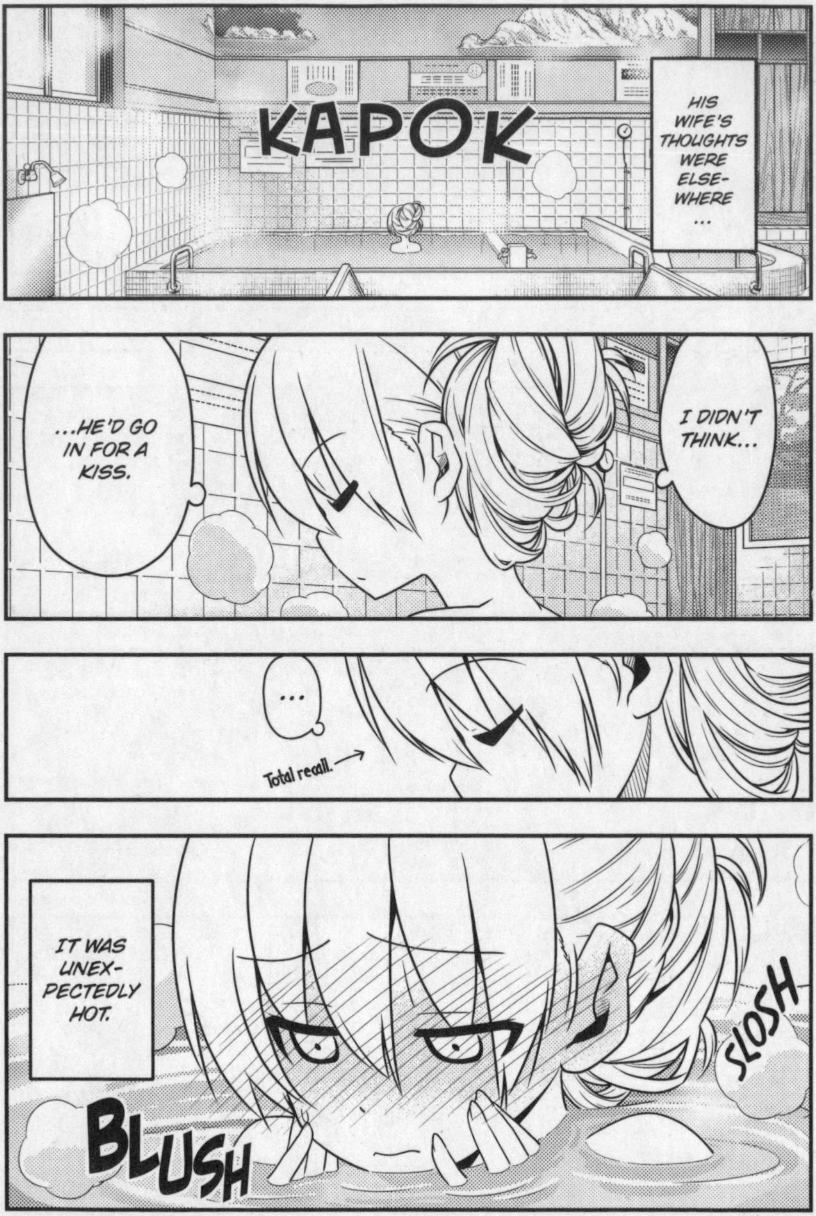
HIS WIFE'S THOUGHTS WERE ELSE-WHERE...
KAPOK
I DIDN'T THINK...
...HE'D GO IN FOR A KISS.
...
Total recall.
SLOSH
IT WAS UNEX-PECTEDLY HOT.
BLUSH

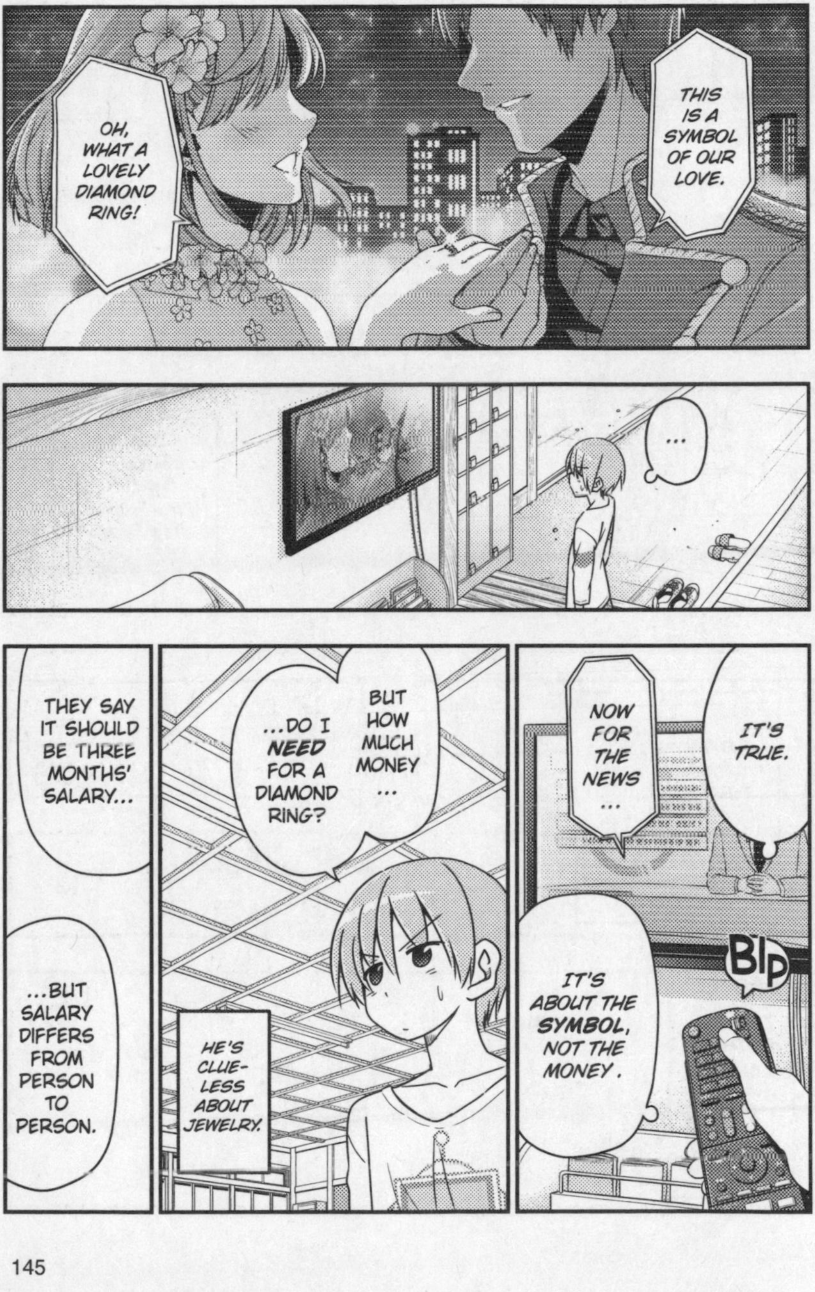
THIS IS A SYMBOL OF OUR LOVE.
OH, WHAT A LOVELY DIAMOND RING!
...
IT'S TRUE.
NOW FOR THE NEWS ...
BIP
IT'S ABOUT THE **SYMBOL**, NOT THE MONEY.
BUT HOW MUCH MONEY ...
...DO I **NEED** FOR A DIAMOND RING?
HE'S CLUELESS ABOUT JEWELRY.
THEY SAY IT SHOULD BE THREE MONTHS' SALARY...
...BUT SALARY DIFFERS FROM PERSON TO PERSON.

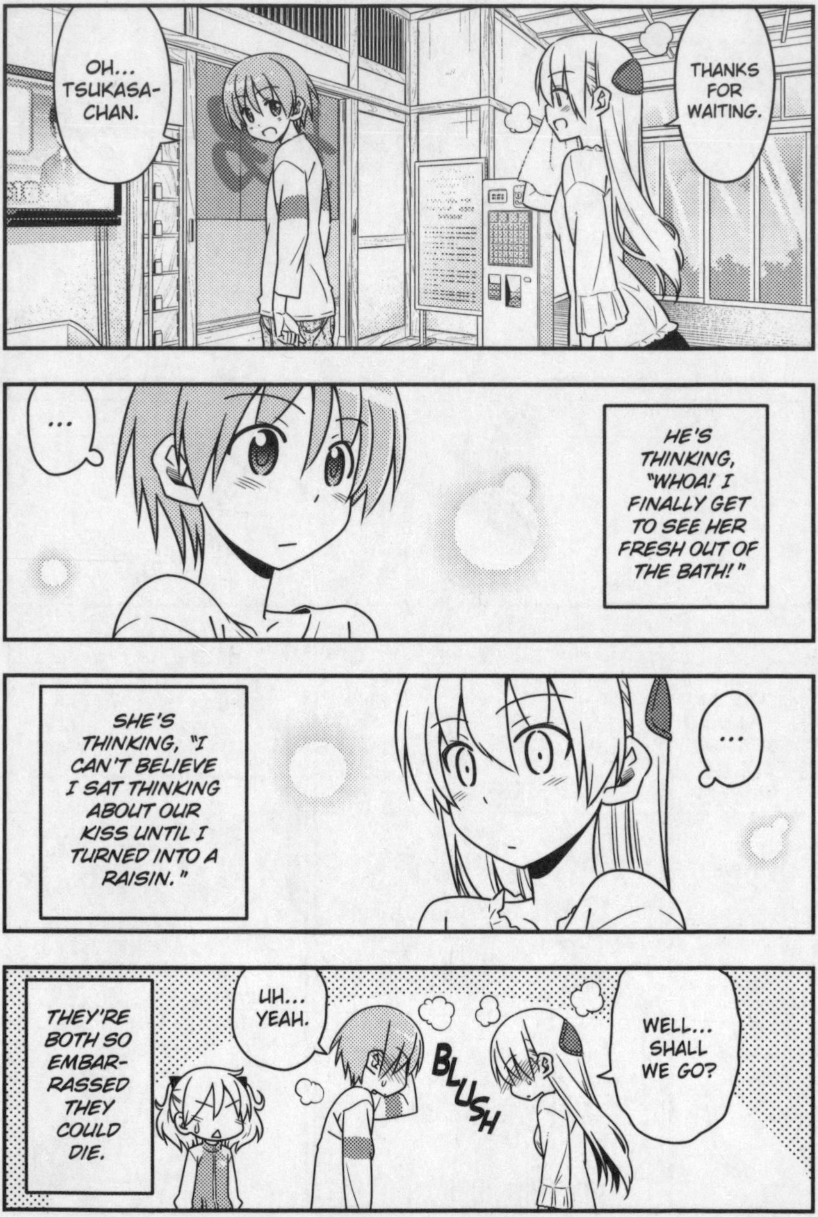
THANKS FOR WAITING.
OH... TSUKASA-CHAN.
HE'S THINKING, "WHOA! I FINALLY GET TO SEE HER FRESH OUT OF THE BATH!"
...
...
SHE'S THINKING, "I CAN'T BELIEVE I SAT THINKING ABOUT OUR KISS UNTIL I TURNED INTO A RAISIN."
WELL... SHALL WE GO?
UH... YEAH.
BLUSH
THEY'RE BOTH SO EMBAR-RASSED THEY COULD DIE.

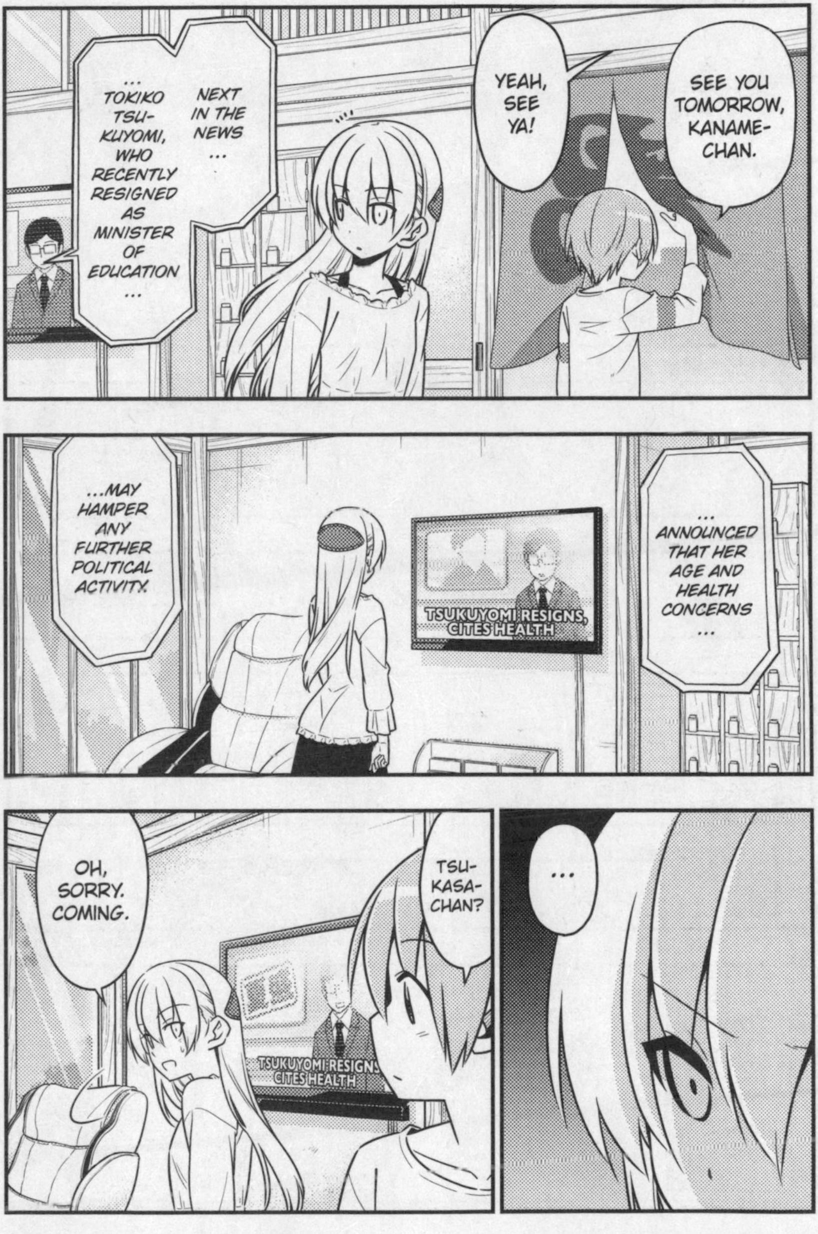
SEE YOU TOMORROW, KANAME-CHAN.
YEAH, SEE YA!
NEXT IN THE NEWS ... ...TOKIKO TSUKUYOMI, WHO RECENTLY RESIGNED AS MINISTER OF EDUCATION ...
... ANNOUNCED THAT HER AGE AND HEALTH CONCERNS ...
TSUKUYOMI RESIGNS, CITES HEALTH
...MAY HAMPER ANY FURTHER POLITICAL ACTIVITY.
...
TSUKASA-CHAN?
OH, SORRY. COMING.
TSUKUYOMI RESIGNS CITES HEALTH

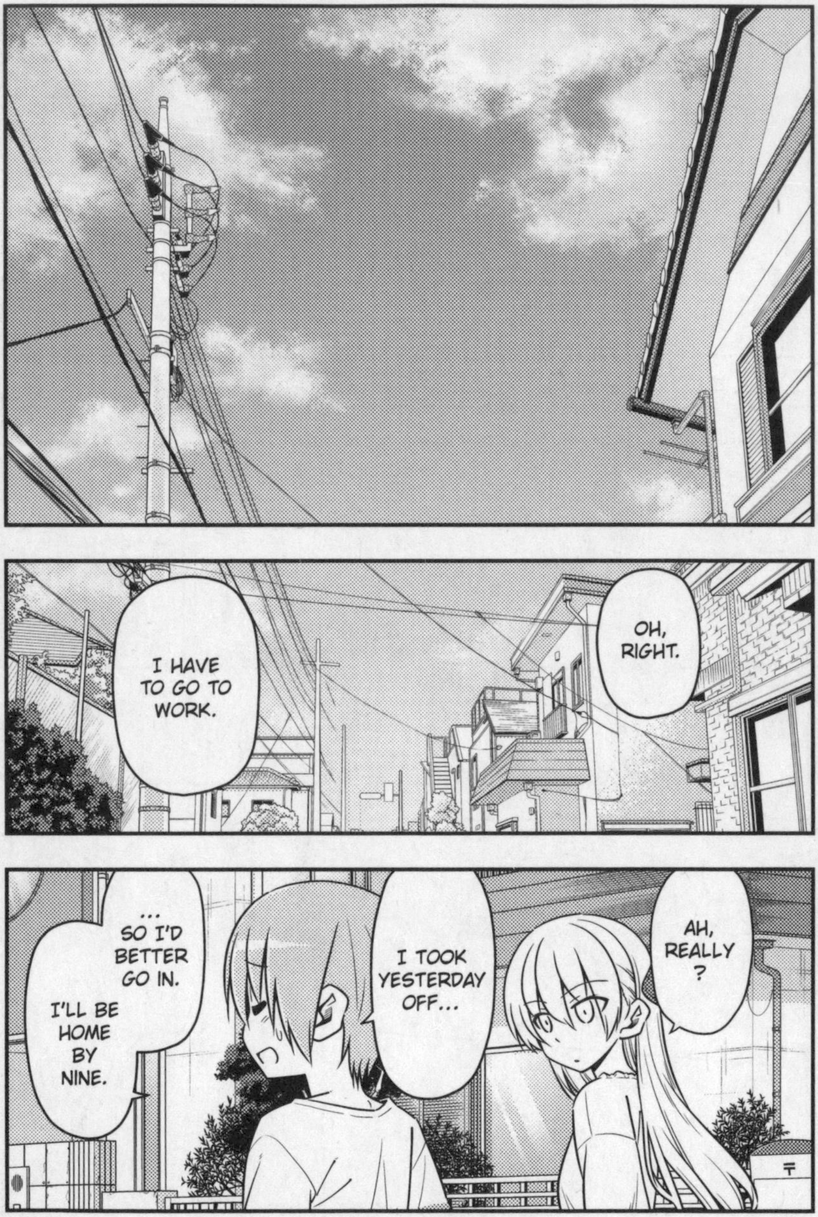
OH, RIGHT.
I HAVE TO GO TO WORK.
AH, REALLY?
I TOOK YESTERDAY OFF...
... SO I'D BETTER GO IN.
I'LL BE HOME BY NINE.

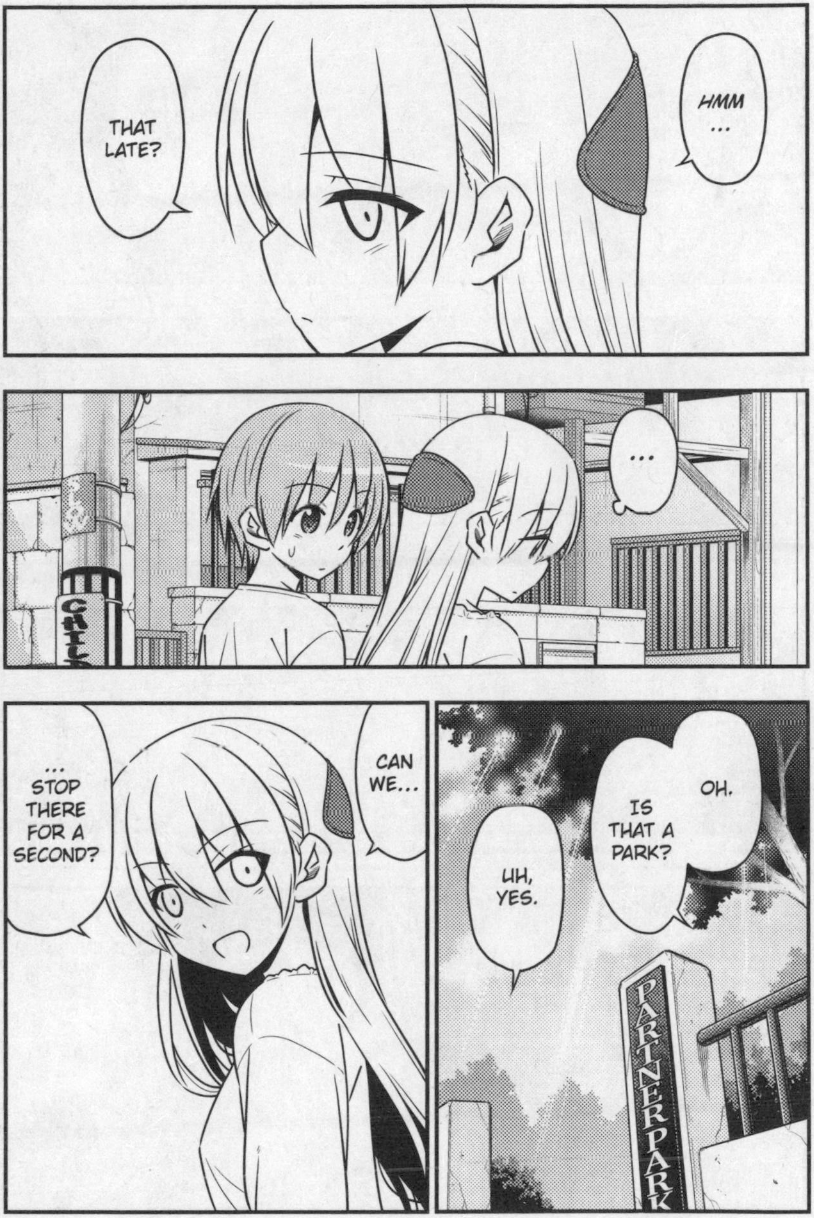
HMM ...
THAT LATE?
...
OH.
IS THAT A PARK?
UH, YES.
PARTNER PARK
CAN WE...
... STOP THERE FOR A SECOND?

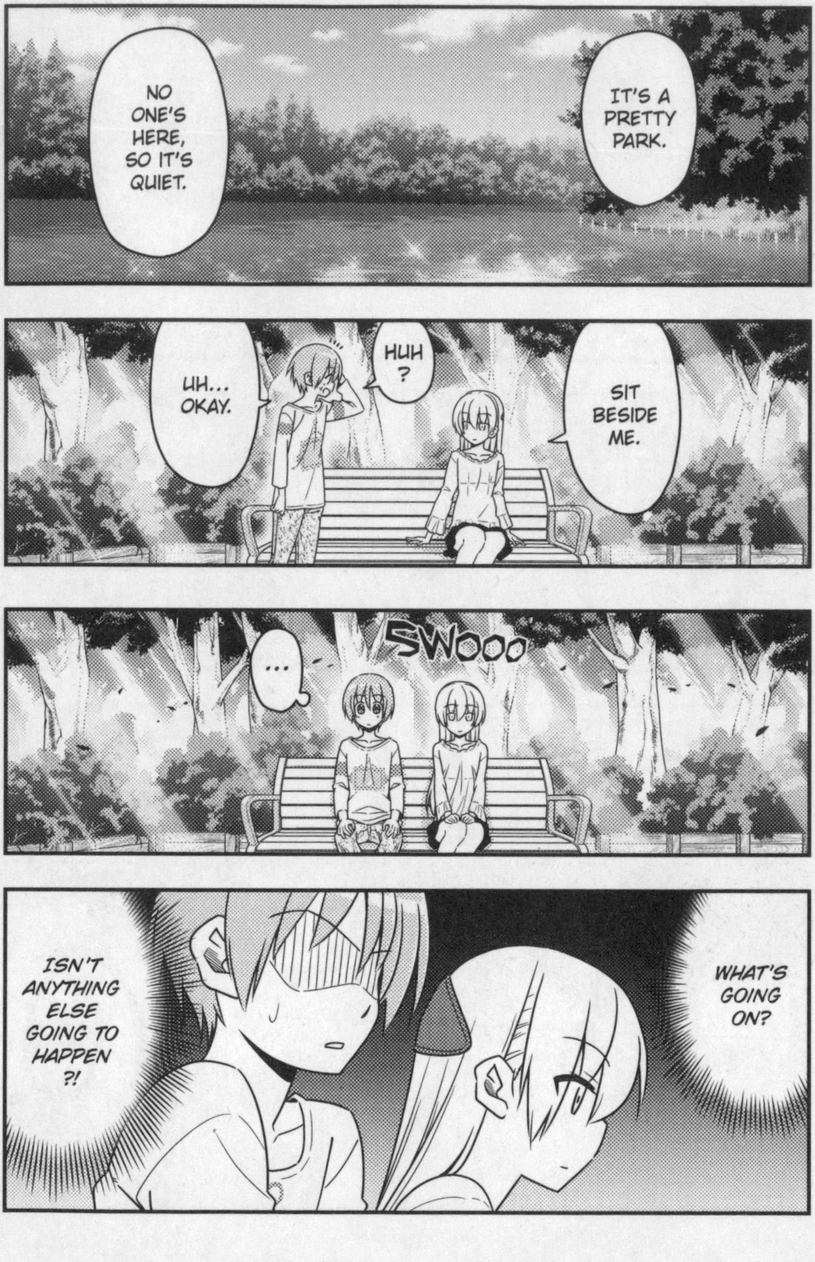
IT'S A PRETTY PARK.
NO ONE'S HERE, SO IT'S QUIET.
SIT BESIDE ME.
HUH?
UH... OKAY.
SWOOO
...
WHAT'S GOING ON?
ISN'T ANYTHING ELSE GOING TO HAPPEN?!

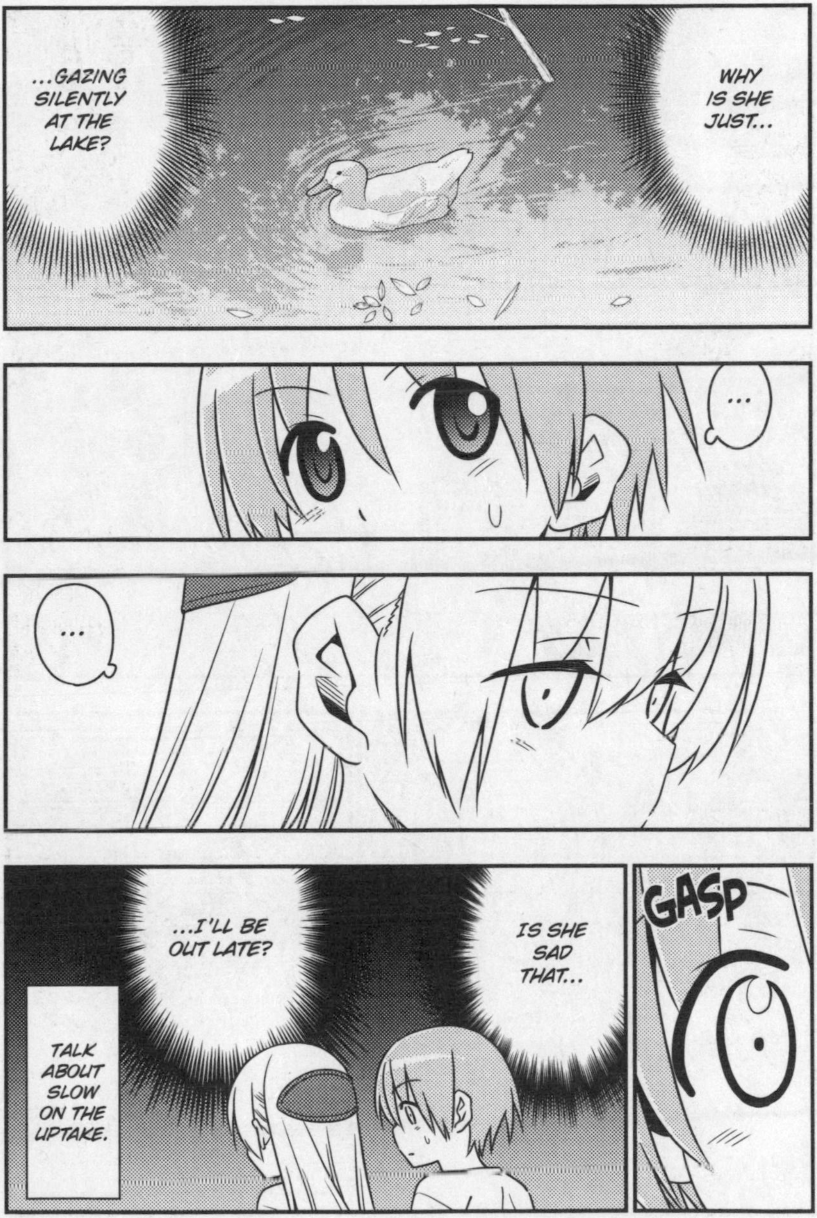
WHY IS SHE JUST...
...GAZING SILENTLY AT THE LAKE?
...
...
GASP
IS SHE SAD THAT...
...I'LL BE OUT LATE?
TALK ABOUT SLOW ON THE UPTAKE.

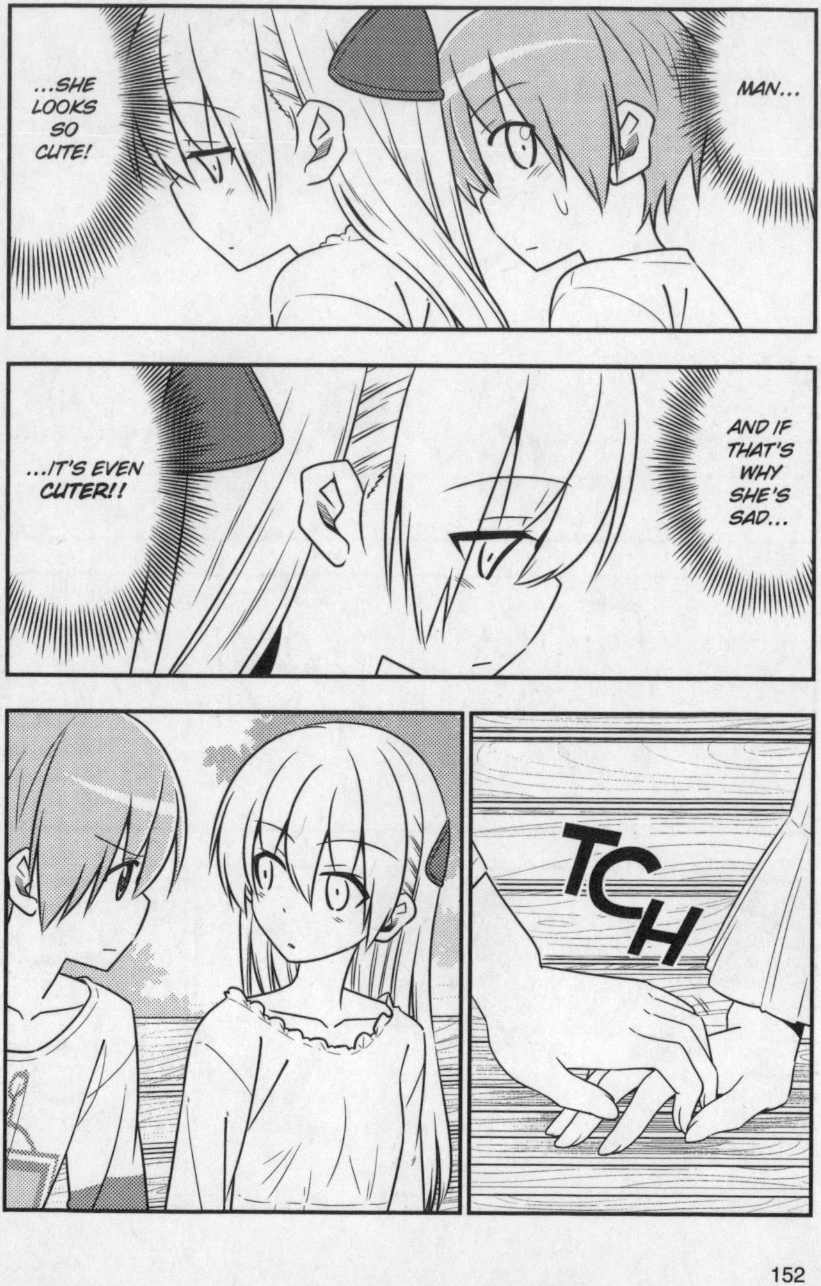
MAN...
...SHE LOOKS SO CUTE!
AND IF THAT'S WHY SHE'S SAD...
...IT'S EVEN CUTER!!
TCH

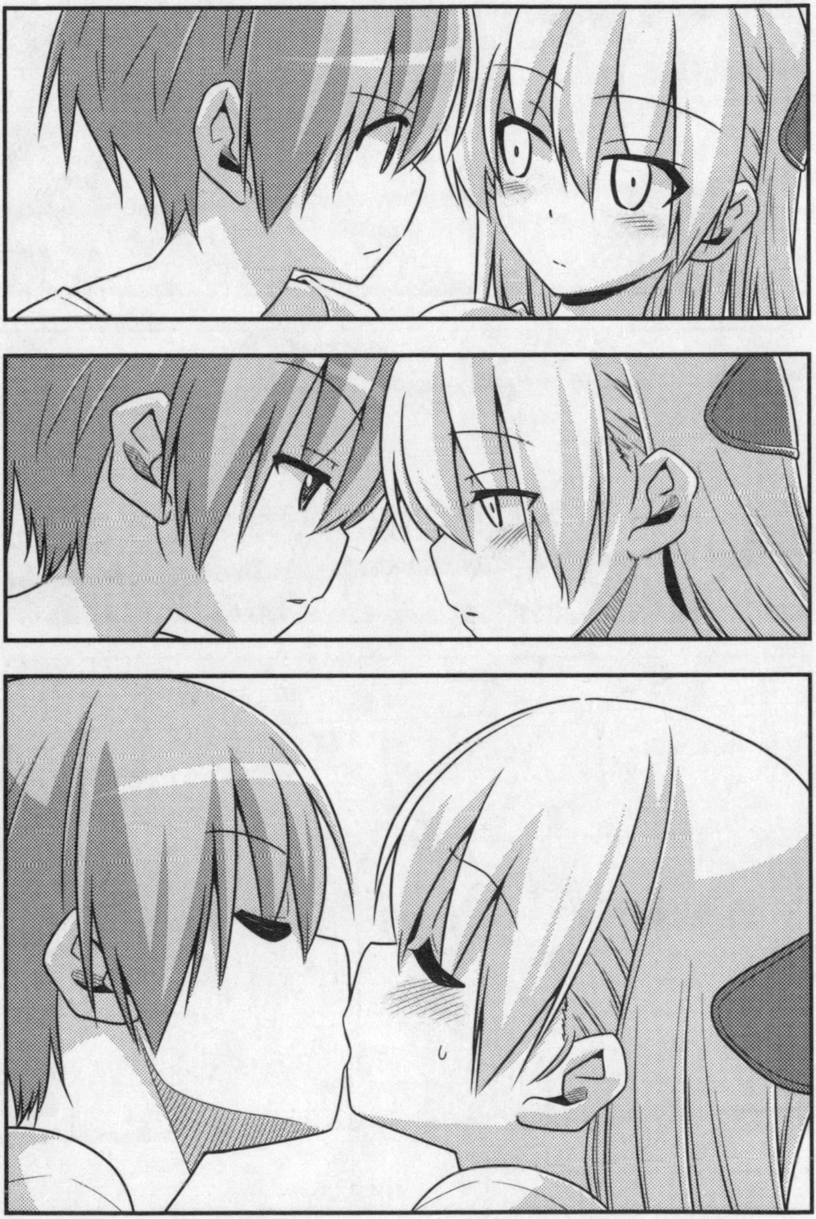

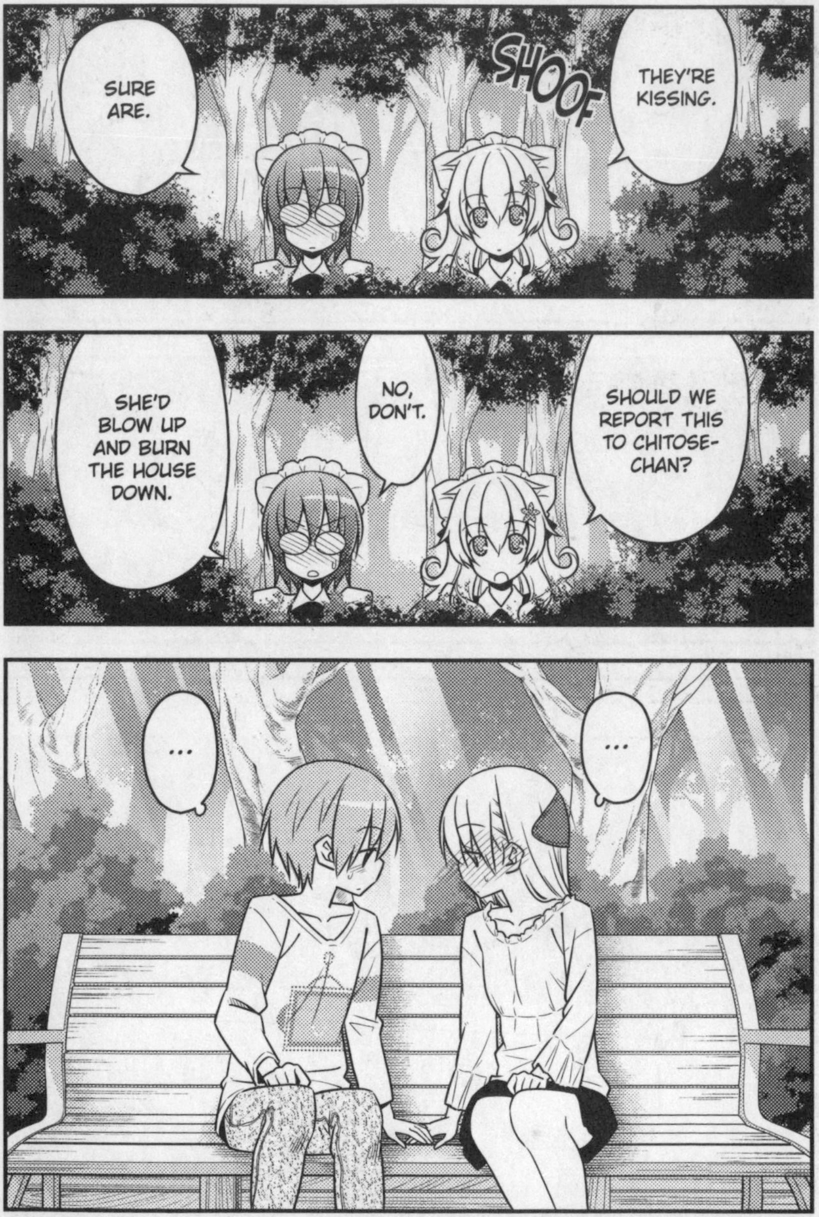
THEY'RE KISSING.
SHOOF
SURE ARE.
SHOULD WE REPORT THIS TO CHITOSE-CHAN?
NO, DON'T.
SHE'D BLOW UP AND BURN THE HOUSE DOWN.
...
...

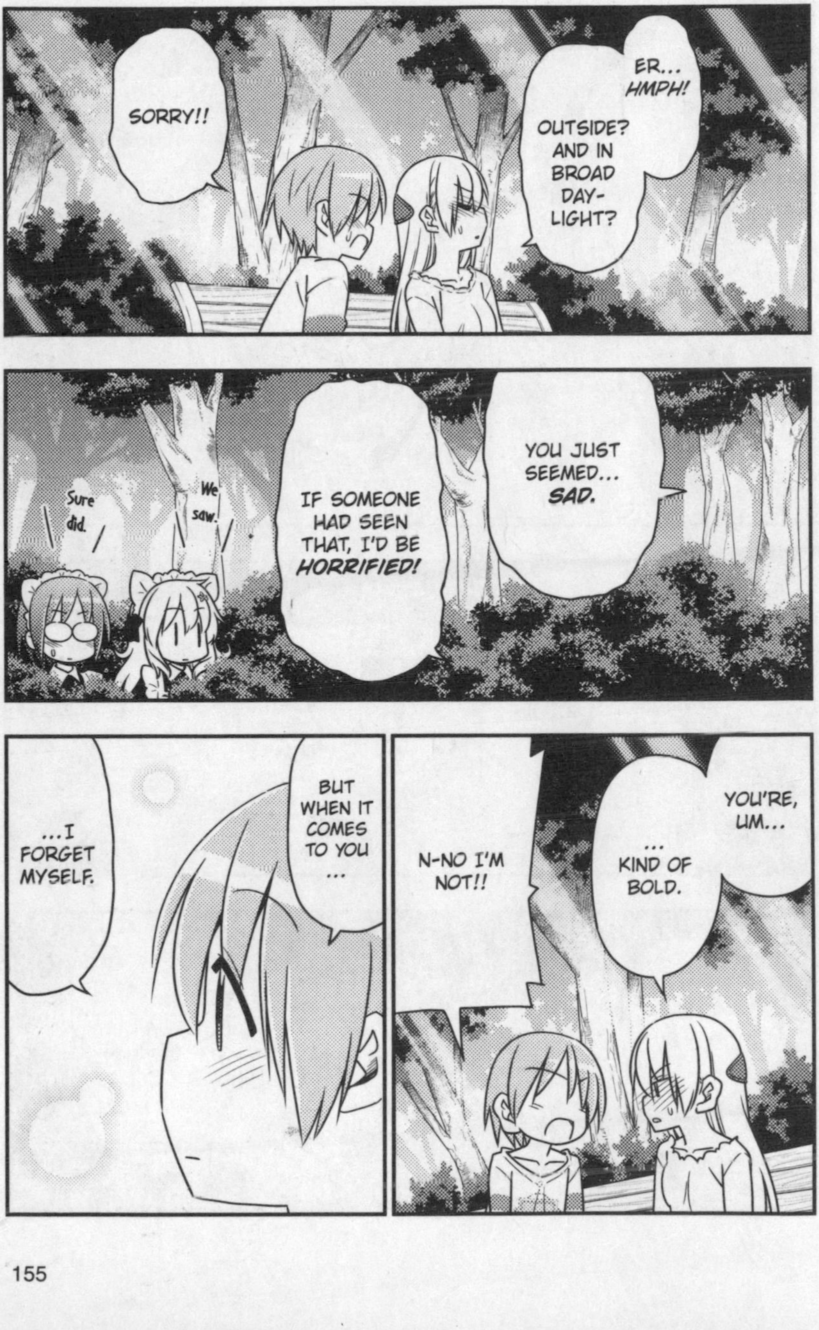
ER... HMPH!
OUTSIDE? AND IN BROAD DAY-LIGHT?
SORRY!!
YOU JUST SEEMED... SAD.
IF SOMEONE HAD SEEN THAT, I'D BE HORRIFIED!
We saw.
Sure did.
YOU'RE, UM...
...KIND OF BOLD.
N-NO I'M NOT!!
BUT WHEN IT COMES TO YOU...
...I FORGET MYSELF.

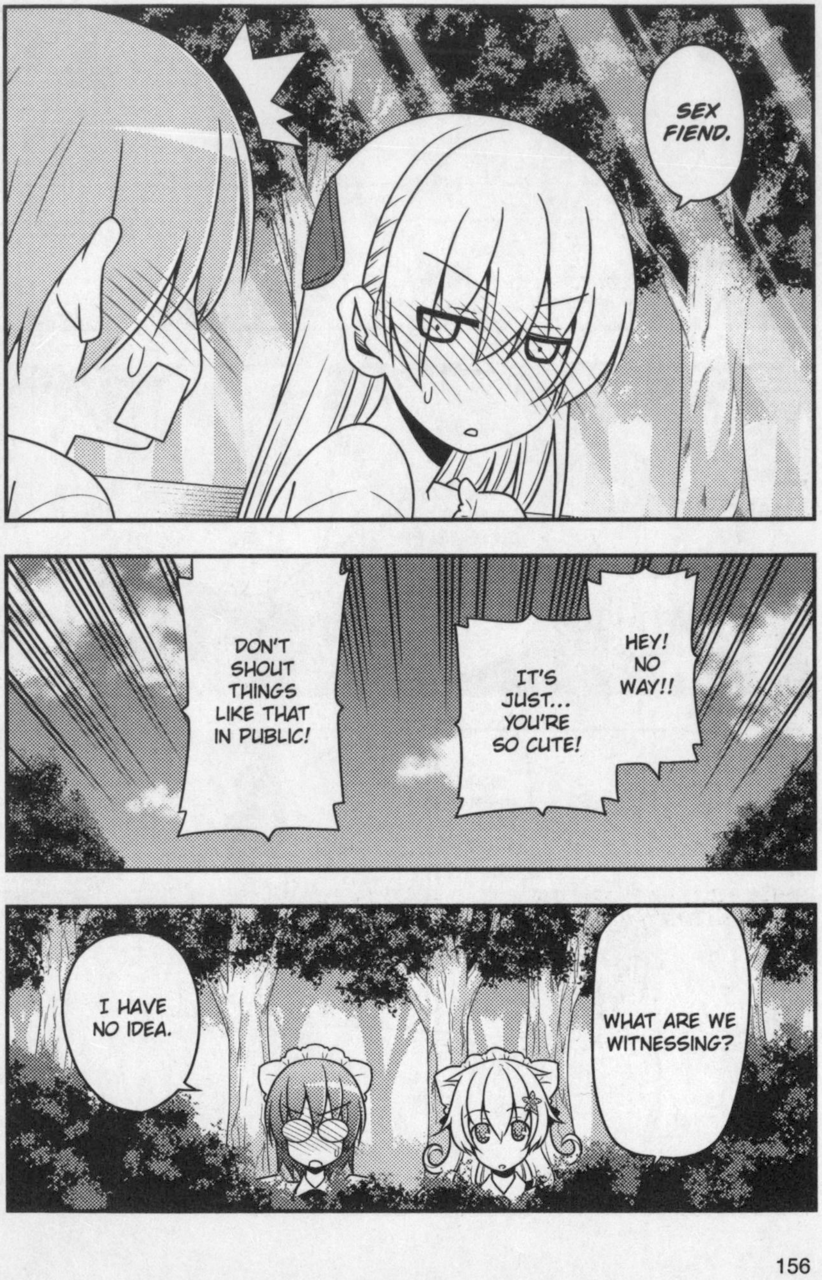
SEX FIEND.
HEY! NO WAY!!
IT'S JUST... YOU'RE SO CUTE!
DON'T SHOUT THINGS LIKE THAT IN PUBLIC!
WHAT ARE WE WITNESSING?
I HAVE NO IDEA.

Chapter 17: "I Hope You Read This While Listening to Kenji Ozawa Sing About Living in Love"

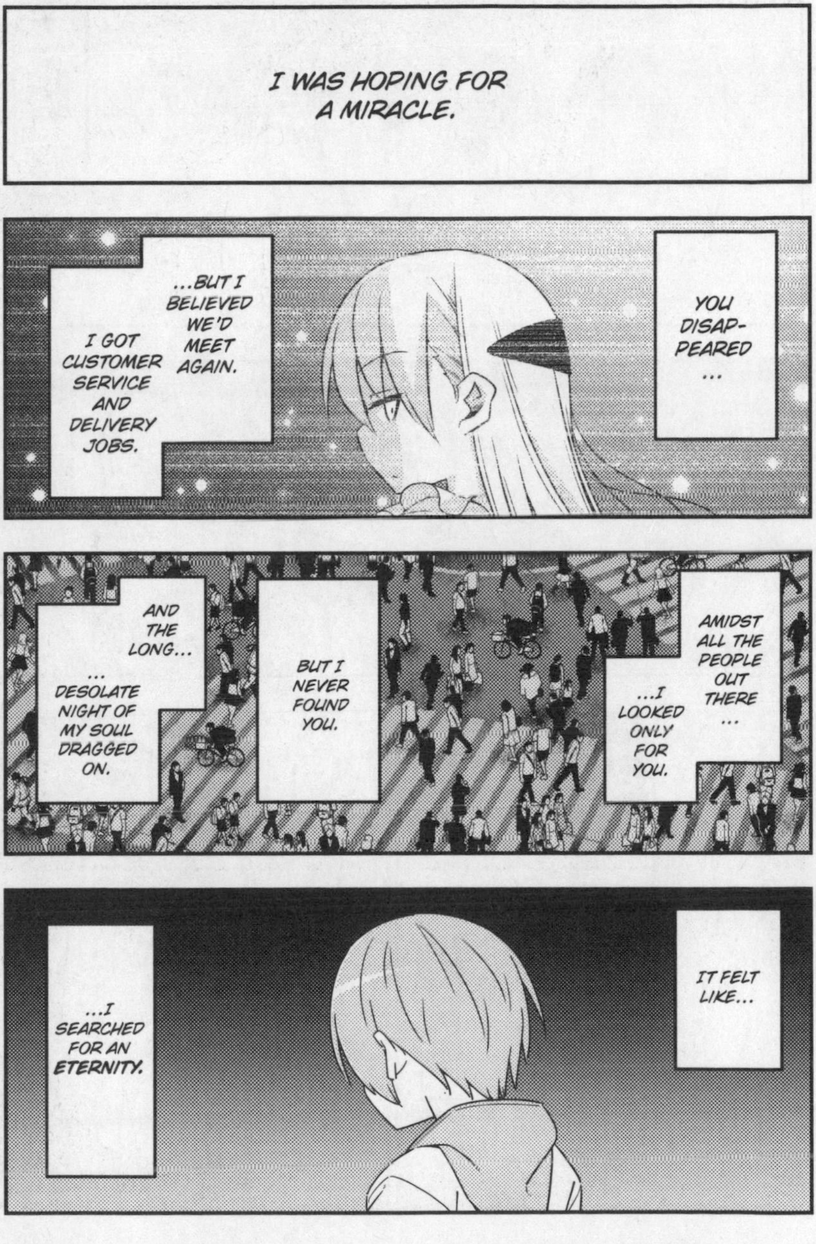
I WAS HOPING FOR A MIRACLE.
YOU DISAPPEARED...
...BUT I BELIEVED WE'D MEET AGAIN.
I GOT CUSTOMER SERVICE AND DELIVERY JOBS.
AMIDST ALL THE PEOPLE OUT THERE...
...I LOOKED ONLY FOR YOU.
BUT I NEVER FOUND YOU.
AND THE LONG...
...DESOLATE NIGHT OF MY SOUL DRAGGED ON.
IT FELT LIKE...
...I SEARCHED FOR AN ETERNITY.

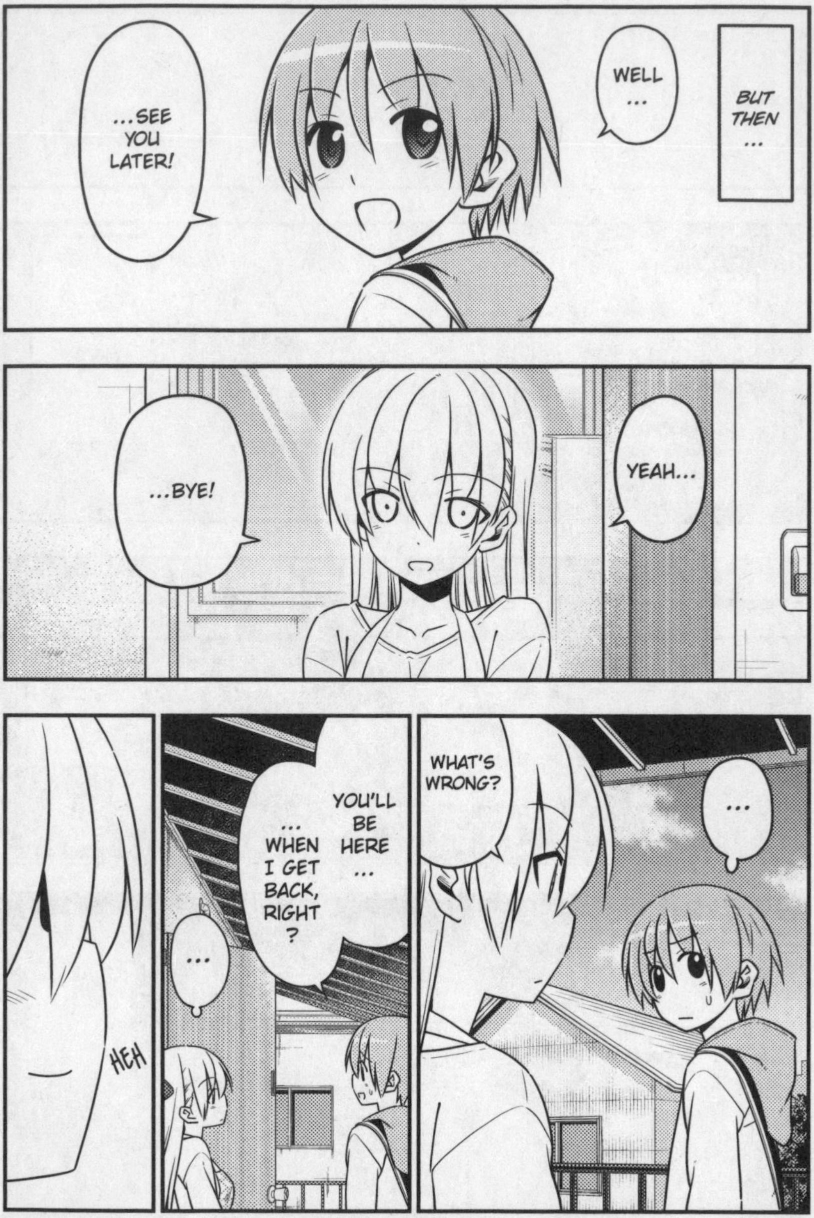
BUT THEN ...
WELL ...
...SEE YOU LATER!
YEAH...
...BYE!
...
WHAT'S WRONG?
YOU'LL BE HERE ...
... WHEN I GET BACK, RIGHT?
...
HEH

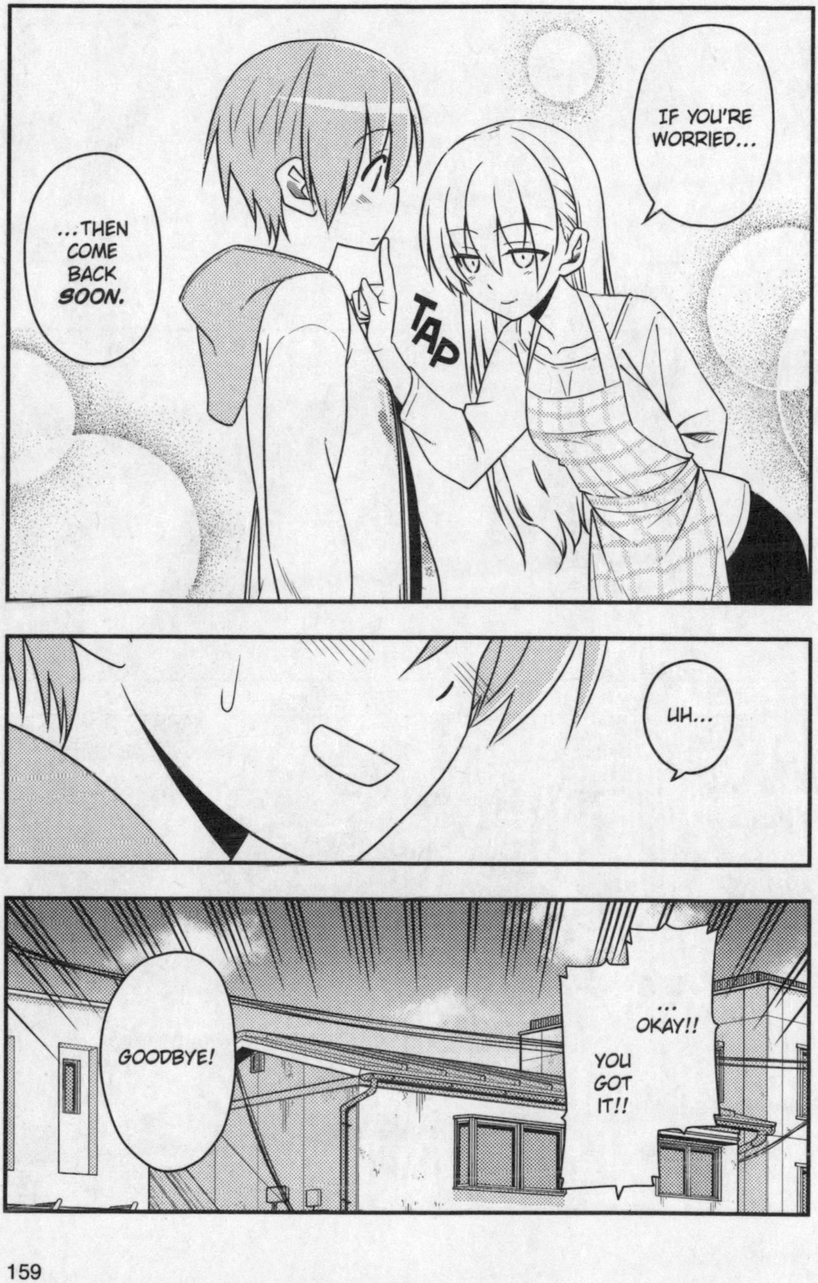
IF YOU'RE WORRIED...
TAP
...THEN COME BACK SOON.
UH...
... OKAY!!
YOU GOT IT!!
GOODBYE!

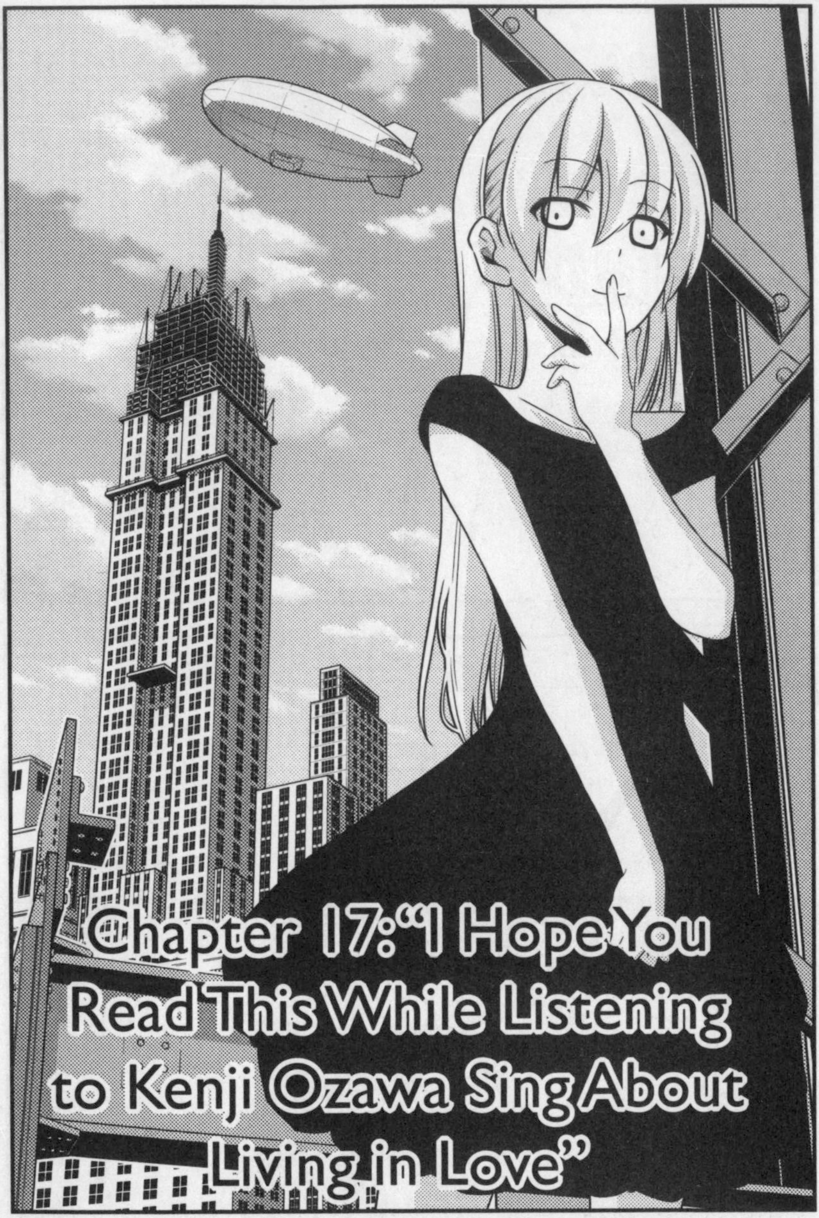
Chapter 17: "I Hope You Read This While Listening to Kenji Ozawa Sing About Living in Love"

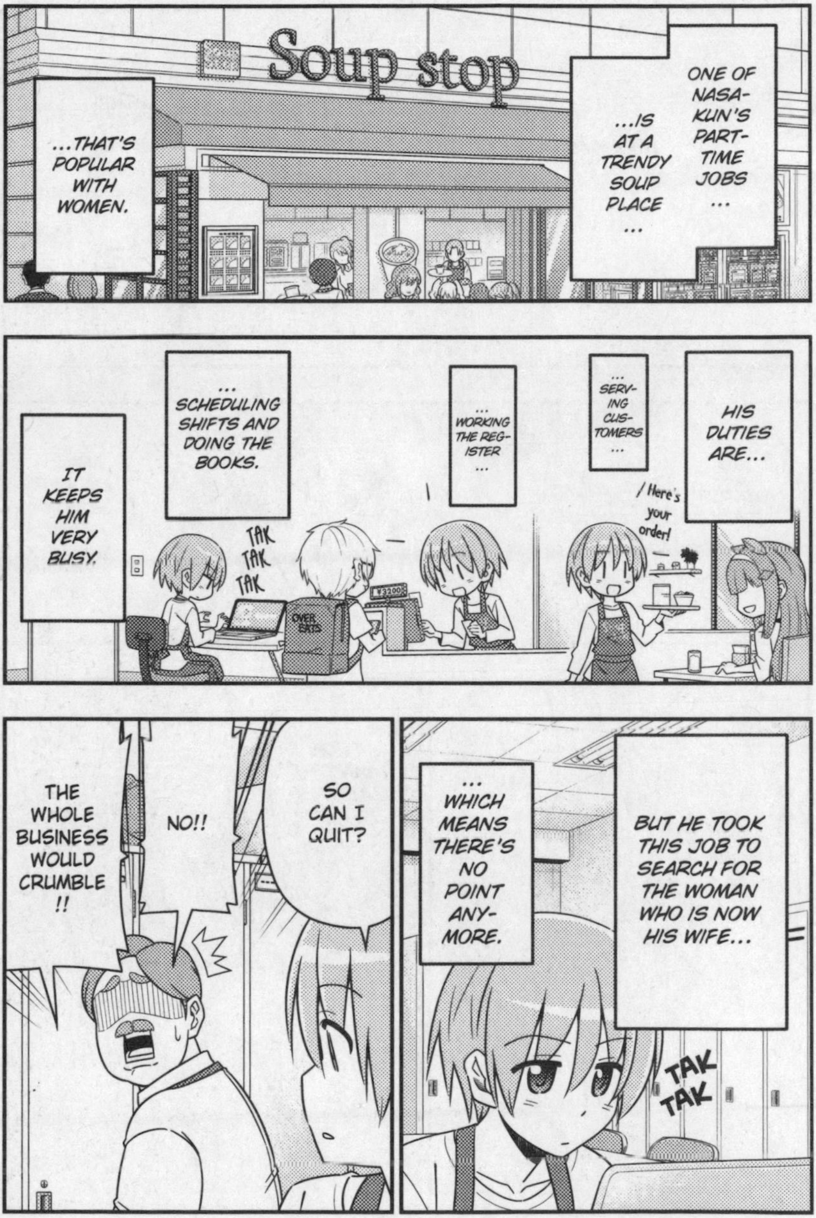
Soup stop
ONE OF NASA-KUN'S PART-TIME JOBS...
...IS AT A TRENDY SOUP PLACE...
...THAT'S POPULAR WITH WOMEN.
HIS DUTIES ARE...
Here's your order!
...SERVING CUSTOMERS...
...WORKING THE REGISTER...
...SCHEDULING SHIFTS AND DOING THE BOOKS.
TAK TAK TAK
¥3200
OVER EATS
IT KEEPS HIM VERY BUSY.
BUT HE TOOK THIS JOB TO SEARCH FOR THE WOMAN WHO IS NOW HIS WIFE...
...WHICH MEANS THERE'S NO POINT ANYMORE.
TAK TAK
SO CAN I QUIT?
NO!!
THE WHOLE BUSINESS WOULD CRUMBLE!!

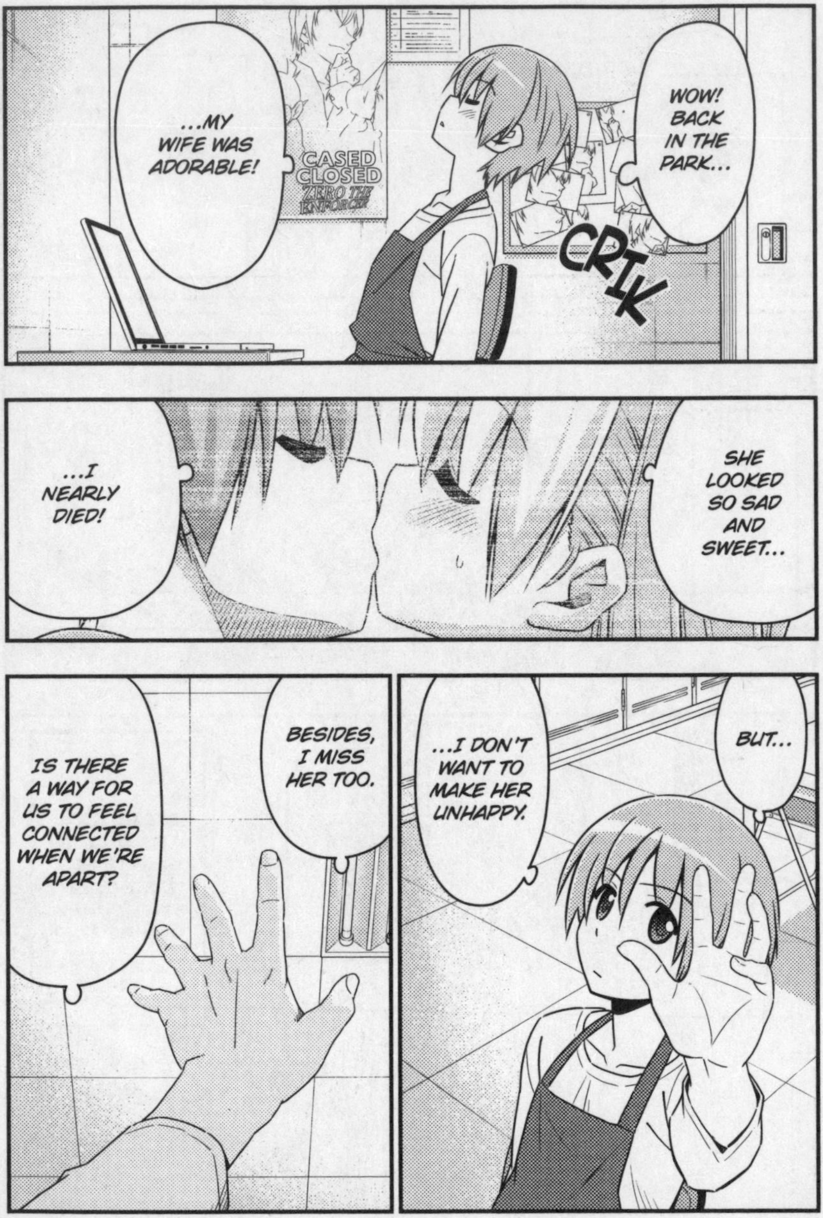
WOW! BACK IN THE PARK...
CRIK
CASED CLOSED
ZERO THE ENFORCER
...MY WIFE WAS ADORABLE!
SHE LOOKED SO SAD AND SWEET...
...I NEARLY DIED!
BUT...
...I DON'T WANT TO MAKE HER UNHAPPY.
BESIDES, I MISS HER TOO.
IS THERE A WAY FOR US TO FEEL CONNECTED WHEN WE'RE APART?

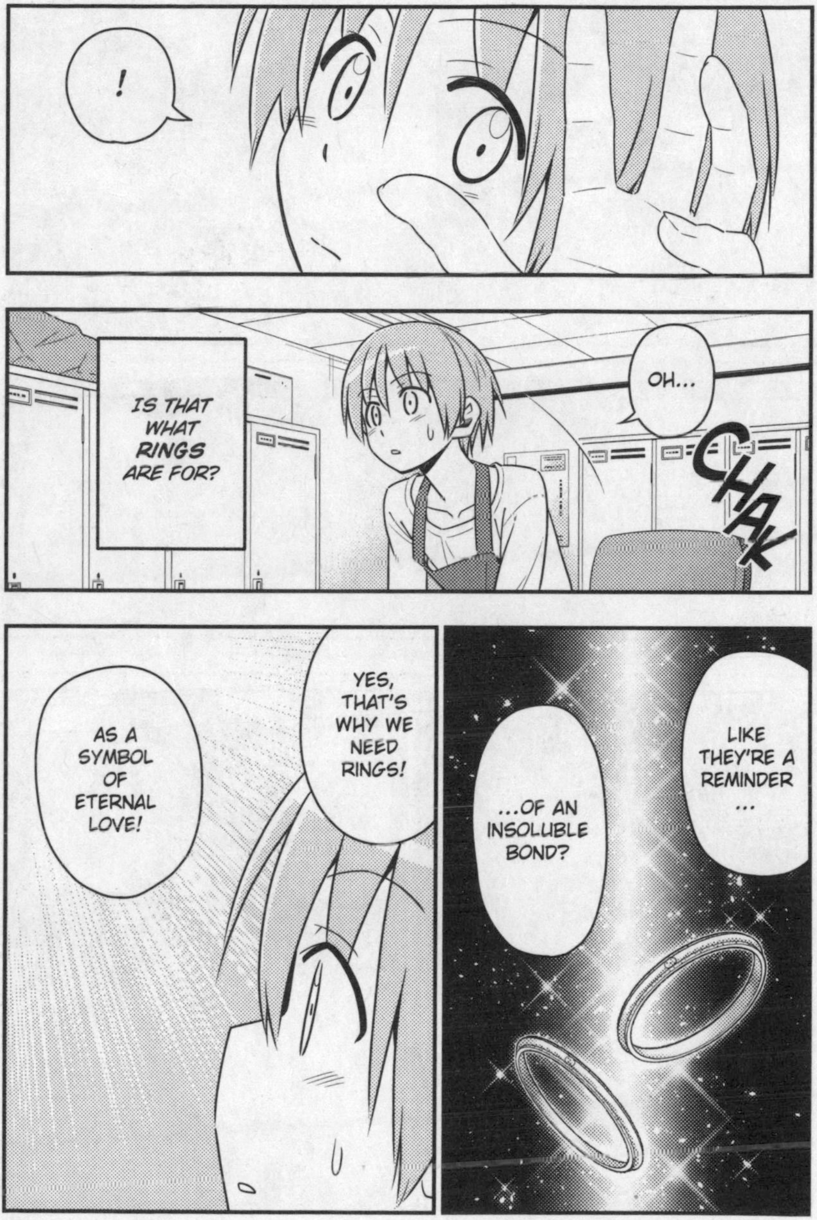
!
OH...
CHAK
IS THAT WHAT RINGS ARE FOR?
LIKE THEY'RE A REMINDER ...
...OF AN INSOLUBLE BOND?
YES, THAT'S WHY WE NEED RINGS!
AS A SYMBOL OF ETERNAL LOVE!

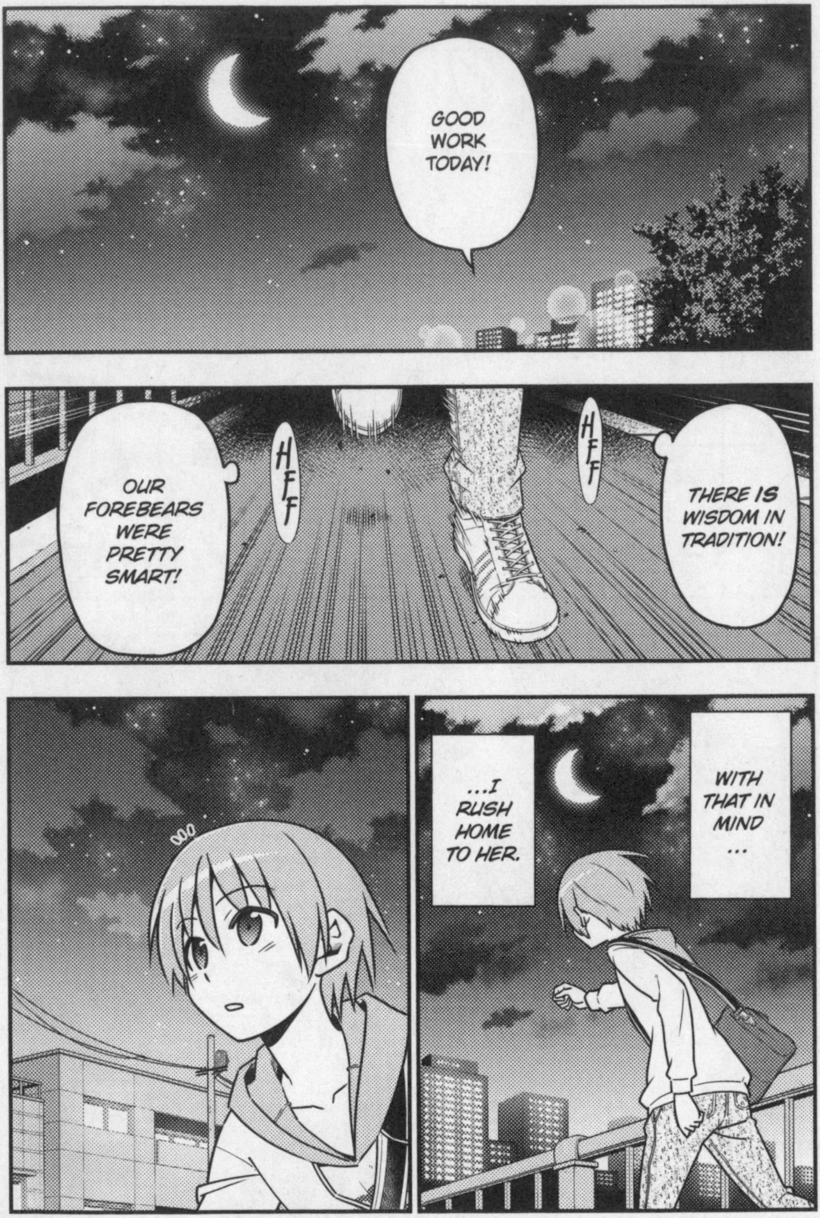
GOOD WORK TODAY!
THERE IS WISDOM IN TRADITION!
HFF
HFF
OUR FOREBEARS WERE PRETTY SMART!
WITH THAT IN MIND ...
...I RUSH HOME TO HER.

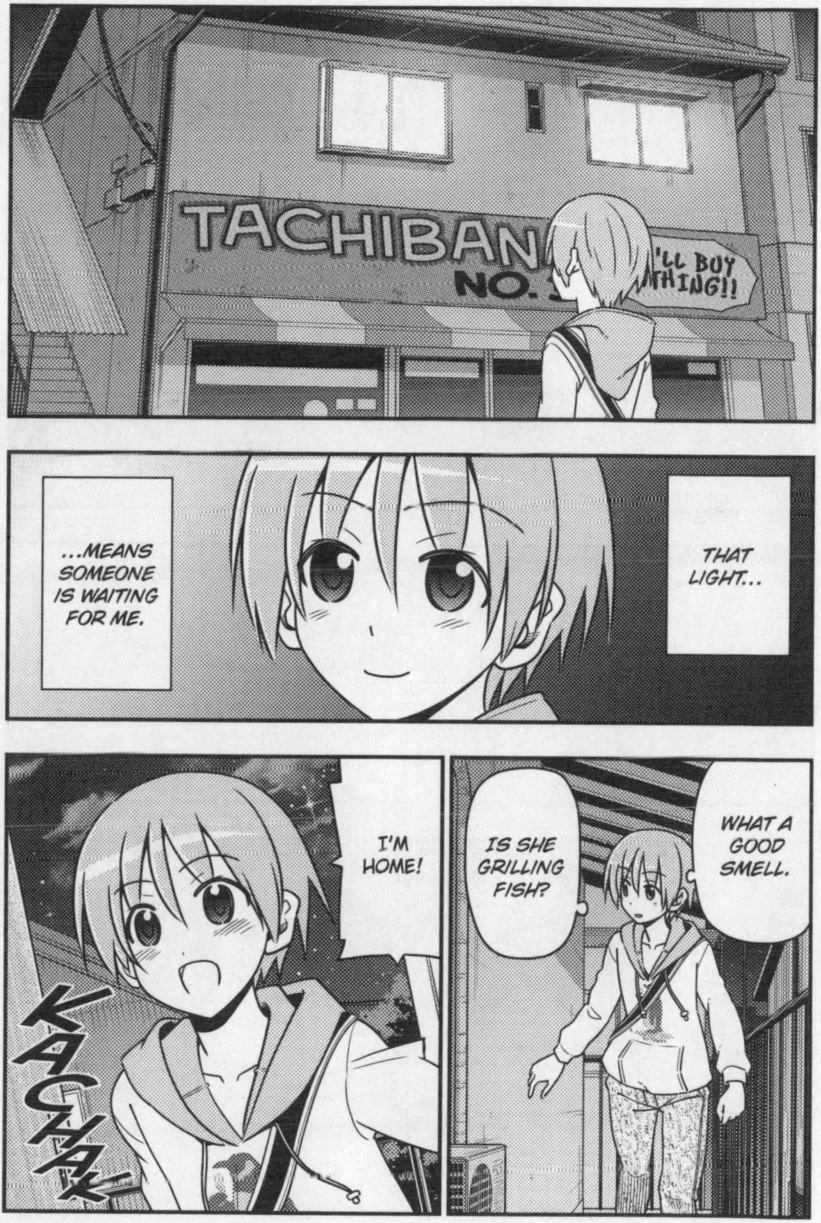
TACHIBAN
NO.
'LL BUY
THING!!
THAT LIGHT...
...MEANS SOMEONE IS WAITING FOR ME.
WHAT A GOOD SMELL.
IS SHE GRILLING FISH?
I'M HOME!
KACHAK

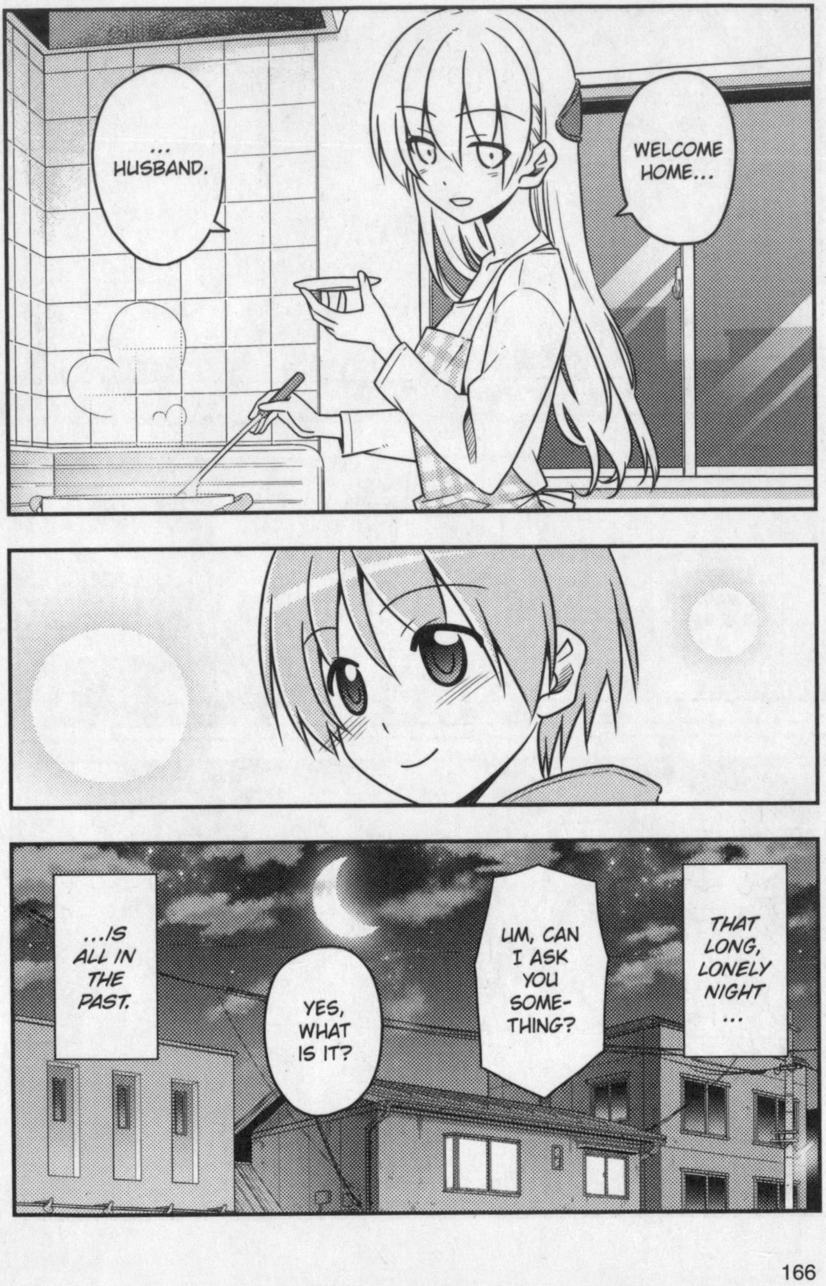
WELCOME HOME...
... HUSBAND.
THAT LONG, LONELY NIGHT ...
UM, CAN I ASK YOU SOME-THING?
YES, WHAT IS IT?
...IS ALL IN THE PAST.

Chapter 18: "After This"

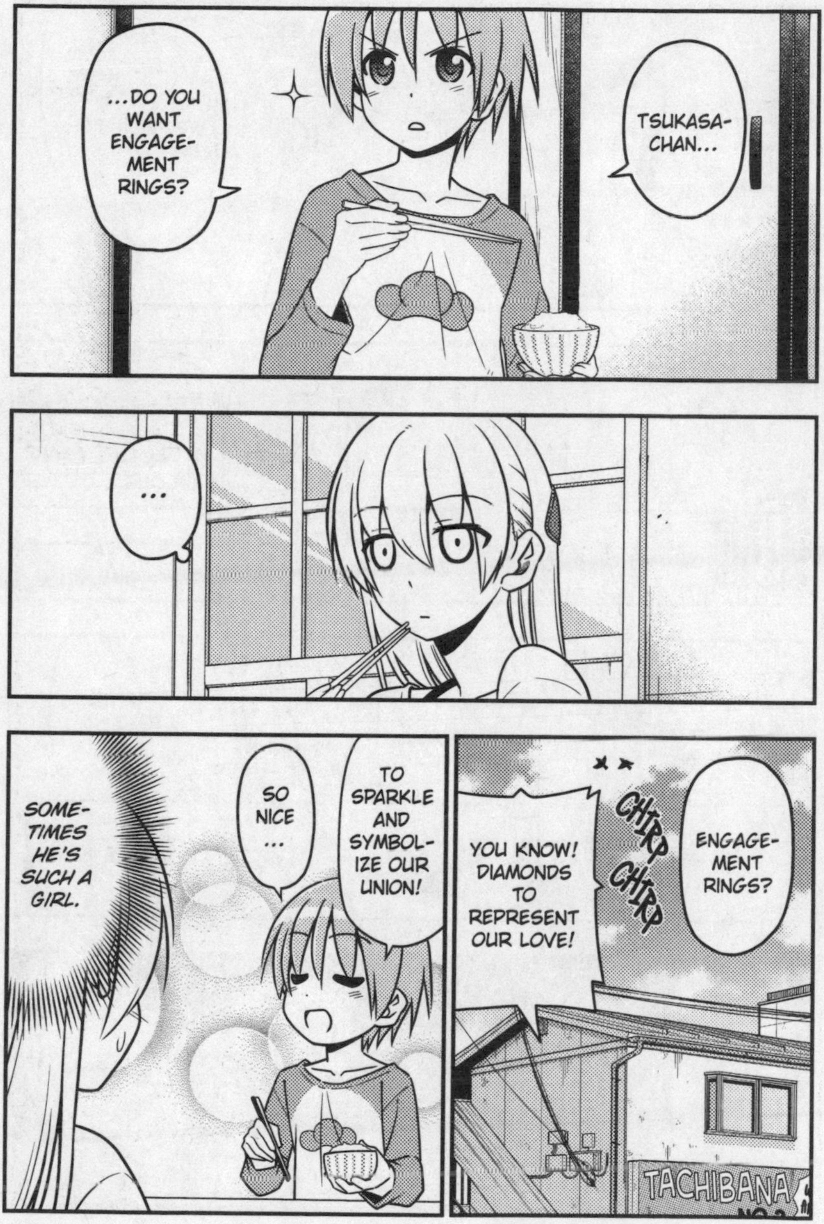

TSUKASA-CHAN...
...DO YOU WANT ENGAGE-MENT RINGS?
...
ENGAGE-MENT RINGS?
CHIRP CHIRP
YOU KNOW! DIAMONDS TO REPRESENT OUR LOVE!
TACHIBANA
TO SPARKLE AND SYMBOL-IZE OUR UNION!
SO NICE ...
SOME-TIMES HE'S SUCH A GIRL.

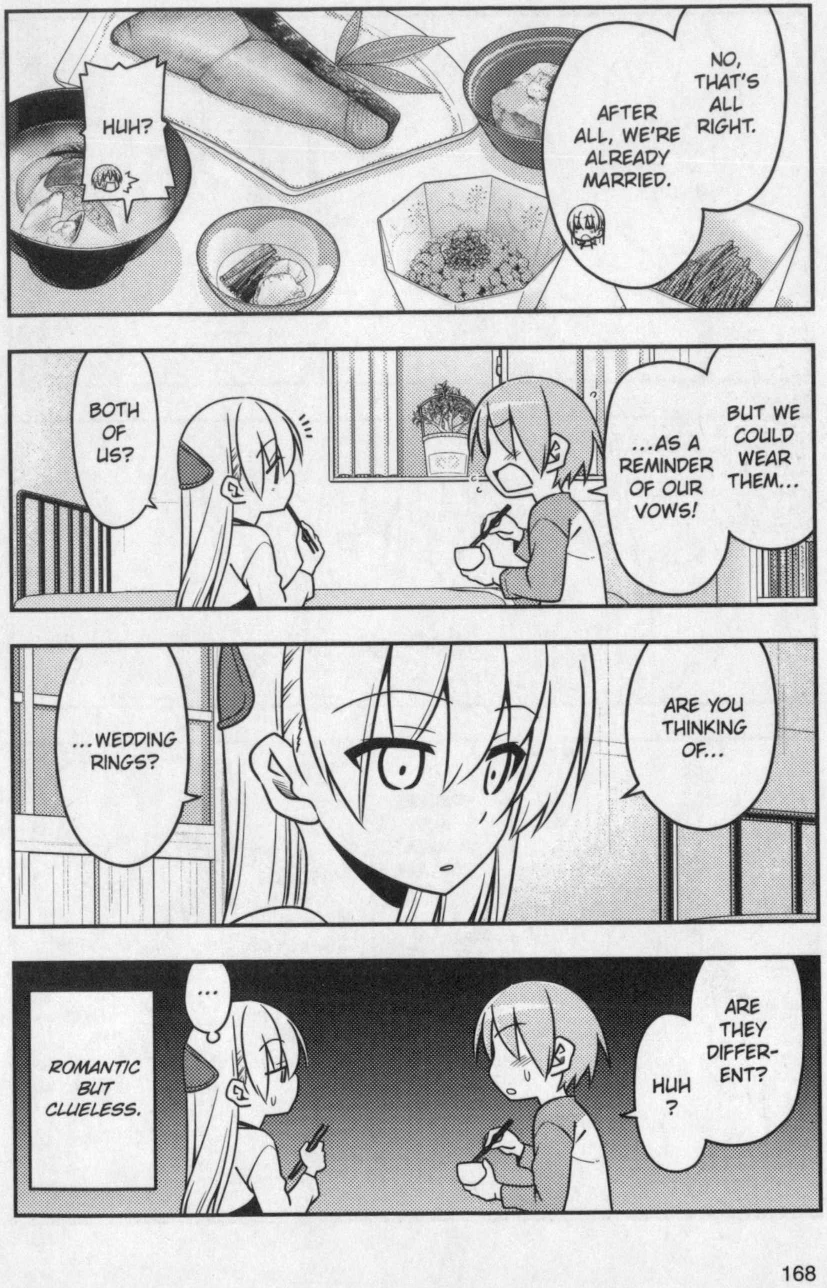
NO, THAT'S ALL RIGHT.
AFTER ALL, WE'RE ALREADY MARRIED.
HUH?
BUT WE COULD WEAR THEM...
...AS A REMINDER OF OUR VOWS!
BOTH OF US?
ARE YOU THINKING OF...
...WEDDING RINGS?
ARE THEY DIFFER-ENT?
HUH?
...
ROMANTIC BUT CLUELESS.

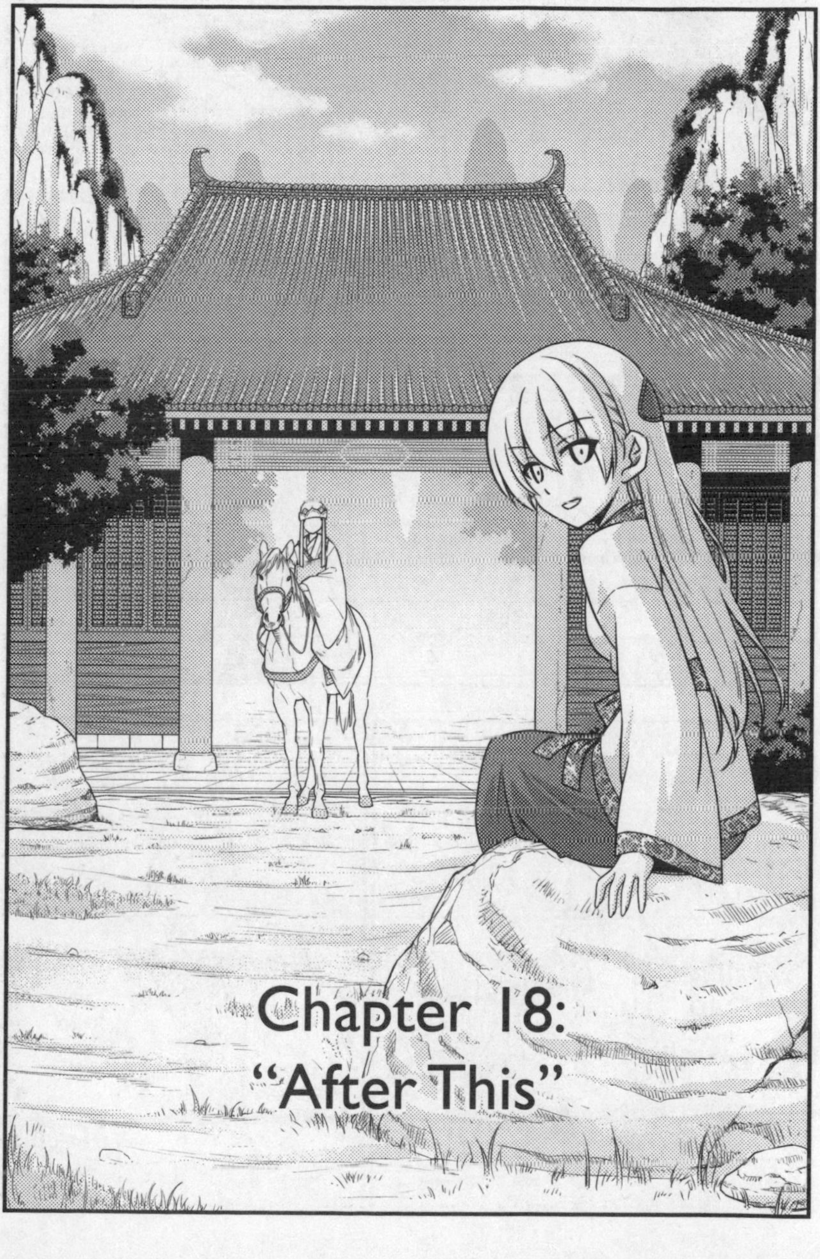
Chapter 18:
"After This"

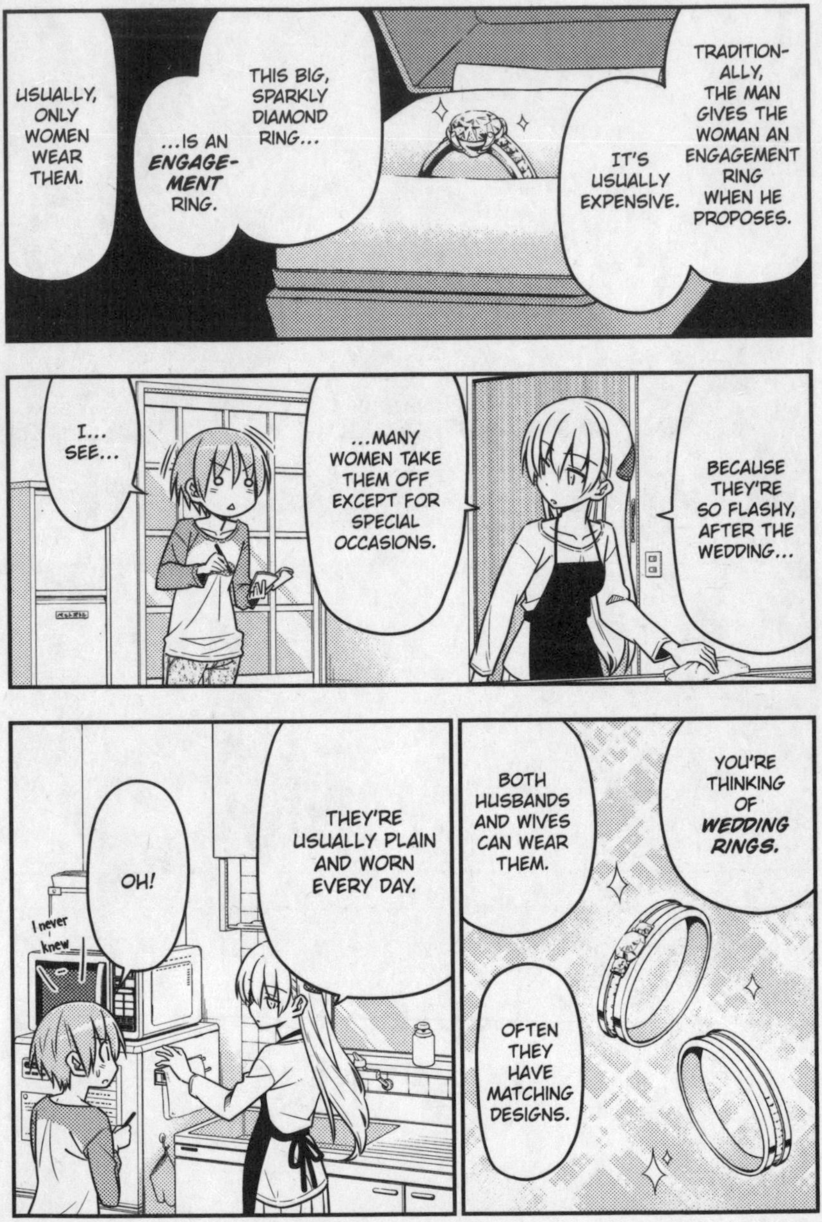
TRADITION-ALLY, THE MAN GIVES THE WOMAN AN ENGAGEMENT RING WHEN HE PROPOSES.
IT'S USUALLY EXPENSIVE.
THIS BIG, SPARKLY DIAMOND RING...
...IS AN ENGAGE-MENT RING.
USUALLY, ONLY WOMEN WEAR THEM.
BECAUSE THEY'RE SO FLASHY, AFTER THE WEDDING...
...MANY WOMEN TAKE THEM OFF EXCEPT FOR SPECIAL OCCASIONS.
I... SEE...
YOU'RE THINKING OF WEDDING RINGS.
BOTH HUSBANDS AND WIVES CAN WEAR THEM.
OFTEN THEY HAVE MATCHING DESIGNS.
THEY'RE USUALLY PLAIN AND WORN EVERY DAY.
OH!
I never knew

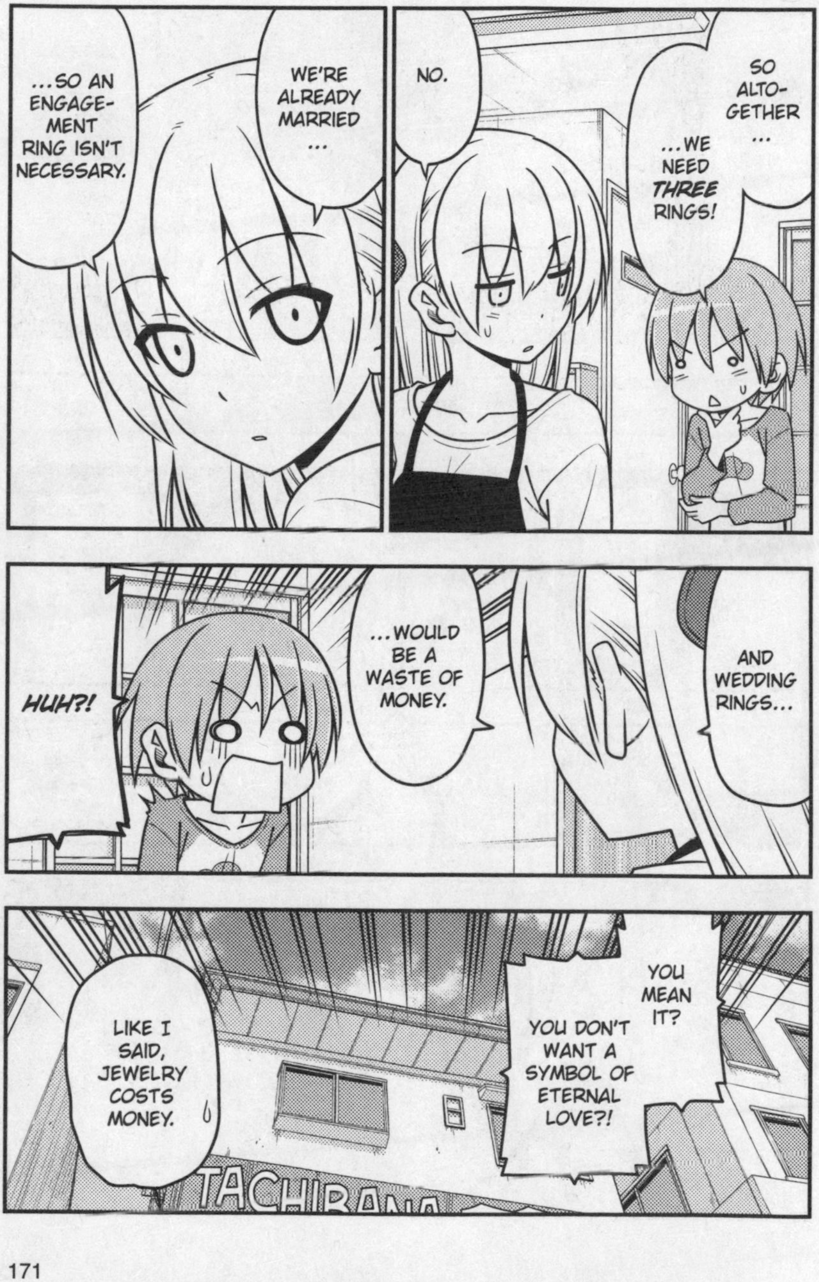
SO ALTO-GETHER...
...WE NEED THREE RINGS!
NO.
WE'RE ALREADY MARRIED...
...SO AN ENGAGE-MENT RING ISN'T NECESSARY.
AND WEDDING RINGS...
...WOULD BE A WASTE OF MONEY.
HUH?!
YOU MEAN IT?
YOU DON'T WANT A SYMBOL OF ETERNAL LOVE?!
LIKE I SAID, JEWELRY COSTS MONEY.
TACHIBANA

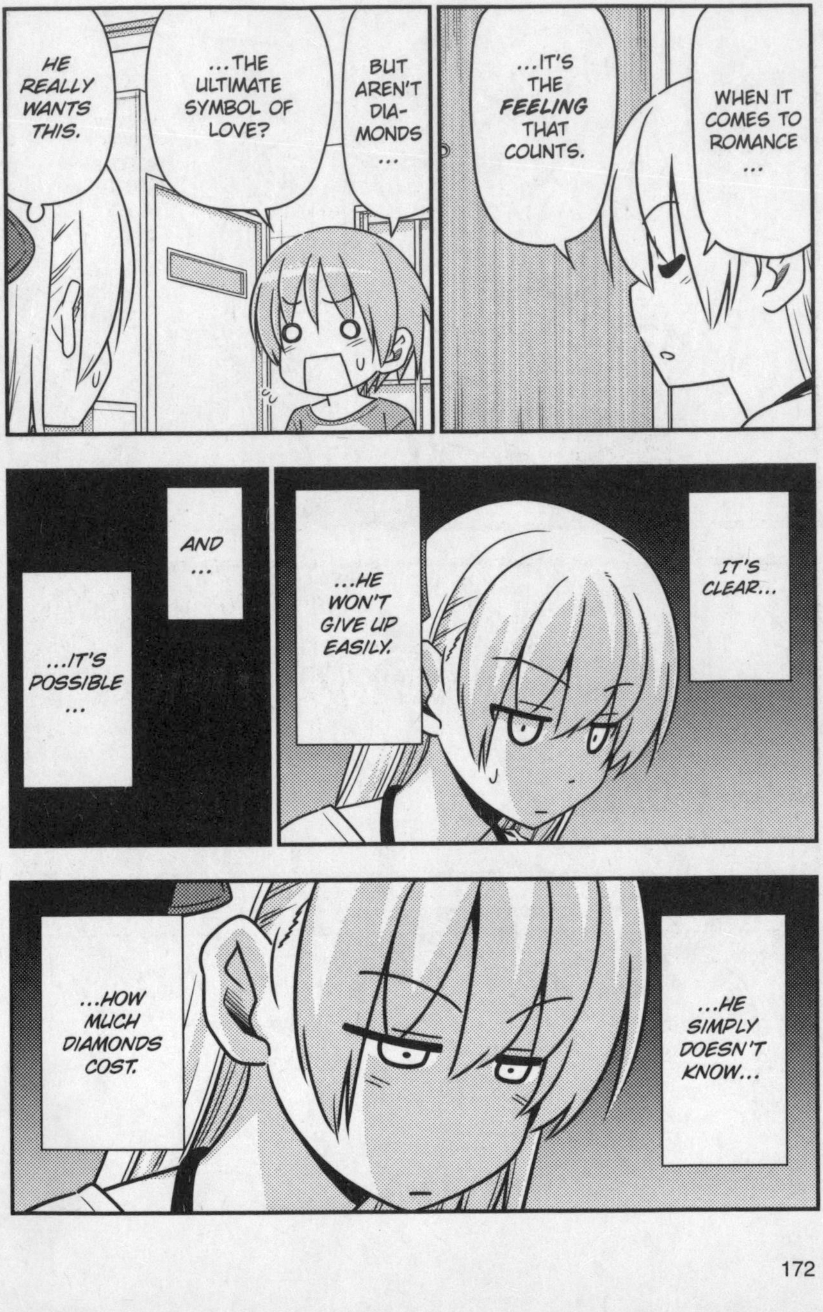
WHEN IT COMES TO ROMANCE ...
...IT'S THE *FEELING* THAT COUNTS.
BUT AREN'T DIA-MONDS ...
...THE ULTIMATE SYMBOL OF LOVE?
HE REALLY WANTS THIS.
IT'S CLEAR...
...HE WON'T GIVE UP EASILY.
AND ...
...IT'S POSSIBLE ...
...HE SIMPLY DOESN'T KNOW...
...HOW MUCH DIAMONDS COST.

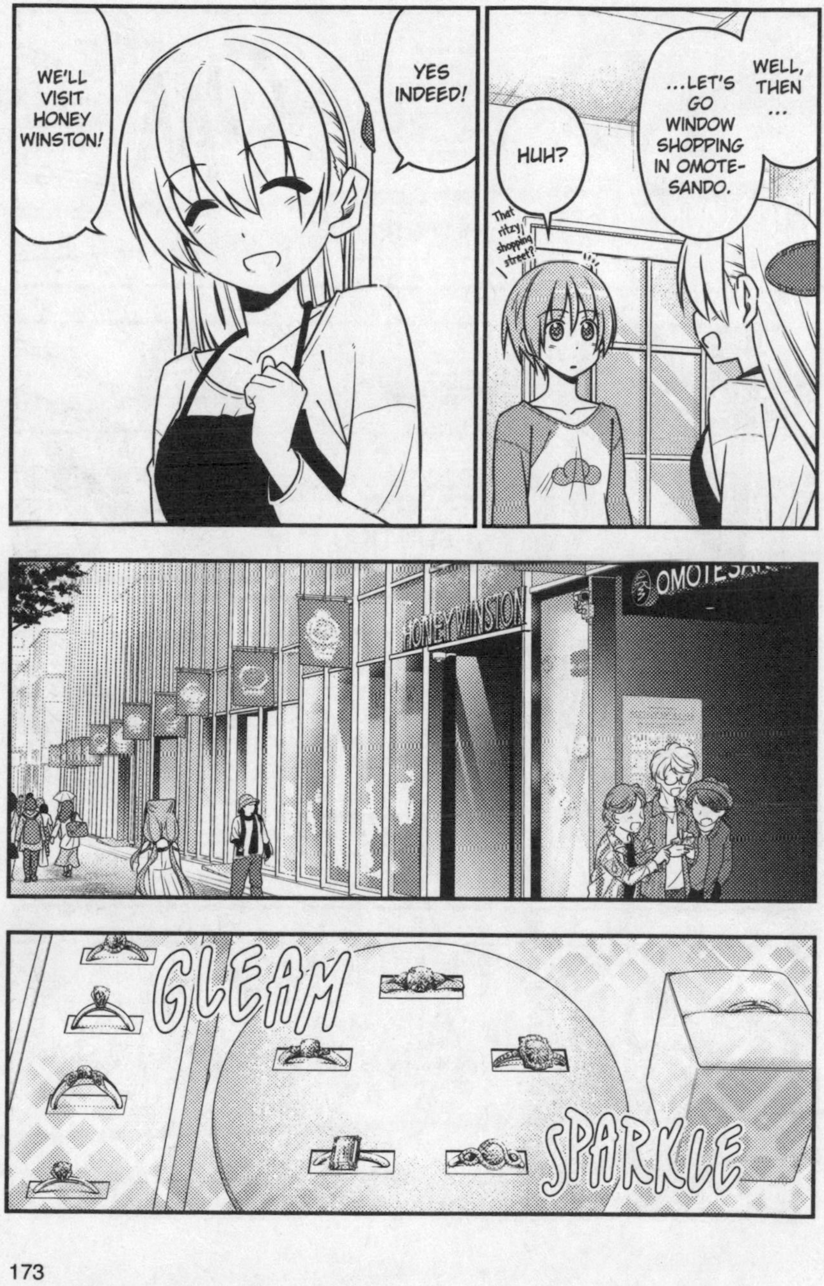
WELL, THEN ...
...LET'S GO WINDOW SHOPPING IN OMOTE-SANDO.
HUH?
That ritzy shopping street?
YES INDEED!
WE'LL VISIT HONEY WINSTON!
HONEY WINSTON
GLEAM
SPARKLE

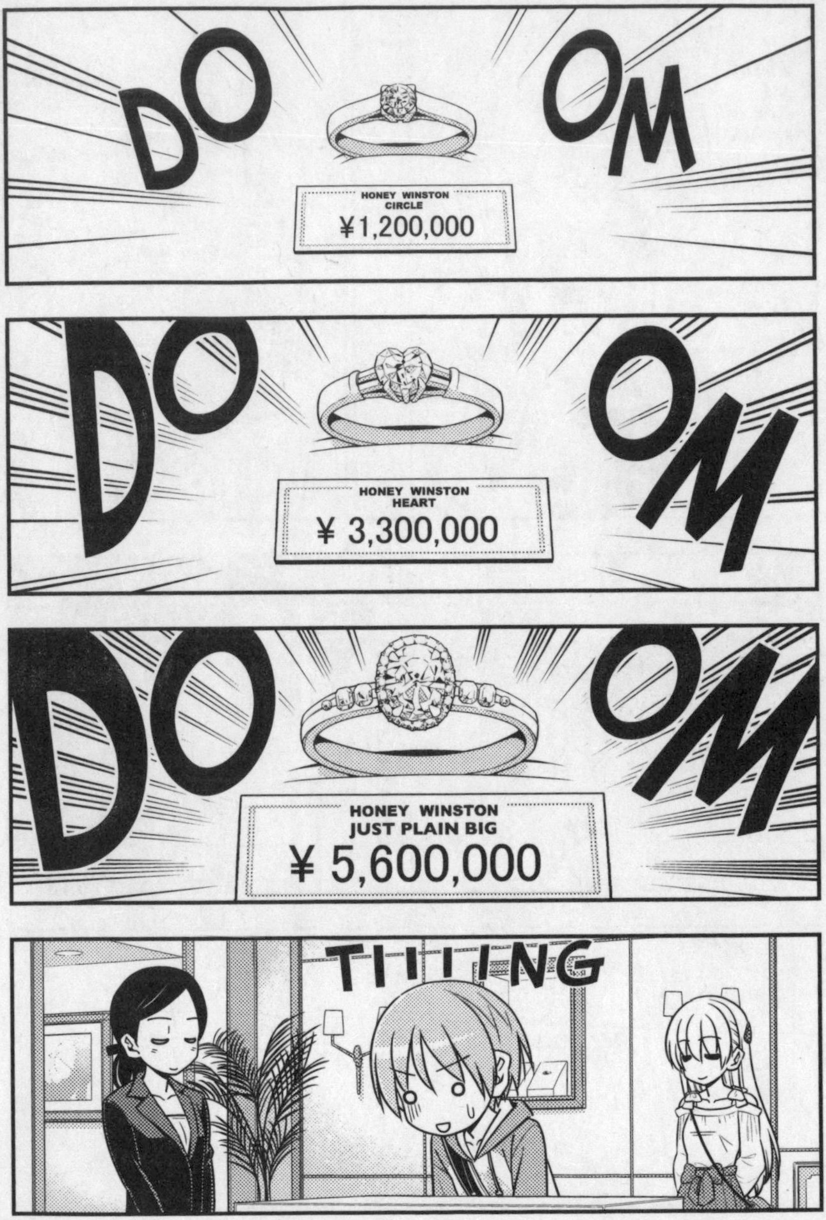
DO OM
HONEY WINSTON CIRCLE
¥1,200,000
DO OM
HONEY WINSTON HEART
¥ 3,300,000
DO OM
HONEY WINSTON JUST PLAIN BIG
¥ 5,600,000
TIIIING

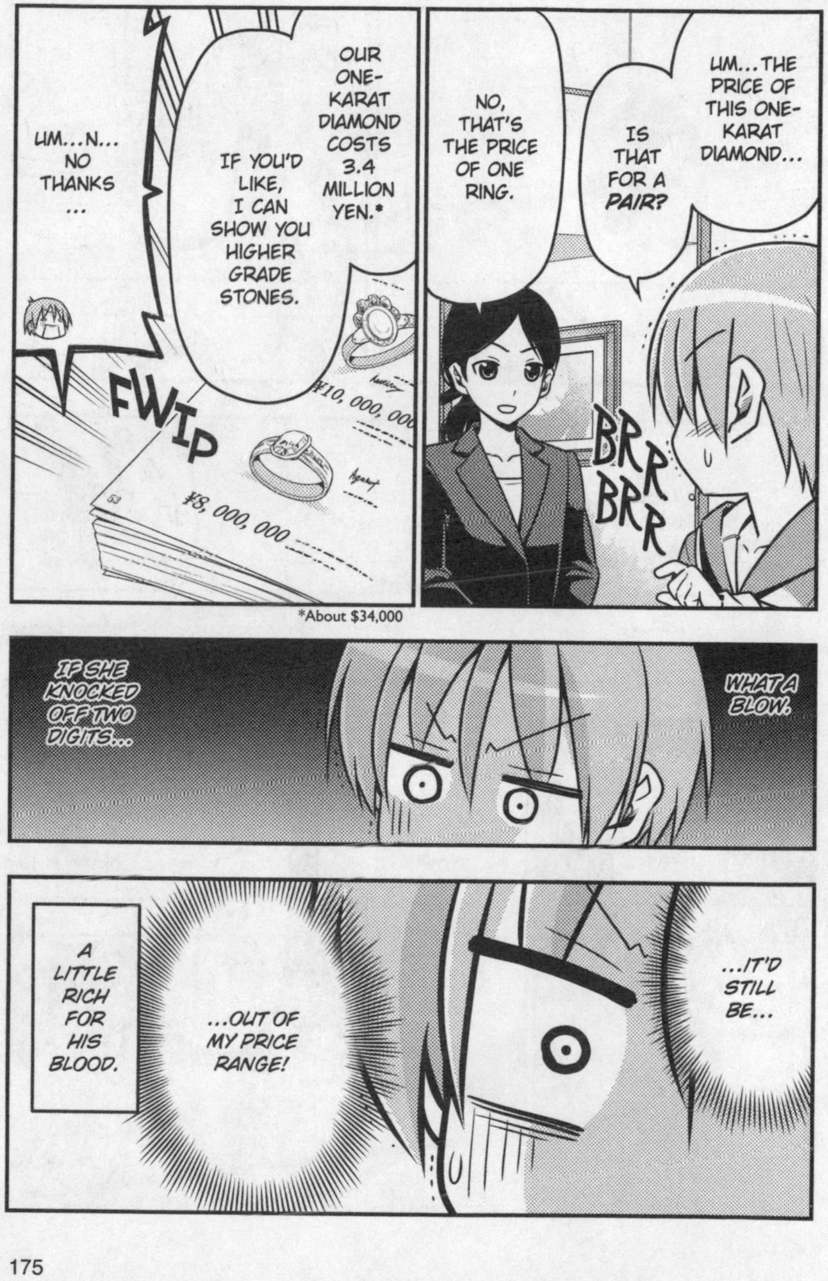
UM...THE PRICE OF THIS ONE-KARAT DIAMOND...
IS THAT FOR A *PAIR?*
NO, THAT'S THE PRICE OF ONE RING.
BRR BRR
OUR ONE-KARAT DIAMOND COSTS 3.4 MILLION YEN.*
IF YOU'D LIKE, I CAN SHOW YOU HIGHER GRADE STONES.
¥10,000,000
¥8,000,000
FWIP
UM...N... NO THANKS...
WHAT A BLOW.
IF SHE KNOCKED OFF TWO DIGITS...
...IT'D STILL BE...
...OUT OF MY PRICE RANGE!
A LITTLE RICH FOR HIS BLOOD.

*About $34,000

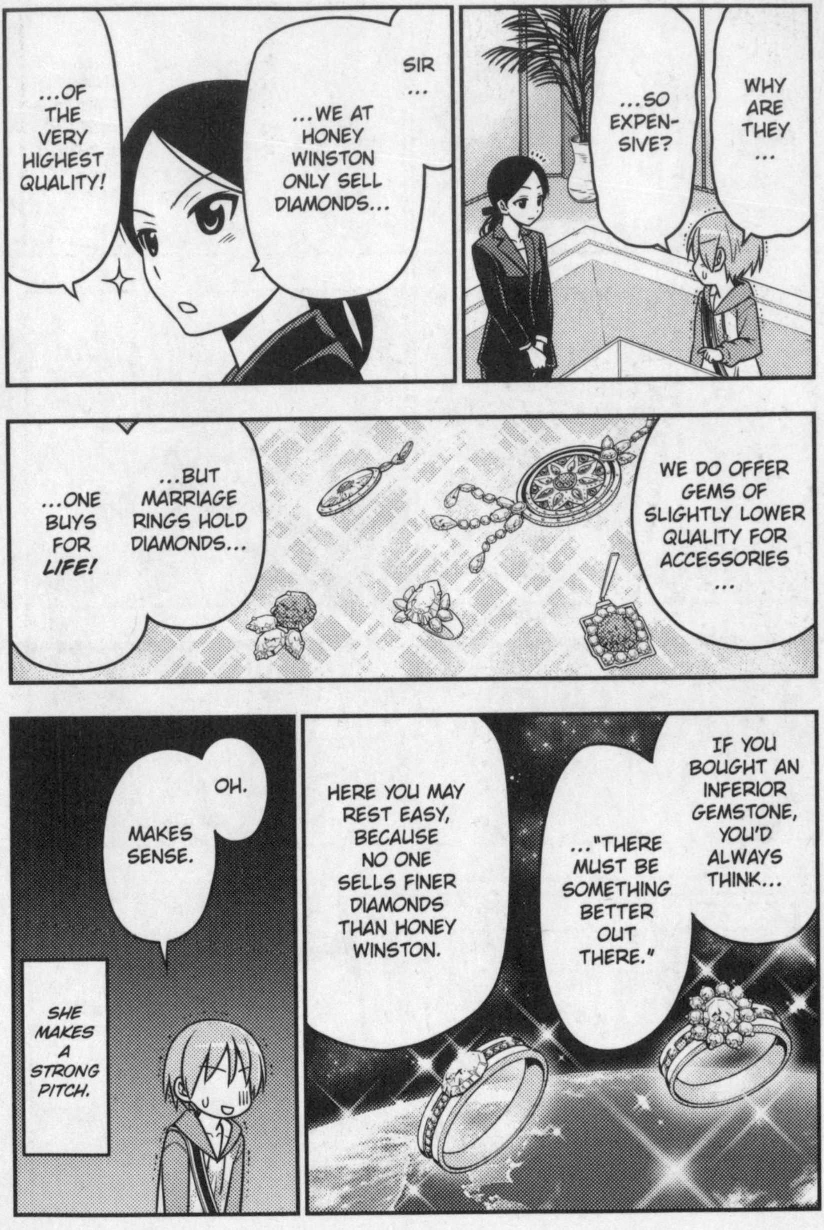
WHY ARE THEY ...
...SO EXPEN-SIVE?
SIR ...
...WE AT HONEY WINSTON ONLY SELL DIAMONDS...
...OF THE VERY HIGHEST QUALITY!
WE DO OFFER GEMS OF SLIGHTLY LOWER QUALITY FOR ACCESSORIES ...
...BUT MARRIAGE RINGS HOLD DIAMONDS...
...ONE BUYS FOR *LIFE!*
IF YOU BOUGHT AN INFERIOR GEMSTONE, YOU'D ALWAYS THINK...
..."THERE MUST BE SOMETHING BETTER OUT THERE."
HERE YOU MAY REST EASY, BECAUSE NO ONE SELLS FINER DIAMONDS THAN HONEY WINSTON.
OH.
MAKES SENSE.
SHE MAKES A STRONG PITCH.

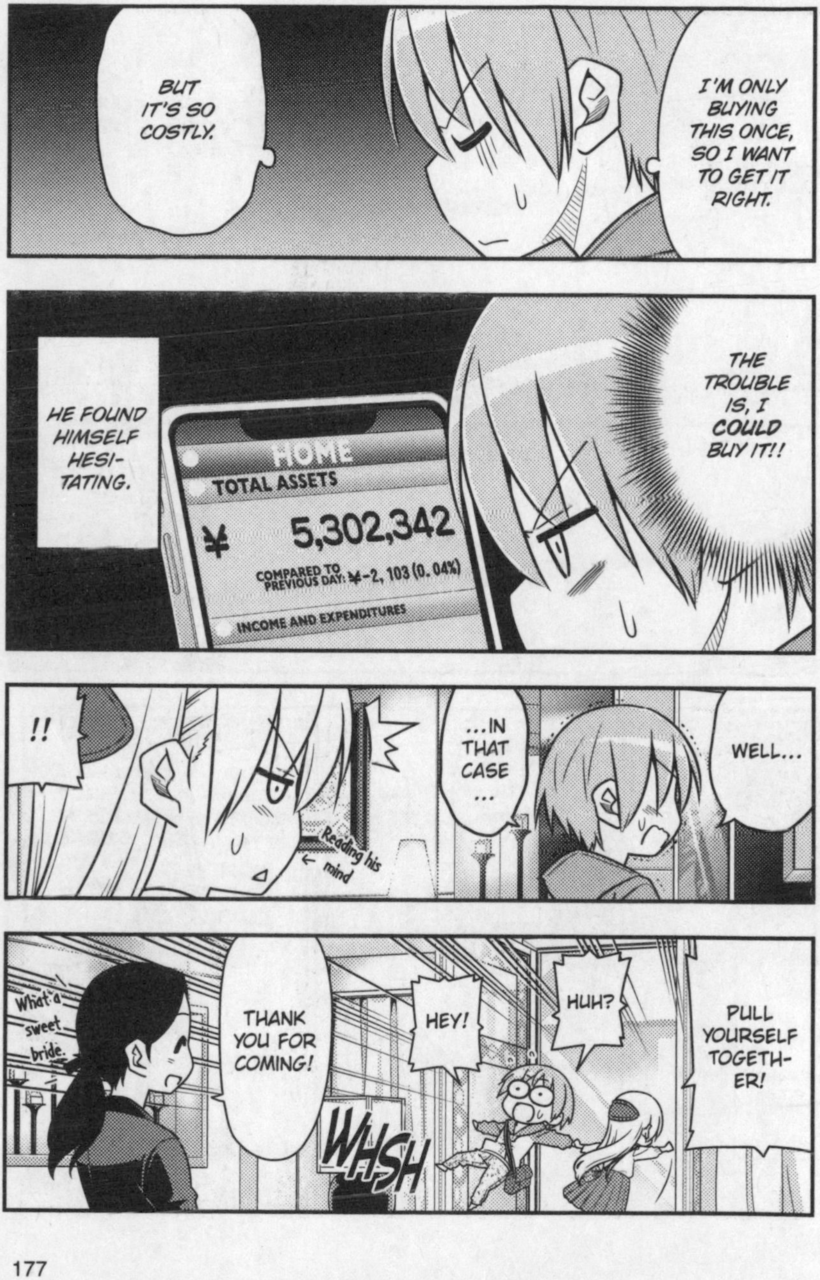
I'M ONLY BUYING THIS ONCE, SO I WANT TO GET IT RIGHT.
BUT IT'S SO COSTLY.
THE TROUBLE IS, I COULD BUY IT!!
HOME
TOTAL ASSETS
¥ 5,302,342
COMPARED TO PREVIOUS DAY: ¥-2, 103 (0. 04%)
INCOME AND EXPENDITURES
HE FOUND HIMSELF HESI-TATING.
WELL...
...IN THAT CASE...
Reading his mind
!!
PULL YOURSELF TOGETH-ER!
HUH?
HEY!
WHSH
THANK YOU FOR COMING!
What a sweet bride.

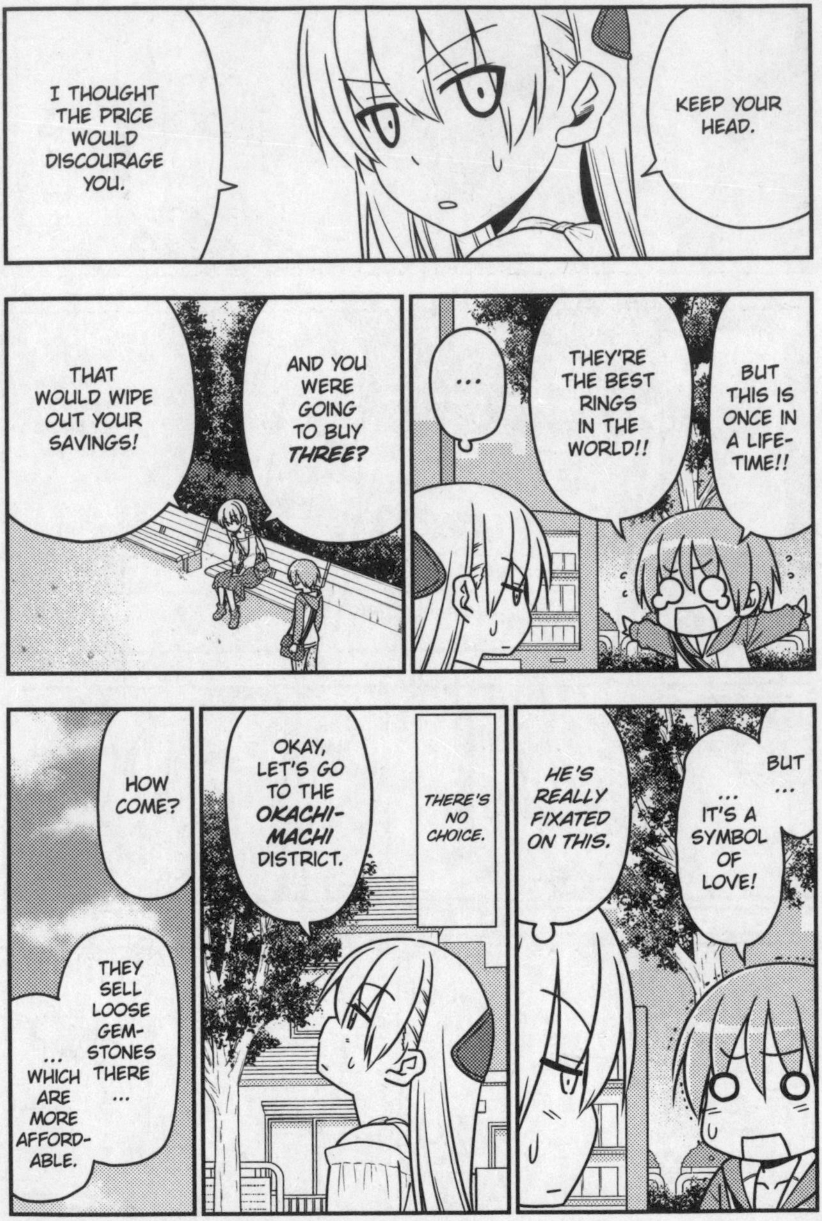
KEEP YOUR HEAD.
I THOUGHT THE PRICE WOULD DISCOURAGE YOU.
BUT THIS IS ONCE IN A LIFE-TIME!!
THEY'RE THE BEST RINGS IN THE WORLD!!
...
AND YOU WERE GOING TO BUY *THREE?*
THAT WOULD WIPE OUT YOUR SAVINGS!
BUT ... IT'S A SYMBOL OF LOVE!
HE'S REALLY FIXATED ON THIS.
THERE'S NO CHOICE.
OKAY, LET'S GO TO THE *OKACHI-MACHI* DISTRICT.
HOW COME?
THEY SELL LOOSE GEM-STONES THERE ... WHICH ARE MORE AFFORD-ABLE.

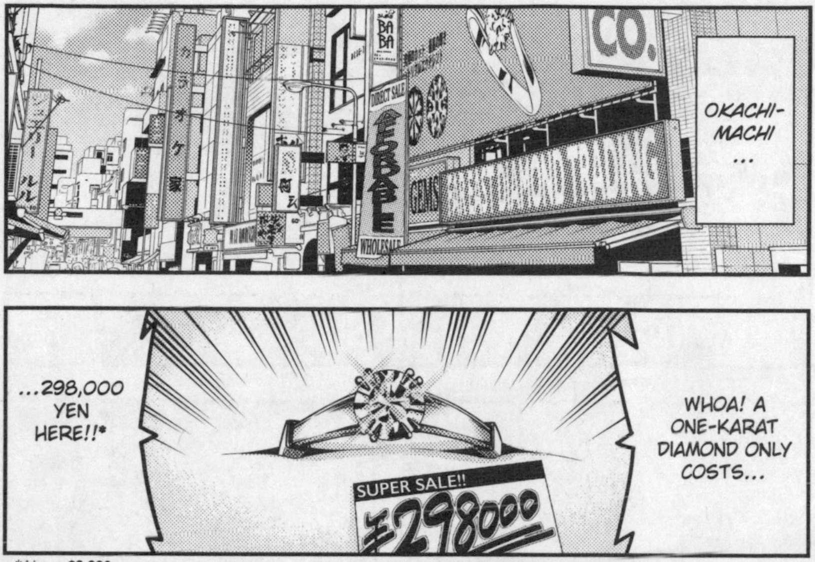
CO.
OKACHI-MACHI...
GEMS
DIRECT SALE
WHOLESALE
BA BA
WHOA! A ONE-KARAT DIAMOND ONLY COSTS...
...298,000 YEN HERE!!*
SUPER SALE!!
¥298000

*About $2,980.

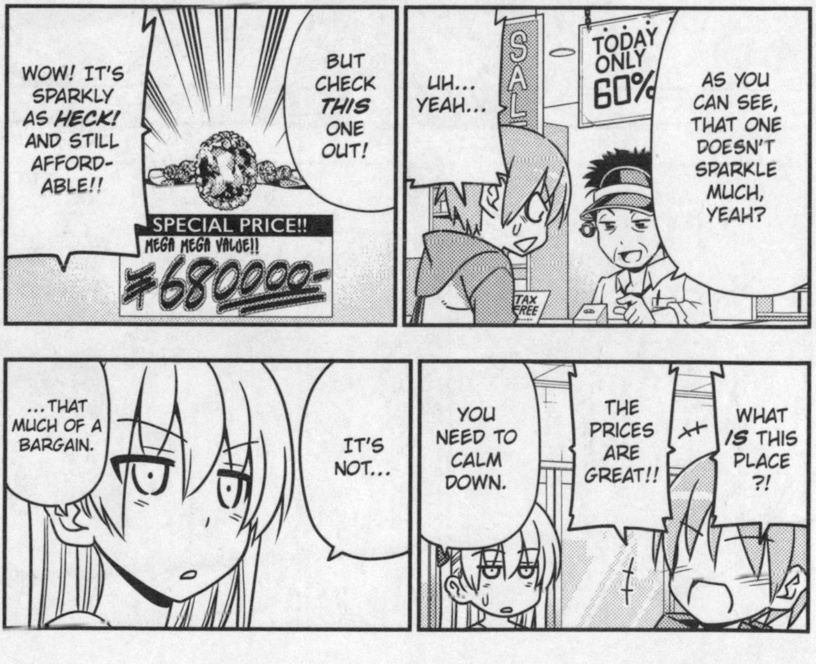
AS YOU CAN SEE, THAT ONE DOESN'T SPARKLE MUCH, YEAH?
TODAY ONLY 60%
UH... YEAH...
TAX FREE
BUT CHECK *THIS* ONE OUT!
WOW! IT'S SPARKLY AS *HECK!* AND STILL AFFORDABLE!!
SPECIAL PRICE!!
MEGA MEGA VALUE!!
¥680000-
WHAT *IS* THIS PLACE?!
THE PRICES ARE GREAT!!
YOU NEED TO CALM DOWN.
IT'S NOT...
...THAT MUCH OF A BARGAIN.

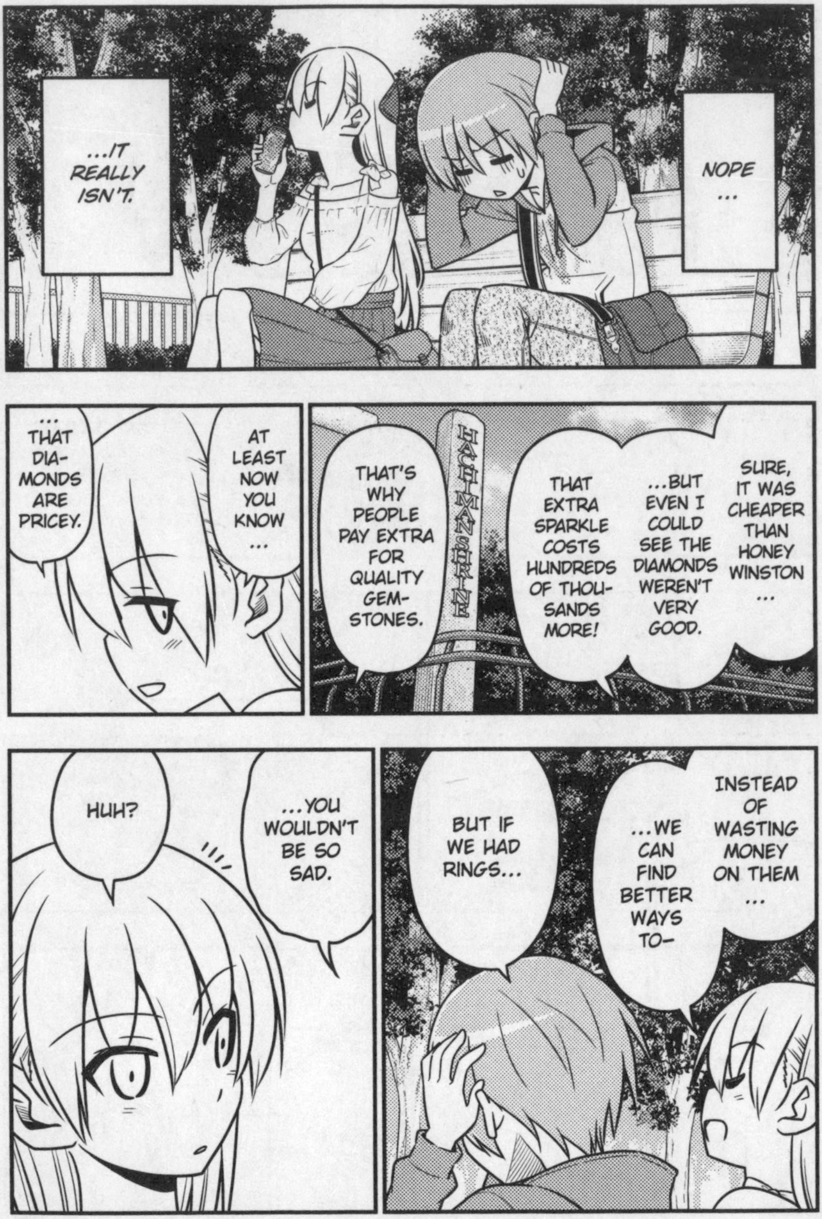
NOPE ...
...IT REALLY ISN'T.
SURE, IT WAS CHEAPER THAN HONEY WINSTON ...
...BUT EVEN I COULD SEE THE DIAMONDS WEREN'T VERY GOOD.
THAT EXTRA SPARKLE COSTS HUNDREDS OF THOUSANDS MORE!
HACHIMAN SHRINE
THAT'S WHY PEOPLE PAY EXTRA FOR QUALITY GEMSTONES.
AT LEAST NOW YOU KNOW ...
... THAT DIAMONDS ARE PRICEY.
INSTEAD OF WASTING MONEY ON THEM ...
...WE CAN FIND BETTER WAYS TO—
BUT IF WE HAD RINGS...
...YOU WOULDN'T BE SO SAD.
HUH?

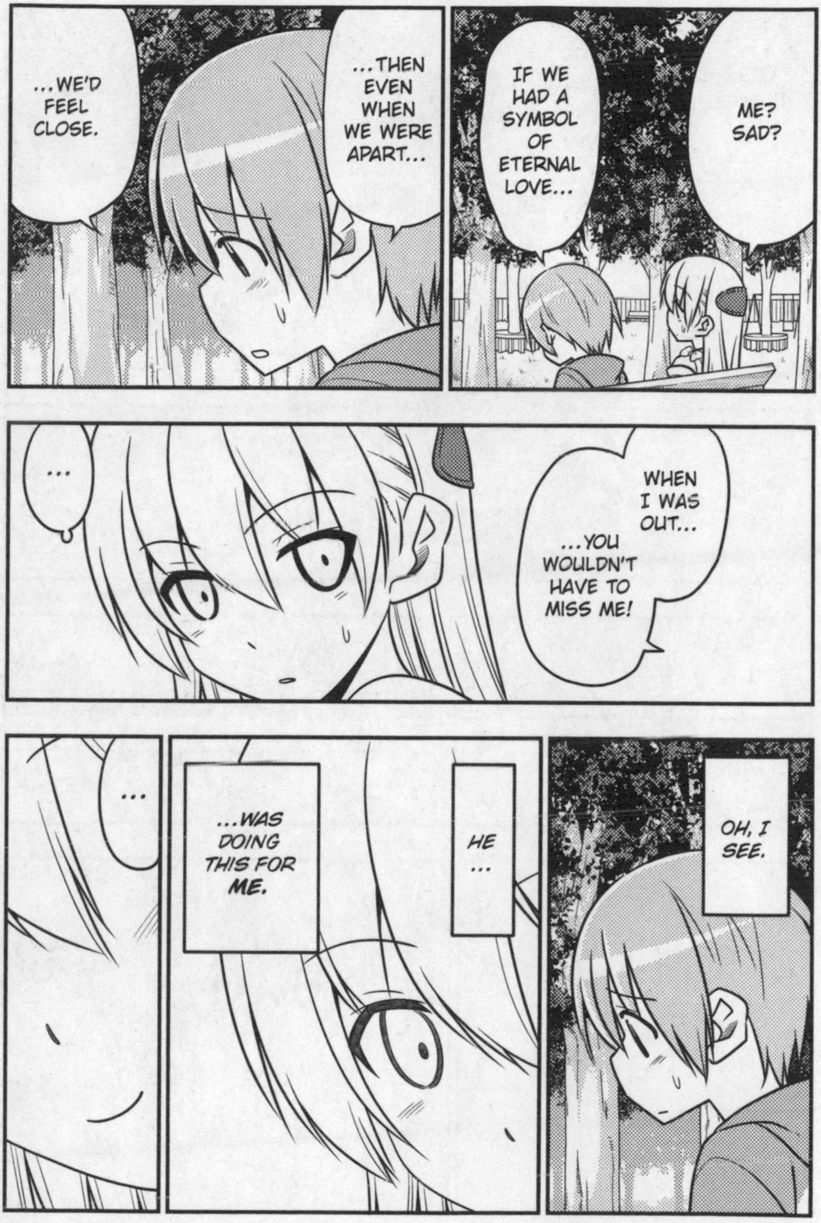
ME? SAD?
IF WE HAD A SYMBOL OF ETERNAL LOVE...
...THEN EVEN WHEN WE WERE APART...
...WE'D FEEL CLOSE.
WHEN I WAS OUT...
...YOU WOULDN'T HAVE TO MISS ME!
...
OH, I SEE.
HE ...
...WAS DOING THIS FOR *ME.*
...

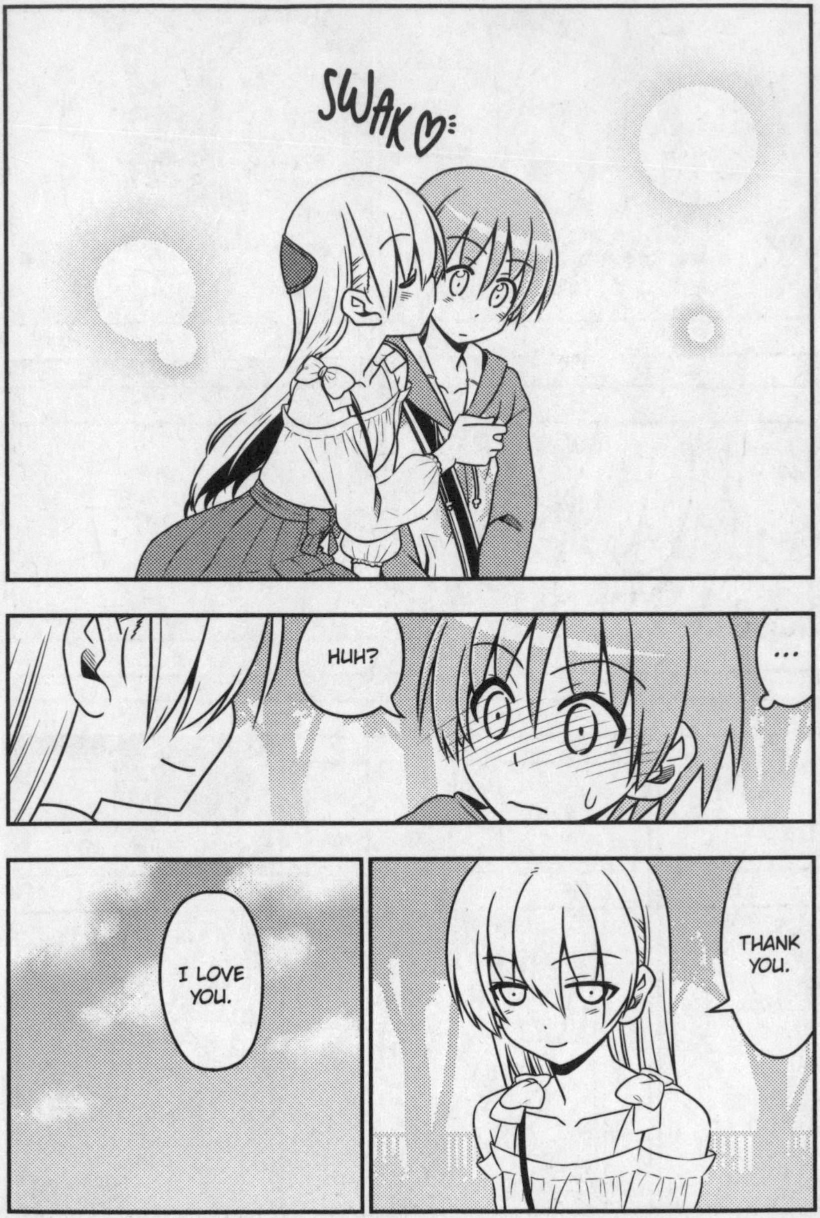
SWAK♡
...
HUH?
THANK YOU.
I LOVE YOU.

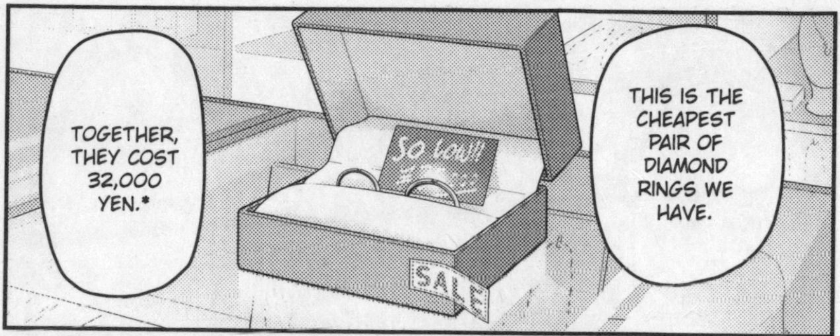
THIS IS THE CHEAPEST PAIR OF DIAMOND RINGS WE HAVE.
TOGETHER, THEY COST 32,000 YEN.*
So low!!
SALE

*About $320.

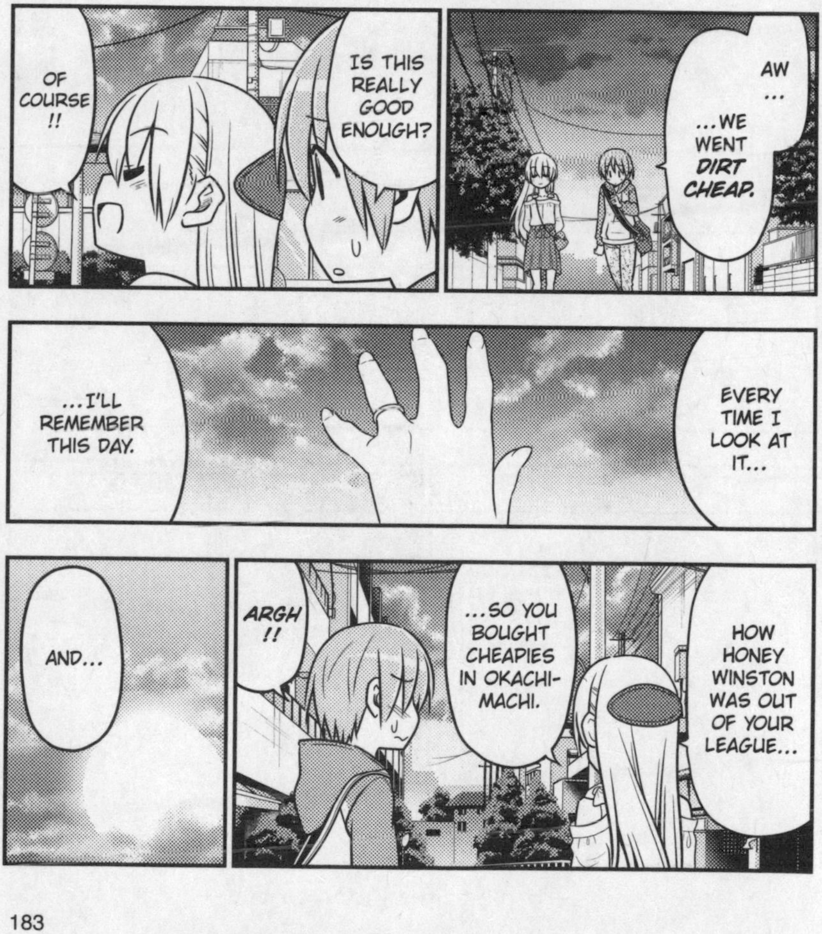
AW...
...WE WENT DIRT CHEAP.
IS THIS REALLY GOOD ENOUGH?
OF COURSE !!
EVERY TIME I LOOK AT IT...
...I'LL REMEMBER THIS DAY.
HOW HONEY WINSTON WAS OUT OF YOUR LEAGUE...
...SO YOU BOUGHT CHEAPIES IN OKACHI-MACHI.
ARGH !!
AND...

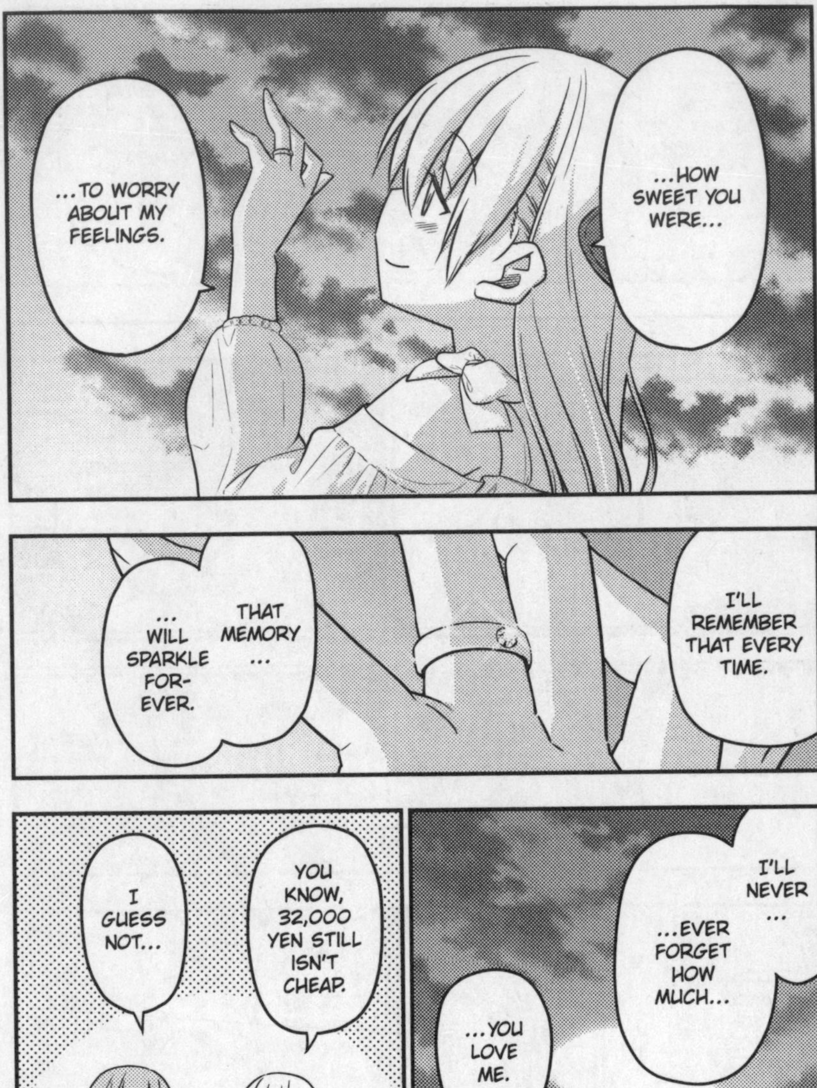
...HOW SWEET YOU WERE...
...TO WORRY ABOUT MY FEELINGS.
I'LL REMEMBER THAT EVERY TIME.
THAT MEMORY ...
... WILL SPARKLE FOR-EVER.
I'LL NEVER ...
...EVER FORGET HOW MUCH...
...YOU LOVE ME.
YOU KNOW, 32,000 YEN STILL ISN'T CHEAP.
I GUESS NOT...

—Fly Me to the Moon 2 / End—

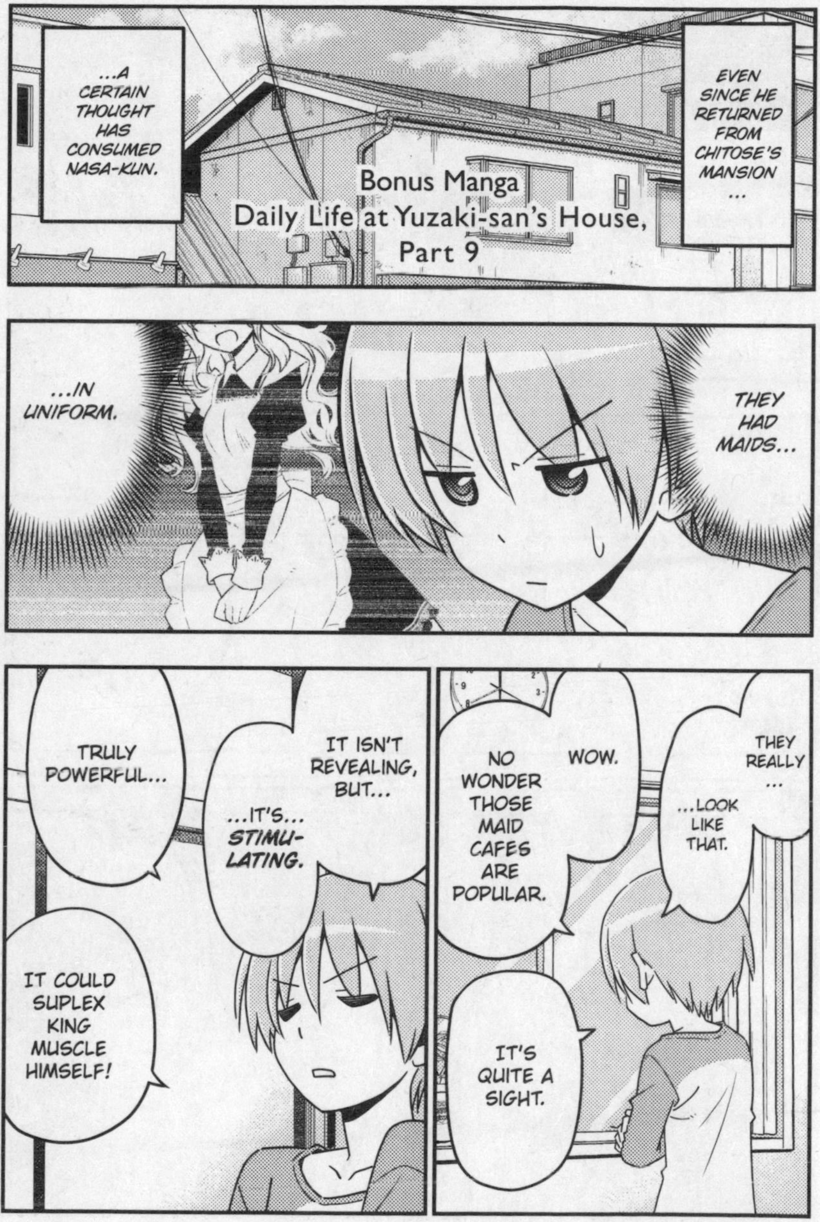
EVEN SINCE HE RETURNED FROM CHITOSE'S MANSION ...
Bonus Manga
Daily Life at Yuzaki-san's House, Part 9
...A CERTAIN THOUGHT HAS CONSUMED NASA-KUN.
THEY HAD MAIDS...
...IN UNIFORM.
THEY REALLY ...
...LOOK LIKE THAT.
WOW.
NO WONDER THOSE MAID CAFES ARE POPULAR.
IT'S QUITE A SIGHT.
IT ISN'T REVEALING, BUT...
...IT'S... STIMULATING.
TRULY POWERFUL...
IT COULD SUPLEX KING MUSCLE HIMSELF!

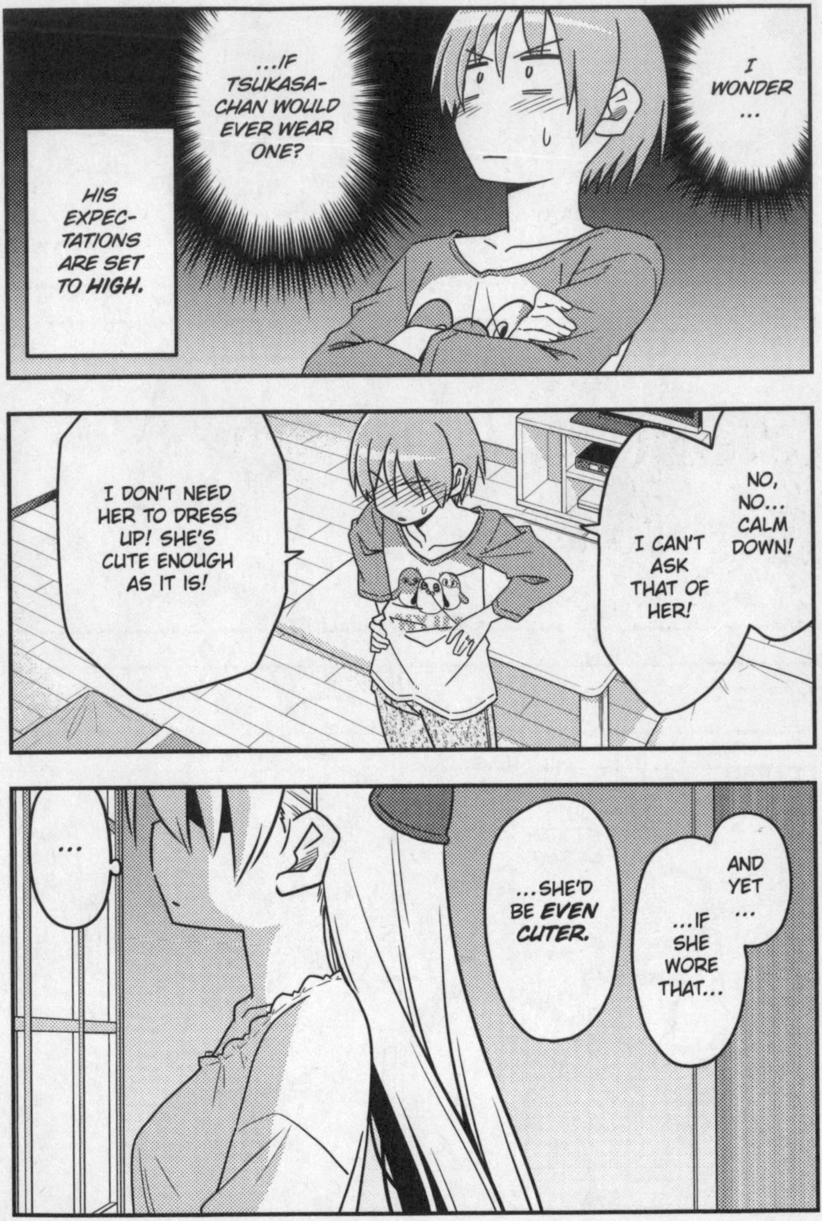
I WONDER ...
...IF TSUKASA-CHAN WOULD EVER WEAR ONE?
HIS EXPECTATIONS ARE SET TO **HIGH.**
NO, NO... CALM DOWN!
I CAN'T ASK THAT OF HER!
I DON'T NEED HER TO DRESS UP! SHE'S CUTE ENOUGH AS IT IS!
AND YET ...
...IF SHE WORE THAT...
...SHE'D BE ***EVEN CUTER.***
...

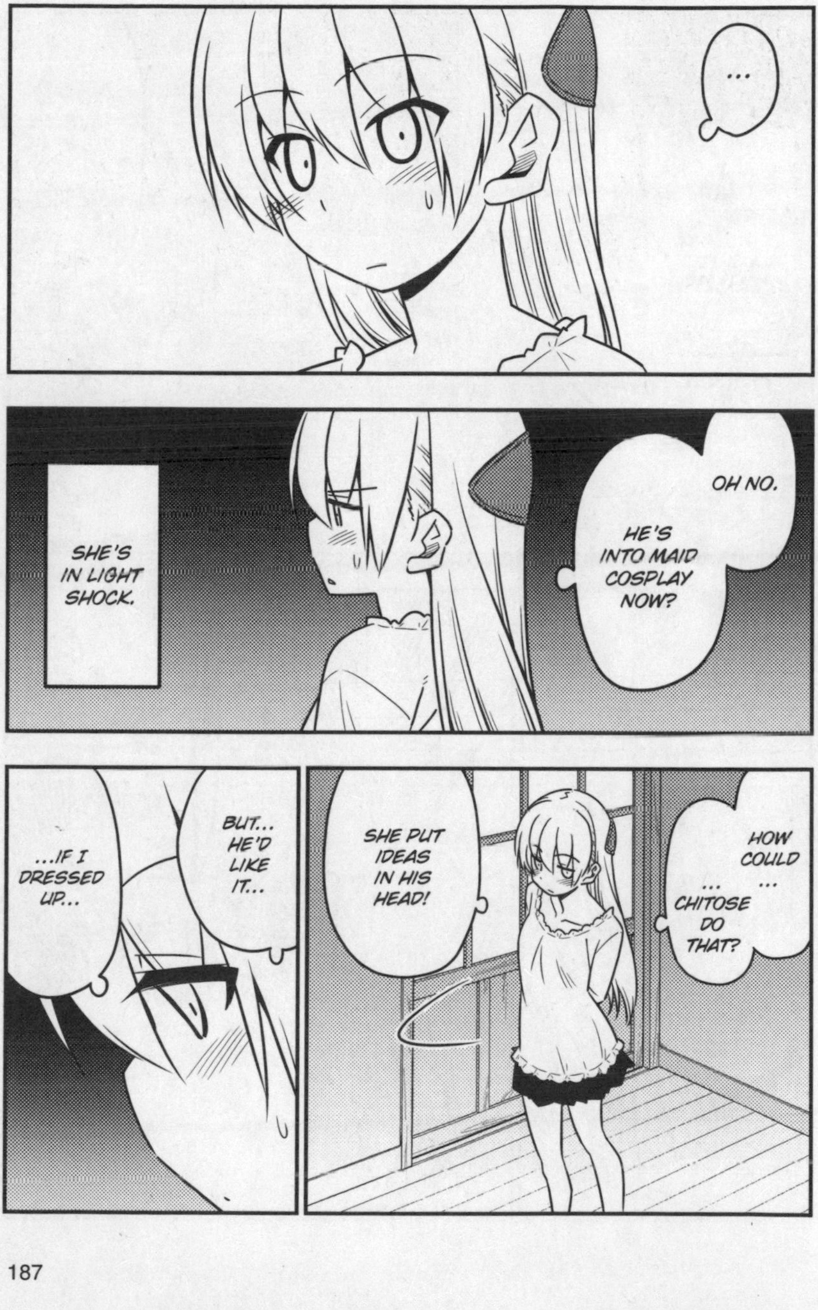
...
OH NO.
HE'S INTO MAID COSPLAY NOW?
SHE'S IN LIGHT SHOCK.
HOW COULD ... ... CHITOSE DO THAT?
SHE PUT IDEAS IN HIS HEAD!
BUT... HE'D LIKE IT...
...IF I DRESSED UP...

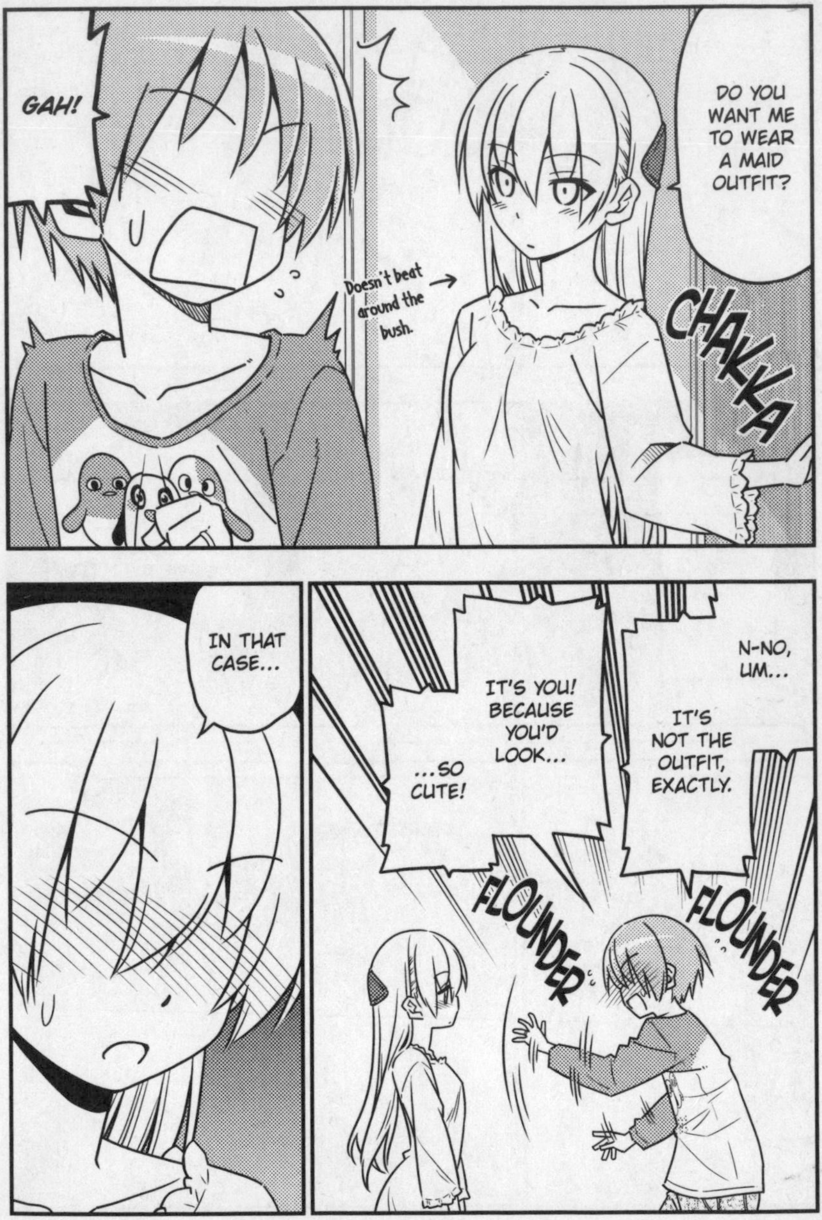
DO YOU WANT ME TO WEAR A MAID OUTFIT?
CHAKKA
Doesn't beat around the bush.
GAH!
N-NO, UM...
IT'S NOT THE OUTFIT, EXACTLY.
IT'S YOU! BECAUSE YOU'D LOOK...
...SO CUTE!
FLOUNDER
FLOUNDER
IN THAT CASE...

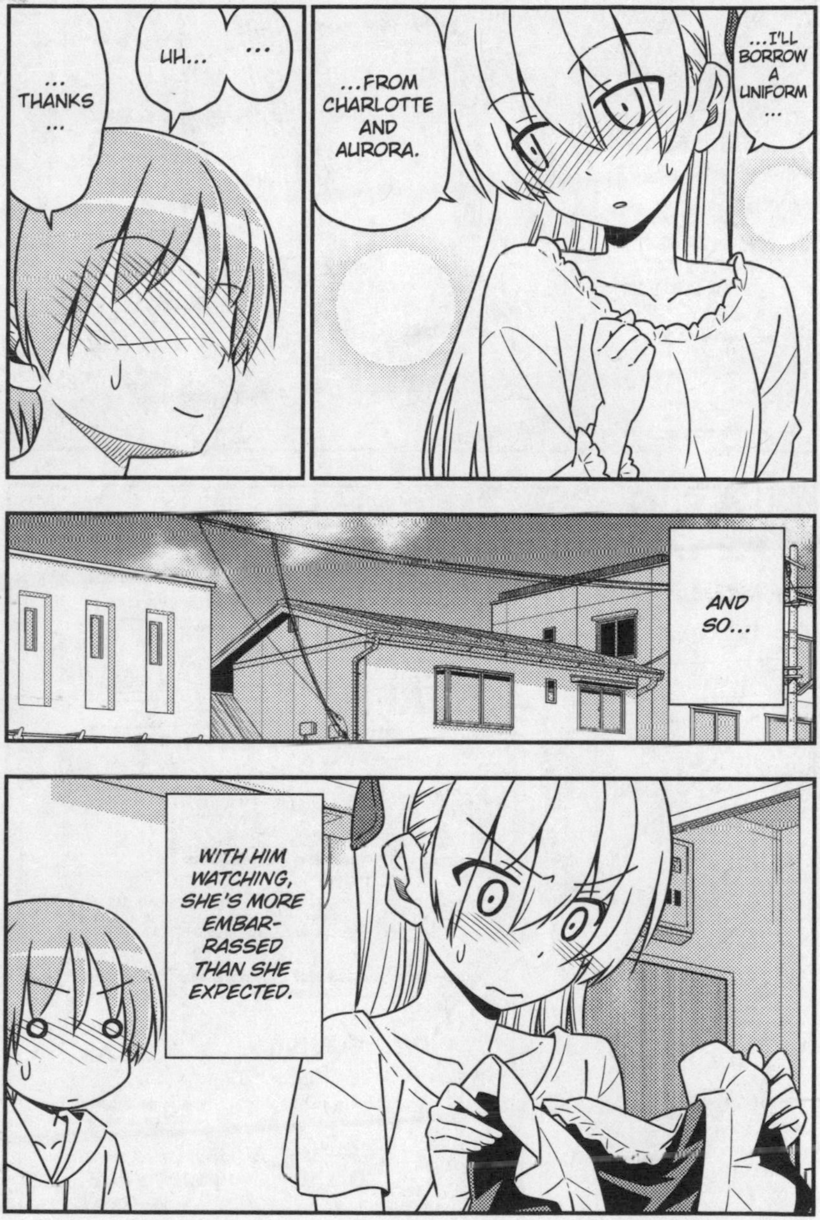
...I'LL BORROW A UNIFORM ...
...FROM CHARLOTTE AND AURORA.
...
UH...
... THANKS ...
AND SO...
WITH HIM WATCHING, SHE'S MORE EMBAR-RASSED THAN SHE EXPECTED.

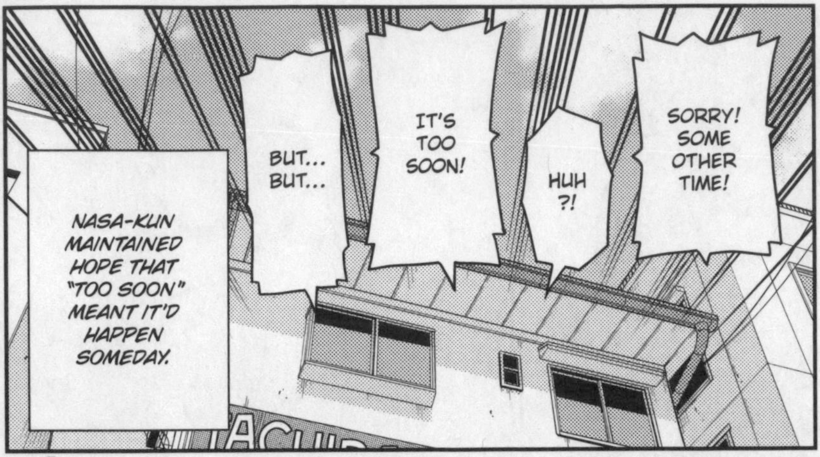
SORRY! SOME OTHER TIME!
HUH ?!
IT'S TOO SOON!
BUT... BUT...
NASA-KUN MAINTAINED HOPE THAT "TOO SOON" MEANT IT'D HAPPEN SOMEDAY.

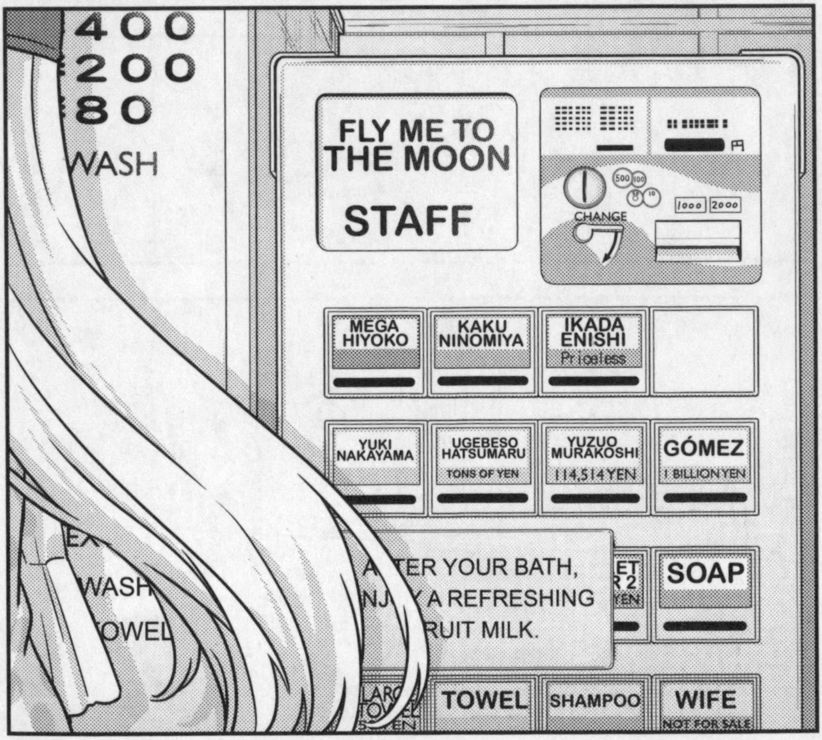
FLY ME TO THE MOON
STAFF
CHANGE
1000
2000
MEGA HIYOKO
KAKU NINOMIYA
IKADA ENISHI
Priceless
YUKI NAKAYAMA
UGEBESO HATSUMARU
TONS OF YEN
YUZUO MURAKOSHI
114,514 YEN
GÓMEZ
1 BILLION YEN
SOAP
TOWEL
SHAMPOO
WIFE
NOT FOR SALE
400
200
80
WASH

The End

FLY ME TO THE MOON

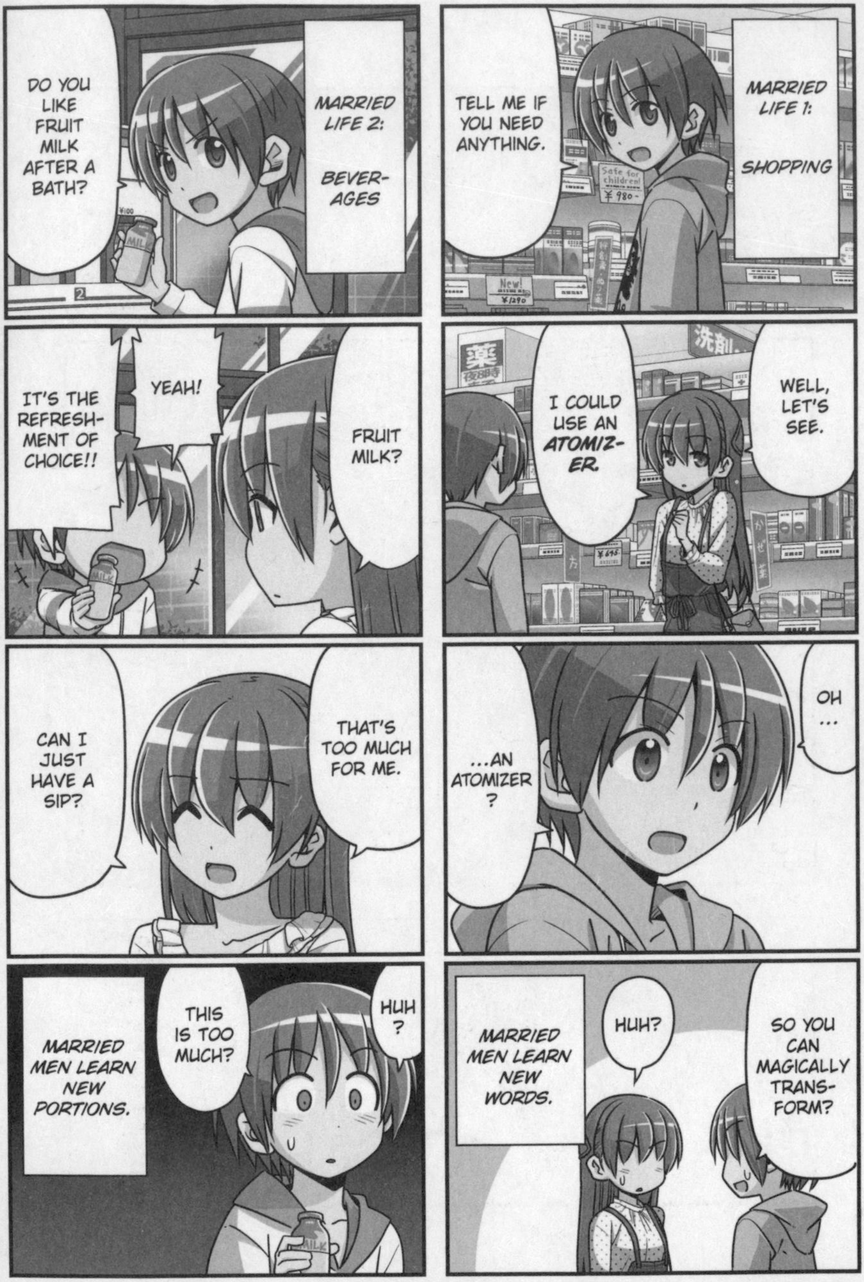
MARRIED LIFE 1: SHOPPING
TELL ME IF YOU NEED ANYTHING.
WELL, LET'S SEE.
I COULD USE AN ATOMIZER.
OH ...
...AN ATOMIZER ?
SO YOU CAN MAGICALLY TRANSFORM?
HUH?
MARRIED MEN LEARN NEW WORDS.
MARRIED LIFE 2: BEVERAGES
DO YOU LIKE FRUIT MILK AFTER A BATH?
FRUIT MILK?
YEAH!
IT'S THE REFRESHMENT OF CHOICE!!
THAT'S TOO MUCH FOR ME.
CAN I JUST HAVE A SIP?
HUH ?
THIS IS TOO MUCH?
MARRIED MEN LEARN NEW PORTIONS.

Fly Me to the Moon

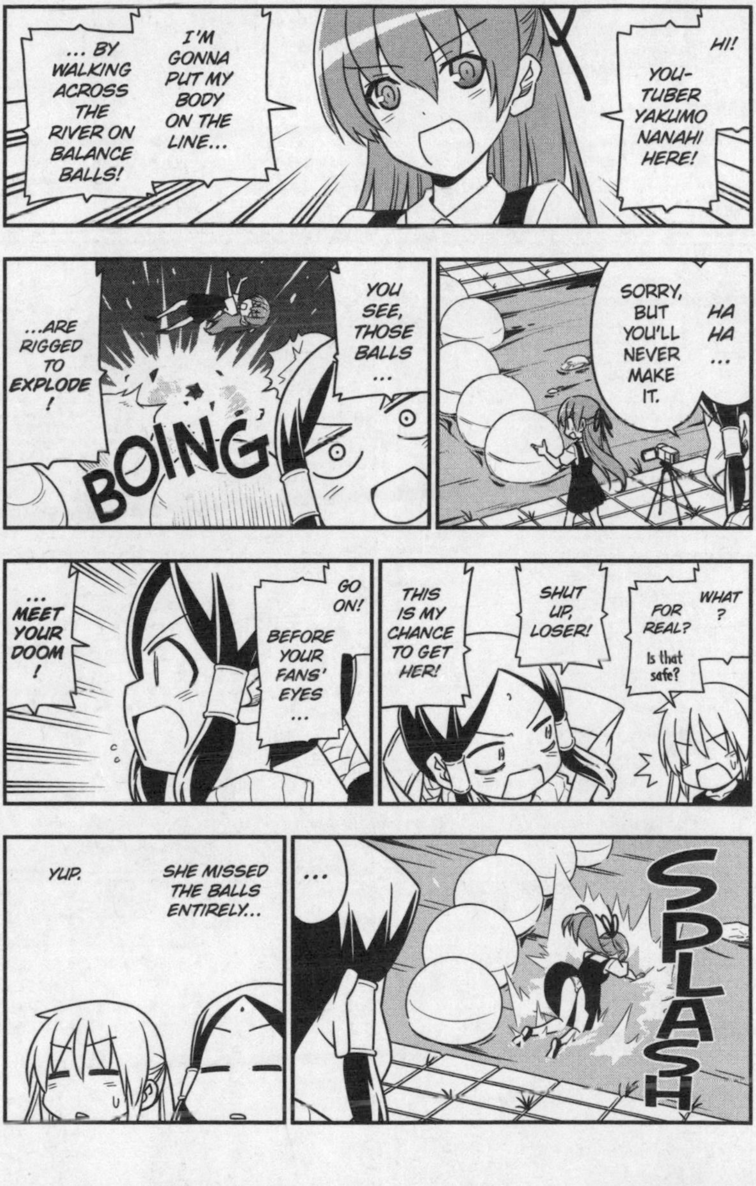
HI!
YOU-TUBER YAKUMO NANAHI HERE!
I'M GONNA PUT MY BODY ON THE LINE...
... BY WALKING ACROSS THE RIVER ON BALANCE BALLS!
HA HA ...
SORRY, BUT YOU'LL NEVER MAKE IT.
YOU SEE, THOSE BALLS ...
...ARE RIGGED TO EXPLODE!
BOING
WHAT?
FOR REAL?
Is that safe?
SHUT UP, LOSER!
THIS IS MY CHANCE TO GET HER!
GO ON!
BEFORE YOUR FANS' EYES ...
... MEET YOUR DOOM!
...
SPLASH
SHE MISSED THE BALLS ENTIRELY...
YUP.

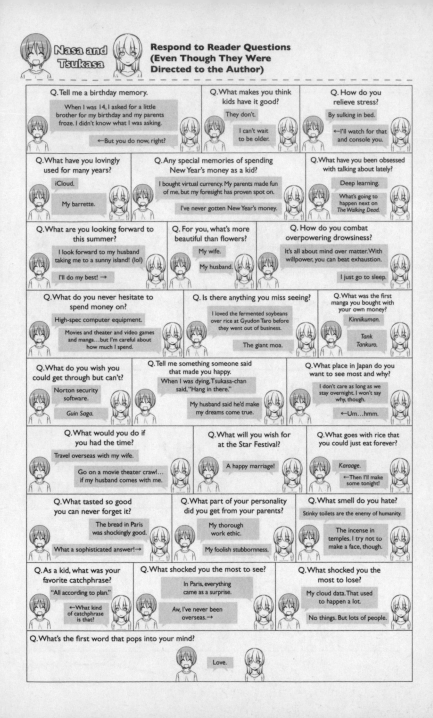

Nasa and Tsukasa

Respond to Reader Questions (Even Though They Were Directed to the Author)

Q. Tell me a birthday memory.

When I was 14, I asked for a little brother for my birthday and my parents froze. I didn't know what I was asking.

←But you do now, right?

Q. What makes you think kids have it good?

They don't.

I can't wait to be older.

Q. How do you relieve stress?

By sulking in bed.

←I'll watch for that and console you.

Q. What have you lovingly used for many years?

iCloud.

My barrette.

Q. Any special memories of spending New Year's money as a kid?

I bought virtual currency. My parents made fun of me, but my foresight has proven spot on.

I've never gotten New Year's money.

Q. What have you been obsessed with talking about lately?

Deep learning.

What's going to happen next on *The Walking Dead*.

Q. What are you looking forward to this summer?

I look forward to my husband taking me to a sunny island! (lol)

I'll do my best! →

Q. For you, what's more beautiful than flowers?

My wife.

My husband.

Q. How do you combat overpowering drowsiness?

It's all about mind over matter. With willpower, you can beat exhaustion.

I just go to sleep.

Q. What do you never hesitate to spend money on?

High-spec computer equipment.

Movies and theater and video games and manga...but I'm careful about how much I spend.

Q. Is there anything you miss seeing?

I loved the fermented soybeans over rice at Gyudon Taro before they went out of business.

The giant moa.

Q. What was the first manga you bought with your own money?

Kinnikuman.

Tank Tankuro.

Q. What do you wish you could get through but can't?

Norton security software.

Guin Saga.

Q. Tell me something someone said that made you happy.

When I was dying, Tsukasa-chan said, "Hang in there."

My husband said he'd make my dreams come true.

Q. What place in Japan do you want to see most and why?

I don't care as long as we stay overnight. I won't say why, though.

←Um...hmm.

Q. What would you do if you had the time?

Travel overseas with my wife.

Go on a movie theater crawl... if my husband comes with me.

Q. What will you wish for at the Star Festival?

A happy marriage!

Q. What goes with rice that you could just eat forever?

Karaage.

←Then I'll make some tonight!

Q. What tasted so good you can never forget it?

The bread in Paris was shockingly good.

What a sophisticated answer!→

Q. What part of your personality did you get from your parents?

My thorough work ethic.

My foolish stubbornness.

Q. What smell do you hate?

Stinky toilets are the enemy of humanity.

The incense in temples. I try not to make a face, though.

Q. As a kid, what was your favorite catchphrase?

"All according to plan."

←What kind of catchphrase is that?

Q. What shocked you the most to see?

In Paris, everything came as a surprise.

Aw, I've never been overseas.→

Q. What shocked you the most to lose?

My cloud data. That used to happen a lot.

No things. But lots of people.

Q. What's the first word that pops into your mind?

Love.

ABOUT THE AUTHOR

Without ever receiving any kind of manga award, Kenjiro Hata's first series, *Umi no Yuusha Lifesavers*, was published in *Shonen Sunday Super*. He followed that up with his smash hit *Hayate the Combat Butler*. His follow-up series, *Fly Me to the Moon*, began serialization in 2018 in *Weekly Shonen Sunday*.

FLY ME TO THE MOON

VOL. 2

Story and Art by **KENJIRO HATA**

SHONEN SUNDAY EDITION

TONIKAKUKAWAII Vol. 2
by Kenjiro HATA

Original Japanese edition published by SHOGAKUKAN.
English translation rights in the United States of America, Canada, the United Kingdom, Ireland, Australia and New Zealand arranged with SHOGAKUKAN.

Original Cover Design: Emi Nakano (BANANA GROVE STUDIO)

Translation
John Werry

Touch-Up Art & Lettering
Evan Waldinger

Design
Jimmy Presler

Editor
Shaenon K. Garrity

Printed in Canada

Published by VIZ Media, LLC
P.O. Box 77010
San Francisco, CA 94107

10 9 8 7 6 5 4 3 2 1
First printing, November 2020

ratings.viz.com RATED T+ OLDER TEEN

PARENTAL ADVISORY
FLY ME TO THE MOON is rated T+ for Older Teen and is recommended for ages 16 and up. This volume contains sexual situations.

VIZ MEDIA
viz.com

MANGA STARTS ON SUNDAY SHONEN SUNDAY
shonensunday.com

A hilarious tale of butlers, love and battles!

Hayate
the Combat Butler

Story and art by
Kenjiro Hata

Since the tender age of nine, Hayate Ayasaki has busted his behind at various part-time jobs to support his degenerate gambler parents. And how do they repay their son's selfless generosity? By selling his organs to the yakuza to cover their debts! But fate throws Hayate a bone... sort of. Now the butler of a wealthy young lady, Hayate can finally pay back his debts, and it'll only take him 40 years to do it.

Komi Can't Communicate

Story & Art by Tomohito Oda

The journey to a hundred friends begins with a single conversation.

Socially anxious high school student Shoko Komi's greatest dream is to make some friends, but everyone at school mistakes her crippling social anxiety for cool reserve. With the whole student body keeping its distance and Komi unable to utter a single word, friendship might be forever beyond her reach.

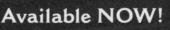

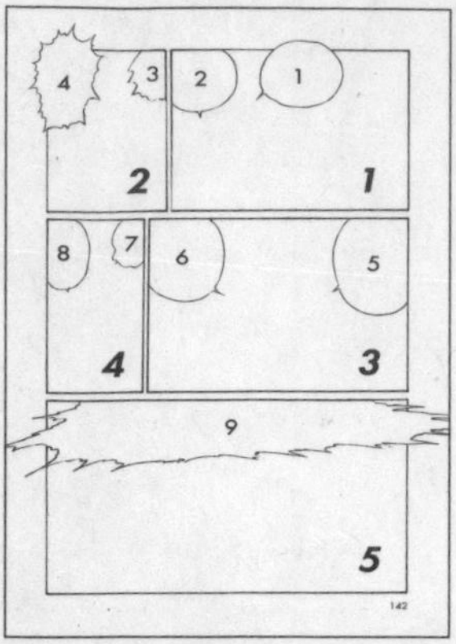

FOLLOW THE ACTION THIS WAY.

Fly Me to the Moon has been printed in the original Japanese format in order to preserve the orientation of the original artwork. Please turn it around and begin reading from right to left.

Unlike English, Japanese is read right to left, so Japanese comics are read in reverse order from the way English comics are typically read. Have fun with it!

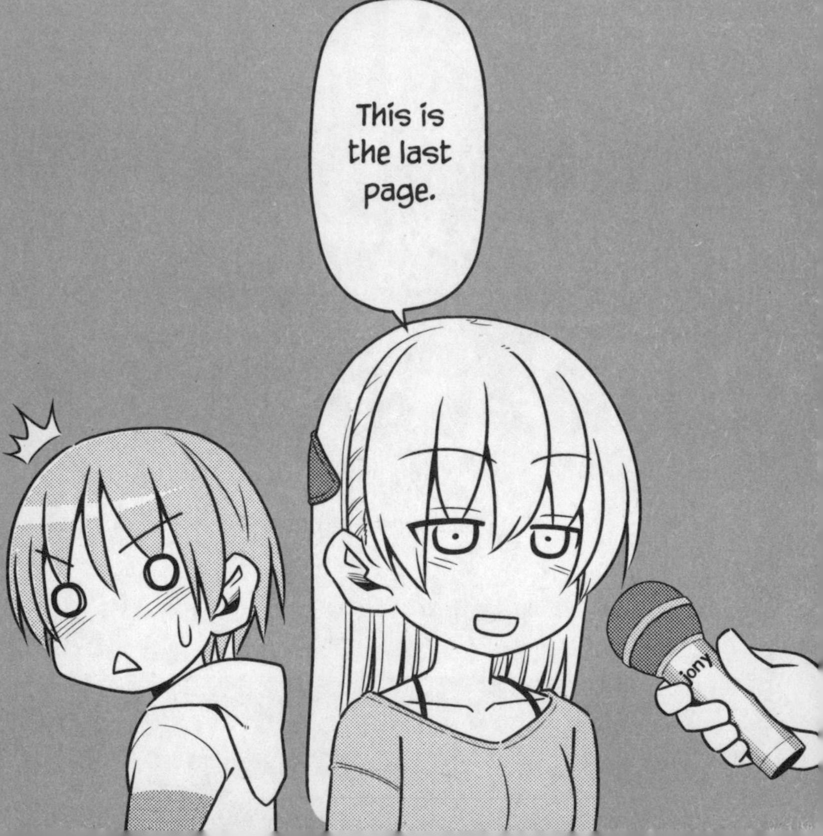

This is the last page.